Infant EEG and Event-Related Potentials

Studies in Developmental Psychology
Published Titles

Series Editor
Charles Hulme, University of York, UK

The Development of Intelligence
Mike Anderson (Ed.)

The Development of Language
Martyn Barrett (Ed.)

The Social Child
Anne Campbell and Steven Muncer (Eds.)

The Development of Memory in Childhood
Nelson Cowan (Ed.)

The Development of Mathematical Skills
Chris Donlan (Ed.)

The Development of Social Cognition
Suzanne Hala (Ed.)

Perceptual Development: Visual, Auditory, and Speech Perception in Infancy
Anne Slater (Ed.)

The Cognitive Neuroscience of Development
Michelle DeHaan and Mark H. Johnson (Eds.)

Connectionist Models of Development
Philip T. Quinlan (Ed.)

Children's Understanding of Society
Martyn Barrett and Eithne Buchanan-Barrow (Eds.)

Infant EEG and Event-Related Potentials

Edited by Michelle de Haan

Psychology Press
Taylor & Francis Group

HOVE AND NEW YORK

First published 2007
by Psychology Press
27 Church Road, Hove, East Sussex BN3 2FA

Simultaneously published in the USA and Canada
by Psychology Press
270 Madison Avenue, New York, NY 10016

*Psychology Press is an imprint of the Taylor & Francis Group,
an informa business*

Typeset in Times by RefineCatch Limited, Bungay, Suffolk
Printed and bound in Great Britain by TJ International Ltd,
Padstow, Cornwall
Cover design by Bob Rowinski

British Library Cataloguing in Publication Data
A catalogue record for this book is available from the British Library

Library of Congress Cataloging-in-Publication Data
Infant EEG and event-related potentials / edited by Michelle de Haan.
      p. ; cm.
   Includes bibliographical references and index.
   ISBN-13: 978-1-84169-583-9
   ISBN-10: 1-84169-583-1
   1. Pediatric neurology – Research – Methodology. 2. Evoked
potentials (Electrophysiology) 3. Electroencephalography. 4. Infants.
I. De Haan, Michelle, 1969– .
   [DNLM: 1. Evoked Potentials. 2. Electroencephalography. 3. Infant.
WL 102 I425 2007]
   RJ488.5.E93I54 2007
   618.92′8047547 – dc22

                                                                2006019610

ISBN: 978-1-84169-583-9

Contents

List of contributors   ix

Introduction   1
MICHELLE ᴅᴇ HAAN

1 Methods for acquiring and analyzing infant event-related potentials 5
TRACY DᴇBOER, LISA S. SCOTT AND CHARLES A. NELSON

Study formation and experimental design 7
Important considerations in developmental populations 8
Data collection systems 12
Participants 16
Data collection 18
Statistical analysis 26
Source separation and localization techniques in ERPs 32
Future directions 33
Acknowledgments 34
References 35

2 Visual evoked potentials in infants   39
DAPHNE L. McCULLOCH

VEP stimulation and recording in infants 40
Maturation of luminance VEPs (flash and flicker) 43
Maturation of standard pattern VEPs 45
Assessment of visual thresholds from VEPs 46
Maturation of visual resolution and contrast sensitivity
  thresholds 50
VEP assessment of other visual functions in infants 51
Clinical applications 58
Conclusions 63

Acknowledgements 64
References 64

3   Development of face-sensitive event-related potentials during infancy   77
MICHELLE DE HAAN, MARK H. JOHNSON AND HANIFE HALIT

Theories and models of face processing 78
Event-related potential studies of face processing 80
General discussion 90
Acknowledgements 93
References 94

4   Visual attention and recognition memory in infancy   101
MICHELLE DE HAAN

Infant ERP components related to recognition memory 101
Late components and slow wave activity 113
How do infant components relate to adult components? 115
Infant ERP studies and theories of memory development 116
Using ERPs to assess infant memory in special
   populations 119
Summary and future directions 121
Acknowledgements 122
Appendix 123
References 139

5   Auditory recognition memory in infancy   145
RAYE-ANN DE REGNIER

The neural pathway for auditory recognition memory 146
Anatomic development of the neural pathway for auditory
   recognition memory 148
Behavioral and evoked potential measures of auditory
   processing 149
Auditory recognition memory in the fetus and newborn 153
Studies of high-risk populations 160
Summary 164
References 165

6   Development of mismatch negativity (MMN) during infancy   171
MARIE CHEOUR

MMN in adults and children 172

Speech-processing MMN studies in healthy infants and
   children 177
MMN studies in clinical pediatric populations 179
Conclusions and future directions 183
References 185

7 **The use of event-related evoked potentials to predict**
   developmental outcomes   199
   DENNIS L. MOLFESE, VICTORIA J. MOLFESE AND NIKKI L. PRATT

   ERPs index speech perception 199
   The use of ERPs to predict language outcomes 200
   ERPs as predictors of language-related outcomes:
      Reading 204
   Mismatch negativity and prediction of language outcomes 208
   Why are ERPs predictive of language development? 211
   Summary and conclusions 213
   Acknowledgments 214
   Appendix 214
   References 221

8 **Infant EEG and ERP in relation to social and**
   emotional development   227
   PETER J. MARSHALL AND NATHAN A. FOX

   EEG band power 227
   EEG asymmetry 230
   Event-related potentials and affective development 234
   Conclusions 242
   References 243

9 **EEG and infant states**   251
   TATIANA A. STROGANOVA AND ELENA V. OREKHOVA

   The problem of infant EEG rhythm identification 252
   Technical questions 254
   Alpha and theta rhythms in infant EEG and their correlations
      with functional states 257
   Concluding remarks 279
   Acknowledgments 280
   References 280

10   Investigating event-related oscillations in infancy   289

GERGELY CSIBRA AND MARK H. JOHNSON

ERO analysis and methods 289
Perceptual "binding" 293
Occluded objects and "object permanence" 296
Conclusions and future prospects 301
Acknowledgements 302
References 302

11   Current and future directions in infant electrophysiology   305

MICHELLE de HAAN

How and why do ERPs and EEG change over infancy? 306
*How do infant ERP components and EEG rhythms relate to
   those in adults? 310*
*What is the role of behavioural measures in ERP/EEG
   research? 311*
*How useful are ERPs and EEG for the study of atypical
   development? 313*
Conclusions 314
References 314

Glossary of ERP/EEG terminology   317

JANE COWNIE

Author index   321
Subject index   331

List of Contributors

Marie Cheour, University of Miami, Department of Psychology, 5665 Ponce de Leon Blvd, FL 33146-0751, USA

Jane Cownie, UCL Institute of Child Health, 30 Guilford Street, London WC1N 1EH, UK

Gergely Csibra, School of Psychology, Birkbeck, University of London, Malet Street, London WC1E 7HX, UK

Tracy DeBoer, M.I.N.D. Institute, University of California, Davis, 2825 50th Street, Sacramento, CA 95817, USA

Michelle de Haan, UCL Institute of Child Health, 30 Guilford Street, London WC1N 1EH, UK

Raye-Ann deRegnier, Northwestern University Feinberg School of Medicine, Prentice Women's Hospital, Room 404B, 333 E. Superior St., Chicago, IL 60611, USA

Nathan A. Fox, Department of Human Development, University of Maryland, College Park, MD 20742, USA

Hanife Halit, School of Psychology, Birkbeck, University of London, Malet Street, London WC1E 7HX, UK

Mark H. Johnson, Centre for Brain and Cognitive Development, School of Psychology, Birkbeck College, University of London, Malet Street, London WC1E 7HX, UK

Peter J. Marshall, Department of Psychology, Temple University, 1701 North 13th Street, Philadelphia, PA 19122, USA

Daphne L. McCulloch, General Secretary of ISCEV, Glasgow Caledonian University, Cowcaddens Road, Glasgow G4 0BA, UK

Dennis L. Molfese, Department of Psychological & Brain Sciences, University of Louisville, Belknap Campus, Louisville, KY 40292, USA

Victoria J. Molfese, Center for Research in Early Childhood, University of Louisville, KY 40014, USA

Charles A. Nelson III, Harvard Medical School, Richard David Scott Chair in Pediatric Developmental Medicine Research, Children's Hospital Boston, DMC Lab of Cognitive Neuroscience, 1 Autumn Street, Mailbox #713, Office AU621, Boston, MA 02215-5365, USA

Elena V. Orekhova, Department of Clinical Neurophysiology, The Sahlgrenska Academy at Goteborg University, Institute of Neuroscience and Physiology, Sahlgrenska University Hospital, S-413 45 Goteborg, Sweden

Nikki L. Pratt, Department of Psychological & Brain Sciences, University of Louisville, Louisville, KY 40292, USA

Lisa S. Scott, Department of Psychology, University of Massachusetts, Amherst, MA 01003, USA

Tatiana A. Stroganova, Brain Research Institute, Russian Academy of Medical Sciences, per. Obukha 5, 103064, Moscow, Russia

Introduction to infant EEG and event-related potentials

Michelle de Haan
Institute of Child Health,
University College London, UK

It is many decades since investigators first employed the electroencephalo-gram (EEG) to study the function of infants' central nervous systems (for reviews see Bell, 1998; Schmidt & Fox, 1998). While initially investigators focused on how changes in the ongoing EEG related to the behavioural states of sleep and wakefulness (Lindsely, 1939; Smith, 1938), in subsequent years they also began to study event-related activity including evoked (e.g., Galambos & Despland, 1980; Sokol & Dobson, 1976) and endogenous responses (e.g., Courchesne, Ganz, & Norcia, 1981; Vaughan, 1975). In recent years, with the growing interest in understanding the neural bases of human perception, cognition, and emotion, there has been increased interest in use of EEG and event-related potentials (ERPs) to study these processes as they develop in human infants. This is because EEG and ERPs are among the only ways to study brain activity in healthy infants (see Meek, 2002, for discussion of another method that can be used with healthy infants, optical imaging). Other brain-imaging methods commonly used with adults and older children pose significant risks or would require sedation in young infants, making them unsuitable unless required for clinical purposes.

That there is now a sufficient body of literature in the field of infant EEG and ERPs to warrant an entire volume on this topic is testament to how quickly the field has grown in the last few years. This is in spite of the fact that these data can be quite challenging to collect from young infants. Cooper-ation with placement of the electrodes and leaving them in place for the duration of the experiment, minimising movement during the experiment to prevent artefacts, and ensuring that the baby participates in the experiment as needed (e.g., by attending to visual stimuli) can all represent challenges (see DeBoer et al., Chapter 1, for discussion of practical aspects of recording infant EEG and ERPs). Once these challenges are overcome, others present themselves in analysis and interpretation of the data, as in many instances the relationship between components observed in infant ERPs and those known in adults is not obvious.

The chapters in this volume demonstrate that these challenges can be overcome and reliable EEG and ERP data can be recorded from infants in a variety of paradigms and ages. Chapter 1 (DeBoer et al.) provides an overview of methods for recording and analysing EEG and ERP, with an emphasis on the special issues related to using these techniques with infants. Chapters 2–4 focus on visual potentials, from visual evoked responses (McCulloch, Chapter 2) to face-sensitive components (de Haan et al., Chapter 3) and components related to visual attention and memory (de Haan, Chapter 4). In Chapter 2, McCulloch outlines techniques for recording visual evoked potentials (VEPs) and describes the picture they provide of the development of the visual system in infancy, in both typical and atypical development. In Chapter 3, de Haan, Johnson, and Halit describe ERP components related to infants' processing of faces, how these relate to components in the adult ERP, and how developmental changes in these components inform theories of the development of face processing. In Chapter 4, de Haan focuses on ERP components related to infant recognition memory and attention, describing the development of the negative central (Nc) component and various slow waves.

Chapters 5–7 focus on auditory potentials, including those related to auditory recognition (deRegnier, Chapter 5), the mismatch negativity (Cheour, Chapter 6), and those related to speech and language (Molfese et al., Chapter 7). In Chapter 5, deRegnier outlines the brain circuits involved in auditory recognition memory and presents data demonstrating differences in ERP response to the mother's vs. a stranger's voice in neonates. When the same auditory recognition paradigm is used with infants at risk for later memory impairment, there is evidence of atypical auditory ERP memory responses very early in life. In Chapter 6, Cheour describes what is perhaps one of the most well-studied ERP components, mismatch negativity (MMN). She discusses issues in identifying the infant MMN, and its differences from and similarities to the adult component, as well as its usefulness in detecting cognitive impairment early in life. In Chapter 7, Molfese, Molfese, and Pratt discuss the use of infant ERPs to predict later language and reading development. They present impressive findings indicating that ERPs to speech and non-speech sounds in neonates and young infants can predict a sizeable amount of the variance in language and reading skills at school age.

Chapters 8–10 focus on other aspects of the EEG, with Chapter 8 (Marshall & Fox) examining ERP and EEG emotion-related responses, Chapter 9 (Stroganova & Orekhova) focusing on EEG and infants' states, particularly different states of wakefulness, and Chapter 10 (Csibra & Johnson) reporting on event-related oscillations in perceptual-cognitive tasks. In Chapter 8, Marshall and Fox report on individual differences in both EEG and ERP responses and how they relate to individual differences in emotion and temperament. Their findings suggest that temperamental differences among infants may be an important factor to consider in interpreting results from ERP group studies. In Chapter 9, Stroganova and Orekhova discuss development of the EEG in relation to infant states, raising important questions regarding variations in the EEG during wakefulness and definition of infant EEG rhythms (e.g., alpha) in relation to those observed in adults. In

Chapter 10, Csibra and Johnson describe a relatively recent approach to analysing infant brain activity, event-related oscillations, and how these have been used to study the neural correlates of perceptual binding and memory for hidden objects in infancy.

Several questions and themes run throughout these chapters, including the usefulness of infant EEG/ERP in early detection of impairments in perception and cognition, and how best to define infant brain activity with respect to adult brain activity, and these and other themes are discussed further in Chapter 11 (de Haan). A glossary of terms is also provided at the end of the book, with the hope that it will make the chapters more accessible to those less familiar with the field and its terminology.

The main purpose of creating this volume was to provide a reference useful to both those active in the field and those new to it. For those already involved in infant EEG and ERP research, the chapters in this book will provide a very useful reference drawing together numerous studies, and may also help to broaden their outlook, as often researchers tend to focus on a particular type of ERP and may not be fully aware of work that is related but carried out in another domain. For those new to the field, it is hoped that the introduction provided by Chapter 1 and the glossary will form the background for informed reading of the remaining chapters devoted to more specific topics. Ideally, the exciting findings reported here will recruit new researchers into the field and help to take the field forward in the decades to come.

REFERENCES

Bell, M. A. (1998). The ontogeny of the EEG during infancy and childhood: Implications for cognitive development. In B. Barreau (Ed.), *Neuroimaging in child neuropsychiatric disorders* (pp. 97–111). Berlin: Springer.

Courchesne, E., Ganz, L., & Norcia, A. M. (1981). Event-related brain potentials to human faces in infants. *Child Development, 52*, 804–811.

Galambos, R., & Despland, P. A. (1980). The auditory brainstem response (ABR) evaluates risk factors for hearing loss in the newborn. *Pediatric Research, 14*, 159–163.

Lindsely, D. B. (1939). A longitudinal study of the occipital alpha rhythm in normal children: Frequency and amplitude standards. *Journal of Genetic Psychology, 55*, 197–213.

Meek, J. (2002). Basic principles of optical imaging and application to the study of infant development. *Developmental Science, 5*, 371–380.

Schmidt, L. A., & Fox, N. A. (1998). Electrophysiological indices I: Quantitative electroencephalography. In C. E. Coffey & R. A. Brumback (Eds.), *Textbook of pediatric neuropsychiatry* (pp. 315–329). Washington, DC: American Psychiatric Press.

Smith, J. R. (1938). The electroencephalogram during normal infancy and childhood: I Rhythmic activities present in the neonate and their subsequent development. *Journal of Genetic Psychology, 53*, 431–453.

Sokol, S., & Dobson, V. (1976). Pattern reversal visually evoked potentials in infants. *Investigative Ophthalmology, 15*, 58–62.

Vaughan, H. G. Jr. (1975). Electrophysiologic analysis of regional cortical maturation. *Biological Psychiatry, 10*, 513–526.

1 Methods for acquiring and analyzing infant event-related potentials

Tracy DeBoer
University of California at Davis, USA

Lisa S. Scott
University of Massachusetts at Amherst, USA

Charles A. Nelson
Harvard Medical School, USA

A primary goal of developmental cognitive neuroscience is to elucidate the relation between brain development and cognitive development (see Nelson & Luciana, 2001). The study of this relation in children older than 5–6 years lends itself to many of the same tools used in the adult, such as functional magnetic resonance imaging (fMRI). However, in children younger than this, limitations in motor and linguistic abilities, coupled with abbreviated attention spans, make the use of such tools impractical. In contrast, electro-encephalography (EEG) and event-related potentials (ERPs) provide some of the only noninvasive methodological techniques in the armamentarium of cognitive neuroscientists that allow researchers to examine the relation between brain and behavior beginning at birth. Both EEG and ERPs measure electrical activity of the brain recorded from scalp electrodes and can be utilized across the entire lifespan, thereby permitting one to use the same methodological tool and dependent measure across a broad range of ages (although comparisons across large age spans may be challenging due to qualitative differences in the EEG and ERP response). In addition, EEG and ERPs do not require an overt behavioral or verbal response and therefore permit the study of phenomena that cannot be studied with behavioral methods (e.g., responses to the simultaneous presentation of multiple stimuli or stimuli presented so briefly as to preclude a behavioral response). However, when a behavioral response is obtainable, EEG and ERPs can also provide an invaluable complement and an additional level of analysis to that behavioral measure by permitting one to glimpse the neural circuits underlying the behavior.

EEG and ERPs both reflect the electrical activity of the brain, and both are collected in a similar manner; however, they represent slightly different aspects of brain function. Whereas EEG is a measure of the brain's ongoing electrical activity, ERPs reflect changes in electrical activity in response to a discrete stimulus or event. ERPs are collected from several trials and then averaged in order to eliminate background noise that is not related to the stimulus of interest. Thus, ERPs are said to be "time-locked" to the stimulus. Both EEG and ERPs contribute to the understanding of brain maturation and cognitive development. EEG provides information regarding the resting state of the brain (as indexed by various EEG patterns or rhythms), synchrony between regions (coherence), or spectral changes in response to a cognitive event (Event-related Synchronization/Desynchronization). In contrast, deflections in the ERP (referred to as components) reflect specific aspects of sensory and cognitive processes associated with various stimuli. Due to the high temporal resolution (on the order of milliseconds), ERPs are well suited to index changes in the mental chronometry of a given neural response.

Although various sources have discussed aspects of electrophysiological research including the historical and neurophysiological background of EEG and ERPs, and issues concerning experimental design, data acquisition, analysis, and interpretation in adult populations in great detail (e.g., Handy, 2004; Regan, 1989), few have addressed utilization of these measures in developmental populations (for an important exception see Taylor & Baldeweg, 2002). This is unfortunate because recording EEG and ERPs in infants and young children differs from recording in adults in some unique ways. Thus, in this chapter we elaborate on the idiosyncrasies of using EEG and ERPs in developmental populations, provide the reader with some practical methodological advice, and call attention to some caveats that arise when using EEG and ERP techniques to investigate the developmental progression of brain–behavior relations early in life. The chapter is designed for the novice developmental EEG/ERP researcher and focuses on issues regarding study formation, experimental design, data collection, and data analysis. The heart of the chapter reviews issues regarding practical acquisition topics such as data acquisition systems, participant selection, data collection (e.g., recording electrophysiological data, artifact rejection, and averaging), and statistical analysis. The chapter closes with an introduction to source separation and localization, as well as challenges and future directions for developmental electrophysiological research.[1]

---

1   The field of developmental electrophysiology is continually evolving; subsequently, what is considered "developmental" electrophysiological research remains broad. At this point in time, the term "developmental" is used not only to refer to authentic change over time (e.g., changes in components, changes in brain structures, or changes in children's behavior) but also to refer to research that, ultimately, will contribute to knowledge regarding such change. Therefore, in this chapter, the term "developmental" will be used to refer to both circumstances (e.g., studying the development of actual entities such as components and the utilization of ERP components in developmental, or child, populations to better understand development more generally).

STUDY FORMATION AND EXPERIMENTAL DESIGN

Hypotheses

Despite increases in the use of EEG and ERPs with developmental popula-tions, several obstacles remain that prevent testable hypotheses from appear-ing more often in the literature. First, since relatively little is known about the specifics of functional human brain development, it can be challenging to derive concrete hypotheses based on the development of discrete neural cir-cuits. Second, almost nothing is known about how physiologic activity in the developing brain propagates to the scalp surface, and thus we do not know what the relation is between activity *in* the brain vs. *at* the scalp. Third, the field has only begun to define ERP components of interest and normative and abnormal patterns of EEG across development; thus much discontinuity remains between age groups and across areas of investigation.

With these caveats in mind, in this chapter we attempt to illustrate the kinds of questions that are particularly amenable to an electrophysiological investigation with developmental populations. We also challenge researchers to perform the appropriate exploratory investigations to ensure that more theoretically driven experiments with testable hypotheses can be conducted.

Task design

Due to the limited attentional capacity and restricted behavioral repertoire of infant populations, several considerations may be necessary when designing an experiment. Some developmental EEG/ERP tasks can be derived from tasks used with adults that are adjusted to take developmental differences into consideration (e.g., decreasing the length of the trials, the number of independent variables, or the complexity of the stimuli). However, as accom-modations such as these are made, it must be acknowledged that infants are not typically tested under the same conditions as adults (e.g., infants do not benefit from instructions, whereas older children do) and, therefore, direct comparisons across large age differences are often difficult to interpret. Other age-appropriate tasks can arise from modified versions of behavioral tasks known to tap certain cognitive functions of interest (e.g., speech discrimin-ation tasks, approach–withdrawal tasks, habituation tasks, or recognition memory tasks).

Many developmental EEG studies to date have compared spectral activity of children with typical cognitive development to that of clinical groups under a variety of circumstances. Common paradigms involve recording rest-ing EEG while infants watch objects such as brightly colored balls tumbling around a bingo wheel, abstract patterns on a video display, or bubbles, for various amounts of time (e.g., Calkins, Fox, & Marshall, 1996; Marshall, Bar-Haim, & Fox, 2002). Additionally, EEG can be recorded during *pro-longed* events such as games of peek-a-boo or a stranger entering the room (e.g., Buss, Malmstadt Schumacher, Dolski, Kalin, Hill Goldsmith, & Davidson, 2003; Dawson, Panagiotides, Klinger, & Spieker, 1997) or emotion-eliciting videos or musical clips (Jones, Field, Fox, Davalos, & Gomez, 2001; Schmidt, Trainor, & Santesso, 2003) as long as precautions are made to minimize movement on the part of the participant.

On the other hand, as mentioned above, ERPs are by definition time-locked to the presentation of a stimulus. Therefore, in both adult and developmental populations, more stringent constraints are placed on the types of tasks amenable to ERP experiments. To date, most developmental ERP studies have used either the standard oddball paradigm or a combination of the oddball paradigm with an infant habituation paradigm. In the former, two or more discrete stimuli (i.e., typically 500 milliseconds in duration) are presented repeatedly, but with different frequencies. For example, in one study 4- to 7-week-old infants were shown pictures of checkerboard patterns and geometric shapes. ERPs were recorded while one stimulus was repeated frequently (80% of the time) and the other stimulus was presented infrequently (20% of the time, Karrer & Monti, 1995). In contrast, the combined oddball/habituation paradigm involves first familiarizing or habituating an infant to a stimulus (e.g., a face), and then presenting a series of stimuli, consisting of the now familiar stimulus and a novel stimulus (e.g., a new face) repeatedly with equal frequency (i.e., 50% of the time for each) while ERPs are recorded (e.g., Pascalis, de Haan, Nelson, & deSchonen, 1998).

IMPORTANT CONSIDERATIONS IN DEVELOPMENTAL POPULATIONS

Beyond paradigm considerations, one must also consider (1) age-related changes in EEG or the morphology and timing of ERP components of interest, and (2) changes in behavioral measures, including the availability, quality, and validity of these measures.

Developmental changes, which are apparent in both EEG rhythms and the morphology of the ERP waveform, are often difficult to describe, and increasingly difficult to explain due to their complex and multifaceted nature. For instance, major developmental changes in synaptic density, myelination, and other physical maturational processes (e.g., changes in skull thickness and closing of the fontanel) may combine to influence amplitude and latency across different ages (Nelson & Luciana, 1998; see also Chapter 11, this volume, for further discussion).

Although great strides have been made in documenting changes in EEG over the first few years of life, much less is known about the developmental trajectories of ERP components (although see Webb, Long, & Nelson, 2005, for an exception). For example, the same EEG frequency bands are typically present throughout development, yet high-frequency bands tend to increase in relative power with increases in age (especially in the band of 6–9Hz:

Marshall et al., 2002; Schmidt et al., 2003; see also Taylor & Baldeweg, 2002, for a review). ERP components tend to vary considerably in both form and function across development. Unexpectedly, ERPs of adults and newborns are similar to each other in amplitude, but very dissimilar compared to ERPs from older infants and young children (see Figure 1.1 for illustration). Furthermore, in the first two years of life, reduced synaptic efficiency results in greater slow wave activity rather than peaked activity, the latter being more typical of adult ERPs. Thus, the infant ERP does not show as many well-defined peaked responses (especially in anterior components) when compared to adult responses. The characteristics of the peaked adult waveform typically begin to emerge when children reach 4 years of age, and continue to develop well into adolescence (Friedman, Brown, Cornblatt, Vaughan, & Erlenmeyer-Kimling, 1984; Nelson & Luciana, 1998). In fact, because the distribution of activity across the scalp (i.e., topography) changes with age, we can infer that important changes are still taking place in the neural substrate generating the components of interest throughout development. Amplitudes may also vary as a function of differing task demands imposed on the participant. Presumably the easier the task, the less effort expended, and the less cortical activation required, which may ultimately result in smaller amplitudes (Nelson & Luciana, 1998). Finally, the general heuristic for changes that take place from early adulthood to later adulthood is that, overall, latencies of several ERP components appear longer and amplitudes appear smaller (see Kurtzberg, Vaughan, Courchesne, Friedman, Harter, & Putnam, 1984; Nelson & Monk, 2001; and Taylor & Baldeweg, 2002 for further discussion).

A major change that also occurs with increasing age is the ability to "ground" the measure in behavior or correlate the brain's electrophysiological response with task performance. Infant EEG/ERP paradigms by necessity do not involve issuing instructions, nor do they require an overt behavioral response. However, most adult ERP paradigms include both instructions and a behavior response (even if only to ensure continued attention to the task). Therefore, due to the differences in testing conditions it is possible that, at some level, differences in ERP morphology are due to differences in task requirements.

The "passive" viewing paradigm (i.e., one in which no instructions are given) is useful for two reasons. First, developmental populations can be tested and their data can be compared to those of adults without modification to the paradigm. Second, passive paradigms may evoke basic perceptual components, without the added activity (or noise) that may be recorded when the participant is engaged in some task and/or a behavioral response is required. The drawback to using a passive task is that it is difficult to determine whether participants maintain attention throughout the task, or whether they are doing the task at all. Depending on the specific hypotheses, one must use other means of monitoring attention, for example in visual paradigms, videotaping participants to ensure they were looking at the

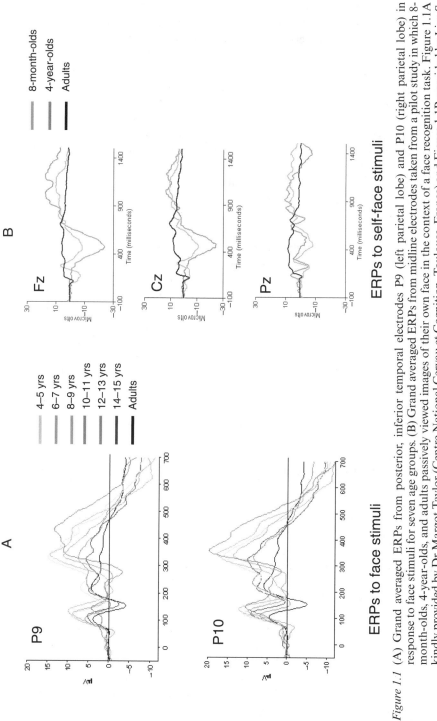

Figure 1.1 (A) Grand averaged ERPs from posterior, inferior temporal electrodes P9 (left parietal lobe) and P10 (right parietal lobe) in response to face stimuli for seven age groups. (B) Grand averaged ERPs from midline electrodes taken from a pilot study in which 8-month-olds, 4-year-olds, and adults passively viewed images of their own face in the context of a face recognition task. Figure 1.1A kindly provided by Dr Margot Taylor (Centre National Cervau et Cognition, Toulouse, France) and Figure 1.1B provided by Lisa S. Scott (Institute of Child Development, University of Massachusetts, Amherst, USA). Visit http://www.psypress.co.uk/dehaan to see this figure in colour.

stimuli, and/or repeating trials in which it was obvious the participants were not attentive. For auditory studies, attention may be a different issue, as ERPs are often recorded during sleep (e.g., deRegnier, Nelson, Thomas, Wewerka, & Georgieff, 2000). During these paradigms, infants may need to be monitored continuously as changes in sleep states (active vs. passive) are thought to influence the ERP response (cf. Martynova, Kirjavainen, & Cheour, 2003).

Although below the age of 4–5 years traditional button-press responses cannot be used, there are some behavioral measures that have been used previously in developmental populations in conjunction with EEG and ERPs. The most informative behavioral measures are those that can be recorded concurrently and therefore directly correlated with the electro-physiological response. For example, in one EEG investigation (Dawson et al., 1997), infants were exposed to several conditions designed to elicit positive and negative emotions while EEG activity was measured (e.g., peek-a-boo with their mothers vs. being approached by a stranger). EEG activity was subsequently analyzed during periods when infants were dis-playing prototypic expressions of emotions. Results from this investigation indicated that, compared with infants of nondepressed mothers, infants of depressed mothers exhibited increased EEG activation in the frontal but not parietal regions when they were expressing negative emotions.

Due to temporal limitations, recording behavior in conjunction with ERP recording has been a slightly greater challenge, although a number of para-digms have been able to record behavior immediately following ERP recording. For example, following a visual oddball paradigm using two stimuli with different presentation frequencies, Karrer and Monti (1995) immediately presented infants with four additional trials during which visual fixations were recorded, analogous to a post-test after a traditional behavioral habituation paradigm. Specifically, one of the two stimuli was presented repeatedly until the infant looked away; followed by the presenta-tion of the other stimulus until the infant again looked away, and so on (Karrer & Monti, 1995). Similarly, Snyder (2002) employed a design analo-gous to a habituation/dishabituation procedure that consisted of recording ERPs during an initial exposure to a stimulus (the habituation phase), and then recording the duration of infants' visual fixations during a dishabitu-ation phase. Snyder's study is unique in that it reflects a composite between ERP methodology and stimulus exposure during a conventional infant con-trolled habituation procedure. During the familiarization phase, trials were continuously presented until the infant either became fussy, or looked away from the screen three times for at least 3 or more seconds each time. After the familiarization phase, infants were shown serial presentations of familiar and novel stimuli and allowed one continuous look at each. Infants' visual prefer-ences for test stimuli were computed as the proportion of fixation to the novel stimulus vs. the total fixation time. Infants were subsequently divided into three groups: infants who showed a novelty preference at test (looked at the novel stimulus 55% or more of the time), those who showed a familiarity preference (looked at the novel stimulus 45% or less of the time), and those who did not show a preference.

This method of combining EEG/ERPs with behavioral measures (facial display of affect or preferential looking) permits researchers to more directly examine relations between behavior and brain activity. A combination of techniques such as these provides information not accessible by either method alone.

Unfortunately, due to the highly constrained testing environment required by EEG and ERPs (e.g., movement restrictions) it is not always feasible to record behavioral measures during or immediately following EEG/ERP data collection. Therefore, some researchers have elected to record behavioral measures separately (e.g., after removing the electrodes when the infant is more attentive or better able to perform a required task). For example, EEG data have been associated with measures of object permanence (Bell & Fox, 1992, 1997), motor development (Bell & Fox, 1996), joint attention (Mundy, Card, & Fox, 2000; Mundy, Fox, & Card, 2003), temperament (Henderson, Fox, & Rubin, 2001), cortisol levels, and withdrawal-related behaviors (Buss et al., 2003), all of which were collected either prior to or sometime after EEG data collection.

Similarly, Carver, Bauer, and Nelson (2000) combined ERP responses with behavioral performance on a deferred imitation task (which has been purported to tap explicit memory functions; see Bauer, 1995; Nelson, 1995). Specifically, *before* recording ERPs, 9-month-old infants were behaviorally exposed to a unique sequence of events (e.g., the experimenter places a red cylinder into a wooden block, which is then pushed into the base of the apparatus causing a green dinosaur puppet to "pop up"). After a 1-week delay, the infants' ERP responses to photographs of the now familiar event sequence and a novel event sequence were recorded. Four weeks later the infants' delayed recall performance on the deferred imitation memory task was assessed. Infants were split into groups based on their behavioral performance: those who recalled the sequence and those who did not. Based on these groupings, Carver and colleagues (2000) examined the electrophysiological responses and found differentiation between the familiar and novel conditions for the infants who demonstrated recall after a 1-month delay, but no such differentiation for the infants who did not display delayed recall.

In sum, although challenging, it is important that researchers continue to ground EEG/ERP measures in behavior. Such a combination will yield converging evidence and lead to more reliable results in predominately exploratory studies typical of the field at this time.

DATA COLLECTION SYSTEMS

Currently, there are several commercial electrophysiological data collection systems available for purchase and use. These systems differ on features such as electrode and montage type, quantity, location, and placement. A major distinction between systems available to date is whether they are high- or low-density electrode montages. A low-density montage provides less coverage over the scalp (ranging from 3 to 32 electrodes), whereas high-density montages refer to greater coverage across the scalp (ranging from 32 to 256 electrodes). The main advantages of high-density systems are increased opportunity for source localization, the use of the average reference, and the relative increased ability to detect subcortical electrical activity. When deciding whether to use a high- or low-density system in developmental populations there are several considerations to be made, such as: (1) where the data will be collected (e.g., a MRI scanner that does not permit the presence of metal), (2) what hypotheses will guide data analysis (e.g., how important is spatial information), (3) what are the components of interest (i.e., what is their distribution across the scalp), (4) the proposed dependent measures for data analysis (e.g., amplitude differences at one electrode site or source localization procedures).

There are two different methods of recording low-density EEG/ERPs that we have utilized in our developmental laboratory. These methods differ in the number of electrodes and the method by which the electrodes are placed on the scalp. For both methods, the location of electrode placement follows the international 10–20 system of electrode placement commonly used in adults (Jasper, 1958). Each electrode is placed a percentage of the distance between the inion and nasion to ensure the ERPs are being recorded from approximately the same neural structures across all individuals regardless of age or head size. In addition, these low-density systems require slight scalp abrasion and the use of conductance cream in order to conduct the signal into the electrode on the scalp. Abrading the scalp may increase the risk of infection, and although it is not likely to occur, certain precautions are necessary (see Ferree, Luu, Russell, & Tucker, 2001; Putnam, Johnson, & Roth, 1992).

The first low-density approach is derived from methods with adults, in which a form of glue (collodion) is used to fix single electrodes filled with conductance cream to the scalp, and a solvent (acetone) is used to remove them. The advantage to this method is that the electrodes remain in the same place throughout the duration of the experiment; however, the disadvantage is that safety glasses, rubber gloves, and ventilation are recommended when using these products due to the fact that they may be irritating to the nose and throat. The modification we have used involves first slightly abrading the scalp with a cleansing solution such as NuPrep© and holding single electrodes filled with conductance cream (EC2 cream©) in place with adhesive-backed foam pads, which in turn are held in place with Velcro headbands (see Figure 1.2A). In studies with newborns or when fewer electrodes are required, disposable electrodes, which stick directly to the infant's scalp, can be used instead of the single electrodes and foam (Figure 1.2B). The advantage is that this procedure is typically no more aversive than putting on a hat. However, the disadvantage is that the foam pads can stick poorly to infants who have a great deal of hair or where the hair is braided, and thus have the

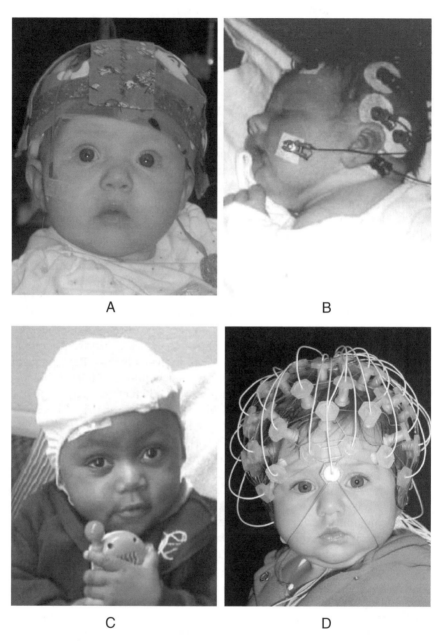

Figure 1.2 Infant wearing (A) 16 electrodes held in place with adhesive foam pads and Velcro headbands, (B) single disposable electrodes typically used in the newborn and NICU nurseries, (C) a 32-channel Electro-Cap©, and (D) a 64-channel Electro Geodesic Sensor net©. Adapted from DeBoer, Scott & Nelson (2004). Visit http://www.psypress.co.uk/dehaan to see this figure in colour.

potential to move around on the scalp unless extra care is taken. Typically 6–12 electrodes are used with this procedure, and are most appropriate for infants under 12 months of age.

The second approach utilizes an electrode cap. Such caps are made out of Spandex-like material that has electrodes sewn into it at standardized coordinates (this method is also commonly used with adults, see Figure 1.2C). The advantage to this procedure is that a greater number of electrodes may be positioned on the scalp in relatively little time in comparison with the Velcro headband procedure, or with using single disposable electrodes. The scalp is lightly abraded and conductance jelly is inserted under each electrode site after the placement of the cap (this is typically done through the use of a blunt-tip syringe and cotton swab). This may be bothersome to some infants as it produces an uncommon sensation of a light scratching on the scalp. The cap is held in place by a chin or chest strap. Although this strap does not wholly ensure that the cap will not shift on the head during the experiment, it does greatly reduce the risk of electrodes moving out of position. A disadvantage is that some infants' heads are asymmetrical and varied in size, which makes it difficult to ensure that the electrodes are fixed in the same location. In addition, the chin or chest strap used to hold the electrodes in place may bother some infants. Typically, electrode caps have 16–32 electrodes and, in our laboratory, have been found to be appropriate for use with infants as young as 9 months of age and through to adulthood.

Recording high-density EEG/ERPs in developmental populations has been made possible by the Geodesic Sensor Net© (GSN), which allows a very large number of electrodes (ranging from 64 to 256) to be applied quickly to the surface of the scalp (Tucker, 1993). The GSN consists of an array of electrodes arranged in an elastic tension structure, which can be relatively quickly and easily slipped on and off the participants' head (see Figure 1.2D). The arrangement of electrodes does not follow the international 10–20 system due to the fact that the tension structure conforms to the geometry of each individual's head, but ensures that the electrodes are all equidistant from one another, even on a variety of head shapes (which is a requirement for localization of underlying dipoles). One advantage of the GSN is its high-operating impedance level, which, when combined with amplifiers that allow high-input impedance, removes the need for scalp abrasion and conductance cream. The net is soaked in an electrolyte solution prior to application, which allows the signal to be conducted, recorded, and amplified by the high-input impedance amplifiers. A second advantage is the use of the average reference, which results in an unbiased estimate of noise across the scalp and thus unconfounds estimates of the amplitude and topography of components with the location of the reference electrode. A third advantage is that high-density montage arrays provide greater coverage of the scalp and thus are able to pick up activity in superficial cortical tissue (which, due to its proximity to the scalp, tends to produce smaller, more discrete patterns of activity, in addition to deeper subcortical structures). Finally, it takes a relatively short amount of time to apply the net (e.g., 5 minutes) in comparison to other procedures (e.g., 15–20 minutes; see Johnson et al., 2001). However, there are a few disadvantages worth mentioning. First, due to the fact that the electrodes are not fixed rigidly to the scalp, movement artifacts are common, and in some cases infants (6 months of age and older) may attempt to grab the net, frequently causing displacement and possible damage to the net (Johnson et al., 2001). A second disadvantage is that high-density systems are considerably more expensive than low-density systems due to the increased cost of equipment and the need for several different net sizes to accommodate small differences in head size among participants. Nets are available in many different sizes that can be used with newborns (64 or 128 electrodes), children up to 6 years of age (64 or 128 electrodes), and children aged 6 years to adults (64, 128, or 256 electrodes). (For a complete review of recording high-density ERPs and strategies for analyzing high-density data with infants using the GNS, see Johnson et al., 2001.)

Thus far, comparisons of ERP data collected from high- and low-density systems appear similar in quality (Carver et al., 1999; Johnson et al., 2001) and the overall advantage of high-density montages is that they may allow for the use of the average reference, source separation, and source localization. Furthermore, due to greater spatial coverage of the scalp, high-density montages may be able to better pick up superficial cortical and subcortical activity. In contrast, low-density systems are more widespread in their use and are less expensive.

PARTICIPANTS

Ages

When selecting participants for a study, rationale should be provided for the selected age group of interest. Common sources of rationale are related to (1) known changes occurring at the neurological or physiological level during some period in development or (2) changes in behavior that are hypothesized to be related to changes in neurological substrates during a specific time in development. It is important, however, to keep in mind that the relation between EEG/ERPs and behavior is associative and not causal (Hood, 2001). Furthermore, as Hood (2001) argues, caution should be used when interpreting EEG/ERP data, due to the fact that EEG/ERPs do not reflect the cause of the behavior nor do they provide an adequate explanation of the behavior. Areas may become activated simply as a consequence of connections with other more relevant areas. Nonetheless, once an age of interest has been selected for a given study, a specific age range must be set, due to changes in the electrophysiological responses that occur with increases in age. The previous discussion of the complex changes in ERPs should help with the conceptualization of the fact that averaging over a wide age range may obscure developmental changes resulting from response variability (Taylor & Baldeweg, 2002). In fact, it is recommended that, in developmental studies, averages of group EEG/ERPs should not be combined over more than 1–2 month intervals in infant studies, 1–2 years in childhood, and 2–3 years in adolescence (Picton et al., 2000; Taylor & Baldweg, 2002). Our laboratory (based on knowledge regarding both brain and child development) typically recommends that averages should not be combined over more than 10 days in infants, 1 month in childhood, and 1 year in adolescence. Final decisions regarding age ranges of participant groups must be based on the specifics of each study, including considerations of task demands, task difficulty, and components of interest.

Screening

As in any research study, participants should be screened for several factors that are thought to influence the dependent variable of interest, although specific exclusion criteria may vary depending on the hypotheses, population, and age group of interest. For most populations it is recommended that the following be described and/or documented, due to presumed or unknown influences that these factors have on the EEG or ERP response: age, gender (Hirayasu, Samura, Ohta, & Ogura, 2000; Lavoie, Robaey, Stauder, Glorieux, & Lefebvre, 1998; Oliver-Rodriguez, Guan, & Johnston, 1999), sensory problems, medications, neurological and psychiatric disorders, and handedness (including handedness of first degree relatives; see Oldfield, 1971, for an example of a handedness assessment). In addition, the following are relevant for developmental populations: pre- or postnatal difficulties, including prematurity (Lavoie et al., 1998; Stolarova, Whitney, Webb, deRegnier, Georgieff, & Nelson, 2003), iron deficiency (deRegnier et al., 2000), head size (circumference, inion to nasion and ear to ear measurements, Polich, Ladish, & Burns, 1990), memory span or intelligence assessment (Polich et al., 1990; Stauder, Van Der Molen, & Molenaar, 1998), time of day (especially in relation to feeding, see Geisler & Polich, 1990), and the main source of nutrition in early months of life (i.e., breast milk or formula).

Sample size

An additional consideration in developmental EEG/ERP studies is the number of participants required to obtain enough power to detect significant results. First, although collecting EEG/ERPs is considered a noninvasive procedure, preparation and participation in an ERP study does require a considerable amount of patience and cooperation on the part of the participant. In developmental populations this requirement is not easily realized. The behavioral and emotional state of young infants and children is extremely variable; many participants are unable to tolerate the preparation procedure or recording and therefore do not produce utilizable data due to extreme fussiness or excessive movement artifacts.

It is currently thought that it is this excessive movement (of the eyes and/or head) that accounts for much of the increased variability in developmental ERP components, although other sources of variability are suspected. Given this increased variability in the ERP response, both between and within participants at younger ages, care must be taken to ensure adequate power. Thus, typical infant ERP studies in our lab have enrollment numbers of 50 participants, with an expected 50–75% retention rate that is highly age dependent (e.g., 65% at 9 months, 50% at 12 months; see also Chapter 4, Table 4.1 for more comparisons of attrition rates over age and in different paradigms).

However, every attempt is made to increase the amount of useable data from every session, such as by using toys to distract the infant during electrode placement, having multiple testing partners who are experienced with children, and testing at a time of day that is best for the infant (see the next section on data collection for more specific suggestions broken down by age group). Due to high and variable rejection rates of developmental data, one must be mindful of differences that may arise due to the differential ability of infants and young children to successfully complete one condition versus another. Therefore, we strongly recommend that manuscript method sections include complete descriptions of rejection criteria including the number of participants indicated by the specific reasons for their exclusion.

DATA COLLECTION

Recording

Due to developmental changes in skull thickness (including closure of fontanels in infancy) and variation in cell density, synaptic efficiency, and other physiological parameters, developmental groups require differences in the set up of the data acquisition system. Specifically, amplifier gain settings (i.e., resolution settings) must be altered in order to adequately resolve the ERP signal; sampling rates (i.e., the analog to digital conversion rate) may need to be adjusted in order to register signals of differing frequencies (with the minimum rate being twice the highest frequency of the signal to be measured); and filtering and scoring parameters need to be specified. For instance, in an ERP experiment with 9-month-olds using a low-density Grass-Astromed© amplifier, we commonly use a gain of 20,000 μV, a sampling rate of 200 Hz, a notch filter at 60 Hz, and headroom of ± 250 μV. However, for the same study in adults, we would use a gain of 50,000 μV, a sampling rate of 200 Hz, a notch filter at 60 Hz, and headroom of ± 100 μV. In short, headroom is a function of the range of values accepted by the A/D board and the gain. For adults, data are typically collected with a ± 100 μV headroom, and this usually does not need to be reduced (or "scored down") any further offline since normal adult brain activity falls within these bounds. However, for infants, due to the large variability and increased amount of movement artifacts, a wider headroom range may be used for data collection. This range is then reduced offline, in order to remove large artifact signals. Although there is still debate about the range of amplitude of typical infant and child brain activity, current consensus is somewhere between $\pm$ 100 and 150 μV. We have provided guidelines for ERP data collection in Table 1.1 from our laboratory; however, these values may differ for various recording systems and in EEG research (which requires a higher sampling frequency). Furthermore, these settings may be changed depending on how the data are to be used. For example, if 6- and 9-month-olds were to be directly compared, it would be appropriate to have the same recording specifications for both ages.

Testing session specifics

There are several factors in developmental EEG/ERP testing sessions that differ from adult testing sessions. For groups of all ages, session length (including preparation) and the number of trials attempted and expected to be completed should be considered. In our laboratory we have found the following recommendations useful regardless of the age of the participant group, whereas in the sections following we make additional recommendations that apply to specific age groups. First, experience with infants and children is desirable, due to the fact that the procedure is often a very novel experience for infants and children and it is important to make the participants and their caregivers comfortable. Second, a welcoming preparation room with many toys and "distractor" items will also help both the child and the caregiver feel comfortable in the unfamiliar surroundings during the introduction to the procedure and preparation. In the actual testing room we

Table 1.1 Recommendations for event-related potential recording parameters in developmental populations

AGE	Amplification factor*(Gain)	Sampling rate	Headroom	Scoring parameters (A/D units)
0–2 months and 6 years and above	50,000	200 Hz***	$\pm$ 100 μV	$\pm$ 100 μV
3 months to 6 years	20,000	200 Hz	$\pm$ 250 μV	$\pm$ 100 to $\pm$ 225 μV**

* High-density systems, such as the EGI© system, have high input impedance amplifiers and gain settings may vary.

** For example, using the following equations: Minimum A/D units: 0 + (headroom/2) – X μV / precision) and Maximum A/D units: 4096 – (headroom/2) – X μV / precision). If headroom is $\pm$ 250 μV, the gain is 20,000, and data that exceed $\pm$ 100 μV need to be rejected, the calculation (using a 16-bit data acquisition board) is: Min A/D units: 0 + (250 – 100) μV / (500/4096)) = ~1229, Max A/D units: 4096 – (250 – 100) μV / (500/4096)) = ~2867.

*** Sampling rates in EEG paradigms are typically higher (500 Hz) as the minimum rate required is twice the highest frequency of the signal to be measured.

recommend placing a screen around the area where the infant or child is sitting and removing any distracting items from the room in order to keep their attention focused on the computer screen. This will help to minimize movement artifacts. Finally, for all age groups, we recommend that the experimenter(s) have some means, either during data collection or during data analysis, to ensure that data are accepted only when the infants are motionless and attending to the stimuli. For example, experimenters could monitor infants' looking during the task and have access to both a repeat button and a pause button. This will reduce artifacts due to either movement or eye blinks, and will allow the experimenter to take short breaks from testing if the infant becomes fussy.

Newborns

Data collection with newborn infants involves "passive" viewing or listening paradigms. During auditory tasks newborns are typically in an active state of sleep or awake, and artifacts are uncommon, due to the newborn's limited range of movement. In fact, most newborn infants are able to complete 50–200 trials, as the experiment can usually be paused to accommodate changes in the newborn's state (e.g., if the newborn becomes fussy). One important consideration when studying newborns is the portability of the data collection system. Often it is desirable to record electrophysiological data within a day of birth and thus requires that these studies take place in a hospital setting, preferably in different hospital rooms so that disturbance of baby and mother is minimal.

Infants

Data collection in infants also typically involves "passive" viewing or listening paradigms. For the most part, infants are easily distracted during preparation by playing with a second experimenter or engaging with toys. Depending on the age and locomotor abilities of the child, we recommend the use of a highchair or self-contained walker to keep the infant from crawling around the room during preparation. During recording, it is preferable if infants remain in a highchair or car seat in front of the computer screen presenting stimuli, with the caregiver seated a little behind and to the side of the infant. It is important to minimize the amount the infant turns to look at his/her caregiver. In some cases, infants may be more comfortable sitting on their caregiver's lap during stimulus presentation and ERP recording but this typically increases movement artifact. If the infant sits on the caregiver's lap, we recommend instructing the caregiver to let the infant move around only as much as necessary, but request that the caregiver not bounce the infant on his/her knee, as such movement creates artifacts in the data. Furthermore, in looking paradigms (such as habituation paradigms) we suggest that the parent be blindfolded to reduce possible biases.

Often, during data collection, infants become inattentive, restless, or fussy. Therefore, in visual experiments an experimenter typically sits next to the infant and directs the infant's attention to the stimuli by tapping or pointing at the screen. (Note: To decrease potential biases in the data due to artifacts that result from consistent movements to only one side, the side on which the experimenter sits should be counterbalanced or randomized.) Additionally, the experimenter who is directing the infants' attention to the stimuli should be naive to stimuli or conditions of interest in order to reduce possible biases.

In auditory ERP studies or during resting EEG data collection, it is also important to achieve eye fixation and reduce movement in order to minimize artifacts. In such cases, providing an interesting screen saver or object (e.g., bubbles) for the infant to watch can be quite useful (for other examples see the section on Task Design earlier in this chapter).

Visual stimuli can either be presented by the computer at a constant rate, with the option to repeat a trial or pause the experiment if the infant is not attending to the stimuli, or the experimenter can control stimulus presentation and only present stimuli when the infant is attending. One experimenter may be needed to control the stimulus presentation and determine when the infant is attending to the stimulus while the other experimenter directs the infants' attention. If necessary, the infant may have a pacifier, bottle, Cheerios™, cookie, or teether, although there is some concern that sucking on such objects may result in movement artifacts and thus should be well documented and examined to determine any influence such items have on the data (cf. Johnson et al., 2001; Picton et al., 2000).

In sum, there are several ways to create a more comfortable atmosphere for infant and child participants and their caregivers both during preparation and EEG/ERP recording. We encourage researchers to try several of the suggestions mentioned above and create new strategies that are appropriate for different types of studies. However, we conclude this section by acknowledging that there is a trade-off between introducing exogenous factors that may influence data (e.g., pacifiers, short breaks, etc.) and keeping participants comfortable and happy in order to acquire useable data.

Reference montages

The appropriate type of recording reference depends largely on the inter-electrode distance. Typically, low-density montages (32 electrodes or less) use a common bipolar. The difference in amplitude between the scalp electrode of interest and a reference electrode that is equidistant from all other electrodes (commonly the vertex or Cz in the 10–20 system) is recorded during data collection, and then the data are re-referenced offline to a mathematically linked reference recorded separately from two single sources (e.g., the ear lobes or mastoids). With high-density montages such as the EGI system (64, 128, 256 electrodes) an average reference is typically used. The average reference is calculated by subtracting the mean of all electrodes from each channel. An important note here is that it is not the density that determines the type of reference per se, but instead the inter-electrode distance. An average reference can be used when the inter-electrode distance is less than 2–3 cm. Junghöfer and colleagues (1997) suggest that the optimal number of electrodes on an adult head is approximately 256 and on the infant head about 128 (although 64, and possibly 32, electrodes can yield a sampling density of less than 3 cm in infants depending on the age of the infant and size of the infant's head; Junghöfer, Elbert, Leiderer, Berg, & Rockstroh, 1997 cited in Johnson et al., 2001).

In our experience, the best way to record a mathematically linked reference is by affixing electrodes to an adhesive foam pad and placing them behind the infant's or child's ears on the mastoid bone. However, this is problematic if the infant has a great deal of hair; the adhesive pad may stick to the hair and not remain in place. Ear clips are also available which clip to the infant's ear lobes, yet our lab has found that these do not consistently remain on the infant's ears and have to be replaced frequently during the recording session. When using the average reference, the data are referenced online to one of the electrodes on the scalp (usually the vertex) and then later re-referenced to the average. The original online recording does not present any unique problems except that one must ensure this essential electrode has a low-impedance connection with the scalp.

It is important to note that different referencing configurations can influence the amplitude and latency of the components of interest. Depending on the distribution of the components and the reference used, amplitudes can be smaller or larger and latencies slower or faster. A recent investigation using a face-processing paradigm in adults reported that both the amplitude and latency of several adult components (VPP, N170, and P300) were influenced by reference type (Abrams, Westerlund, Hersey, Gustafson, & Nelson, 2004). As illustrated in Figure 1.3A, the adult vertex-positive potential (VPP), commonly observed over fronto-central sites, showed a smaller amplitude when an average reference was used compared to either a linked mastoid, linked earlobes, or left mastoid reference. However, as illustrated in Figure 1.3B, the adult N170, which is maximal over posterior-temporal sites, was larger when an average reference was used. Thus, when choosing the referencing montage for any particular study, the components of interest must also be taken into consideration, as a reference proximal to the sources may reduce the ability to distinguish significant differences.

It has also been noted that because activity recorded at the mastoid electrodes may include background noise as well as cephalic activity, using the linked mastoids re-reference can add variability to the data (Abrams et al., 2004). This increased variability may influence the ability to observe consistent differences between conditions or groups. Therefore, caution must be used when comparing data between investigations utilizing different references.

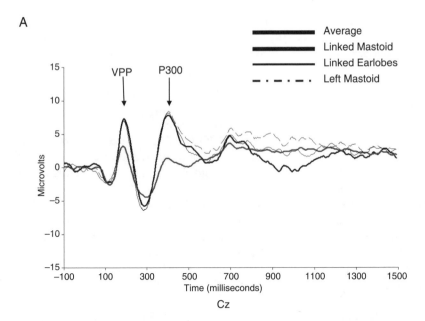

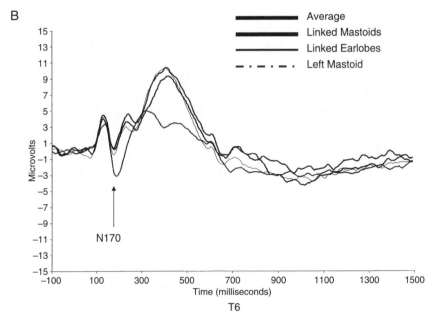

Figure 1.3 Effects of four different references on adult components elicited during a
face-processing paradigm. (A) Components with a fronto-central distribution, such as the vertex-positive potential (VPP) and P300, show decreases
in amplitude when an average reference is used compared to either a linked
mastoid, linked earlobes, or one left mastoid. (B) In contrast, components
that are maximal over posterior-temporal sites, such as the N170, show
increases in amplitude when an average reference is used. (Figure 1.3
kindly provided by and reproduced with permission from Abrams et al.,
2004.) Visit http://www.psypress.co.uk/dehaan to see this figure in colour.

Data reduction

Artifact rejection

Artifacts refer to unwanted noise in the electrophysiological signal that can result from many sources. The largest source of artifact in infant ERPs is movement artifact unrelated to EMG (i.e., high-amplitude or offscale activity as opposed to high-frequency activity of electromyogram, or EMG). However, artifacts can also be caused by EMG (e.g., head or body movements) and eye movements (e.g., blinking). In the previous section we made several suggestions as to how to reduce artifacts and ensure that the infant attends to the stimuli. Far more challenging are artifacts resulting from eye movements, which may disproportionately contaminate anterior recording electrodes. These artifacts may result in the misattribution of the component source to the frontal region of the brain, when it rightly belongs in the eyes and should be excluded from data analysis (Nelson, 1994). Fortunately, the amplitudes of infant ERPs tend to be much larger than adult ERPs (most likely due to physiological differences such as thinner skulls, and less dense cell packing in brain tissue). As a result, developmental researchers have found that it takes considerably more eye activity to contaminate the ERP signal in infants compared to adults (see Nelson, 1994, for further discussion). However, to ensure against contamination due to electrooculogram (EOG) activity, we recommend recording eye movements, using computer algorithms, and visual inspection of the data to identify and delete corrupted trials (see Nelson, 1994, for details).

Specifically, our lab uses a bipolar recording for the EOG recording (i.e., the upper eye electrode is referenced to the lower eye electrode), which provides us with a measure of the eye activity itself. Typically, the recording configuration consists of two electrodes placed on the supra and inferior orbital ridges of the eye. This configuration allows for the detection of blinks and, with somewhat less precision, horizontal eye movements (e.g., saccades). In an ideal situation, recording both vertical and horizontal eye movements is preferable, but from a practical perspective, if participants are not able to tolerate multiple electrodes near the eye, vertical eye movements are considered relatively more problematic and should be recorded. However, if the study involves presenting stimuli in the periphery, it is necessary to record both vertical and horizontal eye movements. Although it is becoming increasingly common with adult participants to use mathematical routines for identifying and subtracting artifacts due to eye movements to preserve the trial for averaging and analysis, this technique should only be used when it is ensured that the infant's eyes were not moving during the time the stimulus was being presented. Moreover, given differences in head size and shape between infants and adults, different propagation factors may dictate the utilization of different algorithms for subtracting EOG artifacts. In practice, our lab has adopted the following procedures for dealing with infant EOG activity. If the slope of the EOG activity is less than 250 μV/100 ms *and* the infant's eyes were fixated during the stimulus presentation, we apply a blink correction algorithm (Gratton, Coles, & Donchin, 1983). After the data have been edited for EOG artifacts, each individual participant's data are visually inspected; if it appears that eye movements were occurring consistently and appear to distort the ERP signal, especially at the anterior electrode sites, we reject those trials from the average and subsequent analyses.

When editing data for artifacts, many benign sources of activity can be detected (e.g., head movements, eye movements, blinks, and so on). In addition, sources of abnormal activity, such as seizure activity, may also become apparent during data collection or data analysis. A final recommendation is that researchers be generally familiar with the appearance of seizure activity and establish procedures for reporting such activity if and when it is suspected (either during or after data collection). Although this is very rare, due to the young age of some participants many seizure disorders may not yet be detected because of the ambiguous way they present themselves behaviorally (situations such as this are similar to incidental findings of structural abnormalities in the brains of normal or typical participants in fMRI studies and should be handled in a similar manner). Notifying the parents of such a possible concern should be done with great care and accompanied with a referral to a competent physician.

Averaging

One issue alluded to above that is highly pertinent to developmental ERP data concerns the large variability in waveforms (both between and within participants). Indeed, Nelson and colleagues report more between-participant variability in infants than in adults and children tested under the same conditions (Nelson, 1994). Although part of this variability is the result of increases in artifacts (as discussed above), there is a great deal of variability between participants as a function of the total number of trials contributed by each infant during the ERP session (Snyder, Webb, & Nelson, 2002). Infants vary widely in the number of trials they complete in an ERP session, with some completing as few as 20 trials and others completing over 100. Importantly, between-participant differences that arise from differences in the number of completed trials have been associated with both amplitude and latency differences in certain components (e.g., the Nc component in 6-month-olds; see Snyder et al., 2002).

In addition to the differences that lead to increased between-participant variability, there is often a great deal of within-participant variability in developmental ERP data. In fact, variability in the infant's brain response to the same stimulus over time has been reported. Differences in topography (of both the Nc and slow wave activity) have been detected in the same participant's data depending on whether the first half or the second half of their data from one testing session was included in their final data set. These differences may depend on the infant's familiarity with the stimulus (Snyder et al., 2002); however, they also may arise from state changes in the infant during data collection (e.g., changes in sleepiness, fussiness, or comfort levels).

Such individual differences are important and can be analyzed separately to answer a different line of questions. However, these differences can result in an extraordinary amount of variability in group data sets. In fact, it is not uncommon to fail to find statistical differences between two experimental conditions that visually appear to be vastly dissimilar from one another. These findings may, of course, reflect the actual equivalence of two experimental conditions. However, null findings can also be due to insufficient power to detect differences due to large between- and within-participant variability. Although methods for analyzing such variability exist (e.g., analyzing variances instead of means), these methods are not common in the literature due to the fact that they are mathematically complex and not easily implemented or interpretable (Nelson, 1994; Taylor & Baldeweg, 2002). Ideally, the signal-to-noise ratio should be maximized both within individual participants, by including a large number of individual trials in a cross average (see Figure 1.4), and between participants, by including a large number of participants in each group (see Figure 1.5). Although it varies from study to study, our current heuristic is to require that an infant contribute *at least* 10–20 artifact-free trials to their individual average and at least 10 infants contribute data for each experimental condition. This same general principle applies to EEG data as well. To obtain stable estimates of spectral power, a minimum of 10–15 seconds of artifact-free EEG is recommended (Davidson, 1995). Without these or more stringent criteria, the signal-to-noise ratio is often compromised and significant results remain elusive despite genuine differences between experimental conditions (i.e., a Type II error). Therefore, we recommend that investigators report estimates of effect size and conduct power analyses to determine the number of participants required to obtain significant effects, and caution the interpretation of null findings with small sample sizes.

STATISTICAL ANALYSIS

In the following sections we comment on the utilization of different techniques used to statistically analyze developmental data, including ANOVA and MANOVA, hierarchical linear modeling (HLM), independent components analysis (ICA), and principal components analysis (PCA). For a full discussion, we refer the reader to other sources regarding these topics (e.g., Handy, 2004; Johnson et al., 2001; Reynolds & Richards, 2003; Richards, 2003a, 2003b), as our discussion will highlight concepts that are especially relevant when working with developmental data.

In EEG studies the dependent variables consist of absolute power, relative power, coherence, or hemispheric asymmetry. More specifically, absolute power is calculated through fast Fourier transform and divided up by spectral frequency for each electrode site. Relative power reflects the percentage of power in a specific frequency bin at each electrode site, relative to total power in all frequency bins. EEG coherence between two electrode sites reflects the power and phase dynamics between two signals, the covariation of which reflects the strength of the relationship (Taylor & Baldeweg, 2002). Finally, hemispheric asymmetries in power reflect the difference in the degree of activation between the left and right hemispheres of the brain (e.g., frontal lobe asymmetries; Fox, Henderson, Rubin, Calkins, & Schmidt, 2001). It is also important to note the common practice of applying a log transformation to the measure of power to normalize the distribution before analyses are conducted.

In adult ERP studies, the typical dependent or response variables include: average or peak amplitude, area below or above the curve, and latency to peak measurements. The independent or predictor variables include condition or task factors. Average amplitude measurements and area measures are typically used with components that do not exhibit a distinctly peaked component. For example, some investigators have used average amplitude to analyze the N400 component (e.g., Bentin & Deouell, 2000; Eimer, 2000). For data occurring in longer latency windows, such as slow wave activity, measurements of area under the curve are typically used. Area measurements tend to be less sensitive to noise but may also underestimate differences between participants, conditions, and electrodes (van Boxtel, 1998). For clearly defined components, such as the N170 or the P300, peak amplitude and corresponding latency measures are often used with similar criteria to those used in adult data (Carmel & Bentin, 2002; Donchin, McCarthy, Kutas, & Ritter, 1983).

Currently, statistical analyses that use the appropriate dependent variables mentioned above are similar if not the same as those analyses conducted with adult ERP data. Both Picton and colleagues (2000) and van Boxtel (1998) provide guidelines for statistical analyses with ERP data that we summarize briefly, but we also refer readers to other relevant sources (e.g., Handy, 2004). It is suggested that the experimenter use statistical analyses that are appropriate to both the nature of the data and the goal of the study. Typically, repeated measures ANOVA models are used to test hypotheses with ERP data. As with any ANOVA, repeated measures ANOVAs test the equality of means. This type of analysis is used when all members of a random sample are measured under a number of different conditions. As the sample is exposed to each condition, the measurement of the dependent variable is repeated (i.e., amplitude or latency at different leads). Using ANOVA techniques is not appropriate in this case because they fail to model the correlation between the repeated measures (the psychophysiological data often violate the ANOVA assumption of independence). To compensate for such violations, the degrees of freedom can be reduced by calculating

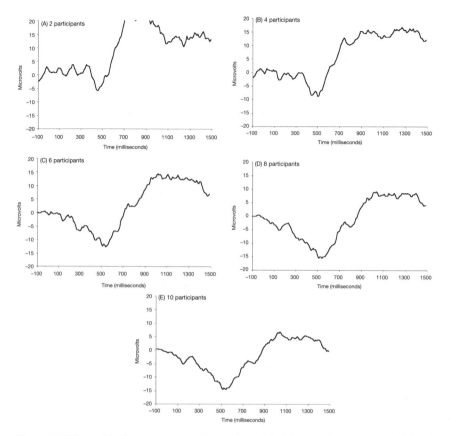

Figure 1.4 Example of a cross averaged waveform (at Cz) created from one individual infant participant using (A) 3 trials, (B) 13 trials, (C) 23 trials, (D) 33 trials, and (E) 43 trials. Note how the variability in the waveform decreases as the number of trials increases. Figure 1.4 kindly provided by Dr Charles Nelson and Alissa J. Westerlund (Developmental Medicine Center, Boston Children's Hospital, Harvard Medical School).

epsilon as described by Greenhouse and Geisser (1959) or Huynh and Feldt (1970).

MANOVA analyses can also be used to analyze ERP data. As long as the sample size exceeds the number of repeated measures by "a few," MANOVA analyses will range from being slightly less powerful than the adjusted method (described above) to infinitely more powerful (Davidson, 1972). Davidson (1972) suggests that the MANOVA approach is the best in cases when one expects small but reliable effects. Furthermore, Davidson (1972) suggests that when using MANOVA, a sample size that exceeds the number of repeated measurements by 20 or more be chosen. Thus, the only case when one should use adjusted ANOVA tests is when the sample size becomes as small as the

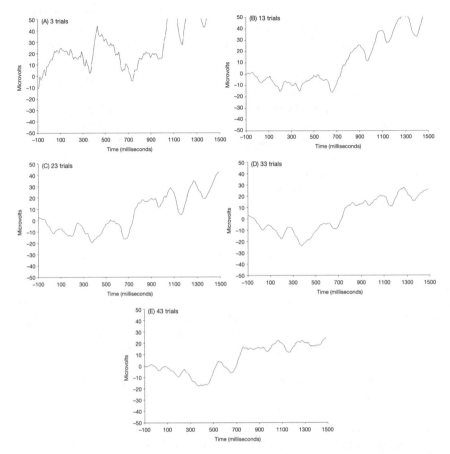

Figure 1.5 Example of a grand mean waveform (at Cz) containing cross averages from (A) 2 participants, (B) 4 participants, (C) 6 participants, (D) 8 participants, and (E) 10 participants. Note how the variability in the waveform decreases as the number of participants increases. Figure 1.5 kindly provided by Dr Charles Nelson and Alissa J. Westerlund (Developmental Medicine Center, Boston Children's Hospital, Harvard Medical School).

number of repeated measurements in the design. These typical statistical methods used with ERP data in adults (ANOVA, MANOVA, etc.), which can also be utilized for the statistical analysis of developmental ERP data, have several assumptions. For instance, (1) there cannot be any missing data (cases are deleted listwise), (2) all participants must be measured at the same equally spaced time points (e.g., using the same leads across all participants), (3) the response variable must be normally distributed, and (4) there is homogeneity of variance (either across time or across measurements). Violations in the above assumptions that, unfortunately, are common in developmental ERP data, result in deletion of cases and an unbalanced design. However, recent statistical advances such as the use of hierarchical linear modeling (HLM) to analyze longitudinal and repeated measure data sets may be especially relevant for developmental ERP data, due to the fact that it is not constrained by these assumptions. For example, HLM can accommodate unbalanced designs or data sets by estimating missing data. This accommodation may allow researchers to include more data that ultimately results in an increase in the retention rate. HLM can be used to include data from participants who may have unusable or artifact-contaminated data at specific electrode locations (e.g., participants with data that were selectively contaminated at anterior electrode sites by eye artifacts). Furthermore, infants will often only finish one of two experimental conditions (e.g., due to fussiness). The use of HLM may allow one to keep data from the first condition for subsequent data analysis, as opposed to deleting all of the participant's data.

SOURCE SEPARATION AND LOCALIZATION TECHNIQUES IN ERPs

An increase in the number of electrodes, and a concomitant decrease in inter-electrode distances, results in increased spatial resolution in high-density recording methods. Conventional methods of analyzing electrophysiological data do not take advantage of this added spatial information, thus several investigators have used source separation and localization techniques to statistically identify source generators in the brain (for further illustration see Johnson et al., 2001; Reynolds & Richards, 2003; Richards, 2000).

A well-known challenge in ERP research is localizing activity that is volume conducted to the scalp surface. This problem, known as the inverse problem, refers to the relative difficulty we have in calculating the distribution of electrical current in the brain from surface measurements. Electrical recordings taken from the scalp reflect a mixture of the activity of a number of underlying neural sources (dipoles) in the brain. Source separation consists of identifying sources that account for the largest portion of variance in ERP data. One method of source separation is independent component analysis (ICA), which decomposes spatiotemporal data into separate, or independent, components. ICA can be thought of as an extension of a more commonly applied method, principal component analysis (PCA). PCA uses factor analysis to identify the components that account for the largest amount of variance in the data, then the next largest, and so on. Compared to ICA, which is not restricted to normally distributed components, PCA yields statistically independent components if they are normally distributed (Johnson et al., 2001). ICA assumes that electrical activity recorded at scalp electrode sites represents a linear combination of the concurrent electrical activity evoked by networks of neurons within the brain. It is assumed that these networks are spatially fixed and operate independently in time. However, the "sources" of ICA components may be (one or more) distributed brain networks rather than modularly active brain regions. Source localization procedures assume that brain networks (or dipoles) are physically isolated from one another, whereas ICA procedures only assume that brain networks act independently. Therefore, ICA may be useful as a preprocessing step prior to attempting source localization (Makeig, Bell, Jung, & Sejnowski, 1996). However, this does not solve the problem of source localization. Johnson and colleagues (2001) suggest that ICA may be useful in reducing intertrial variability in analyses of infant ERP data. They state that ICA may be able to extract components from more noisy data (common in infant data) that are similar to those extracted from a data set that has been previously corrected for artifacts. In sum, for developmental ERP data, ICA could provide a method for examining both intersubject and intertrial variability.

Source localization is a different process from source separation. Source localization attempts to identify the location, orientation, and magnitude of dipoles in the brain that may be responsible for specific ERP components (Nunez, 1990). The software package Brain Electrical Source Analysis (BESA$^©$) identifies candidate dipoles in the brain by analyzing the distribution of electrical activity recorded at the scalp (Scherg & Berg, 1996). This activity is applied to simplified models of the head in order to determine neural sources. Johnson and colleagues (2001) voice several concerns regarding the use of source localization methods in infants. First, skull thickness, density, and fontanel closure are different in adults relative to infants. Thus, localization techniques used with adults may not be applicable to all developmental populations. Second, the spherical head model used in source localization may be less appropriate for developmental populations, as factors such as skull thickness and head circumference may be more variable in infant compared to adult populations. There are currently no software packages (such as BESA) that attempt to compensate for these differences. Developmentally appropriate head models may increase the feasibility of source localization in developmental populations. Although high-density ERP techniques appear to provide researchers with the ability to estimate sources of neural activity, it is recommended that source localization only be combined with strong theoretical foundations concerning anatomical localization (e.g., Richards, 2003a). In fact, Hood argues that although relatively specific areas may "light up" under some conditions, such localization is of limited value on its own as explanation, and provocatively claims that "in most cases it [source localization] simply confirms the experimenter's expectation that there is event-related activity occurring in the brain" (Hood, 2001, p. 215).

FUTURE DIRECTIONS

There are several areas of developmental EEG/ERP research in need of improvement. First, further headway in grounding developmental EEG/ERP research in behavior is needed. New behavioral measures need to be utilized (especially in conjunction with ERP measures), and new paradigms, which facilitate a convergence of behavioral and electrophysiological data, need to be designed. Second, future research should aim to explore the development of ERP components (e.g., Webb et al., 2005). Such knowledge can be combined with our increasing knowledge of the development of EEG rhythms and the brain in order to refine data collection parameters. This will allow ERP recordings to accurately capture the dynamic development of the brain. Third, statistical methods, which accommodate missing data, should be applied to developmental data sets. This strategy will help to ensure that valuable information is not lost due to insufficient statistical techniques. In addition, algorithms used to identify artifacts in adult EEG/ERP data analysis should be altered to accommodate the wide variability in infant data. This will ensure that similar techniques can be used across age groups. Finally, if researchers continue to use source localization techniques, parameters suitable for infant and child data need to be developed and established in available software.

In conclusion, the challenges of developmental research include issues ranging from designing studies that are sufficiently interesting in order to recruit and sustain infants' attention, to successfully placing the desired number of electrodes on infants' heads, to the careful reduction of variability in data and rejection of artifact-contaminated data. However, the ultimate challenge in conducting developmental EEG/ERP research is to take what is known from other areas of research, which utilize different methodologies, and combine this information with electrophysiological data in innovative ways to produce converging evidence, which support theoretical claims. The use of consistent and appropriate methods will, we hope, contribute to this goal. Furthermore, we hope that methods for developmental EEG/ERP research will continue to be refined after the publication of this chapter. We underscore the importance of a collaborative approach that will prove to be the most powerful tool in examining complex developmental changes in the brain from infancy through the lifespan.

ACKNOWLEDGMENTS

The authors would like to thank Michelle de Haan, the members of the Developmental Cognitive Neuroscience Lab, and the Cognition in the Transition Lab at the University of Minnesota for their comments on the chapter. Support for the writing of this chapter was made possible by grants to the first author from the Thomas F. Wallace Endowed Fellowship at the

University of Minnesota, to the second author by a training grant from the National Institute of Child Health & Human Development to the Center for Cognitive Sciences at the University of Minnesota (5T32 HD07151), and to the third author from the National Institute of Health (NS329976 and NS32755). Portions of this chapter first appeared (with permission from MIT Press) in DeBoer, T., Scott, L. S., & Nelson, C. A. (2004). Event-related potentials in developmental populations. In T. C. Handy (Ed.), *Event-related potentials: A methods handbook* (pp. 263–297). MIT Press. Correspondence regarding this chapter should be directed to the third author at Harvard Medical School, Developmental Medicine Center, Laboratory of Cognitive Neuroscience, Boston Children's Hospital, 1 Autumn Street, #713 6th floor, Boston, MA 02115 or charles.nelson@childrens.harvard.edu

REFERENCES

Abrams, J. M., Westerlund, A., Hersey, M. A., Gustafson, E. C., & Nelson, C. A. (2004, April). *Is the N170 a reference-specific component?* Poster presented at the Annual Meeting of the Cognitive Neuroscience Society, San Francisco, CA.

Bauer, P. J. (1995) Recalling past events: From infancy to early childhood. *Annals of Child Development, 11*, 25–71.

Bell, M. A., & Fox, N. A. (1992). The relations between frontal brain electrical activity and cognitive development during infancy. *Child Development, 63*, 1142–1163.

Bell, M. A., & Fox, N. A. (1996). Crawling experience is related to changes in cortical organization during infancy: Evidence from EEG coherence. *Developmental Psychobiology, 29*, 551–561.

Bell, M. A., & Fox, N. A. (1997). Individual differences in object permanence performance at 8 months: Locomotor experience and brain electrical activity. *Developmental Psychobiology, 31*, 287–297.

Bentin, S., & Deouell, L. Y. (2000). Structural encoding and identification in face processing: ERP evidence for separate mechanisms. *Cognitive Neuropsychology, 17*, 35–54.

Buss, K. A., Malmstadt Schumacher, J. R., Dolski, I., Kalin, N. H., Hill Goldsmith, H., & Davidson, R. J. (2003). Right frontal brain activity, cortisol, and withdrawal behavior in 6-month-old infants. *Behavioral Neuroscience, 117*, 11–20.

Calkins, S. D., Fox, N. A., & Marshall, T. R. (1996). Behavioral and physiological antecedents of inhibited and uninhibited behavior. *Child Development, 67*, 523–540.

Carmel, D., & Bentin, S. (2002). Domain specificity versus expertise: Factors influencing distinct processing of faces. *Cognition, 83*, 1–29.

Carver, L. J., Bauer, P. J., & Nelson, C. A. (2000). Associations between infant brain activity and recall memory. *Developmental Science, 3*, 234–246.

Carver, L. J., Wewerka, S. S., Gary, J. W., Panagiotides, H., Tribby-Walbridge, S. R., Rinaldi, J. A. et al. (1999, April). *Neural correlates of recognition memory during the second year of life.* Poster presented at the Biennial Meeting of the Society for Research in Child Development, Albuquerque, NM.

Davidson, M. L. (1972). Univariate versus multivariate tests in repeated-measures experiments. *Psychological Bulletin, 77*, 446–452.

Davidson, R. J. (1995). Cerebral asymmetry, emotion, and affective style. In R. J. Davidson & K. Hugadahl (Eds.), *Brain asymmetry* (pp. 361–387). Cambridge, MA: MIT Press.

Dawson, G., Panagiotides, H., Klinger, L. G., & Spieker, S. (1997). Infants of depressed and nondepressed mothers exhibit differences in frontal brain electrical activity during the expression of negative emotions. *Developmental Psychology, 33*, 650–656.

deRegnier, R.-A., Nelson, C. A., Thomas, K., Wewerka, S., & Georgieff, M. K. (2000). Neurophysiologic evaluation of auditory recognition memory in healthy newborn infants and infants of diabetic mothers. *Journal of Pediatrics, 137*, 777–784.

Donchin, E., & McCarthy, G., Kutas, M., & Ritter, W. (1983). Event-related brain potentials in the study of consciousness. In R. J. Davidson, G. E. Schwartz, & D. Shapiro (Eds.), *Consciousness and self-regulation* (Vol. 3, pp. 81–121). New York: Plenum Press.

Eimer, M. (2000). Effects of face inversion on the structural encoding and recognition of faces: Evidence from event-related brain potentials. *Cognitive Brain Research, 10*, 145–158.

Ferree, T. C., Luu, P., Russell, G. S., & Tucker, D. M. (2001). Scalp electrode impedance, infection risk, and EEG data quality. *Clinical Neurophysiology, 112*, 536–544.

Fox, N. A., Henderson, H. A., Rubin, K. H., Calkins, S. D., & Schmidt, L. A. (2001). Continuity and discontinuity of behavioral inhibition and exuberance: Psycho-physiological and behavioral influences across the first four years of life. *Child Development, 72*, 1–21.

Friedman, D., Brown, C. III, Cornblatt, B., Vaughan, H. G., & Erlenmeyer-Kimling, L. (1984). Changes in the late task-related brain potentials during adolescence. *Annals of the New York Academy of Sciences, 425*, 344–352.

Geisler, M. W., & Polich, J. (1990). P300 and time of day: Circadian rhythms, food intake, and body temperature. *Biological Psychology, 31*, 117–136.

Gratton, G., Coles, M. G. H., & Donchin, E. (1983). A new method of off-line removal of ocular artifact. *Electroencephalography and Clinical Neurophysiology, 55*, 468–484.

Greenhouse, S. W., & Geisser, S. (1959). On methods in the analysis of profile data. *Psychometrika, 24*, 95–112.

Handy, T. C. (2004). *Event related potentials: A methods handbook*. Cambridge, MA: MIT Press.

Henderson, H. A., Fox, N. A., & Rubin, K. H. (2001). Temperamental contributions to social behavior: The moderating roles of frontal EEG asymmetry and gender. *Journal of the American Academy of Child & Adolescent Psychiatry, 40*, 68–74.

Hirayasu, Y., Samura, M., Ohta, H., & Ogura, C. (2000). Sex effects on rate of change of P300 latency with age. *Clinical Neurophysiology, 111*, 187–194.

Hood, B. M. (2001). Combined electrophysiological and behavioral measurement in developmental cognitive neuroscience: Some cautionary notes. *Infancy, 2*, 213–217.

Huynh, H., & Feldt, L. S. (1970). Conditions under which mean square ratios in repeated measures designs have exact F-distributions. *Journal of the American Statistical Association, 65*, 1582–1589.

Jasper, H. H. (1958). The Ten–Twenty electrode system of the international federation. *Electroencephalography Clinical Neurophysiology, 10*, 371–375.

Johnson, M. H., de Haan, M., Oliver, A., Smith, W., Hatzakis, H., Tucker, L. A. et al. (2001). Recording and analyzing high-density event-related potentials with infants using the geodesic sensor net. *Developmental Neuropsychology*, *19*, 295–323.

Jones, N. A., Field, T., Fox, N. A., Davalos, M., & Gomez, C. (2001). EEG during different emotions in 10-month-old infants of depressed mothers. *Journal of Reproductive & Infant Psychology*, *19*, 295–312.

Junghöfer, M., Elbert, T., Leiderer, P., Berg, P., & Rockstroh, B. (1997). Mapping EEG-potentials on the surface of the brain: A strategy for uncovering cortical sources. *Brain Topography*, *9*, 203–217.

Karrer, R., & Monti, L. A. (1995). Event-related potentials of 4–7-week-old infants in a visual recognition memory task. *Electroencephalography and Clinical Neurology*, *94*, 414–424.

Kurtzberg, D., Vaughan, H. G. Jr., Courchesne, E., Friedman, D., Harter, M. R., & Putnam, L. E. (1984). Developmental aspects of event-related potentials. *Annals of the New York Academy of Sciences*, *425*, 300–318.

Lavoie, M. E., Robaey, P., Stauder, J. E. A., Glorieux, J., & Lefebvre, F. (1998). Extreme prematurity in healthy 5-year-old children: A re-analysis of sex effects on event-related brain activity. *Psychophysiology*, *35*, 679–689.

Makeig, S., Bell, A. J., Jung, T.-P., & Sejnowski, T. J. (1996). Independent component analysis of electroencephalographic data. *Advances in Neural Information Processing Systems*, *8*, 145–151.

Marshall, P. J., Bar-Haim, Y., & Fox, N. A. (2002). Development of the EEG from 5 months to 4 years of age. *Clinical Neurophysiology*, *113*, 1199–1208.

Martynova, O., Kirjavainen, J., & Cheour, M. (2003). Mismatch negativity and late discriminative negativity in sleeping human newborns. *Neuroscience Letters*, *340*, 75–78.

Mundy, P., Card, J., & Fox, N. (2000). EEG correlates of the development of infant joint attention skills. *Developmental Psychobiology*, *36*, 325–338.

Mundy, P., Fox, N., & Card, J. (2003). EEG coherence, joint attention and language development in the second year. *Developmental Science*, *6*, 48–54.

Nelson, C. A. (1994). Neural correlates of recognition memory in the first postnatal year of life. In G. Dawson & K. Fischer (Eds.), *Human behavior and the developing brain* (pp. 269–313). New York: Guilford Press.

Nelson, C. A. (1995). The ontogeny of human memory: A cognitive neuroscience perspective. *Developmental Psychology*, *31*, 723–738.

Nelson, C. A., & Luciana, M. (1998). Electrophysiological studies II: Evoked potentials and event-related potentials. In C. E. Coffey & R. A. Brumback (Eds.), *Textbook of pediatric neuropsychiatry* (pp. 331–356). Washington, DC: American Psychiatric Press, Inc.

Nelson, C. A., & Luciana, M. (2001). *Handbook of developmental cognitive neuroscience*. Cambridge, MA: MIT Press.

Nelson, C. A., & Monk, C. (2001). The use of event-related potentials in the study of cognitive development. In C. A. Nelson & M. Luciana (Eds.), *Handbook of developmental cognitive neuroscience* (pp. 125–136). Cambridge, MA: MIT Press.

Nunez, P. L. (1990). Physical principles and neurophysiological mechanisms underlying event-related potentials. In J. W. Rohrbach, R. Parasuraman, & R. Johnson (Eds.), *Event-related potentials: Basic issues and applications* (pp. 19–36). New York: Oxford University Press.

Oldfield, R. C. (1971). The assessment and analysis of handedness: The Edinburgh inventory. *Neuropsychologia, 9*, 97–113.

Oliver-Rodriguez, J. C., Guan, Z., & Johnston, V. S. (1999). Gender differences in late positive components evoked by human faces. *Psychophysiology, 36*, 176–185.

Pascalis, O., de Haan, M., Nelson, C. A., & de Schonen, S. (1998). Long term recognition memory assessed by visual paired comparison in 3- and 6-month-old infants. *Journal of Experimental Psychology: Learning, Memory, and Cognition, 24*, 1–12

Picton, T. W., Bentin, S., Berg, P., Donchin, E., Hillyard, S. A., Johnson, R. Jr. et al. (2000). Guidelines for using human event-related potentials to study cognition: Recording standards and publication criteria. *Psychophysiology, 37*, 127–152.

Polich, J., Ladish, C., & Burns, T. (1990). Normal variation of P300 in children: Age, memory span, and head size. *International Journal of Psychophysiology, 9*, 237–248.

Putnam, L. E., Johnson, R. Jr., & Roth, W. T. (1992). Guidelines for reducing the risk of disease transmission in the psychophysiology laboratory. SPR Ad Hoc Committee on the Prevention of Disease Transmission. *Psychophysiology, 29*, 127–141.

Regan, D. (1989). *Human brain electrophysiology: Evoked potentials and evoked magnetic fields in science and medicine*. New York: Elsevier.

Reynolds, G., & Richards, J. (2003, April). *The impact of familiarization on electrophysiological correlates of recognition memory in infants*. Poster presented the Annual Meeting of the Cognitive Neuroscience Society, New York City, NY.

Richards, J. E. (2000). Localizing the development of covert attention in infants with scalp event-related potentials. *Developmental Psychology, 36*, 91–108.

Richards, J. E. (2003a). Attention affects the recognition of briefly presented visual stimuli in infants: An ERP study. *Developmental Science, 6*, 312–328.

Richards, J. E. (2003b). Cortical sources of event-related potentials in the prosaccade and antisaccade task. *Psychophysiology, 40*, 878–894.

Scherg, M., & Berg, P. (1996). *BESA—Brain Electromagnetic Source Analysis user manual (Version 2.2)*. Munchen, Germany: MEGIS Software GmbH.

Schmidt, L. A., Trainor, L. J., & Santesso, D. L. (2003). Development of frontal electroencephalogram (EEG) and heart rate (ECG) responses to affective musical stimuli during the first 12 months of post-natal life. *Brain & Cognition, 52*, 27–32.

Snyder, K., Webb, S. J., & Nelson, C. A. (2002). Theoretical and methodological implications of variability in infant brain response during a recognition memory paradigm. *Infant Behavior and Development, 25*, 466–494.

Snyder, K. A. (2002, April). *Neurophysiological correlates of habituation and novelty preferences in human infants*. Presented at the International Conference on Infant Studies, Toronto, Canada.

Stauder, J. E. A., Van Der Molen, M. W., & Molenaar, P. C. M. (1998). Changing relations between intelligence and brain activity in late childhood: A longitudinal event-related potential study. *Brain & Cognition, 37*, 119–122

Stolarova, M., Whitney, H., Webb, S., deRegnier, R.-A., Georgieff, M., & Nelson, C. A. (2003). Electrophysiological brain responses of six-month-old low-risk premature infants during a visual priming task. *Infancy, 4*, 437–450.

Taylor, M. J., & Baldeweg, T. (2002). Application of EEG, ERP and intracranial recordings to the investigation of cognitive functions in children. *Developmental Science, 5*, 318–334.

Tucker, D. (1993). Spatial sampling of head electrical fields: The geodesic sensor net. *Electroencephalography and Clinical Neurophysiology, 87,* 154–163.

van Boxtel, G. (1998). Computational and statistical methods for analyzing event related potential data. *Behavior Research Methods, Instruments and Computers, 30,* 87–102.

Webb, S. J., Long, J. D., & Nelson, C. A. (2005). A longitudinal investigation of visual event-related potentials in the first year of life. *Developmental Science, 8,* 605–616.

2   Visual evoked potentials in infants

Daphne L. McCulloch
Glasgow Caledonian University, UK

Visual evoked potentials (VEPs) are used to assess the integrity and maturity of the visual system in infants and young children (Fulton, Hartmann, & Hansen, 1989; Hartmann, 1995; Mackie & McCulloch, 1995; Mellor & Fielder, 1980; Skarf, 1989; Taylor & McCulloch, 1992). The retinae and visual pathways develop very rapidly during the last trimester of gestation and the early months of life, which is reflected in dramatic changes in VEPs. Following this period of very rapid development, maturation of VEPs proceeds more gradually throughout infancy and childhood. VEPs are particularly useful in infants as they are easily recorded and precise normal limits have been established for a range of functions.

By convention, VEPs are defined as cortical potentials that are time-locked to repeated presentations of a visual stimulus, in the absence of a defined task and without significant cognitive content. However, the distinction between VEPs and event-related potentials to visual targets is never absolute, as both visual and cognitive processing mature in tandem. In this chapter, it is presumed that VEPs to repetitive visual stimuli reflect visual functions such as resolution, contrast, colour, and motion, while cognitive processing such as novelty and memory make minimal contributions to the resulting VEP.

In adults, the first major component of VEPs to commonly used pattern stimuli likely arise from surface negative activity of the primary visual cortex around the calcarine sulcus, V1. The generators of the other early components, those within 200 ms of the stimulus, are generated in V1 and in several visually active cortical areas in the occipital and parietal cortex (Di Russo et al., 2005; Schroeder, Teneke, Givre, Arezzo, & Vaughn, 1991; Vanni, Warnking, Dojat, Delon-Martin, Bullier, & Segebarth, 2004). Infant VEPs have relatively few components with broad scalp distributions and there is very little information available regarding their cortical origins. It seems likely that the cortical sources of immature VEPs would be relatively extended. Source locations for individual components in infants may overlap and may evolve during the maturational process.

VEP STIMULATION AND RECORDING IN INFANTS

VEP stimuli

VEPs are classified according to both the rate and the type of visual stimulation. Those elicited by abrupt stimulation followed by relatively long inter-stimulus intervals are called transient VEPs and consist of a series of components that are usually labelled according to their peak time relative to the stimulus onset. In adults, stimulation below four times per second will elicit a transient VEP. In infants, transient VEP stimuli are typically presented twice per second in healthy infants after 10 weeks of age, and once per second for very young infants or those at risk for abnormal development.

Rapid repeated visual stimulation elicits VEPs that overlap in time producing a continuous oscillating waveform. These are called steady-state VEPs. The oscillating components of steady-state VEPs coincide with the frequency of the stimulation and its harmonics so that this type of VEP is usually analysed in the frequency domain (Bach & Meigen, 1999). Most strategies for rapid VEP signal detection and threshold estimation use steady-state VEPs.

Although virtually any type of visual stimulus will elicit a VEP, stimuli are selected to isolate an underlying visual function. Luminance VEPs can be elicited by transient luminance stimuli (flash, onset or offset of light) or by steady-state luminance stimulation (flicker).

Stimuli that isolate pattern vision are usually designed with constant average luminance so that the resulting VEP depends solely on processing of pattern information. Pattern VEPs can be designed to test a wide range of visual functions, such as resolution, orientation tuning, contrast detection, motion, and binocular visual functions.

VEP testing strategies for infants

Although infants do not follow instructions about fixation and attention, they are naturally attracted to visual stimuli. Thus, VEP recording is straightforward in alert, attentive infants. Infant VEP amplitudes are larger than those of adults, allowing good quality VEP recording with shorter recording times. These large amplitudes are in part due to the thin infant skull that allows the electrode to be positioned close to the cortex with much lower electrical insulation than that of the thicker adult skull. Additionally, neural synchrony may be greater in the infant visual cortex compared with that in a more developed brain.

To facilitate recording VEPs in infants, the stimulus should be positioned away from distracting objects and people: a testing booth or moveable screens are useful. Fixation should be monitored and VEP recording interrupted during fixation losses. Useful strategies to improve fixation include dangling and tapping the fixation screen with small objects (usually keys) and superimposing or interrupting the stimulus with interesting pictures, animation, or input from a live camera (for example, a parent encouraging fixation). Although such strategies introduce random interruption of the stimulus, the improved attention and fixation greatly outweigh the disadvantages (Fulton et al., 1989; Kriss & Russell-Eggitt, 1992; Skarf, 1989). Finally, young infants are best tested using a flexible approach that allows the infant to adopt his/her preferred position (sitting, reclining, over a shoulder) and ensures appropriate breaks for feeding, changing, or rest (Figure 2.1).

ISCEV Standard VEP tests

Standardised VEPs are the basic tests used to assess the integrity of an infant's visual system. Standard VEP stimuli and recording methods are defined in the VEP standard of the International Society of Clinical Electrophysiology of Vision (ISCEV) (Odom et al., 2004). This standard as well as guidelines for calibration (Brigell, Bach, Barber, Moskowitz, & Robson, 2003) and standards for other electrophysiological tests of the visual system are regularly updated (http://www.iscev.org/standards). The standards specify recording conditions and define standard flash and pattern stimuli.

For flash VEPs the standard stimulus is brief flash from an extended source (strobe or screen flash of at least 20 degrees of visual angle) with a flash luminance between 1.5 and 3 candela seconds per metre squared.[1] Although standard flash VEPs demonstrate high inter-subject variability, they are particularly useful for those with poor fixation, reduced vision, or defects affecting the optics of the eyes.

Standard stimuli for pattern VEPs are defined as high-contrast, black and white checkerboards with large checks (check width, 1 degree of visual angle) and with small checks (check width, 0.25 degree). Checkerboards are visually complex, but they have been adopted as the standard because they are used widely and because they elicit large amplitude VEPs. The preferred presentation mode for standard checkerboards is pattern-reversal, abrupt alternation of black and white checks without a change in average luminance. This ensures that there will be no stimulus present if the pattern is not resolved. Pattern-reversal VEPs have low intra-subject variability in waveform and in peak latencies, particularly of the major positivity, P100, which peaks approximately 100 ms after pattern reversal in adults. The alternative mode of presentation for standard check stimuli is onset/offset, in which the pattern is abruptly substituted for a diffuse grey background. As the onset and offset must be achieved with no absolute or transient change in the average luminance or colour, this stimulus is technically more difficult to achieve compared with pattern reversal. Onset/offset VEPs have greater inter-subject variability

1   A brief flash is within the neural integration time of the retina, which varies with background and adaption levels. These stimuli should last less than 5 ms. Brief flashers are specified by the "total luminance integrated over the flash duration", often abbreviated "flash luminance".

Figure 2.1 Infants prepared for VEP testing. In this case, disposable orthopaedic wrap is used to keep the electrodes secure. The young infant has adopted his preferred position, looking over the adult's shoulder (upper). When older the infant prefers to be seated with an object to keep his attention.

compared with pattern reversal VEPs, but they are more robust in cases of poor fixation and nystagmus (Apkarian, 1994a; Hoffmann, Seufert, & Bach, 2004; Saunders, Brown, & McCulloch, 1998).

An ISCEV standard VEP is, in general, quick and easy to record in most infants. All paediatric laboratories should incorporate standard VEP testing into every protocol to document the integrity of the visual system in a way that is comparable with other laboratories and with published normative data.

MATURATION OF LUMINANCE VEPs (FLASH AND FLICKER)

The earliest indication of an intact visual pathway from the retina to the brain is a transient VEP to flash stimulation, which can be recorded from the occipital scalp in premature infants from approximately 24 weeks after conception (Ellingson, 1960; Gross, Harding, Wilton, & Bissenden, 1989; Taylor, Menzies, MacMillan, & Whyte, 1987a). The premature flash VEP is dominated by a slow, broad negativity, usually called N3, at about 300 ms. Between 30 and 36 weeks after conception, N3 is typically a bifid peak (Ellingson, 1986; Tsuneishi, Casaer, Fock, & Hirano, 1995). From 35 weeks after conception, the flash VEP of healthy infants typically has several components with a prominent positivity, P2, preceding the N3. Between term age and 15 weeks after term, there is a phase of rapid maturation of the flash VEP. This phase is characterised by the emergence of an earlier positivity (P1), an overall shortening and sharpening of all peak latencies, and the disappearance of the N3 component. The waveform of the flash VEP during early maturation is illustrated in Figure 2.2. After 15 weeks of age, flash VEP maturation progresses much more slowly and the mean peak latencies for infant VEPs fall within the range of adult values (McCulloch, Skarf, & Taylor, 1993).

Flash VEPs in young infants have generally been studied in hospital settings often without calibrated, standard flash stimuli. Hand-held strobes and LED flashing goggles give qualitatively similar VEPs with overlapping normal ranges for peak latencies (Taylor et al., 1987a). However, even within a single study, the flash VEP has a broad normal range in healthy infants so that only gross delays or non-recordable flash VEPs are associated with increased visual or neurological risk (Shepherd, Saunders, McCulloch, & Dutton, 1996b; Taylor & McCulloch, 1992).

Sleep is a confounding factor in the study of the flash VEP of young infants. Quiet sleep is a convenient and artifact-free opportunity to test very young infants but VEPs recorded during sleep differ from those of alert infants with both longer peak latencies and smaller amplitudes (Apkarian, 1993; Apkarian, Mirmiran, & Tijssen, 1991b; Shepherd, Saunders, & McCulloch, 1999a; Shepherd et al., 1999b).

Steady-state luminance stimulation (flicker) elicits optimal VEP amplitude at a stimulation frequency of 4–5 Hz in young infants from birth to 3 months

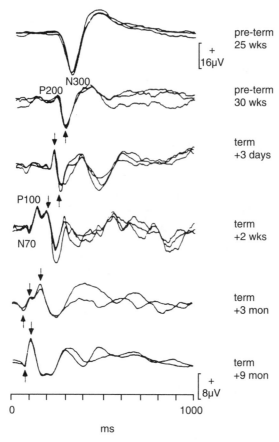

Figure 2.2 Maturation of the flash VEP waveform is illustrated for pre-term (<40 weeks gestation) and post-term infants. Traces are overlaid to show reproducibility. The major components N3, P2, and P1 are labelled at their first occurrence and indicated by an arrow thereafter. (Figure courtesy of Margot J. Taylor.)

of age (Ellingson, 1960; Pieh, McCulloch, Shahani, & Bach, 2005; Regal, 1981). Infants show maturation of this optimum stimulus frequency in the first year of life, but the adult value for optimum frequency of 12–15 Hz is not reached by 15 months of age (Pieh et al., 2005; Regan, 1986). The temporal resolution limit—that is, the highest flicker frequency that elicits a detectable VEP—is more difficult to determine and shows high inter-subject variability. At birth, the highest values for this limit are around 15 Hz in infants during quiet sleep (Ellingson, 1986). Apkarian (1993) used bright sinusoidally modulated flicker in alert infants and reported that the temporal resolution limit is below 20 Hz for young infants and matures to over 50 Hz by 8 months of age. Maturation proceeded slowly in the first month of life, rapidly between 2 and 6 months, and more gradually thereafter.

MATURATION OF STANDARD PATTERN VEPs

The dominant feature of the standard pattern reversal VEP is a major positive peak centred at Oz on the occipital scalp (Figure 2.3). This peak, conventionally labelled P100 based on its nominal peak latency in adults, has a large amplitude and low inter-subject variability. The pattern reversal VEP waveform remains dominated by this positive component throughout the developmental period. P100 peaks at 250–300 ms in full-term neonates and in premature infants from 32 weeks gestation (Harding, Grose, Wilton,

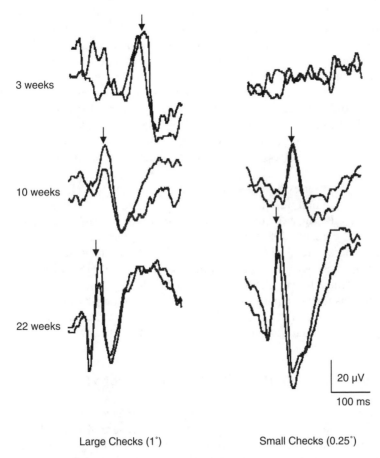

Large Checks (1°)   Small Checks (0.25°)

Figure 2.3 Representative pattern reversal VEPs are illustrated for standard high-contrast large checks (1°) and small checks (0.25 ° = 15 min. of arc) in healthy infants aged 3 weeks, 10 weeks, and 22 weeks after birth at full term. Overlaid traces show reproducibility. The P100 peak for the averaged traces, indicated by an arrow (↓) for the large checks is at 247, 136, and 108 ms after pattern reversal respectively from youngest to oldest. For the small checks, P100 is not recordable in the youngest infant and is at 153 and 118 ms for the older two infants.

& Bissenden, 1989; Roy, Gosselin, Hanna, Orquin, & Chemtob, 2004). It shifts to around 100 ms before 6 months of age and matures only slightly thereafter (Aso et al., 1988; Brecelj, 2003; Brecelj et al., 2002; McCulloch & Skarf, 1991; Moskowitz & Sokol, 1983).

It is widely held that normative data for VEPs may not be comparable across laboratories, and guidelines recommend that laboratories collect their own normative data (American EEG Society, 1984; Odom et al., 2004). However, collection of sufficient normative data for testing young infants throughout the period of early maturation is impractical for many laboratories, as pattern VEP components mature by as much as 10 ms per week during the first 4 months of life. Although none of the published studies of pattern VEP maturation matches the current standards on all of the relevant parameters (i.e., reversal rate, check size, luminance, field size, reference electrode location, and band pass filtering), studies show remarkable agreement when methods broadly similar to standard VEPs are used (McCulloch, Orbach, & Skarf, 1999). The general agreement among laboratories is illustrated for eight published studies (Figure 2.4). However, this masks small systematic differences in the VEPs. Specifically, the P100 has a shorter peak latency for larger stimuli (Crognale, Kelly, Chang, Weiss, & Teller, 1997; McCulloch & Skarf, 1991) and lower contrast produced longer latencies (Fiorentini & Trimarchi, 1992).

Several laboratories have also reported data for infant VEPs elicited by small checks similar to those of the ISCEV standard 0.25-degree checks (Birch, Birch, Petrig, & Uauy, 1990; McCulloch & Skarf, 1991; Moskowitz & Sokol, 1983; Porciatti, 1984). For very young and premature infants no data for small checks are available because these VEPs are not detectable before 8–10 weeks post term age (McCulloch & Skarf, 1991). Smaller patterns give consistently longer P100 peak times but follow a similar pattern of maturation as for large patterns: early rapid maturation followed by a more gradual change. For both standards, the logistic curve provides an efficient description of the maturation of P100 (McCulloch et al., 1999).

ASSESSMENT OF VISUAL THRESHOLDS FROM VEPs

The basic question "How well does the infant see?" requires not only confirmation of an intact visual pathway but also a measure of visual threshold. Measuring visual acuity, the visual resolution threshold for high-contrast stimuli, is the aim of most studies of visual threshold in infants. However, VEPs have been used to measure contrast thresholds and a range of other visual functions.

Using conventional signal averaging, near-threshold visual stimuli do not elicit VEPs that are recognisable and reproducible to an experienced observer. In good recording conditions the critical stimulus of the conventional VEP (i.e., the weakest stimulus that elicits a detectable VEP) is two to three times

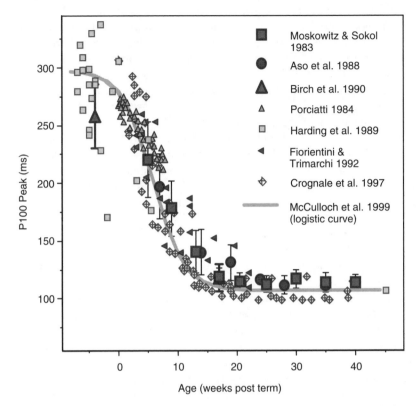

Figure 2.4 Maturation of P100 the pattern reversal VEP elicited by stimuli similar to the ISCEV standard large checks. The studies illustrated include infant VEP studies using abrupt pattern reversal presented on video monitors (average luminance 43–100 cd/m²), with high contrast (= 50%), visual field sizes of 12 degrees or greater and an active occipital electrode (1–2.5 cm above the inion).

stronger than the psychophysical threshold and there are large variations from this in some individuals (Katsumi, Kronheim, Mehta, Tetsuka, & Hirose, 1993; Mackie et al., 1995). In conditions of elevated noise or limited cooperation the disparity between thresholds for conventional VEPs and subjective thresholds is greater.

Strategies to estimate thresholds from steady-state VEPs are based on extrapolation, quantitative signal detection, or both. Extrapolation is possible because the amplitude of steady-state VEPs decreases in a linear fashion as the stimulus approaches threshold. When vision is good, extrapolation to zero amplitude or to the noise level is a useful strategy to estimate visual thresholds in both infants and adults (Jenkins, Douthwaite, & Peedle, 1985; Katsumi, Hirose, Larson, Skladzien, & Tsukada, 1986; Marechal & Faidherbe, 1990; Marg, Freeman, Peltzman, & Goldstein, 1976; Ohn, Katsumi, Matsui,

Tetsuka, & Hirose, 1994). However, extrapolation may be unreliable when vision is poor and VEPs to supra-threshold stimuli are small in amplitude (Bane & Birch, 1992; Ridder, McCulloch, & Herbert, 1998; Sokol, 1978). Extrapolation using components of transient VEPs is not recommended as there are non-linearities near threshold and success rates for linear fitting are low (McCormack & Tomlinson, 1979; McCulloch & Skarf, 1994; Sokol & Jones, 1979).

Signal detection of steady-state VEPs can be approached quantitatively using the frequency spectra (Bach & Meighen, 1999; Regan, 1985). Steady-state stimuli evoke cortical activity at the stimulation frequency and at its harmonics. Using a noise estimate, usually calculated from nearby frequencies, steady-state VEP signals can be quantified in terms of a specific signal-to-noise ratio. Signal detection is further enhanced with adaptive filters that estimate the phase of the VEP signal and by considering the VEP at more than one harmonic frequency (Tang & Norcia, 1995; Zemon, Hartmann, Gordon, & Prunte Glowazki, 1997). The signal-to-noise ratio is improved further by recording from appropriately placed surrounding electrodes and calculating the differential signal (Laplacian derivation). Using some or all of these strategies, the VEP is detectable at or near the psychophysical threshold (Bach, 2005; Beers, Riemslag, & Spekreijse, 1992; Eizenman, McCulloch, Hui, & Skarf, 1989; Mackay, Hamilton, & Bradnam, 2003; Tang & Norcia, 1995).

The step VEP is a technique that uses steady-state VEPs to measure acuity (see Figure 2.5). Real-time analysis of EEG allows automated reduction of stimulus size on detection of a steady-state VEP using a successive approximation, staircase protocol to find a threshold (Bach, Wolfe, & Maurer, 2005; Eizenman et al., 1989; Mackay et al., 2003). Threshold is determined in less than a minute for patients with good fixation. To this end, the step VEP spends minimal time testing below the acuity threshold.

The method known as the sweep VEP is more widely applied to the study of infant visual thresholds (Norcia & Tyler, 1985a, 1985b). The sweep VEP is elicited by a continuous sequence of steady-state visual stimuli, each presented for a few seconds. The stimuli are ordered in an increasing or decreasing sequence. For example, in a typical "visual acuity sweep" black and white gratings are presented in either pattern reversal or onset–offset modes, beginning with very fine gratings and progressing through medium to wide gratings. The VEP elicited by this "swept" stimulus sequence is then analysed using extrapolation of the steady-state VEP amplitudes to rapidly estimate visual thresholds (Regan, 1977). Figure 2.6 illustrates sweep VEPs for typically developing infants.

VEP measures of infant visual thresholds usually record greater sensitivity levels than those derived from behavioural techniques. Although part of this difference can be attributed to differences between static and reversing stimuli, thresholds based on VEPs also show a different time course of development from that measured from behaviour (Sokol, Hansen, Moskowitz,

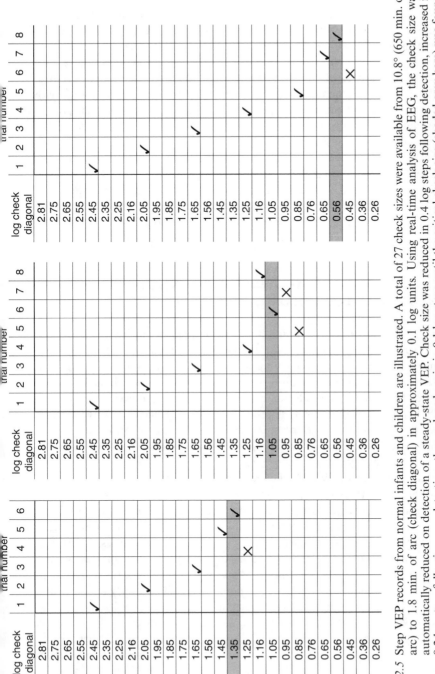

Figure 2.5 Step VEP records from normal infants and children are illustrated. A total of 27 check sizes were available from 10.8° (650 min. of arc) to 1.8 min. of arc (check diagonal) in approximately 0.1 log units. Using real-time analysis of EEG, the check size was automatically reduced on detection of a steady-state VEP. Check size was reduced in 0.4 log steps following detection, increased in 0.2 log steps following non-detection, then reduced again in 0.1 log steps until the critical check size (shaded grey here) was found. Equivalent behavioural acuity is estimated using data from artificially fogged adults tested both behaviourally and with the step VEP. (a) 10-week-old infant, critical check 23 min. of arc (1.35 log), estimated acuity 6/56. (b) 6-month-old infant, critical check 11.3 min. of arc (1.05 log), estimated acuity 6/24. (c) 8-year-old child, critical check 3.6 min. of arc (0.56 log), estimated acuity 6/7.5. (Figure courtesy of Alison M. Mackay and Ruth Hamilton.)

Greenfield, & Towle, 1983; Sokol & Moskowitz, 1985; Sokol, Moskowitz, & McCormack, 1992a). When comparing acuity thresholds derived from sweep VEPs in adults with visual acuity measured using eye charts, the results are correlated but are not equivalent. In general, acuity charts record better acuity in those with good vision and sweep VEP acuity is better in those with poor vision (Bane & Birch, 1992; Hoyt, 1986; Katsumi, Denno, Arai, Faria, & Hirose, 1997). When comparing sweep VEP thresholds in infants with visual acuity based on fixation preference behaviour, there is even greater uncertainty (Katsumi, Mehta, Larsonpark, Skladzien, & Hirose, 1994; Westall, Ainsworth, & Buncic, 2000).

Success rates are generally high for recording visual thresholds in infants with sweep VEPs (Birch & Petrig, 1996; Norcia & Tyler, 1985a; Norcia, Tyler, & Hamer, 1988) and validity is similar to that for adults (Suttle, Banks, & Candy, 2000). However, accuracy is limited so that the sweep VEP is a good method to estimate vision in populations, but caution should be used for assessing individuals (Lauritzen et al., 2004; Ridder et al., 1998).

MATURATION OF VISUAL RESOLUTION AND CONTRAST SENSITIVITY THRESHOLDS

At birth, visual resolution (visual acuity) is limited by both the optical and neural systems (Candy & Banks, 1999; Odom & Green, 1984; Skoczenski & Norcia, 1998). However, very young infants resolve large contours and show evidence of selective adaptation based on spatial frequency (Shahani, Mana-hilov, & McCulloch, 2001; Suter, Armstrong, Suter, & Powers, 1991). Poor visual acuity in young infants is reflected in the absence of a VEP to small patterns such as the standard small checks (15 min. of arc). Early rapid improvement is indicated by emergence of the small check VEP in the majority of healthy infants before 11 weeks of age (Crognale et al., 1997; McCulloch & Skarf, 1991; Moskowitz & Sokol, 1983).

Visual acuity thresholds in infants are usually measured from black and white gratings and expressed as either the angular size of a "stripe" at thresh-old or as grating spatial frequency in cycles per degree of visual angle. Regardless of the pattern used, the VEP amplitude near threshold relates to the fundamental or largest spatial frequency element in the pattern (Tobimatsu et al., 1993). Threshold detection strategies, like those described in the previous section, are used to define a visual acuity threshold and characterise the time course of its maturation.

Studies of VEP acuity in infants show rapid improvement in the early months of life (Fiorentini, Pirchio, & Spinelli, 1983; Norcia & Tyler, 1985a; Sokol, 1978). Figure 2.7 illustrates maturation of visual acuity derived from standard VEPs, from extrapolation of steady-state VEPs and from sweep VEPs. Acuity plotted on a logarithmic scale improves in an approximately linear fashion throughout the first 7 months of life. Differences in VEP threshold values reflect not only differences in extrapolation methods but also differences in the temporal stimulation rate, which interacts with the VEP amplitude (Orel-Bixler & Norcia, 1987; Norcia, Pettet, Candy, Skoczenski, & Good, 1999; Norcia & Tyler, 1985b).

Figure 2.6 also illustrates that behavioural thresholds are substantially poorer than those derived from VEPs. Part of this difference can be accounted for by differences in the stimuli (behavioural studies usually use static stimuli), but even with matched stimuli behavioural thresholds are different from VEP thresholds (Katsumi et al., 1993, 1997; Sokol et al., 1992a). Behavioural methods require attention and motor responses as well as sensory input to meet the threshold criterion, so equivalence is not expected.

Visual acuity defines the upper resolution limit for high-contrast patterns, whereas the contrast sensitivity function is a comprehensive description of contrast thresholds in spatial vision. Thresholds for contrast detection vary with stimulus size (i.e., with the spatial frequency of the stimulus). Extrapolation of steady-state VEPs can be used to calculate the contrast thresholds across a range of spatial frequencies (Atkinson, Braddick, & French, 1979; Parker & Salzen, 1977; Pirchio, Spinelli, Fiorentini, & Maffei, 1978; Porciatti, Vizzoni, & vonBerger, 1982). With rapid VEP techniques such as the sweep VEP, it is feasible to measure the entire contrast sensitivity function in infants within a single visit (Norcia et al., 1988, 1990).

Contrast sensitivity matures rapidly in the early months of life in tandem with maturation of visual acuity (Atkinson et al., 1979). Young infants under 10 weeks of age show maximal contrast sensitivity for large patterns (low spatial frequencies). The optimum then shifts to higher spatial frequencies, accompanied by an overall increase in contrast sensitivity, which is more marked at the higher spatial frequencies. By 6 months of age the contrast sensitivity function parallels that of adults but is approximately one octave below adult sensitivity levels. Both visual acuity and contrast sensitivity decline rapidly away from the centre of the visual field. In the paracentral field (8–16 degrees from fixation), maturation of both contrast sensitivity and visual acuity proceed at similar rates to those in the central field (Allen, Tyler, & Norcia, 1996).

VEP ASSESSMENT OF OTHER VISUAL FUNCTIONS IN INFANTS

A number of important elements of infant visual perception have been investigated using VEPs, including chromatic (colour) perception, orientation selectivity, motion perception, binocular functions, and maturation of the functional subsystems in the visual pathways.

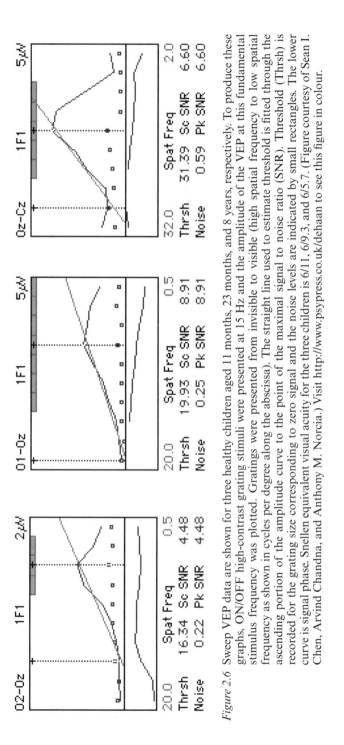

Figure 2.6 Sweep VEP data are shown for three healthy children aged 11 months, 23 months, and 8 years, respectively. To produce these graphs, ON/OFF high-contrast grating stimuli were presented at 15 Hz and the amplitude of the VEP at this fundamental stimulus frequency was plotted. Gratings were presented from invisible to visible (high spatial frequency to low spatial frequency as shown in cycles per degree along the abscissa). The straight line used to estimate threshold is fitted through the ascending portion of the amplitude curve to the point of the maximal signal to noise ratio (SNR). Threshold (Thrsh) is recorded for the grating size corresponding to zero signal and the noise levels are indicated by small rectangles. The lower curve is signal phase. Snellen equivalent visual acuity for the three children is 6/11, 6/9.3, and 6/5.7. (Figure courtesy of Sean I. Chen, Arvind Chandna, and Anthony M. Norcia.) Visit http://www.psypress.co.uk/dehaan to see this figure in colour.

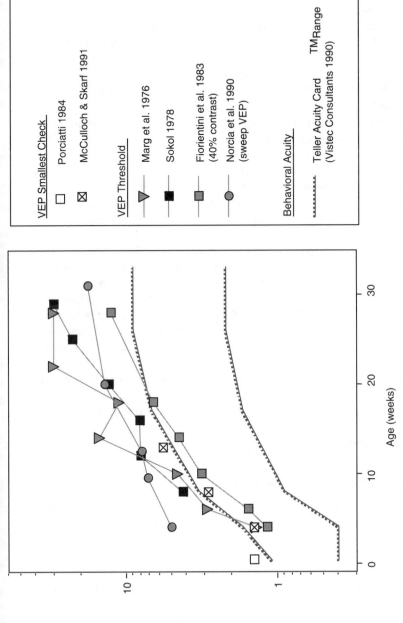

Figure 2.7 Visual acuity maturation in the first 7 months of life is shown using various measurement techniques. The normal range for the behavioural method based on fixation preference is shown with dashed lines (95% confidence intervals for Teller Acuity Cards™). The smallest recordable check size using standard VEP techniques is comparable with the upper limits of this behavioural acuity range (McCulloch & Skarf, 1991; Porciatti, 1984). Extrapolation of VEP amplitudes and other signal detection techniques usually indicate better resolution and more rapid maturation of visual acuity. Visit http://www.psypress.co.uk/dehaan to see this figure in colour.

Colour vision

This can be studied using purely chromatic stimuli; specifically alternating, unpatterned light stimuli with equal luminance but different chromaticity (spectral constitution). These studies rely on first determining isoluminance for light with different chromaticity. As luminance differences evoke larger VEPs than those evoked by chromatic differences, isoluminance can be identified at the VEP amplitude minimum by varying luminance in a stimuli with fixed chromatic differences. Isoluminant stimuli in infants are generally similar to those of adults throughout the developmental period (Bieber, Volbrecht, & Werner, 1995; Pereverzeva, Chien, Palmer, & Teller, 2002). However, VEPs to isoluminant chromatic stimuli are considerably less mature than those elicited by luminance and the time course of chromatic VEP maturation is relatively protracted (Crognale, Kelly, Weiss, & Teller, 1998; Madrid & Crognale, 2000).

Colour vision, however, is not isolated from spatial vision and purely chromatic contrast stimuli can be produced with isoluminant pattern elements. Maturation of VEPs to chromatic contrast lags behind that for luminance contrast VEPs, although both processes show similar shifts in spatial scale (Allen, Banks, & Norcia, 1993; Kelly, Borchest, & Teller, 1997; Rudduck & Harding, 1994). Morrone and colleagues (Morrone, Burr, & Fiorentini, 1993; Morrone, Fiorentini, & Burr, 1996) reported that maturation of both chromatic and luminance contrast VEPs is slow in the early weeks of life. Others found that the chromatic VEP is undetectable before 7 weeks of age (Rudduck & Harding, 1994). After 8 weeks of age, VEP development accelerates for all stimuli, but this acceleration is more rapid for luminance VEPs compared with that for chromatic VEPs, which develop more slowly and over a longer time course (Morrone et al., 1993, 1996).

Chromatic contrast VEPs in both adults and infants are larger for isoluminant red-green stimuli than for blue-yellow chromatic contrast. Blue-yellow VEPs mature even more gradually than do the red-green responses (Crognale et al., 1998) and they are undetectable up to 4 months of age using the sweep VEP technique (Suttle, Banks, & Graf, 2002).

Orientation sensitivity and vernier offset

VEPs to large shifts in the orientation of a grating develop rapidly at around 6 weeks of age when they can be differentiated from the VEP to pattern reversal of similar gratings (Atkinson, Hood, Wattam-Bell, Anker, & Tricklebank, 1988; Braddick, Wattam-Bell, & Atkinson, 1986). Orientation tuning (sensitivity to small shifts of orientation) can be identified when pre-adaptation to gratings selectively suppresses the VEP to similarly oriented stimuli (Candy, Skoczenski, & Norcia, 2001). Orientation tuning of VEPs is broad in very young infants; double that of the tuning bandwidth in adults. This shows rapid maturation to adult levels between 6 and 12 weeks of age (Shahani et al., 2002).

Vernier acuity, the ability to detect offsets in linear stimuli, can be isolated in a rapid sweep VEP strategy (Norcia, Wesemann, & Manny, 1999b; Wesemann, Norcia, & Manny, 1996). Infants show striking immaturity in vernier acuity relative to the maturation of pattern vision and orientation sensitivity (Skoczenski & Norcia, 1999).

Motion perception

In visual neurophysiology, motion is distinguished from other dynamic aspects of vision by the criterion of directional selectivity (Braddick, Atkinson, & Wattam-Bell, 2003). When a motion reversal stimulus is alternated with pattern reversal, very young infants show no difference between the pattern and the motion reversal phases in the resulting VEP (Wattam-Bell, 1991). Between 10 and 12 weeks of age, there is a velocity-dependent emergence of the motion-reversal-specific VEP (Hamer & Norcia, 1994). This motion reversal VEP develops later than that for the orientation reversal VEP even when these similar strategies were used in the same group of infants (Atkinson, Wattam-Bell, & Braddick, 2002). Relative to adult VEP thresholds, thresholds for oscillatory motion in infants lag far behind those for contrast reversal until well into the second year of life. Although cortical motion processing has its onset before 3 months of age, aspects of this complex system such as coherence sensitivity and velocity range continue to develop throughout childhood (Braddick et al., 2003).

In normal infants, directional asymmetry in motion processing is revealed only under uniocular viewing conditions (Norcia, Garcia, Humphry, Holmes, Hamer, & Orel-Bixler, 1991). Temporalward motion elicits stronger VEPs than those elicited by nasalward motion (Mason, Braddick, Wattam-Bell, & Atkinson, 2001). This uniocular motion asymmetry constitutes only a brief developmental period; it is absent in very young infants, maximal at 2–3 months of age, and disappears around 6 months of age (Birch, Fawcett, & Stager, 2000; Braddick, Mercuri, Atkinson, & Wattam-Bell, 1998). Uniocular motion asymmetry has attracted considerable attention, not least because it persists to adulthood in those with strabismus or amblyopia who lack normal binocular vision (Birch et al., 2000; Norcia, 1996; Shea, Chandna, & Norcia, 1999). The directional asymmetry in VEPs is in the opposite direction and independent of the asymmetry found in the reflex optokinetic eye movements of young infants, which are strongest for nasalward motion (Atkinson & Braddick, 1981; Naegele & Held, 1982; Wilson, Noyd, Aiyer, Norcia, Mustari, & Boothe, 1999). The apparent paradox can be explained by considering the anatomical separation of the underlying neural systems. Optokinetic eye movements for nasalward motion are processed subcortically in the midbrain nuclei, which are functional from birth. The temporalward optokinetic eye movements are mediated by cortical pathways and are functional only after the development of cortical motion processing (Braddick et al., 2003).

Binocular vision

The afferent visual pathways from each eye are segregated until they reach the primary visual cortex. In those with equal vision in the two eyes, uniocular stimulation produces very similar levels of cortical activation. For standard pattern reversal VEPs, amplitudes for left and right eye stimulation of the same individual agree within 20% and peak latencies agree within five milliseconds, similar to the trial-to-trial variations found when stimulating the same eye (Shors, Ary, Eriksen, & Wright, 1986). The fact that binocular VEPs differ from the linear sum of the uniocular VEPs is evidence for binocular interactions. In adults, binocular VEP amplitudes exceed those of uniocular VEPs and peak latencies are slightly shorter (diSumma et al., 1997; Sloper & Collins, 1998). However, during early development, binocular VEPs are relatively much larger, which could indicate less binocular interaction and greater passive summation of monocular inputs (Shea, Aslin, & McCulloch, 1987). Difficulties arise in comparing monocular and binocular VEP amplitudes, however, as both cooperation and the quality of fixation and accommodation are poorer with monocular viewing in infants (cf. Hamer, Norcia, Tyler, & Hsu-Winges, 1989; McCulloch & Skarf, 1991).

Basic binocular interaction is unequivocally demonstrated by the non-linear combination of flicker stimulation delivered to the two eyes at different temporal frequencies. In adults with normal binocular vision, the VEP to such stimuli contains components at the frequency of stimulation for each eye as well as at the sum and difference frequencies, called binocular beat frequencies (Baitch & Levi, 1989). Beat frequencies are absent when binocular interactions are abnormal in conditions such as strabismus and amblyopia (Baitch, Ridder, Harwerth, & Smith, 1991). Beat frequencies are present in infants as young as 7 weeks of age, indicating the existence of basic binocular interactions (Baitch & Srebro, 1991; Stevens, Berman, Schmeisser, & Baker, 1994).

Non-linear binocular interactions also occur when patterns are presented to each eye that reverse or oscillate at different rates (Brown, Candy, & Norcia, 1999; Norcia, Harrad, & Brown, 2000). As with luminance beats, these binocular interactions in pattern VEPs are a characteristic of normal binocular vision. Although pattern VEP interactions are present in young infants, there is immaturity in the inhibitory interactions (suppression) when the gratings are cross-oriented throughout the first 15 months of life (Brown et al., 1999).

More advanced binocular functions include fusion of images in the two eyes and stereopsis (depth perception) based on disparities between fused images. These advanced binocular functions can be investigated with VEPs using dynamic random dot correlogram and stereogram stimuli (Julez, 1971; Julez, Kropfl, & Petrig, 1980). For both stimuli, correlated random dot patterns are presented separately to each eye. Regular updating of the dot patterns masks changes that are visible uniocularly. Dynamic random dot correlograms switch between correlated and anti-correlated phases. In stereo-grams, changes in apparent depth occur when image disparity is switched within the correlated dot patterns. Studies of infants using correlograms have shown that binocular fusion develops before 2 or 3 months of age (Birch & Petrig, 1996; Braddick, Atkinson, Julez, Kropfl, Bodis-Wollner, & Raab, 1980; Braddick, Wattam-Bell, Day, & Atkinson, 1983; Eizenman et al., 1999; Petrig, Julez, Lehnann, & Lang, 1982). The onset of stereopsis follows the onset of binocular fusion and is adult-like by 5–6 months of age (Braddick, 1996; Birch & Petrig, 1996).

Functional sub-systems

The primate visual system is organised into several functional sub-systems that are anatomically and pharmacologically distinct. These can be defined along three dichotomous dimensions: excitatory versus lateral inhibitory, ON versus OFF, and magnocellular versus parvocellular. Although there has been much recent attention to the fact that the functions of these sub-systems overlap, the basic dichotomies are clear and the substrates for maturational differences exist (Livingstone & Hubel, 1988; Schiller, 1992). Standard VEP stimuli do not differentiate the functional sub-systems. Zemon and Ratliff (1984) used specially designed "windmill-dartboard" stimuli in adults to identify VEP components associated with lateral inhibitory processing, which are dissociated from the direct, excitatory system. In this excitatory/lateral inhibitory sub-system, long-range lateral inhibition was shown to be well developed at 2 months of age, while short-range inhibitory mechanisms mature later, at around 6 months of age (Grose et al., 1989; Sokol, Zemon, & Moskowitz, 1992b; Zemon, Pinkhasov, & Gordon, 1989). Target and flanking stimuli presented at different temporal frequencies have provided evidence that non-specific lateral interactions are functional early in infancy; lateral inhibition that is tuned to orientation develops in parallel with orienta-tion sensitivity, between 6 and 30 weeks of age, but position-specific lateral inhibition is immature throughout infancy (Candy et al., 2001; Hou, Pettet, Sampath, Candy, & Norcia, 2004).

ON and OFF pathways can be investigated using contrast increments and decrements, respectively, within a stimulus grid. Evolutionarily these ON and OFF sub-systems can be viewed as efficient systems to detect light and dark objects (Schiller, 1992). Adults show larger VEPs to contrast decrements (OFF stimulation) when contrasting squares are smaller than 100 min. of arc, but equal VEP amplitudes for ON and OFF when stimuli are larger (Zemon, Gordon, & Welch, 1988). This asymmetry of OFF and ON path-ways is established in infants before 2 months of age, although pattern processing by both sub-systems is clearly immature (Hartmann, Hitchcox, & Zemon, 1992; Sokol & Moskowitz, 1990; Zemon et al., 1988; Zemon, Schneider, Gordon, & Eisner, 1996).

The major sub-divisions of the primary visual pathways, the magnocellular and parvocellular pathways, are anatomically separated from the retinae to the visual cortex with separate layers in the lateral geniculate nucleus (LGN). VEP studies of these sub-systems are surprisingly scarce, perhaps because the considerable functional overlap between the pathways makes them difficult to isolate. However, the large neurons of the magnocellular pathway clearly process primarily motion, flicker, and positional information, while the smaller cells of the parvocellular pathway process primarily high-resolution and colour information. Using a range of strategies that preferentially stimulate each pathway, there is a general consensus that the magnocellular pathway matures earlier and more rapidly than the parvocellular pathway: VEPs to stimuli that are primarily parvocellular, such as chromatic or high spatial frequency stimuli, mature more slowly throughout infancy and childhood than do VEPs to stimuli that are primarily magnocellular, such as low contrast and high temporal frequency stimuli (Gordon & McCulloch, 1999; Hammarrenger, Lepore, Lippe, Labrosse, Guillemot, & Roy, 2003; Madrid & Crognale, 2000).

CLINICAL APPLICATIONS

VEPs are particularly valuable in paediatric clinical practice, as infants cannot report symptoms or respond to standard tests of vision. They are used to detect, quantify, and monitor dysfunction of the visual system and to provide a non-invasive, physiological measure of vision that is complementary to behavioural oculomotor and clinical assessment.

In general, standard VEPs are used to address the question "Are the visual pathways intact and developing normally?" VEP threshold measures are used to quantify visual function. VEPs depend on clear optics of the eyes as well as on the healthy functioning of the retinae, optic nerves, and visual pathways, at least to the level of the primary visual cortex. Thus, an abnormal VEP is a non-specific finding, which nonetheless may be invaluable in the differential diagnosis of conditions such as infantile nystagmus (Shawkat, Kriss, Russell-Eggitt, Taylor, & Harris, 2001). As both luminance and pattern VEPs predominantly reflect processing of the central 5–10 degrees of the visual field, they are of little use in detecting conditions that affect only the peripheral fields.

At least one standard VEP is required in any clinical study, although other stimuli can be added to address specific clinical questions. Results should be compared with age-matched normal ranges. Prolonged P100 peak latency of a standard VEP can reflect the presence and severity of conditions such as amblyopia, delayed visual maturation, and other forms of visual impairment (Arden & Barnard, 1979; Mackie & McCulloch, 1995a; Mellor & Fielder, 1980; Moskowitz, Sokol, & Hansen, 1987; Skarf, 1989; Sokol, 1983; Taylor & McCulloch, 1992). Amplitude measures have limited clinical utility as VEP amplitude has large variations among individuals and can be degraded by both artifact and inattention (Cigánek, 1969; Sokol & Jones, 1979). In adults, VEPs are usually recorded separately from the right and left eyes to help identify the site of any lesion. As the relevant issue in paediatric practice is often an assessment of vision with optimal attention and fixation, binocular recording is usually the priority (Odom et al., 2004). Whenever cooperation is sufficient, at least one VEP should be recorded from each eye to assess interocular symmetry. Major clinical applications of VEPs in paediatric practice are reviewed below.

Visual acuity

Visual development requires early visual experience, so detection and intervention in infants with subnormal visual acuity is crucial to prevent or minimise amblyopia. Even when visual impairment is untreatable, intervention in the early developmental period improves motor and cognitive learning in visually impaired infants (Sonksen & Dale, 2002; Sonksen, Petrie, & Drew, 1991). Thus in paediatric practice, estimation of visual acuity by sweep or other methods has broad applications, as some disorders, congenital glaucoma or macular hypoplasia for example, may result in widely varied levels of visual acuity. Visual acuity is also a useful measure in infants who are at risk for visual dysfunction, such as those with cerebral palsy or developmental delays, even if normal fixation and following is present. Finally, VEP acuity measurements can aid in the diagnosis of infants with behavioural signs of visual dysfunction.

Amblyopia

Amblyopia, the most common visual disorder affecting infants and children, has a prevalence of 2% of the population. Amblyopia is the failure or regression of visual development, which results from poor quality or misaligned optical images. Most often amblyopia is uniocular and associated with squint or uniocular refractive error but other conditions such as congenital cataract and ptosis lead to a more severe form of deprivation amblyopia.

Although VEP testing is not currently routine in the management of amblyopia, both standard and sweep VEPs are sensitive tools for detection and monitoring of treatment regimes (Arden, Barnard, & Mushin, 1974; Odom, Hoyt, & Marg, 1981; Regan, 1977, 1985; Sokol, 1983). Amblyopia affects not only visual resolution but also a range of other visual abilities, and there is an extensive literature demonstrating VEP abnormalities in functions such as binocular integration, lateral interactions, and contrast sensitivity (cf. Chadna, Pennefather, Kovacs, & Norcia, 2001; Levi & Harwerth, 1978; Norcia et al., 2000). Clinical studies often emphasise the benefits of VEP testing and monitoring in infants treated very early or particularly high-risk groups such as infants with ptosis or congenital cataract (McCulloch & Skarf, 1994; McCulloch & Wright, 1993; Salomao & Birch, 1997).

VEPs and visual maturation

In addition to measuring visual function, VEPs indicate the state of maturation of the visual system, which is particularly useful in clinical trials. For example, VEPs have been used as a measure of neural maturation when assessing the outcomes of infant lipid nutrition (Birch, Hoffman, Uauy, Birch, & Prestidge, 1998; Jorgensen, Hernell, Hughes, & Michaelsen, 2001; Khedr, Farghaly, Amry, & Osman, 2004; Makrides, Neumann, Simmer, & Gibson, 2000; Malcolm, McCulloch, Montgomery, Shepherd, & Weaver, 2003). Similarly, VEP studies have demonstrated maturational delays associated with prenatal exposure to drugs or other adverse conditions (Hamer, Dobson, & Mayer, 1984; Scher et al., 1998; Till, Rovet, Koren, & Westall, 2003).

Even very young infants should be visually attentive when they are alert, so that inattention is always a reason for concern. In a large series of visually inattentive infants without a diagnosed disorder of the visual system, approximately half had uncomplicated, idiopathic delayed visual maturation (Fielder, Russell-Eggitt, Dodd, & Mellor, 1985). In delayed visual maturation, VEPs are usually present but may be abnormally immature. Full recovery of VEPs in conjunction with development of normal visual function and visually guided behaviour typically occurs before 6 months of age. In visually inattentive infants with other concurrent disorders, such as developmental delays and seizure disorders, recovery may be slow or incomplete (Hartel, Holtzman, & Fiensod, 1983; Hoyt, Jastrzebski, & Marg, 1983). Infants with permanent visual impairment are differentiated from those with delayed visual maturation as they have severely abnormal or undetectable VEPs that do not recover (Derek, Leguire, Rogers, & Bremer, 1990; Weiss, Kelly, & Phillips, 2001).

Disorders of the eye

When ocular examination is prevented by congenital cataract or corneal opacity, luminance (flash or flicker) VEPs provide useful pre-surgical information about the integrity of the central retinae and visual pathways.

In congenital retinal dystrophies such as Leber's amaurosis, achromatopsia, and congenital stationary night blindness, the retinal appearance in infancy is often within normal limits. Thus, it is useful to investigate retinal function using the electroretinogram (ERG) when examining paediatric patients. If retinal dystrophy is suspected, the ERG is specifically indicated. Standard diagnostic ERG testing requires pupil dilation, dark adaptation, and a contact lens electrode (Marmor, Holder, Seeliger, & Yamamoto, 2004). Sedation may be required to complete standard ERGs (Fulton, Hansen, & Westall, 2003; Jandeck, Kellner, Kraus, & Foerster, 1997; Westall, Panton, & Levin, 1999), so screening ERG procedures may be useful when investigating paediatric patients (Brecelj, 2003; Brecelj & Stirn-Kranjc, 2004; Kriss,

1994). In its simplest form, a screening ERG can be recorded from the lower eyelid with a skin electrode or from a DTL thread electrode in contact with the conjunctiva using a stroboscopic flash stimulus (Kriss, 1994). The ERG is a large retinal potential consisting of an early negative A-wave followed by a positive B-wave. The ERG to a bright flash is well developed at birth, although amplitude is immature and develops throughout infancy and childhood (Berezovsky, Moraes, Nusinowitz, & Salomao, 2003; Westall et al., 1999). Full ERG testing is required to follow up an abnormal or undetectable screening ERG.

The afferent visual pathways

In paediatric neuro-ophthalmology, VEPs are useful to demonstrate the degree of functional loss, to monitor progression or recovery, and to monitor visual development in infants who may improve. Appropriate radiological studies are required to make a definitive diagnosis of a visual pathway lesion. Disorders of the afferent visual pathways may involve (1) the anterior pathways (optic nerves and tracts), (2) the posterior pathways (optic radiations), or (3) the entire pathway. Common paediatric disorders of the anterior visual pathways include congenital optic nerve hypoplasia, optic nerve atrophy, glioma, and compressive lesions. In general, pattern VEPs are used to give a sensitive measure of function in these disorders (Groswasser, Kriss, Halliday, & McDonald, 1985). However, flash VEPs are useful when function is seriously impaired, for example in infants with optic nerve hypoplasia (Borchert, McCulloch, Rother, & Stout, 1995). Recently, the clinical utility of flicker VEPs was demonstrated for monitoring childhood gliomas (Trisciuzzi et al., 2004).

Albinism is associated with an abnormality of optic stalk development that leads to misrouting of the anterior visual pathways. Specifically, nearly all of the optic nerve fibres from the temporal retinae anomalously decussate at the optic chiasm (Kasmann-Kellner, Schafer, Krick, Ruprecht, Reith, & Schmitz, 2003). Mapping of the visual fields in the midbrain and visual cortex is disrupted. All phenotypes of albinism have this chiasmal misrouting but the other signs, foveal hypoplasia, hypopigmentation of the skin and ocular structures, and nystagmus, overlap with those of other conditions (Apkarian, 1994a; Dorey, Neveu, Burton, Sloper, & Holder, 2003). Chiasmal misrouting can be reliably diagnosed by comparing the lateralisation of uniocular VEPs across three to five occipital electrodes. Although the VEP can be asymmetric across the scalp in individuals with normal optic routing, such individuals have very similar VEP topography from the right and left eyes. In those with misrouting, there is a characteristic asymmetry in the topography of VEPs recorded from each eye (Soong, Levin, & Westall, 2000). This intraocular VEP asymmetry test for misrouting may be reliable using flash stimulation even in the first few days of life (Apkarian, Eckhardt, & Vanschooneveld, 1991a). Pattern onset stimulation improves accuracy for those over 3 years of age (Apkarian, 1994; Apkarian & Tijssen, 1992).

The posterior visual pathway, specifically the optic radiations around the lateral ventricles, are vulnerable in infancy. In particular, infants born prematurely are at risk for periventricular leucomalacia and those with hydrocephalus characteristically show periventricular damage. In premature infants, pattern VEP recording is difficult before 36 weeks after conception, as these infants sleep most of the time and visual resolution is limited by inaccurate fixation, poor optical quality of eye, and by retinal and neural immaturity. However the flash VEP has prognostic utility as the absence or abnormality of the simple waveform in the premature flash VEP is associated with a poor prognosis for survival and with neurological dysfunction among survivors (Pike & Marlow, 2000; Shepherd et al., 1999b).

In hydrocephalus, increased intracranial pressure can affect the peri-ventricular visual pathways. VEPs reliably demonstrate that this damage is reversible on successful shunting in young infants (George & Taylor, 1987). In older infants and children, the association between intracranial pressure and VEPs is not as clear, perhaps because acute and long-standing tissue damage is confounded.

In generalised neurodegenerative and white matter diseases, both the anterior and posterior visual pathways may be affected. VEPs can aid in the detection, differentiation, and monitoring of conditions such as the hereditary ataxias, ceroid lipofucnosis (Batten's disease), and various forms of leucodystrophy (De Meilier, Taylor, & Logan, 1988; Tobimatsu, Fukai, Kato, Kobayashi, & Kuroiwa, 1985). Multimodal evoked potentials, neuro-radiography, metabolic testing, and genetic studies are often used together in these serious paediatric disorders (Taylor & McCulloch, 1992).

Cortical visual impairment

Cortical visual impairment is visual impairment associated with damage to the visual cortex. As dysfunction is rarely isolated to the cortex without associated damage to the posterior visual pathways, some prefer the term "cerebral visual impairment". An operational definition is visual impairment in the absence of dysfunction of the eyes and anterior visual pathways with intact pupillary reflexes. For all aetiologies, pattern VEPs and VEP estimates of visual thresholds are useful indicators of visual function (Gottlob, Fendick, Guo, Zubcov, Odom, & Renecke, 1990; Odom & Green, 1984; Orel-Bixler, Haegerstrom-Portnoy, & Hall, 1989). An important caveat is that VEPs reflect visual function at the level of the visual cortex but affected individuals are at high risk for concurrent impairment of cognitive function. Thus, abnormal VEPs indicate limitations to visual function, but normal VEPs do not ensure normal visual behaviour. When cortical damage is focal, such as in cerebral haemorrhage, congenital malformations or tumours, the utility of VEPs is limited. Variations in cortical topography and the large cortical areas that respond to flash or pattern stimuli contribute to poor sensitivity and specificity of VEPs for assessing visual function (Bodis-Wollner, Atkin, Raab, & Wolkstein, 1977; Frank & Tores, 1979; Whiting, Jan, Wong, Floodmark, Farrell, & McCormick, 1985; Wong, 1991).

When cortical damage is widespread, in aetiologies such as asphyxia, intracranial infection, or toxic agents, not only do pattern VEPs provide an indication of visual function, but flash VEPs also have prognostic value for recovery (Barnet, Mason, & Wilner, 1970; Bodis-Wollner & Mylin, 1987; Duchowney, Weiss, Majlessi, & Barnet, 1974; McCulloch & Taylor, 1992; McCulloch, Taylor, & Whyte, 1991; Regan, Regal, & Tribbles, 1982; Taylor & McCulloch, 1991). More specifically, a normal flash VEP is associated with recovery and abnormal or undetectable flash VEPs have good sensitivity for identifying those who may not recover. However, accuracy is limited—some infants with abnormal flash VEPs show visual recovery (Clarke, Mitchell, & Gibson, 1997).

Other applications

The visual pathways traverse the brain and VEPs are simple non-invasive measures of function. Thus, VEPs can be used to monitor general neurological function. In addition to the conditions described above, VEPs are used to assess neuro-toxic effects of medications with paediatric applications such as deferoxanmine (Taylor, Keenan, Gallant, Skarf, Freedman, & Logan, 1987b), viagabatrin (Morong, Westall, Buncic, Snead, Logan, & Weiss, 2003), and chemotherapy drugs (Packer, Meadows, Roark, Goldwein, & D'Angio, 1987). Flash VEPs have prognostic value in childhood coma, although for this condition somatosensory evoked potentials have greater accuracy (De Meirlier & Taylor, 1987).

CONCLUSIONS

Since the 1970s, clinical scientists have used VEPs to understand visual maturation in human infants. These early VEP studies provided the basis for understanding that visual development is very rapid in the early months of life (Harris, Atkinson, & Braddick, 1976; Harter & Suitt, 1970; Marg et al., 1976; Sokol & Dobson, 1976). The applications of VEPs in paediatrics are broad and limited only by our ability to design innovative strategies for testing visual functions within the attention span of infant subjects.

Standard VEP testing has a well-established role in paediatric neuro-ophthalmology practice. Innovations in areas such as signal detection have added to the accuracy of VEP testing in infants.

In the context of event-related potentials in infants, it is important to consider a VEP as a prerequisite for testing visual cognitive processes. VEPs to repetitive visual stimuli provide evidence of the function of the eyes and afferent visual pathways subserving vision.

ACKNOWLEDGEMENTS

I gratefully acknowledge Ruth E. Hamilton, Alison M. Mackay, and Michael Bach for assistance with the topic of threshold detection. For contributing original figures, I thank Margot J. Taylor, Alison M. Mackay, Ruth Hamilton, Sean I. Chen, Arvind Chandna, and Anthony M. Norcia.

REFERENCES

Allen, D., Banks, M. S., & Norcia, A. M. (1993). Does chromatic sensitivity develop more slowly than luminance sensitivity? *Vision Research*, *33*, 2553–2562.

Allen, D., Tyler, C. W., & Norcia, A. M. (1996). Development of grating acuity and contrast sensitivity in the central and peripheral visual field of the human infant. *Vision Research*, *36*, 1945–1953.

American Encephalographic Society. (1984). Guidelines for clinical evoked potential studies. *Journal of Clinical Neurophysiology*, *1*, 3–53.

Apkarian, P. (1993). Temporal frequency responsivity shows multiple maturational phases—state-dependent visual-evoked potential luminance flicker fusion from birth to 9 months. *Visual Neuroscience*, *10*, 1007–1018.

Apkarian, P. (1994a). Visual evoked potential assessment of visual function in pediatric neuroophthalmology. In D. M. Albert & F. A. Jakobiec (Eds.), *Principles and practice of ophthalmology* (1st ed., pp. 622–647). Philadelphia, PA: WB Saunders.

Apkarian, P. (1994b). Electrodiagnosis in pediatric ophthalmogenetics. *International Journal of Psychophysiology*, *16*, 229–243.

Apkarian, P., Eckhardt, P. G., & Vanschooneveld, M. J. (1991a). Detection of optic pathway misrouting in the human albino neonate. *Neuropediatrics*, *22*, 211–215.

Apkarian, P., Mirmiran, M., & Tijssen, R. (1991b). Effects of behavioral state on visual processing in neonates. *Neuropediatrics*, *22*, 85–91.

Apkarian, P., & Tijssen, R. (1992). Detection and maturation of VEP albino asymmetry—An overview and a longitudinal study from birth to 54 weeks. *Behavioral Brain Research*, *49*, 57–67.

Arden, G. B., & Barnard, W. M. (1979). Effect of occlusion on the VER in amblyopia. *Transactions of the Ophthalmology Society UK*, *99*, 419–426.

Arden, G. B., Barnard, W. M., & Mushin, A. S. (1974). Visually evoked responses in amblyopia. *British Journal of Ophthalmology*, *58*, 1183–1192.

Aso, K., Watanabe, K., Negro, T., Takaetsu, E., Furune, S., Takahashi, I. et al. (1988). Developmental changes of pattern reversal visual evoked potentials. *Brain Development*, *10*, 154–159.

Atkinson, J., & Braddick, O. J. (1981). Development of optokinetic nystagmus in infants: An indicator of cortical binocularity? In D. F. Fisher, R. A. Monty, & J. W. Senders (Eds.), *Eye movements: Cognition and visual perception* (pp. 53–64). Hillsdale, NJ: Lawrence Erlbaum Associates Inc.

Atkinson, J., Braddick, O. J., & French, J. (1979). Contrast sensitivity of the human neonate measured by the visual evoked potential. *Investigative Ophthalmology and Visual Science*, *18*, 210–213.

Atkinson, J., Hood, B., Wattam-Bell, J., Anker, S., & Tricklebank, J. (1988). Development of orientation discrimination in infancy. *Perception*, *17*, 587–595.

Atkinson, J., Wattam-Bell, J., & Braddick, O. J. (2002). Development of directional and orientational-selective VEP responses: Relative functional onset of dorsal and ventral stream processing in human infants. *Investigative Ophthalmology and Visual Science, 43,* 3992.

Bach, M., & Meigen, T. (1999). Do's and don'ts in Fourier analysis of steady-state potentials. *Documenta Ophthalmologica, 99,* 69–82.

Bach, M., Wolfe, M. E., & Maurer, J. P. (2005). *YAVA—Yet Another VEP-based Visual Acuity Assessment*. Paper presented at the 43rd meeting of the International Society of Clinical Electrophysiology of Vision, Glasgow, UK.

Baitch, L. W., & Levi, D. M. (1989). Binocular beats—psychophysical studies of binocular interaction in normal and stereoblind humans. *Vision Research, 29,* 27–35.

Baitch, L. W., Ridder, W. H., Harwerth, R. S., & Smith, E. L. III (1991). Binocular beat VEPs—losses of cortical binocularity in monkeys reared with abnormal visual experience. *Investigative Ophthalmology and Visual Science, 32,* 3096–3103.

Baitch, L., & Srebro, R. (1991). Nonlinear binocular interactions in strabismus and amblyopia – trying to beat a dead synapse. *Investigative Ophthalmology and Visual Science, 32,* 709.

Bane, M. C., & Birch, E. E. (1992). VEP acuity, FPL acuity and visual behavior of visually impaired children. *Journal of Pediatric Ophthalmology & Strabismus, 29,* 202–209.

Barnet, A. B., Mason, J. I., & Wilner, E. (1970). Acute cerebral blindness in childhood. *Neurology, 20,* 1147–1156.

Beers, A. P. A., Riemslag, F. C., & Spekreijse, H. (1992). Visual evoked potential estimation of acuity with a Laplacian derivation. *Documenta Ophthalmologica, 79,* 383–389.

Berezovsky, A., Moraes, N. S. B., Nusinowitz, S., & Salomao, S. R. (2003). Standard full-field electroretinography in healthy preterm infants. *Documenta Ophthalmologica, 107,* 243–249.

Bieber, M. L., Volbrecht, V. J., & Werner, J. S. (1995). Spectral efficiency measured by heterochromatic flicker photometry is similar in human infants and adults. *Vision Research, 35,* 1385–1392.

Birch, E. E., Birch, D. G., Petrig, B., & Uauy, R. (1990). Retinal and cortical function of very low birth weight infants at 36 and 57 weeks post conception. *Clinical Vision Science, 5,* 363–373.

Birch, E. E., Fawcett, S., & Stager, D. (2000). Co-development of VEP motion response and binocular vision in normal infants and infantile esotropes. *Investigative Ophthalmology and Visual Science, 41,* 1719–1723.

Birch, E. E., Hoffman, D. R., Uauy, R., Birch, D. G., & Prestidge, C. (1998). Visual acuity and the essentiality of docosahexaenoic acid and arachidonic acid in the diet of term infants. *Pediatric Research, 44,* 201–209.

Birch, E., & Petrig, B. (1996). FPL and VEP measures of fusion, stereopsis and stereoacuity in normal infants. *Vision Research, 36,* 1321–1327.

Bodis-Wollner, I., Atkin, A., Raab, E., & Wolkstein, M. (1977). Visual association cortex and vision in man: Pattern evoked occipital potentials in a blind boy. *Science, 198,* 629–631.

Bodis-Wollner, I., & Mylin, L. (1987). Plasticity of monocular and binocular vision following cerebral blindness—evoked-potential evidence. *Neurophysiology, 68,* 70–74.

Borchert, M., McCulloch, D., Rother, C., & Stout, A. U. (1995). Clinical assessment of optic disc measurements, and visual-evoked potentials in optic nerve hypoplasia. *American Journal of Ophthalmology, 120*, 605–612.

Borchert, M. S., McCulloch, D. L., Rother, C., & Stout, A. K. (1995). Clinical value of disc measurements and VEP in optic nerve hypoplasia. *American Journal of Ophthalmology, 120*, 605–612.

Braddick, O. J. (1996). Binocularity in infancy. *Eye, 10*, 182–188.

Braddick, O. J., Atkinson, J., Julez, B., Kropfl, W., Bodis-Wollner, I., & Raab, E. (1980). Cortical binocularity in infants. *Nature, 288*, 363–365.

Braddick, O. J., Atkinson, J., & Wattam-Bell, J. (2003). Normal and anomalous development of visual motion processing: Motion coherence and dorsal-stream vulnerability. *Neuropsychologia, 41*, 1769–1784.

Braddick, O., Mercuri, E., Atkinson, J., & Wattam-Bell, J. (1998). Basis of the naso-temporal asymmetry in infants' VEPs to grating displacements. *Investigative Ophthalmology and Visual Science, 39*, S884.

Braddick, O. J., Wattam-Bell, J., & Atkinson, J. (1986). Orientation-specific cortical responses develop in early infancy. *Nature, 320*, 617–619.

Braddick, O. J., Wattam-Bell, J., Day, J., & Atkinson, J. (1983). The onset of binocular function in human infants. *Human Neurobiology, 2*, 65–69.

Brecelj, J. (2003). From immature to mature pattern ERG and VEP. *Documenta Ophthalmologica, 107*, 215–224.

Brecelj, J., & Stirn-Kranjc, B. (2004). Visual electrophysiological screening in diagnosing infants with congenital nystagmus. *Clinical Neurophysiology, 115*, 461–470.

Brecelj, J., Strucl, M., Zidar, I., & Tekavcic-Pompe, M. (2002). Pattern ERG and VEP maturation in schoolchildren. *Clinical Neurophysiology, 113*, 1764–1770.

Brigell, M., Bach, M., Barber, C., Moskowitz, A., & Robson, J. (2003). Guidelines for calibration of stimulus and recording parameters used in clinical electrophysiology of vision. *Documenta Ophthalmologica, 107*, 185–193.

Brown, R. J., Candy, T. R., & Norcia, A. M. (1999). Development of rivalry and dichoptic masking in human infants. *Investigative Ophthalmology and Visual Science, 40*, 3324–3333.

Candy, T. R., & Banks, M. S. (1999). Use of an early nonlinearity to measure optical and receptor resolution in the human infant. *Vision Research, 39*, 3386–3398.

Candy, T. R., Skoczenski, M., & Norcia, A. M. (2001). Normalization models applied to orientation masking in the human infant. *Journal of Neuroscience, 21*, 4530–4541.

Chandna, A., Pennefather, P. M., Kovacs, I., & Norcia, A. M. (2001). Contour integration deficits in anisometropic amblyopia. *Investigative Ophthalmology and Visual Science, 42*, 875–878.

Cigánek, L. (1969). Variability of the human visual evoked potential: Normative data. *Electroencephalography & Clinical Neurophysiology, 27*, 35–42.

Clarke, M. P., Mitchell, K. W., & Gibson, M. (1997). The prognostic value of flash visual evoked potentials in the assessment of non-ocular visual impairment in infancy. *Eye, 11*, 398–402.

Crognale, M. A., Kelly, J. P., Chang, S., Weiss, A. H., & Teller, D. Y. (1997). Development of pattern VEPs: Longitudinal measurements in human infants. *Optometry and Visual Science, 74*, 808–815.

Crognale, M. A., Kelly, J. P., Weiss, A. H., & Teller, D. Y. (1998). Development of the spatio-chromatic visual evoked potential (VEP): A longitudinal study. *Vision Research, 10*, 3283–3292.

De Meirlier, L. J., & Taylor, M. J. (1987). Prognostic utility of SEPs in comatose children. *Pediatric Neurology, 3*, 78–82.

De Meirlier, L. J., Taylor, M. J., & Logan, W. J. (1988). Multimodal evoked potential studies in leukodystrophies of children. *Canadian Journal of Neurological Science, 15*, 26–31.

Derek, R. J., Leguire, L. E., Rogers, G. L., & Bremer, D. L. (1990). The predictability of infant VER testing on future visual acuity. *Annals of Ophthalmology, 22*, 432–438.

Di Russo, F., Pitzalis, S., Spitoni, G., Aprile, T., Patria, F., Spinelli, D. et al. (2005). Identification of the neural sources of the pattern-reversal VEP. *NeuroImage, 24*, 874–886.

diSumma, A., Polo, A., Tinazzi, M., Zanette, G., Bertolasi, L., Bongiovanni, L. G. et al. (1997). Binocular interaction in normal vision studied by pattern-reversal visual evoked potentials (PR-VEPS). *Italian Journal of Neurological Science, 18*, 81–86.

Dorey, S. E., Neveu, M. M., Burton, L. C., Sloper, J. J., & Holder, G. E. (2003). The clinical features of albinism and their correlation with visual evoked potentials. *British Journal of Ophthalmology, 87*, 767–772.

Duchowney, M. S., Weiss, I. P., Majlessi, H., & Barnet, A. B. (1974). Visual evoked responses in childhood cortical blindness after head trauma and meningitis. *Neurology, 24*, 933–940.

Eizenman, M., McCulloch, D. L., Hui, R., & Skarf, B. (1989). Detection of threshold visual evoked potentials. *Noninvasive assessment of the visual system: Technical digest series* (pp. 88–94). Washington, DC: Optical Society of America.

Eizenman, M., Westall, C. A., Geer, I., Smith, K., Chatterjee, S., Panton, C. M. et al. (1999). Electrophysiological evidence of cortical fusion in children with early-onset esotropia. *Investigative Ophthalmology and Visual Science, 40*, 354–362.

Ellingson, R. J. (1960). Cortical electrical responses to visual stimulation in the human infant. *Electroencephalography & Clinical Neurophysiology, 16*, 633–677.

Ellingson, R. J. (1986). Development of visual evoked potentials and photic driving responses in normal full-term, low risk premature and trisomy–21 infants during the first year of life. *Investigative Ophthalmology and Visual Science, 63*, 306–316.

Fielder, A. R., Russell-Eggitt, I. R., Dodd, K. L., & Mellor, D. H. (1985). Delayed visual maturation. *Transactions of the Ophthalmological Societies of the United Kingdom, 104*, 653–661.

Fiorentini, A., Pirchio, M., & Spinelli, D. (1983). Electro-physiological evidence for spatial-frequency selective mechanisms in adults and infants. *Vision Research, 23*, 119–127.

Fiorentini, A., & Trimarchi, C. (1992). Development of temporal properties of pattern electroretinogram and visual evoked potentials in infants. *Vision Research, 32*, 1609–1621.

Frank, Y., & Torres, F. (1979). Evoked potentials in evaluation of cortical blindness in children. *Annals of Neurology, 6*, 126–129.

Fulton, A. B., Hansen, R. M., & Westall, C. A. (2003). Development of ERG responses: The ISCEV rod, maximal and cone responses in normal subjects. *Documenta Ophthalmologica, 107*, 235–241.

Fulton, A. B., Hartmann, E. E., & Hansen, R. M. (1989). Electrophysiologic testing techniques for children. *Documenta Ophthalmologica, 71*, 341–354.

George, S. R., & Taylor, M. J. (1987). VEPs and SEPs in hydrocephalic infants before and after testing. *Clinical Neurology & Neurosurgery, SI*, 96.

Gordon, G. E., & McCulloch, D. L. (1999). A VEP investigation of parallel visual pathways in primary school age children. *Documenta Ophthalmologica, 99*, 1–10.

Gottlob, I., Fendick, M. G., Guo, A., Zubcov, A. A., Odom, J. V., & Renecke, R. D. (1990). Visual acuity measurements by swept spatial frequency visual-evoked–cortical potentials: Clinical applications in children with various visual disorders. *Journal of Pediatric Ophthalmology and Strabismus, 27*, 40–47.

Grose, J., Harding, G. F. A., Wilton, A. Y., & Bissenden, J. G. (1989). The maturation of pattern reversal VEP and flash ERG in pre-term infants. *Clinical Vision Science, 4*, 239–246.

Groswasser, Z., Kriss, A., Halliday, A. M., & McDonald, W. I. (1985). Pattern- and flash-evoked potentials in the assessment and management of optic nerve gliomas. *Journal of Neurology, Neurosurgery & Psychiatry, 48*, 1125–1134.

Hamer, R. D., Dobson, V., & Mayer, M. J. (1984). Absolute thresholds in human infants exposed to continuous illumination. *Investigative Ophthalmology and Visual Science, 25*, 381–388.

Hamer, R. D., & Norcia, A. M. (1994). The development of motion sensitivity during the first year of life. *Vision Research, 16*, 2387–2402.

Hamer, R. D., Norcia, A. M., Tyler, C. W., & Hsu-Winges, C. (1989). The development of monocular and binocular VEP acuity. *Vision Research, 29*, 397–408.

Hammarrenger, B., Lepore, F., Lippe, S., Labrosse, M., Guillemot, J. P., & Roy, M. S. (2003). Magnocellular and parvocellular developmental course in infants during the first year of life. *Documenta Ophthalmologica, 107*, 225–233.

Harding, G. F. A., Grose, J., Wilton, A. Y., & Bissenden, J. G. (1989). The pattern reversal VEP in short-gestation infants. *Electroencephalography & Clinical Neurophysiology, 74*, 76–80.

Harris, L., Atkinson, J., & Braddick, O. (1976). Visual contrast sensitivity of a 6-month-old infant measured by the evoked potential. *Nature, 264*, 570–571.

Hartel, S., Holtzman, M., & Fiensod, M. (1983). Delayed visual maturation. *Archives of Disease in Childhood, 58*, 289–309.

Harter, M. R., & Suitt, C. D. (1970). Visually-evoked cortical responses and pattern vision in the infant: A longitudinal study. *Psychonomic Science, 18*, 235–237.

Hartmann, E. E. (1995). Infant visual development: An overview of studies using visual evoked potential measures from Harter to the present. *International Journal of Neuroscience, 80*, 203–235.

Hartmann, E. E., Hitchcox, S. M., & Zemon, V. (1992). Development of pattern responses to contrast-increment and decrement stimuli in infants: A VEP measure of functional sub-systems. *Investigative Ophthalmology and Visual Science, 33*, 1351.

Hoffmann, M. B., Seufert, P., & Bach, M. (2004). Simulated nystagmus suppresses pattern-reversal but not pattern-onset visual evoked potentials. *Clinical Neurophysiology, 115*, 2659–2665.

Hou, C., Pettet, M. W., Sampath, V., Candy, T. R., & Norcia, A. M. (2003). Development of the spatial organization and dynamics of lateral interactions in the human visual system. *Journal of Neuroscience, 23*, 8630–8640.

Hoyt, C. S. (1986). Objective techniques of visual-acuity assessment in infancy. *Australian and New Zealand Journal of Ophthalmology, 14*, 205–209.

Hoyt, C. S., Jastrzebski, G., & Marg, E. (1983). Delayed visual maturation in infancy. *British Journal of Ophthalmology, 67*, 127–130.

Jandeck, C., Kellner, U., Kraus, H., & Foerster, M. H. (1997). Electrophysiologic evaluation according to ISCEV standards in infants less than 10 years of age. *Ophthalmologe, 94*, 796–800.

Jenkins, T. C., Douthwaite, W. A., & Peedle, J. E. (1985). The VER as a predictor of normal visual acuity in the adult human eye. *Ophthalmic & Physiological Optics, 5*, 441–449.

Jorgensen, M. H., Hernell, O., Hughes, E. L., & Michaelsen, K. F. (2001). Is there a relation between docosahexaenoic acid concentration in mothers' milk and visual development in term infants? *Journal of Pedatric Gastroenterology and Nutrition, 32*, 293–296.

Julez, B. (1971). *Foundations of cyclopean perception.* Chicago, IL: University of Chicago Press.

Julez, B., Kropfl, W., & Petrig, B. (1980). Large evoked potentials to dynamic random dot correlograms and stereograms permit quick determination of stereopsis. *Proceedings of the National Academy Science USA, 77*, 2348–2351.

Kasmann-Kellner, B., Schafer, T., Krick, C. M., Ruprecht, K. W., Reith, W., & Schmitz, B. L. (2003). Anatomical differences in optic nerve, chiasma and tractus opticus in human albinism as demonstrated by standardised clinical and MRI evaluation. *Klinische Monatsblat Augenheilkunde, 220*, 334–344.

Katsumi, O., Denno, S., Arai, M., Faria, J. D., & Hirose, T. (1997). Comparison of preferential looking acuity and pattern reversal visual evoked response acuity in pediatric patients. *Graefe's Archives for Clinical and Experimental Ophthalmology, 235*, 684–690.

Katsumi, O., Hirose, T., Larson, E. W., Skladzien, C. J., & Tsukada, T. (1986). A new method to measure the pattern reversal visual evoked-response in infants and young children. *Japanese Journal of Ophthalmology, 30*, 420–430.

Katsumi, O., Kronheim, J. K., Mehta, M. C., Tetsuka, H., & Hirose, T. (1993). Measuring vision with temporally modulated stripes in infants and children with ROP. *Investigative Ophthalmology and Visual Sciences, 34*, 496–502.

Katsumi, O., Mehta, M. C., Larsonpark, E. W., Skladzien, C. J., & Hirose, T. (1994). Pattern reversal visual evoked response and Snellen visual acuity. *Graefe's Archives for Clinical and Experimental Ophthalmology, 232*, 272–278.

Kelly, J. P., Borchert, K., & Teller, D. Y. (1997). The development of chromatic and achromatic contrast sensitivity in infancy tested with sweep VEP. *Vision Research, 37*, 2057–2072.

Khedr, E. H. M., Farghaly, W. M. A., Amry, S. E., & Osman, A. A. A. (2004). Neural maturation of breastfed and formula-fed infants. *Acta Paediatrica, 93*, 734–738.

Kriss, A. (1994). Skin ERGs—their effectiveness in pediatric visual assessment, confounding factors, and comparison with ERGs recorded using various types of corneal electrode *International Journal of Psychophysiology, 10*, 137–146.

Kriss, A., & Russell-Eggitt, I. (1992). Electrophysiological assessment of visual pathway function in infants. *Eye, 6*, 145–153.

Lauritzen, L., Jorgensen, M. H., Mikkelsen, T. B., Skovgaard, I. M., Straarup, E. M., Olsen, S. F. et al. (2004). Maternal fish oil supplementation in lactation: Effect on visual acuity and n-3 fatty acid content of infant erythrocytes. *Lipids, 39*, 195–206.

Levi, D. M., & Harwerth, R. (1978). Contrast evoked potentials in strabismic and anisometropic amblyopia. *Investigative Ophthalmology and Visual Sciences, 17*, 571–575.

Livingstone, M. S., & Hubel, D. (1988). Segregation of form, colour, movement, and depth: Anatomy, physiology and perception. *Science, 240*, 740–749.

Mackay, A. M., Hamilton, R., & Bradnam, M. S. (2003). Faster and more sensitive VEP recording in children. *Documenta Ophthalmologica, 107,* 251–259.

Mackie, R. T., & McCulloch, D. L. (1995a). Assessment of visual acuity in multiply handicapped children. *British Journal of Ophthalmology, 79,* 260–269.

Mackie, R. T., McCulloch, D. L., Saunders, K. J., Ballantyne, J., Day, R. E., Bradnam, M. S. et al. (1995b). Comparison of visual assessment tests in handicapped children. *Eye, 9,* 136–141.

Madrid, M., & Crognale, M. A. (2000). Long-term maturation of visual pathways. *Visual Neuroscience, 17,* 831–837.

Makrides, M., Neumann, M. A., Simmer, K., & Gibson, R. A. (2000). A critical appraisal of the role of dietary long-chain polyunsaturated fatty acids on neural indices of term infants: A randomized, controlled trial. *Pediatrics, 105,* 32–38.

Malcolm, C. A., McCulloch, D. L., Montgomery, C., Shepherd, A., & Weaver, L. T. (2003). Maternal docosahexaenoic acid supplementation during pregnancy and visual evoked potential development in term infants: A double blind, prospective, randomised trial. *Archives of Disease in Childhood, 88,* F383–F390.

Marechal, L., & Faidherbe, J. (1990). Objective evaluation of visual acuity and its maturation by measurement of visual evoked-potential [in French]. *Archives Internationales de Physiologie, de Biochemie et de Biophysique, 98,* TD7–96.

Marg, E., Freeman, D. N., Peltzman, P., & Goldstein, P. J. (1976). Visual acuity measurement in human infants: Evoked potential measures. *Investigative Ophthalmology & Visual Science, 15,* 150–153.

Marmor, M. F., Holder, G. E., Seeliger, M. W., & Yamamoto, S. (2004). Standard for clinical electroretinography (update). *Documenta Ophthalmologica, 108,* 107–114.

Mason, A. J. S., Braddick, O. J., Wattam-Bell, J., & Atkinson, J. (2001). Directional motion asymmetry in infant VEPs—which direction? *Vision Research, 41,* 201–211.

McCormack, G. L., & Tomlinson, A. (1979). Human visual acuity assessed through linear extrapolation to threshold of bar grating VERs. *American Journal of Optometry and Physiological Optics, 56,* 480–489.

McCulloch, D. L., Orbach, H., & Skarf, B. (1999). Maturation of the pattern-reversal VEP in human infants: A theoretical framework. *Vision Research, 39,* 3673–3680.

McCulloch, D. L., & Skarf, B. (1991). Development of the human visual system: Monocular and binocular pattern VEP latency. *Investigative Ophthalmology & Visual Science, 32,* 2372–2381.

McCulloch, D. L., & Skarf, B. (1994). Pattern VEPs following unilateral congenital cataract. *Archives of Ophthalmology, 112,* 510–518.

McCulloch, D. L., Skarf, B., & Taylor, M. J. (1993). A two-stage linear model for maturation of visual evoked potential (VEP) latency in infants. *Investigative Ophthalmology & Visual Science, 34,* 1353.

McCulloch, D. L., & Taylor, M. J. (1992). Cortical blindness in children: Utility of flash VEPs. *Pediatric Neurology, 8,* 156.

McCulloch, D. L., Taylor, M., & Whyte, H. (1991). Visual evoked potentials and visual prognosis following perinatal asphyxia. *Archives of Opthalmology, 109,* 229–233.

McCulloch, D. L., & Wright, K. W. (1993). Unilateral congenital ptosis: Compensatory head posturing and amblyopia. *Ophthalmic Plastic & Reconstructive Surgery, 9,* 196–200.

Mellor, D. H., & Fielder, A. R. (1980). Dissociated visual development: Electrodiagnostic studies of infants who are "slow to see". *Developmental Medicine and Child Neurology*, *22*, 327–335.

Morong, S. E., Westall, C. A., Buncic, R. J., Snead, O. C., Logan, W. J., & Weiss, S. (2003). Sweep visual evoked potentials in infants with infantile spasms before and during Vigabatrin treatment. *Investigative Ophthalmology & Visual Science*, *44*, S2720.

Morrone, M. C., Burr, D. C., & Fiorentini, A. (1993). Development of infant contrast sensitivity to chromatic stimuli. *Vision Research*, *33*, 2535–2552.

Morrone, M. C., Fiorentini, A., & Burr, D. C. (1996). Development of the temporal properties of visual evoked potentials to luminance and colour contrast in infants. *Vision Research*, *36*, 3141–3155.

Moskowitz, A., & Sokol, S. (1983). Developmental changes in the human visual system as reflected in the pattern reversal VEP. *Electrophysiology & Clinical Neurophysiology*, *56*, 1–15.

Moskowitz, A., Sokol, S., & Hansen, V. (1987). Rapid assessment of visual function in pediatric patients using pattern VEPs and acuity cards. *Clinical Vision Science*, *2*, 11–20.

Naegele, J. R., & Held, R. (1982). The postnatal development of monocular optokinetic nystagmus in infants. *Vision Research*, *22*, 341–346.

Norcia, A. M. (1996). Abnormal motion processing and binocularity: Infantile esotropia as a model system for effects of early interruptions of binocularity. *Eye*, *10*, 259–265.

Norcia, A. M., Garcia, H., Humphry, R., Holmes, A., Hamer, R. D., & Orel-Bixler, D. (1991). Anomalous motion VEPs in infants and infantile esotropia. *Investigative Ophthalmology & Visual Science*, *32*, 436–439.

Norcia, A. M., Harrad, R. A., & Brown, R. J. (2000). Changes in cortical activity during suppression in stereoblindness. *NeuroReport*, *11*, 1007–1012.

Norcia, A. M., Pettet, M. W., Candy, R. C., Skoczenski, A., & Good, W. V. (1999a). Optimizing the stimulus for sweep VEP acuity estimation. *Investigative Ophthalmology & Visual Science*, *40*, 4321.

Norcia, A. M., & Tyler, C. W. (1985a). Spatial frequency sweep VEP: Visual acuity during the first year of life. *Vision Research*, *25*, 1399.

Norcia, A. M., & Tyler, C. W. (1985b). Infant VEP acuity measurement—Analysis of individual differences and measurement error. *Electroencephalography & Clinical Neurophysiology*, *61*, 359–369.

Norcia, A. M., Tyler, C. W., & Hamer, R. D. (1988). High visual contrast sensitivity in the young human infant. *Investigative Ophthalmology & Visual Science*, *29*, 44–49.

Norcia, A. M., Tyler, C. W., & Hamer, R. D. (1990). Development of contrast sensitivity in the human infant. *Vision Research*, *30*, 1475–1486.

Norcia, A. M., Wesemann, W., & Manny, R. E. (1999b). Electrophysiological correlates of vernier and relative motion mechanisms in human visual cortex. *Visual Neuroscience*, *16*, 1123–1131.

Odom, J. V., Bach, M., Barber, C., Brigell, M., Marmor, M. F., Tormene, A. P. et al. (2004). Visual evoked potentials standard (2004). *Documenta Ophthalmologica*, *108*, 115–123.

Odom, J. V., & Green, M. (1984). Developmental physiological optics and visual acuity—a brief review. *Experientia*, *40*, 1178–1181.

Odom, J. V., Hoyt, C. S., & Marg, E. (1981). Effect of natural deprivation and unilateral eye patching on visual acuity of infants and children—evoked-potential measurements. *Archives of Ophthalmology*, *99*, 1412–1416.

Ohn, Y. H., Katsumi, O., Matsui, Y., Tetsuka, H., & Hirose, T. (1994). Snellen visual acuity versus pattern-reversal visual-evoked response acuity in clinical applications. *Ophthalmic Research*, *26*, 240–252.

Orel-Bixler, D. A., Haegerstrom-Portnoy, G., & Hall, A. (1989). Visual assessment of the multiply handicapped patient. *Optometry and Vision Science*, *66*, 530–536.

Orel-Bixler, D. A., & Norcia, A. M. (1987). Differential growth of acuity for steady-state pattern reversal and transient pattern onset–offset VEPs. *Clinical Vision Science*, *2*, 1–9.

Packer, R. J., Meadows, A. T., Roark, L. B., Goldwein, J. L., & D'Angio, G. (1987). Long term sequellae of cancer treatment on the central nervous system in childhood. *Medical and Pediatric Oncology*, *15*, 241–253.

Parker, D. M., & Salzen, E. A. (1977). Latency changes in the human visual evoked response to sinusoidal gratings. *Vision Research*, *17*, 1201–1204.

Pereverzeva, M., Chien, S. H. L., Palmer, J., & Teller, D. Y. (2002). Infant photometry: Are mean adult isoluminance values a sufficient approximation to individual infant values? *Vision Reserach*, *42*, 1639–1649.

Petrig, B., Julesz, B., Lehmann, D., & Lang, J. (1982). Assessment of stereopsis in infants and children, using dynamic random dot pattern evoked potentials. In G. Niemeyer & C. H. Huber (Eds.), *Techniques in clinical electrophysiology of vision*. The Hague, The Netherlands: Dr W Junk Publishers.

Pieh, C., McCulloch, D. L., Shahani, U., & Bach, M. (2005). *Maturation of the visual system reflected in the temporal frequency transfer function of the flash VEP*. Paper presented at the 43rd meeting of the International Society of Clinical Electrophysiology of Vision, Glasgow, UK.

Pike, A. A., & Marlow, N. (2000). The role of cortical evoked responses in predicting neuromotor outcome in very preterm infants. *Early Human Development*, *57*, 123–135.

Pirchio, M., Spinelli, D., Fiorentini, A., & Maffei, L. (1978). Infant contrast sensitivity evaluated by evoked potentials. *Brain Research*, *141*, 179–184.

Porciatti, V. (1984). Temporal and spatial properties of the pattern-reversal VEPs in infants below 2 months of age. *Human Neurobiology*, *3*, 97–102.

Porciatti, V., Vizzoni, L., & vonBerger, G. P. (1982). Neurological age determination by evoked potentials. In J. Francios & M. Maione (Eds.), *Paediatric ophthalmology* (pp. 345–348). New York: John Wiley & Sons.

Regal, D. M. (1981). Development of critical flicker frequency in human infants. *Vision Research*, *21*, 549–555.

Regan, D. (1977). Speedy assessment of visual acuity in amblyopia by the evoked potential method. *Ophthalmologica*, *175*, 159–164.

Regan, D. (1985). Evoked-potentials and their applications to neuroophthalmology. *Neuro-Ophthalmology*, *5*, 73–108.

Regan, D. (1986). *Evoked-potentials in science and medicine*. New York: Chapman & Hall, Wiley.

Regan, D., Regal, D. M., & Tribbles, J. A. R. (1982). Evoked potentials during recovery from blindness recorded serially from an infant and his normally sighted twin. *Electroencephalography & Clinical Neurophysiology*, *54*, 465–468.

Ridder, W. H. III, McCulloch, D. L., & Herbert, A. M. (1998). Stimulus duration, neural adaptation and sweep VEP acuity estimates. *Investigative Ophthalmology & Visual Science*, *39*, 2759–2768.

Roy, M. S., Gosselin, J., Hanna, N., Orquin, J., & Chemtob, S. (2004). Influence of the state of alertness on the pattern visual evoked potentials (PVEP) in very young infant. *Brain Development, 26*, 197–202.

Ruddick, G. A., & Harding, G. F. A. (1994). Visual electrophysiology to achromatic and chromatic stimuli in premature and full-term infants. *International Journal of Psychophysiology, 16*, 3209–3218.

Salomao, S. R., & Birch, E. E. (1997). Visual acuity outcomes measured by sweep-VEP in infants with dense congenital unilateral cataract. *Investigative Ophthalmology & Visual Science, 38*, 4625.

Saunders, K. J., Brown, G., & McCulloch, D. L. (1998). Pattern onset VEPs: More useful than pattern reversal for patients with nystagmus. *Documenta Ophthalmologica, 94*, 265–274.

Scher, M. S., Richardson, G. A., Robles, N., Geva, D., Goldschmidt, L., Dahl, R. E. et al. (1998). Effects of prenatal substance exposure: Altered maturation of visual evoked potentials. *Pediatric Neurology, 18*, 236–243.

Schiller, P. H. (1992). The ON and OFF channels of the visual system. *Trends in Neurosciences, 15*, 86–92.

Schroeder, C. E., Teneke, C. E., Givre, S. J., Arezzo, J. C., & Vaughn, H. G. (1991). Striate cortical contribution to the surface recorded pattern-reversal VEP in the alert monkey. *Vision Research, 31*, 1143–1157.

Shahani, U., Manahilov, V., & McCulloch, D. L. (2001). Maturation of spatial-frequency and orientation selectivity of primary visual cortex. In J. Nenonen, R. J. Ilmoniemi, & T. Katila (Eds.), *Biomag 2000: Proceedings of the 12th International Conference on Biomagnetism* (pp. 153–156). Amsterdam: Elsevier.

Shawkat, F. S., Kriss, A., Russell-Eggitt, I., Taylor, D., & Harris, C. (2001). Diagnosing children presenting with asymmetric pendular nystagmus. *Developmental Medicine and Child Neurology, 43*, 622–627.

Shea, S. L., Aslin, R. N., & McCulloch, D. L. (1987). Binocular summation of visually evoked potentials in infant and stereodeficient adults. *Investigative Ophthalmology & Visual Science, 28*, 356–365.

Shea, S. J., Chandna, A., & Norcia, A. M. (1999). Oscillatory motion but not pattern reversal elicits monocular motion VEP biases in infantile esotropia. *Vision Research, 39*, 1803–1811.

Shepherd, A. J., Saunders, K. J., & McCulloch, D. L. (1999a). Effect of sleep state on the flash visual evoked potential—A case study. *Documenta Ophthalmologica, 98*, 247–256.

Shepherd, A. J., Saunders, K. J., McCulloch, D. L., & Dutton, G. N. (1999b). The prognostic value of visual evoked potentials in preterm infants. *Developmental Medicine & Child Neurology, 41*, 9–16.

Shors, T. J., Ary, J. P., Eriksen, K. J., & Wright, K. W. (1986). P100 amplitude variability of the pattern visual evoked-potential. *Electroencephalography & Clinical Neurophysiology, 65*, 316–319.

Skarf, B. (1989). Clinical use of visual evoked potentials. *Ophthalmology Clinics of North America, 2*, 499–518.

Skoczenski, A. M., & Norcia, A. M. (1998). Neural noise limitations on infant visual sensitivity. *Nature, 391*, 697–700.

Skoczenski, A. M., & Norcia, A. M. (1999). Development of VEP Vernier acuity and grating acuity in human infants. *Investigative Ophthalmology & Visual Science, 40*, 2411–2417.

Sloper, J. J., & Collins, A. D. (1998). Reduction in binocular enhancement of the visual-evoked potential during development accompanies increasing stereoacuity. *Journal of Pediatric Ophthalmology and Strabismus*, *35*, 154–158.

Sokol, S. (1978). Measurement of infant visual acuity from pattern reversal evoked potentials. *Vision Research*, *18*, 33–39.

Sokol, S. (1983). Abnormal evoked potential latencies in amblyopia. *British Journal of Ophthalmology*, *67*, 310–314.

Sokol, S., & Dobson, V. (1976). Pattern reversal visually evoked potentials in infants. *Investigative Ophthalmology & Visual Science*, *15*, 58–62.

Sokol, S., Hansen, V. C., Moskowitz, A., Greenfield, P., & Towle, V. L. (1983). Evoked potential and preferential looking estimates of visual acuity in pediatric patients. *American Journal of Ophthalmology*, *90*, 552–562.

Sokol, S., & Jones, K. (1979). Implicit time of pattern evoked potentials in infants: an index of maturation of spatial vision. *Vision Research*, *19*, 747–755.

Sokol, S., & Moskowitz, A. (1985). Comparison of pattern VEPs and preferential-looking behavior in 3-month-old infants. *Investigative Ophthalmology & Visual Science*, *26*, 359–365.

Sokol, S., & Moskowitz, A. (1990). Development of ON and OFF brightness pathways in human infants. *Investigative Ophthalmology & Visual Science*, *34*, 251.

Sokol, S., Moskowitz, A., & McCormack, G. (1992a). Infant VEP and preferential looking acuity measured with phase alternating gratings. *Investigative Ophthalmology & Visual Science*, *33*, 3156–3161.

Sokol, S., Zemon, V., & Moskowitz, A. (1992b). Development of lateral interactions in the infant visual system. *Visual Neuroscience*, *8*, 3–8.

Sonksen, P. M., & Dale, N. (2002). Visual impairment in infancy: Impact on neurodevelopmental and neurobiological processes. *Developmental Medicine & Child Neurology*, *44*, 782–791.

Sonksen, P. M., Petrie, A., & Drew, K. J. (1991). Promotion of visual development of severely visually impaired babies: Evaluation of a developmental based programme. *Developmental Medicine and Child Neurology*, *33*, 320–335.

Soong, F., Levin, A. V., & Westall, C. A. (2000). Comparison of techniques for detecting visually evoked potential asymmetry in albinism. *Journal of the American Association for Pediatric Ophthalmology and Strabismus*, *4*, 302–310.

Stevens, J. L., Berman, J. L., Schmeisser, E. T., & Baker, R. S. (1994). Dichoptic luminance beat visual-evoked potentials in the assessment of binocularity in children. *Journal of Pediatric Ophthalmology & Strabismus*, *31*, 368–373.

Suter, S., Armstrong, C. A., Suter, P. S., & Powers, J. C. (1991). Spatial-frequency-tuned attenuation and enhancement of the steady-state VEP by grating adaptation. *Vision Research*, *31*, 1167–1175.

Suttle, C. M., Banks, M. S., & Candy, T. R. (2000). Does a front-end nonlinearity confound VEP acuity measures in human infants? *Vision Research*, *11*, 3665–3675.

Suttle, C. M., Banks, M. S., & Graf, E. W. (2002). FPL and sweep VEP to tritan stimuli in young human infants. *Vision Research*, *42*, 2879–2891.

Tang, Y., & Norcia, A. M. (1995). An adaptive filter for steady-state evoked-responses. *Electroencephalography & Clinical Neurophysiology: Evoked Potentials*, *96*, 268–277.

Taylor, M. J., Keenan, N. K., Gallant, T., Skarf, B., Freedman, M. H., & Logan, W. J. (1987b). Subclinical abnormalities in patients on chronic deferoxamine therapy: Longitudinal studies. *Electroencephalography & Clinical Neurophysiology*, *68*, 81–87.

Taylor, M. J., & McCulloch, D. L. (1991). The prognostic value of VEPs in young children with acute onset cortical blindness. *Pediatric Neurology*, *7*, 111–115.

Taylor, M. J., & McCulloch, D. L. (1992). Visual evoked potentials in infants and children. *Journal of Clinical Neurophysiology*, *9*, 357–372.

Taylor, M. J., Menzies, R., MacMillan, L. J., & Whyte, H. E. (1987a). VEPs in normal full-term and premature neonates: Longitudinal versus cross-sectional data. *Electrophysiology & Clinical Neurophysiology*, *68*, 20–27.

Till, C., Rovet, J. F., Koren, G., & Westall, C. A. (2003). Assessment of visual functions following prenatal exposure to organic solvents. *Neurotoxicology*, *24*, 725–731.

Tobimatsu, S., Fukai, R., Kato, M., Kobayashi, T., & Kuroiwa, Y. (1985). Multi-modality evoked potentials in patients and carriers with adrenoleucodystrophy and adrenomyeloneuropathy. *Electrophysiology & Clinical Neurophysiology*, *62*, 18–24.

Tobimatsu, S., Kuritatashima, S., Nakayamahiromatsu, M., & Kato, M. (1993). Effect of spatial-frequency on transient and steady-state VEPs—stimulation with checkerboard, square-wave grating and sinusoidal grating patterns. *Journal of Neurological Sciences*, *118*, 17–24.

Trisciuzzi, M. T. S., Riccardi, R., Piccardi, M., Iarossi, G., Buzzonetti, L., Dickmann, A. et al. (2004). A fast visual evoked potential method for functional assessment and follow-up of childhood optic gliomas. *Progress in Brain Research*, *115*, 217–226.

Tsuneishi, S., Casaer, P., Fock, J. M., & Hirano, S. (1995). Establishment of normal values for flash visual-evoked potentials (VEPs) in preterm infants—a longitudinal-study with special reference to 2 components of the N1 wave. *Electrophysiology & Clinical Neurophysiology: Evoked Potentials*, *96*, 291–299.

Vanni, S., Warnking, J., Dojat, M., Delon-Martin, C., Bullier, J., & Segebarth, C. (2004). Sequence of pattern onset responses in the human visual areas: An fMRI constrained source analysis. *Neuroimage*, *21*, 801–817.

Wattam-Bell, J. (1991). The development of motion-specific cortical responses in infants. *Vision Research*, *31*, 287–297.

Weiss, A. H., Kelly, J. P., & Phillips, J. O. (2001). The infant who is visually unresponsive on a cortical basis. *Ophthalmology*, *108*, 2076–2087.

Wesemann, W., Norcia, A. M., & Manny, R. E. (1996). Measurement of vernier and motion sensitivity with the rapid sweep-VEP. *Klinische Monatsblat. Augenheilkunde*, *208*, 11–17.

Westall, C. A., Ainsworth, J. R., & Buncic, J. R. (2000). Which ocular and neurologic conditions cause disparate results in visual acuity scores recorded with visually evoked potential and teller acuity cards? *Journal of the American Association for Pediatric Ophthalmology and Strabismus*, *4*, 295–301.

Westall, C. A., Panton, C. M., & Levin, A. V. (1999). Time courses for maturation of electroretinogram responses from infancy to adulthood—ERG responses mature at different ages. *Documenta Ophthalmologica*, *96*, 355–379.

Whiting, S., Jan, J. E., Wong, P. K. H., Floodmark, O., Farrell, K., & McCormick, A. Q. (1985). Permanent cortical visual impairment in children. *Developmental Medicine & Child Neurology*, *27*, 730–739.

Wilson, J. R., Noyd, W. W., Aiyer, A. D., Norcia, A. M., Mustari, M. J., & Boothe, R. G. (1999). Asymmetric responses in cortical visually evoked potentials to motion are not derived from eye movements. *Investigative Ophthalmology & Visual Science*, *40*, 2435–2439.

Wong, V. C. (1991). Cortical blindness in children: A study of etiology and prognosis. *Pediatric Neurology*, *7*, 178–185.

Zemon, V., Gordon, J., & Welch, J. (1988). Asymmetries in on and off visual pathways of humans revealed using contrast-evoked cortical potentials. *Visual Neuroscience*, *1*, 145–150.

Zemon, V., Hartmann, E. E., Gordon, J., & Prunte Glowazki, A. (1997). An electrophysiological technique for assessment of the development of spatial vision. *Investigative Ophthalmology & Visual Science*, *74*, 708–716.

Zemon, V., Pinkhasov, E., & Gordon, J. (1989). Electrophysiological tests of neural models—evidence for nonlinear binocular interactions in humans. *Proceedings of the National Academy of Sciences USA*, *90*, 2975–2978.

Zemon, V., & Ratliff, F. (1984). Intermodulation components of the visual evoked-potential—responses to lateral and superimposed stimuli. *Biological Cybernetics*, *50*, 401–408.

Zemon, V., Schneider, S., Gordon, J., & Eisner, W. (1996). Lateral interactions within ON and OFF pathways: A VEP analysis. *Investigative Ophthalmology & Visual Science*, *37*, 2036.

3 Development of face-sensitive event-related potentials during infancy

Michelle de Haan
Institute of Child Health,
University College London, UK

Mark H. Johnson and Hanife Halit
Centre for Brain & Cognitive Development,
Birkbeck College, London, UK

A growing literature documents the existence and properties of components in adult event-related potentials related to the perception and recognition of faces. For example, the N170 has been related to the structural encoding of physical information in faces (Bentin, Allison, Puce, Perez, & McCarthy, 1996; Eimer, 2000a, 2000b), while later components, such as the N400 and P600, have been related to the recognition of facial identity (Eimer, 2000b). In contrast to the numerous studies of these components in adults, much less attention has been paid to their emergence during development. A developmental approach can provide unique insight into understanding the neural correlates of face processing in several ways. First, because different aspects of face processing may emerge at different ages, development provides the possibility of dissociating these aspects and studying them in isolation in a way not possible in adults. For example, in adults there is disagreement over whether the N170 reflects eye detection (Bentin et al., 1996) or encoding of the entire configuration of facial features (Eimer, 2000b). A recent study showing that the N170 response to eyes alone matures by 11 years of age, while that to the full face is not mature until adulthood (Taylor, Edmonds, McCarthy, & Allison, 2001), can be seen as supporting the view that there are separate eye-detection and face-detection generators of the N170 (e.g., Shibata et al., 2002).

Second, studying development of ERP components related to face processing can provide information that is important for putting constraints on debates about the degree of modularity and the role of expertise in face recognition. For example, recent studies showing that N170-like components observed in infants during the first year of life are less stimulus specific than the adult N170 (de Haan, Pascalis, & Johnson, 2002; Halit, de Haan, & Johnson, 2003) provide evidence against the view that face-specific cortical systems are present from birth. In this chapter we provide a brief and selective review of models of the mature and developing face-processing system and of ERP components related to face processing in children and adults, together with a more detailed review of the development during infancy of ERP components related to face processing. We close by discussing the implications of the work with infants for understanding the mechanisms underlying face processing by adults.

THEORIES AND MODELS OF FACE PROCESSING

Face processing by adults

Evidence from a range of sources suggests that, in adults, face processing is mediated by neural and cognitive mechanisms that are to some extent different from those used to process most other classes of object. At the neural level, evidence showing that (1) certain neurons in monkeys' temporal and frontal lobes fire more to faces than a variety of other stimuli (reviewed in Gauthier & Logothetis, 2000), (2) in human adults face or object processing can be selectively impaired following brain damage (de Renzi, Perani, Carlesimo, Silveri, & Fazio, 1994), and (3) particular areas of ventral and lateral occipito-temporal cortex in human adults are more active during viewing of faces than a variety of comparison stimuli (Puce, Allison, Gore, & McCarthy, 1995), collectively suggests that there are cortical areas devoted preferentially to the processing of faces. The results of several studies also suggest that the face-related cortical areas of the right hemisphere are more extensive or are more critical for face processing than the homologous regions in the left hemisphere (De Renzi et al., 1994; Gauthier, Tarr, Anderson, Skudlarski, & Gore, 1999; Kanwisher, McDermott, & Chun, 1997). At the cognitive level, it has been proposed that the type of information encoded and remembered for faces differs from that for objects. Although the difference in the nature of processing has been described in various ways (e.g., compare Diamond & Carey, 1986; Farah, 1990; Rhodes, Carey, Byatt, & Proffitt, 1998), the essence of all these approaches is that objects are represented mainly in terms of their isolated features or parts, whereas faces are represented in terms of global patterns or relations among parts. The main line of evidence in support of this view is the face inversion effect: stimulus inversion disproportionately impairs face compared to object processing. The most common explanation for this effect is that inversion disrupts the relational encoding used for faces more than parts-based encoding used to encode objects. The right hemisphere is believed to play a more prominent role than the left in relation encoding, providing a cognitive explanation for the right-hemisphere bias in face processing.

While these lines of evidence support the existence of a neurocognitive system dedicated to processing of human faces, this conclusion is challenged by investigations of visual expertise with other object categories. For example, the same regions of the fusiform gyrus that are preferentially activated by faces can also be activated by other categories with which the perceiver has extensive experience (Gauthier, Skudlarski, Gore, & Anderson, 2000). These results have been used to argue that the mechanisms involved in the processing of faces are no different from those involved in any task that requires visual expertise for discriminating among exemplars of other categories with complex, visually similar members.

Development of face processing

Models of the development of face processing have largely focused on the question of how the differences in face and object processing observed in adults arise. There are currently several views that differ from one another on two main points (reviewed in de Haan & Halit, 2001): (a) whether the cortical face-processing system is domain specific, and (b) whether the degree of domain specificity changes with development. According to one account, the neural mechanisms underlying face processing are genetically determined and specific to faces, and thus a cortical module specifically dedicated to this process exists from birth (Farah, 2000; Farah, Rabinowitz, Quinn, & Liu, 2000). Evidence in support of this view comes from a patient who suffered brain damage at one day of age and subsequently, at age 16, showed disproportionate impairment in face recognition compared to object recognition (Farah et al., 2000). The authors interpret these results as evidence that the distinction between face and object recognition, and the anatomical localisation of face recognition, are genetically explicitly pre-specified.

In contrast to this view, two alternative accounts argue that the cortical face-processing system is initially not specific to faces, and both accounts emphasise the critical role of experience of viewing faces in development of the system. One such account argues that the neural specialisation for faces arises during development due to processes that parallel perceptual learning in adults (Diamond & Carey, 1986; Gauthier & Nelson, 2001). In this view, the mechanisms that are involved in the processing of faces are no different from those involved in tasks that require visual expertise for discriminating among exemplars of other categories with complex, visually similar members. These domain-general learning mechanisms appear to be specific to faces only because faces are a stimulus category for which all humans consistently develop a relatively high level of expertise. Evidence to support this view comes from studies showing that effects previously thought to be specific to faces can be obtained for other categories for which participants show expertise (Gauthier et al., 1999, 2000; Rossion, Gauthier, Goffaux, Tarr, & Crommelinck, 2002; Tarr & Gauthier, 2000).

A third perspective also argues that the cortical system used to process faces is initially not specific to faces, but postulates that there are developmental mechanisms that generate increasingly specialised processing within cortical areas (Johnson, 2000, 2001; Nelson, 2001). In this view, two distinct brain systems are proposed to underlie development during infancy (Johnson & Morton, 1991): (a) "Conspec", a system operating from birth that functions to bias the newborn to orient their visual attention towards faces, and (b) "Conlern", a system sensitive to the effects of experience through passive exposure. In this model, Conspec is mediated by primitive, possibly largely subcortical, circuits, whereas Conlern is mediated by developing cortical circuits in the ventral visual pathway. The purpose of Conspec is to bias the input to the still-plastic cortical circuits underlying Conlern, providing the first step towards the eventual emergence of the specialised circuits for face processing observed in adults. From this perspective, early in life a given region of cortical tissue may be activated by a broad range of stimuli, but over time its selectivity increases so that it responds only to certain kinds of inputs, e.g., upright human faces. In this way the face-processing system may develop from a broadly tuned, non-specific, complex figure recognition system into one tuned to the type of faces seen most frequently in the natural environment, i.e., upright human faces (Nelson, 1993, 2001). This view is supported by a recent study showing a decrease in discrimination abilities for non-human faces with age: 6-month-olds can discriminate between individual humans and individual monkeys, while 9-month-olds and adults tested with the same procedure discriminate only between members of their own species (Pascalis, de Haan, & Nelson, 2002).

EVENT-RELATED POTENTIAL STUDIES OF FACE PROCESSING

ERPs have provided a very useful tool in studying the face-processing system. Their excellent temporal resolution allows investigation of how the neuro-cognitive operations involved in face processing unfold over time, and they also provide one way of assessing the domain specificity of these processes. These studies have provided evidence relating the P1 and the N170 to encoding of faces, the N250r to the recognition of familiarity (Schweinberger, Pickering, Burton, & Kaufmann, 2002a), and longer-latency ERP components (> 400 ms after stimulus onset) to recognition of facial identity (e.g., Barrett & Rugg, 1989; Begleiter, Porjesz, & Wang, 1995; Eimer, 2000b; Itier & Taylor, 2002; Schweinberger et al., 2002a; Schweinberger, Pickering, Jentzsch, Burton, & Kaufmann, 2002b; Uhl, Lang, Spieth, & Deecke, 1990) and/or retrieval of semantic information related to faces (Paller, Gonsalves, Grabowecky, Bozic, & Yamada, 2000).

Relatively few studies have examined the neural correlates of face recognition during infancy. ERPs provide an ideal tool for this type of study, as they are non-invasive and can be obtained passively, without a behavioural response being required from the participant. Among the questions that can be addressed are: (a) Can the precursors of components observed in children and adults be observed in infants? (b) To what degree are these responses specific to faces? Answers to these questions can help to place constraints on theoretical debates about the degree of modularity and the role of expertise in face recognition. Below, components observed in infant ERPs during face processing are discussed in order of the temporal occurrence in the waveform, and possible links to similar components observed in adults and children are explored. Note that we focus on infant components for which responses to upright human faces have been compared to inverted faces, animal faces, or objects, and do not provide an exhaustive review of all components previously reported in the infant visual event-related potentials.

P1

The P1 is reliably elicited in response to visual stimuli in individuals of all ages, and has been shown to be influenced by manipulations of spatial (Hofp & Mangun, 2000) and other visual (Taylor, McCarthy, Saliba, & Degiovanni, 1999) information. Some investigators have argued for the existence of a "global, holistic" stage of face processing in adults around 110 ms, reflected in the P1 (Itier & Taylor, 2002). The main lines of evidence in support of this view are that: (a) from 4 years of age the P1 is of shorter latency to faces than objects (flowers; Taylor et al., 2001a; but see Itier & Taylor, 2004a), (b) from age 4 years it is of shorter latency and in adults it is of smaller amplitude for upright than inverted faces (Taylor et al., 2001a; Itier & Taylor, 2002, 2004a), and (c) its amplitude is modulated by displacement of facial features, a manipulation that affects perception of facial configuration (Halit, de Haan, & Johnson, 2000). However, an effect of inversion on the P1 has not been documented in all studies (Rossion et al., 1999), and the specificity of the inversion effect to faces is not well documented. Thus, the degree to which the processes reflected in the P1 are specific to faces remains somewhat unclear. Alternative explanations are that the modulations observed reflect top-down influences during the early encoding of faces (Taylor, 2002) and/or that they reflect more general visual attentional effects (e.g., differential allocation of attention within or between blocks of trials (Hillyard & Anllo-Vento, 1998).

The only relevant study in infants did find a difference in amplitude over the P1 at the midline occipital electrode for faces compared to objects (de Haan & Nelson, 1999). However, because the stimuli were not controlled for low-level physical differences that might influence the P1, the interpretation of this effect is unclear.

N290

The infant N290 is a negative-going deflection most prominent over midline and paramidline posterior electrodes whose peak latency decreases from approximately 350 ms to 290 ms between 3 and 12 months of age (Halit et al., 2003). The N290 may be a developmental precursor of the N170, a component observed in infants and adults that has been termed "face-sensitive", because the presence of a face causes systematic changes in its amplitude and/or latency compared to a wide range of other classes of object. Thus, while N170s of varying amplitudes can be elicited by non-face objects (Itier & Taylor, 2004a; Rossion et al., 2000), the response to human faces is consistently of larger amplitude and often shorter latency than that to any other object category tested (Bentin et al., 1996; Carmel & Bentin, 2002; Itier & Taylor, 2004a; Rossion et al., 2000; Taylor et al., 1999). The component is thought to be related to stages of structural encoding of the physical information in faces rather than to recognition of individual identity, as it is unaffected by the familiarity of individual faces (Bentin & Deouell, 2000; Eimer, 2000c, Rossion et al., 1999; Schweinberger et al., 2002a). Hemispheric differences in the amplitude of the component are not always present, but when they appear they tend to favour larger amplitudes over the right than left for faces (e.g., Itier & Taylor, 2002) but not for scrambled faces or objects (Taylor et al., 2001a). Further evidence that the N170 is a face-sensitive component comes from studies demonstrating that its amplitude and latency in response to faces are affected by manipulations thought to disrupt the encoding of configural information in faces. For example, several studies report that N170 amplitude is larger and/or latency is longer for inverted compared to upright faces (Bentin et al., 1996; de Haan et al., 2002; Eimer, 2000c; Itier, Latinus, & Tayor, 2006; Itier & Taylor, 2002, 2004a; Rossion et al., 2000) or faces with features intact compared to scrambled (George, Evans, Fiori, Davidoff, & Renault, 1996). The N170 is not larger or slower for inverted compared to upright exemplars of non-face object categories (Bentin et al., 1996; Itier et al., 2006; Rebai, Poiroux, Bernard, & Lalonde, 2001; Rossion et al., 2000; but see Rossion, Joyce, Cottrell, & Tarr, 2003), even animal (monkey/ape) faces that share the basic eyes-nose-mouth arrangement with the human face (de Haan et al., 2002; Itier et al., 2006; but see Rousselet, Mace, & Fabre-Thorpe, 2004). The N170 is also observed in children as young as 4 years of age, although its amplitude is smaller and latency longer than in adults (Taylor et al., 1999, 2001a).

The N290 has been implicated as a possible precursor to the adult N170 in two types of studies: (1) comparing faces to noise, and (2) comparing upright and inverted faces. In one study comparing responses to faces with responses to noise composed of the same outer contour and amplitude and colour spectra, 3-month-olds showed a larger N290 to faces than noise (Halit, Csibra, Volein, & Johnson, 2004). These results paralleled those obtained for the N170 with adults under the same procedure (Halit et al., 2004). In other studies, infants' and adults' ERPs were recorded in response to upright and inverted human and monkey faces, in order to determine whether infants, like adults, show an ERP inversion effect that is specific to human faces. The results of these studies show that at 12 months of age the amplitude of the N290 is modulated by stimulus inversion in the same way as is the adult N170: inversion increases the amplitude of the N290 for human but not monkey faces (Halit et al., 2003; see Figure 3.1). However, at 3 and 6 months

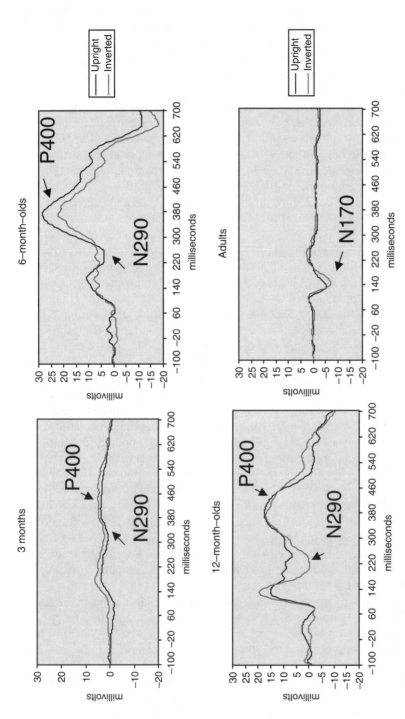

Figure 3.1 Event-related potentials to upright and inverted human faces at 3, 6, and 12 months of age and adulthood. Adapted from de Haan et al. (2002) and Halit et al. (2003).

the N290 is unaffected by stimulus inversion (de Haan et al., 2002; Halit et al., 2003). This is not because younger infants cannot discriminate between upright and inverted faces, as at both ages inversion does influence the P400 (see below) that follows the N290. Thus, the N290 appears to become more sensitive to upright human faces with age (de Haan et al., 2002; Halit et al., 2003).

While some characteristics of the infant N290 are similar to the adult N170 by 12 months of age, there are also some differences between the two components in terms of their temporal and spatial characteristics. The N290 is of longer peak latency (290 ms vs 170 ms), and has a more medial distribution and a smaller peak amplitude to human faces than the adult N170. The differences in amplitude and latency are not unexpected, as studies of the N170 during childhood show an increase in amplitude and decrease in peak latency with age (Taylor et al., 1999). In fact, the latency of the N290 at 12 months of age is only 15–20 ms longer than the latency of the N170 in 4- to 5-year-olds (Taylor et al., 1999, 2001a). In terms of response properties, the 12-month-old's N290 and adults' N170 are also not identical. First, while the latency of the adult N170 is delayed by inversion, no effect of inversion is observed for the latency of the infant N290 at any age tested (de Haan et al., 2002; Halit et al., 2003). Second, while the amplitude of the adult N170 is larger for monkey faces than human faces, the infant N290 shows the opposite pattern at all ages tested (de Haan et al., 2002; Halit et al., 2003). Third, while the amplitude of the adult N170 is not affected by direction of gaze (Taylor, Itier, Allison, & Edmonds, 2001b), the amplitude of the infant N290 is larger for faces with direct than averted gaze (Farroni, Csibra, Simion, & Johnson, 2002). While these last two findings are consistent with a role for the N290 in face processing, they suggest that the information that is processed from the face may still differ for infants compared to adults. One possibility is that modulation of the N290 by eye gaze indicates that this component is primarily sensitive to eyes, an interpretation consistent with the view that eye detection develops more quickly than face detection (Taylor et al., 2001a) and with behavioural studies showing that the eyes are perhaps the most salient feature of the face, at least during the first months of life (Maurer, 1985). This interpretation could be consistent with the fact that the N290 differs for upright compared to inverted faces, even though both have eyes present with direct gaze, if the inversion effect is primarily driven by the eye region (see Itier et al., 2006).

With respect to latency, it is interesting to note that it appears the latency of the N290 at 12 months of age is only ~20 ms longer than the latency of the N170 observed at 4–5 years of age (Taylor et al., 1999, 2001a). This is especially striking since the N170 latency decreases more rapidly, by 35 ms, between 4–5 and 6–7 years of age (Taylor et al., 1999, 2001a). One possible explanation for the relatively slow change in latency between 1 and 4 years is that it is due to methodological differences between the studies that may affect peak amplitudes and latencies (e.g., filtering, reference, size of stimuli). However, the fact that the latency of the N170 in adults was similar in the different studies (approx. 160 ms in de Haan et al., 2002; approx 160 ms in Taylor et al., 1999; approx 150 ms in Taylor et al., 2001a) is not consistent with this explanation. Another possibility is that the time between 1 and 4 years represents a period of relatively slow development of face processing and/or that the time between 4 and 7 years represents a period of relatively rapid development of face processing. The fact that the N170 in 4- to 5-year-olds, but not in infants or teenagers, appears to show a double peak (Taylor et al., 2001a), might make estimates of its latency less reliable at this age and/or support the idea that it is an important period of change in face processing. Given the absence of reports on the development of the N170 between 1 and 4 years of age and the relatively limited number of behavioural studies in the same age range, it is difficult to evaluate these possibilities.

P400

The P400 is a positive component most prominent over posterior lateral electrodes whose peak latency decreases from approximately 450 to 390 ms between 3 and 12 months of age. It has also been suggested as a precursor of the adult N170. Although the P400 differs in polarity from, and peaks at a later latency than, the N170, it is similar to the N170 in two ways: (a) like the N170, the P400 is more prominent at lateral than medial electrodes (de Haan et al., 2002; Halit et al., 2003), and (b) like the adult N170, the peak latency of the P400 is faster in response to faces compared to objects (de Haan & Nelson, 1999).

By 3 months of age the P400 differs for inverted compared to upright faces (Halit et al., 2003) as well as intact versus distorted faces and bodies (Gliga & Dehaene-Lambertz, 2005; but see Macchi Cassia, Kuefner, Westerlund, & Nelson, 2006). However, the response to inversion is not adult-like even by 6 months of age, as it is not specific to human faces (see Figure 3.1; de Haan et al., 2002). In contrast, by 12 months of age the latency of the P400 is influenced by inversion in a manner similar to the adult N170: latency is longer for inverted than upright human faces, but does not differ for inverted compared to upright monkey faces (Halit et al., 2003). Thus, like the N290, the P400 appears to become more finely tuned to human faces with age.

Negative central (Nc)

The negative central (Nc) component is one of the most well-studied components of the infant cognitive visual ERP (see Chapter 4, this volume, for further discussion of the Nc). It is a negative deflection occurring between 400 and 800 ms after stimulus onset in 6-month-olds, most prominent over fronto-central electrodes. It is sensitive to stimulus probability, and tends to be of larger amplitude for infrequent compared to frequent events in oddball paradigms (Courchesne, Ganz, & Norcia, 1981; Karrer & Ackles, 1987;

Karrer & Monti, 1995; Richards, 2002). In this context, the Nc has been interpreted as reflecting either the infant's allocation of attention, with the greater negativity to the infrequently presented face reflecting greater allocation of attention to the novel or more unexpected face (Courchesne et al., 1981; Nelson, 1994), or a more generalised arousal elicited by novel stimuli (Richards, 2002).

The Nc also appears to reflect aspects of recognition, as its amplitude is affected by stimulus familiarity even when items are present with equal probability. At 6 months of age, the Nc is larger for the mother's face than a stranger's face, and for familiar toys than novel ones (see Figure 4.1 in Chapter 4, this volume; de Haan & Nelson, 1997, 1999; Nelson, Wewerka, Thomas, Tribby-Walbridge, deRegnier, & Georgieff, 2000; but see Webb, Long, & Nelson, 2005). The spatial distribution of this recognition effect differs for faces compared to toys: for faces it is observed over midline and right anterior temporal sites (T4), while for objects it is observed for midline and bilateral anterior temporal sites (T3, T4). The right lateralisation of the response for recognition of faces is consistent with split visual field investigations of infants in this age range, demonstrating a left visual field (right hemisphere) advantage for recognition of the mother's face (de Schonen & Mathivet, 1990).

The difference in Nc amplitude to familiar compared to novel items may reflect greater allocation of attention to the familiar items, although in tests of visual attention infants of this age do not look longer at the mother's face than a stranger's face (de Haan & Nelson, 1997; Robinson, 2002). It may also reflect processing of semantic and/or emotional information related to the mother's face, as Nc amplitude is also known to be modulated by the emotional content of the face in infants of a similar age (de Haan, Belsky, Reid, Volein, & Johnson, 2004; de Haan & Nelson, 1999; Nelson & de Haan, 1996). In support of the view that the response is related to the relative salience of the face, the direction of the differences in amplitude between mother's and stranger's faces, but not between familiar and unfamiliar objects, changes with age. Children younger than 24 months show a larger Nc to mother's face compared to stranger's face, but children older than 45 months show a larger Nc to stranger's face compared to mother's face (Carver et al., 2003). The authors interpret this result as indicating that the caregiver's face is particularly salient in the first years of life, as children are forming their relationship with and mental representation of the caregiver, but these are well established enough by 4 years that children begin to devote more resources to processing strangers' faces.

Interestingly, modulation of the midline Nc by familiarity of a face is observed only when mother's and stranger's faces are perceptually quite distinct. When the faces are similar looking, the midline Nc amplitude is not affected by familiarity and instead a positive slow wave over bilateral posterior temporal electrodes is larger for stranger's than mother's faces (de Haan & Nelson, 1997). Positive slow wave activity has been linked to updating information in memory representations (see below). It is possible that, for similar-looking face pairs, no difference is observed in the Nc because both faces are "recognised" as mother, but that, because of the stranger's greater perceptual difference from the stored representation of mother, it elicits a positive slow wave.

Further evidence linking the Nc to recognition comes from a study investigating 2- to 5-year-old children with autism and typically developing children (Dawson, Carver, Meltzoff, Panagiotides, McPartland, & Webb, 2001). Typically developing children showed the expected pattern with different amplitude of the Nc for familiar compared to unfamiliar items, and a more widespread distribution of this response for objects than for faces. In contrast, children with autism, a developmental disorder characterised by impairments in face perception and social skills, showed evidence of recognition of objects, but not of faces.

How the Nc relates to components elicited during adults' recognition of faces is unclear, since adults have not been tested under the same conditions. However, several studies have compared responses to briefly familiarised or famous faces with responses to unfamiliar faces. While some studies have found no difference (e.g., Schweinberger, Sommer, & Stiller, 1993), others have shown three time windows in which components are larger for familiar than unfamiliar faces: (a) a negative component occurring 250–600 ms (Eimer, 2000b; Smith & Halgren, 1987; Uhl et al., 1990), (b) a positive component peaking at approximately 520 ms (Eimer, 2000b; Smith & Halgren, 1987), and (c) a negative slow wave following the positive component, that also tends to be larger over the right than the left hemisphere (Smith & Halgren, 1987; Uhl et al., 1990; but see Barrett, Rugg, & Perrett, 1988).

The specificity of the memory-related components elicited during recognition of facial identity in adults has not been a frequent focus of investigation. Some investigators have addressed this question indirectly by comparison to language processing. These studies have focused on the N400, a component that in studies of language is larger for words appearing in an unexpected context than words appearing in an expected context (e.g., Kutas & Van Petten, 1988). Investigators have been interested in determining whether this effect is specific to language or also occurs for non-verbal stimuli such as faces. For faces, the N400 is elicited in tasks where participants are asked to decide if two sequentially presented faces match or mismatch. Some studies have concluded that, for both faces and words, the N400 response to mismatch is usually bilaterally symmetric and without a distinctive topography (Barrett & Rugg, 1989; Barrett et al., 1988; the exact topography appears to depend on factors such as the reference used), suggesting it reflects processing common in linguistic and non-linguistic domains (Barrett & Rugg, 1989). However, in a study in which the amount of verbal information associated with faces was systematically varied, the timing and topography of the N400 varied with verbal loading. There was a predominant right posterior temporal localisation in the condition involving "pure" face processing that differed from the pattern observed in the various verbal loading conditions (Olivares, Iglesias, & Rodinguez-Holquin, 2003). These results suggest that there may be a non-linguistic N400 related to purely visual information. Whether there is a response specific to faces within the visual domain is unknown, but another study that also found a right-lateralised mismatch effect for upright faces did find that the mismatch effect for inverted faces was of longer latency and bilaterally distributed (Mills, Alvarez, St. George, Appelbaum, Bellugi, & Neville, 2000).

Whether the Nc reflects the developmental precursor of any of these components remains an open question. Future studies in which infants and adults are tested under the same conditions with familiar and unfamiliar faces may provide some answers.

Positive slow wave

Positive slow wave activity beginning approximately 800 ms after stimulus onset has been linked to the updating of memory representations in infants (Nelson, 1994, 1997) and is detectable by 3 months of age in visual studies (Pascalis, de Haan, Nelson, & de Schonen, 1998). Thus, in the context of face recognition, it might reflect encoding processes related to creating new and/or modifying perceptual representations of known faces (de Haan & Nelson, 1999). The observation that the slow wave diminishes in amplitude and returns to baseline across repeated presentations is consistent with this view (Webb, Snyder, & Nelson, 2001).

In order to investigate further the influence of stimulus type on expression of the positive slow wave, we conducted an experiment aimed at determining whether the positive slow wave differed during encoding of different stimulus categories. Because these results are previously unpublished, we will describe the methods and results in some detail here (full details of the methods can be obtained from Johnson, 2000, in which the results from the Oz electrode in this experiment are also described).

We presented 6-month-old infants ($n = 22$; M age = 185 days, SD = 5 days; 14 boys) with a series of coloured images of upright faces, inverted faces, and objects (infant toys) while recording ERPs (Cz, Pz, Fz,T3, T3, T5, T6, referenced to averaged ears; sampling rate 100 Hz, bandpass 0.1–30 Hz with a 60-Hz notch filter; further details of recording can be found in Johnson et al., 2001). Each category was presented with equal probability so that any category-related effects were not due to stimulus probability. Within each category, there were five different exemplars that were presented repeatedly (six times each), to allow opportunity for encoding of face/object identity.

Mean amplitude of the slow wave between 800 and 1500 ms was analysed in separate repeated measures ANOVAs for midline (Electrode [Pz, Cz, Fz] by Stimulus Type [Upright Face, Inverted Face, Object) and lateral (Hemisphere [Right, Left] by Anterior-Posterior [Anterior Temporal, Posterior Temporal] by Stimulus Type [Upright Face, Inverted Face, Object] electrode groupings.

At midline electrodes, the component did not differ between upright and inverted faces or toys, $F(2, 42) = 0.03, p > .1$. At temporal electrodes there was a Stimulus Type by Hemisphere interaction, $F(2, 42) = 3.41, p < .05$, illustrated in Figure 3.2. For upright faces, there was a positive slow wave over the right hemisphere electrodes (M = 5.23 µv) but a return to baseline over left hemisphere electrodes (–0.91 µv). For inverted faces there was a bilateral negative slow wave more prominent over left (–7.5 µv) than right (–3.5 µv) hemisphere electrodes, while for toys there was a bilateral positive slow wave more prominent over left (10.23 µv) than right (4.45 µv) hemisphere electrodes.

Since positive slow wave activity is thought to reflect updating of memory for a partially encoded stimulus, neural activity underlying memory representations of the faces and toys may occur bilaterally for upright toys but more unilaterally on the right for upright faces. This spatial pattern is qualitatively similar to that pattern of lateralisation observed for the Nc during recognition of familiar faces and toys. It has been suggested that the positive slow wave may reflect activity of the hippocampus (Nelson, 1994; see also Reynolds & Richards, 2005). This interpretation is consistent with studies showing that the right hippocampal-parahippocampal region is involved in encoding of faces in adults (Grady et al., 1994; Haxby, Ungerleider, Horwitz, Maisog, & Grady, 1994).

In contrast to the upright faces and toys, inverted faces elicited a negative slow wave bilaterally. The negative slow wave is thought to reflect detection of novelty (Nelson, 1994). It is possible that this activity reflects infants' perception of inverted faces as unusual or unfamiliar. The greater similarity for infants' responses to faces and toys than to inverted faces suggests that

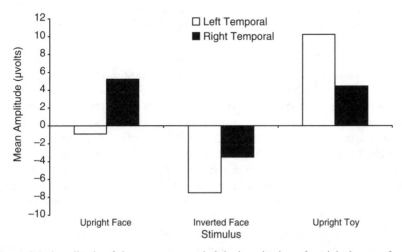

Figure 3.2 Amplitude of slow waves recorded during viewing of upright human faces, inverted human faces, and objects (toys without faces) in 6-month-old infants.

infants' familiarity with a category may influence how they encode new exemplars. They may have mental schemas for upright faces and toys which allow them to more easily begin to form mental representations of individual items within these categories, while they may not have a similar schema for inverted faces and therefore respond to them as novel.

The relation of these slow wave responses to those observed during adults' face processing is not entirely clear. In general, investigations of the effects of repeating visual stimuli on adults' ERPs tend to find greater positivity for repeated face and nonface stimuli (e.g., Doyle & Rugg, 1998; Eimer, 2000b; Smith & Halgren, 1987; Uhl et al., 1990). One study that compared infants' and adults' ERPs to a single familiar face and a single novel face found that adults showed a larger positive slow wave to the novel face while infants showed a larger positive slow wave to the familiar face (Nelson, Thomas, de Haan, & Wewerka, 1998). However, it is not clear whether the difference in pattern of responding was due to developmental differences in the function/response properties of the slow wave or to the different familiarisation procedures used for infants compared to adults. Future studies, in which adults and infants are tested under the same conditions, will provide a clearer picture of the relations among these components.

GENERAL DISCUSSION

ERP studies in adults have been very useful in addressing questions as to the timing and domain specificity of the perceptual-cognitive processes involved in face recognition. Although there are relatively few studies to date, investigating the development of the ERP correlates of face processing during infancy not only can provide insight into the nature of specific ERP components identified in adults, but also has broader implications for theories of the development of face processing.

In studies of adults, ERP components can be identified by examining their peak latencies, morphology, and spatial distribution. For example, a target-elicited P300 might be described as a positive component peaking between 300 and 500 ms with a parietal maximum. Identifying the infant equivalents of such components is not simply a matter of applying the same criteria to the younger age group, as investigations of ERPs during childhood and old age have clearly shown that timing and topography of components can change across the lifespan (e.g., Taylor & Pang, 1999). This problem is not unique to the study of face processing, and has been tackled in other studies questioning, for example, whether there is an infant equivalent of the adult P300 (e.g., McIsaac & Polich, 1992; Nelson et al., 1998). One basic approach to identifying the infant and child equivalents of adult ERP components has been a functional one: test younger and older participants under the same conditions and look for ERP components that show similar stimulus- or task-related modulations across age. While this approach has proved useful in practice, it is important to keep in mind that it makes the assumption that there will be no change in functionality with age.

In the field of face processing, this functional approach has been used most extensively to study the developmental trajectory of the N170. As discussed earlier, developmental studies through childhood have identified the N170 as a negative deflection over posterior temporal scalp regions that, like the adult N170, is larger in amplitude and often shorter in latency for faces compared to other objects (Taylor et al., 1999). These studies show that the peak latency of the N170 decreases with age into adolescence, and that the peak amplitude over the right hemisphere increases over this time (Taylor et al., 1999; Taylor et al., 2001a).

With respect to the components described in infants as potential precursors of the N170, two components have been identified based on their response properties. The N290 component is similar to the N170 in that it shows an adult-like effect of face inversion on amplitude, and a relatively similar timing and polarity. However, the basic question of whether the N290 differs for faces versus objects (a defining characteristic of the adult N170) remains to be tested. The P400 is like the N170 in that it is of shorter latency for faces than objects (de Haan & Nelson, 1999), and shows an adult-like effect of face inversion on peak latency by 12 months of age (Halit et al., 2003). With respect to spatial distribution, the P400, like the N170, shows a more lateral distribution. However, the P400 differs in latency and polarity from the N170. Overall, these findings suggest that both the N290 and P400 reflect processes that in the adult may become integrated in time in the N170 component. In other words, the structural encoding of faces may be spread out over a longer time of processing in infants than adults. It is possible that, as they become more automated, the processes involved in face processing are carried out more quickly and/or in a parallel rather than serial fashion. Currently, there is a gap between those studies that have examined face-related ERPs up to 12 months, and studies of older children that begin at 60 months, which prevents a firm conclusion.

Both the N290 and P400 show changes in their spatial-temporal distribution over the first year of life. Their latencies decrease from 3 to 12 months, a change likely in part to reflect general changes in information processing rather than changes specific to face processing. Decreases in latency of ERP components with age are commonly reported (e.g., Karrer & Ackles, 1987; Nelson, 1997) and are often interpreted as reflecting the increased speed of neural processing with myelination. Whether there are changes in amplitude and latency with age for the N290 and P400 that are specific to faces remains to be carefully investigated by directly contrasting the responses to a wider variety of stimuli over different ages. The spatial distribution of both the N290 and P400 also changes from 3 to 12 months, with the location of peak amplitude shifting laterally for both. In addition, the maxima of these components appear more superior than in adults, a result consistent with studies of children finding a shift from superior to inferior maximum of the N170 with age (Taylor et al., 2001a). In this way, both become more like the adult N170 with age, as the N170 peaks maximally over lateral (T5/T6) electrodes. One possibility is that this reflects a change in the configuration of generators underlying these components with age. Several areas, including regions of the fusiform gyrus (Shibata et al., 2002), the posterior inferior temporal gyrus (Bentin et al., 1996; Shibata et al., 2002), superior temporal sulcus (Henson, Goshen-Gottstein, Ganel, Otten, Quayle, & Rugg, 2003; Itier & Taylor, 2004b) and lateral occipito-temporal cortex (Bentin et al., 1996; Schweiberger et al., 2002b) have been proposed as underlying the adult N170. It is possible that several or all of these regions do contribute to the N170, but that different generators develop at different rates and lead to a change in the spatial distribution of the component with age. Another possible explanation for the shift and spatial distribution with age is that it occurs incidentally as a consequence of brain growth, which may cause the generators of the components to shift in location or orientation. Results of one source analysis study suggests that areas including the lateral occipital area, right fusiform gyrus and right superior temporal sulcus contribute to the infant N290, suggesting similarity in the generators involved in the infant N290 and adult N170 (Johnson et al., 2005). Future studies modelling and comparing the generators of the infant, child, and adult component can help to further detail the degree of stability or change in the configuration of generators underlying the N170 over development.

While existing studies allow a potential link between the N290/P400 and the adult N170, the correspondence between other infant and adult components is less clear. The two components that have been linked most strongly to infants' recognition of familiar faces, the Nc and the positive slow wave, may relate to the N400 and P600 identified in adults during identity recognition tasks (Eimer, 2000b). However, because there are no studies of recognition of facial identity that have tested infants and adults under the same conditions, such interpretations remain very speculative. The studies with infants and adults differ in factors such as the response demands (passive tasks with infants but active behavioural responses in adults) and definitions of familiarity, and thus are difficult to compare directly.

It is also more difficult to draw conclusions regarding the stimulus specificity of the later-latency ERP components. There is evidence of right lateralisation of the Nc and positive slow wave for faces but not objects in infants (de Haan & Nelson, 1997, 1999), a result consistent with the hypothesis that the right hemisphere is more involved than the left in processing of faces. However, studies of recognition of identity in adults have tended not to compare faces directly with other categories. Those that do have tended to compare faces with verbal stimuli in order to contrast verbal and nonverbal processing, an approach that does not address the question of whether there are differences in processing for different categories within the visual domain.

The results of infant ERP studies of face processing have implications for theories of the development of the mechanisms underlying face processing in adults. Young infants, who are not considered experts in face recognition, show many of the characteristics of adult face processing (e.g., right hemisphere bias, inversion effects). These results are consistent with the view that regions involved in face processing in adults are also active during infancy. However, these regions may be competitively selected from an initially larger set of activated areas (Johnson, 2001), and may initially respond to a wider range of stimuli. In terms of the three perspectives on the development of face processing discussed earlier, we suggest that the current ERP evidence is most consistent with the third perspective in which a series of biases combine during development to ensure that some cortical regions become specialised for face processing. The early appearance of characteristics of face processing may be one difference (or be indicative of differences) between the process of development and process of adult learning.

The results of infant ERP studies also clearly show that components elicited during face processing in infants are less specific to upright human faces than is the adult N170 component. These results show a gradual increase in the specificity of two components, the N290 and P400 over the first year of life. However, even by 12 months of age the components and their response properties are not adult-like. The gradual emergence of the specificity of response is consistent with the view that experience in viewing faces plays an important role in the ultimate emergence of the adult face-processing system. Results from a recent behavioural study support this view. In this study, individuals who were deprived of pattern visual input in the first months of life later showed impairments in encoding configural information from faces, in spite of normal encoding of featural information in faces and configural information in geometric patterns (Le Grand, Mondloch, Maurer, & Brent, 2001).

In summary, the P1, N290, P400, Nc, and positive slow wave are all elicited during infants' processing of faces. The relation of these components to those elicited in children and adults remains an open question for study, although there is convincing evidence relating both the N290 and P400 to the adult N170. Further investigations that document changes across a number of time points in development, particularly from 12 to 60 months, and using the same procedure across ages, are needed. Use of high-density recordings in these studies will help to clarify questions regarding changes in the generators underlying particular components with age.

ACKNOWLEDGEMENTS

This chapter is reprinted from *International Journal of Psychophysiology* (Vol. 51, de Haan, M., Johnson, M. H., & Halit, H. Development of face-sensitive event-related potentials during infancy: A review. Pp. 45–58). Copyright (2003) with permission from Elsevier. Minor modifications have been made for purposes of updating.

REFERENCES

Barrett, S. E., & Rugg, M. D. (1989). Event-related potentials and the semantic matching of faces. *Neuropsychologia, 27*, 913–922.

Barrett, S. E., Rugg, M. D., & Perrett, D. I. (1988). Event-related potentials and the matching of familiar and unfamiliar faces. *Neuropsychologia, 26*, 105–117.

Begleiter, H., Porjesz, B., & Wang, W. (1995). Event-related potentials differentiate priming and recognition to familiar and unfamiliar faces. *Electroencephalography and Clinical Neurophysiology, 94*, 41–49.

Bentin, S., Allison, T., Puce, A., Perez, E., & McCarthy, G. (1996). Electrophysiological studies of face perception in humans. *Journal of Cognitive Neuroscience, 8*, 551–565.

Bentin, S., & Deouell, L. Y. (2000). Structural encoding and identification in face processing: ERP evidence for separate mechanisms. *Cognitive Neuropsychology, 17*, 35–54.

Carmel, D., & Bentin, S. (2002). Domain specificity versus expertise: Factors influencing distinct processing of faces. *Cognition, 83*, 1–29.

Carver, L. J., Dawson, G., Panagiotides, H., Meltzoff, A. N., McPartland, J., Gray, J. et al. (2003). Age-related differences in neural correlates of face recognition during the toddler and preschool years. *Developmental Psychobiology, 42*, 148–159.

Courchesne, E., Ganz, L., & Norcia, A. M. (1981). Event-related potentials to human faces in infants. *Child Development, 52*, 804–811.

Dawson, G., Carver, L., Meltzoff, A. N., Panagiotides, H., McPartland, J., & Webb, S. J. (2002). Neural correlates of face and object recognition in young children with autism spectrum disorder, developmental delay, and typical development. *Child Development, 73*, 700–717.

de Haan, M., Belsky, J., Reid, V., Volein, A., & Johnson, M. H. (2004). Maternal personality and infants' neural and visual responsivity to facial expressions of emotion. *Journal Child Psychology and Psychiatry, 45*, 1209–1218.

de Haan, M., & Halit, H. (2001). The development and neural basis of face processing during infancy. In A. F. Kalverboer & A. Gramsbergen (Eds.), *Brain and behavior in human development: A sourcebook* (pp. 921–937). Dordrecht: Kluwer Academic Publishers.

de Haan, M., & Nelson, C. A. (1999). Brain activity differentiates face and object processing by 6-month-old infants. *Developmental Psychology, 34*, 1114–1121.

de Haan, M., & Nelson, C. A. (1998). Discrimination and categorization of facial expressions of emotion during infancy. In A. Slater (Ed.), *Perceptual development: Visual, auditory, and language development in infancy* (pp. 287–309). London: University College London Press.

de Haan, M., & Nelson, C. A. (1997). Recognition of the mother's face by six month-old infants: A neurobehavioral study. *Child Development, 68*, 187–210.

de Haan, M., Pascalis, O., & Johnson, M. H. (2002). Specialization of neural mechanisms underlying face recognition in human infants. *Journal of Cognitive Neuroscience, 14*, 199–209.

De Renzi, E., Perani, D., Carlesimo, G. A., Silveri, M. C., & Fazio, F. (1994). Prosopagnosia can be associated with damage confined to the right hemisphere—an MRI and PET study and review of the literature. *Neuropsychologia, 32*, 893–902.

de Schonen, S., & Mathivet, E. (1990). Hemispheric asymmetry in a face discrimination task in infants. *Child Development, 61*, 1192–1205.

Diamond, R., & Carey, S. (1986). Why faces are and are not special: An effect of expertise. *Journal of Experimental Psychology: General, 115,* 107–117.

Doyle, M. C., & Rugg, M. D. (1998). Word repetition within- and across-visual fields: An event-related potential study. *Neuropsychologia, 36,* 1403–1415.

Eimer, M. (2000a). The face-specific N170 component reflects late stages in the structural encoding of faces. *Neuroreport, 11,* 2319–2324.

Eimer, M. (2000b). Event-related brain potentials distinguish processing stages involved in face perception and recognition. *Clinical Neurophysiology, 111,* 694–705.

Eimer, M. (2000c). Effects of face inversion on the structural encoding and recognition of faces. Evidence from event-related brain potentials. *Brain Research: Cognitive Brain Research, 10,* 145–158.

Farah, M. J. (1990). *Visual agnosia.* Cambridge, MA: MIT Press.

Farah, M. J. (2000). *The cognitive neuroscience of vision.* Malden, MA: Blackwell.

Farah, M. J., Rabinowitz, C., Quinn, G. E., & Liu, G. (2000). Early commitment of neural substrates for face recognition. *Cognitive Neuropsychology, 17,* 117–123.

Farroni, T., Csibra, G., Simion, F., & Johnson, M. H. (2002). Eye contact detection in humans from birth. *Proceedings of the National Academy of Science, USA, 99,* 9602–9605.

Gauthier, I., & Logothetis, N. (2000). Is face recognition not so unique after all? *Cognitive Neuropsychology, 17,* 125–142.

Gauthier, I., & Nelson, C. A. (2001). The development of face expertise. *Current Opinion in Neurobiology, 11,* 219–224.

Gauthier, I., Skudlarski, P., Gore, J. C., & Anderson, A. W. (2000). Expertise for cars and birds recruits brain areas involved in face recognition. *Nature Neuroscience, 3,* 191–197.

Gauthier, I., Tarr, M. J., Anderson, A. W., Skudlarski, P., & Gore, J. C. (1999). Activation of the middle fusiform "face area" increases with expertise in recognizing novel objects. *Nature Neuroscience, 2,* 568–573.

George, N., Evans, J., Fiori, N., Davidoff, J., & Renault, B. (1996). Brain events related to normal and moderately scrambled faces. *Brain Research: Cognitive Brain Research, 4,* 65–76.

Gliga, T., & Dehaene-Lambertz, G. (2005). Structural encoding of the human body parallels that of the human face. *Journal of Cognitive Neuroscience, 17,* 1328–1340.

Grady, C. L., Maisog, J. M., Horwitz, B., Ungerleider, L. G., Mentis, M. J., Salerno, J. A. et al. (1994). Age related changes in cortical blood flow activation during visual processing of faces and location. *The Journal of Neuroscience, 14,* 1450–1462.

Halit, H., Csibra, G., Volein, A., & Johnson, M. H. (2004). Face-sensitive cortical processing in early infancy. *Journal of Child Psychology and Psychiatry, 45,* 1228–1234.

Halit, H., de Haan, M., & Johnson, M. H. (2000). Modulation of event-related potentials by prototypical and atypical faces. *Neuroreport, 11,* 1871–1875.

Halit, H., de Haan, M., & Johnson, M. H. (2003). Cortical specialisation for face processing: Face-sensitive event-related potential components in 3 and 12 month old infants. *Neuroimage, 19,* 1180–1193.

Haxby, J. V., Ungerleider, L. G., Horwitz, B., Maisog, J. M., & Grady, C. L. (1994). Neural systems for encoding and retrieving new long-term visual memories: A PET-rCBF study. *Investigative Ophthalmology and Visual Science, 35,* 1813.

Henson, R. N., Goshen-Gottenstein, Y., Ganel, T., Otten, L. J., Quayle, A., &

Rugg, M. D. (2003). Electrophysiological and haemodynamic correlates of face perception, recognition and priming. *Cerebral Cortex, 13,* 793–805.

Hillyard, S. A., & Anllo-Vento, L. (1998). Event-related brain potentials in the study of visual selective attention. *Proceedings of the National Academy of Science USA, 95,* 781–787.

Hopf, J. M., & Mangun, G. R. (2000). Shifting visual attention in space: An electro-physiological analysis using high spatial resolution mapping. *Clinical Neuro-physiology, 111,* 1241–1257.

Itier, R. J., Latinus, M., & Taylor, M. J. (2006). Face, eye and object early processing: What is the face specificity? *Neuroimage, 29,* 667–676.

Itier, R. J., & Taylor, M. J. (2002). Inversion and contrast reversal affect both encoding and recognition of faces: A repetition study using ERPs. *Neuroimage, 15,* 353–372.

Itier, R. J., & Taylor, M. J. (2004a). N170 or N1? Spatiotemporal differences between object and face processing using ERPs. *Ceberal Cortex, 14,* 132–142.

Itier, R. J., & Taylor, M. J. (2004b). Source analysis of the N170 to faces and objects. *Neuroreport, 15,* 1261–1265.

Johnson, M. H. (2000). Functional brain development in infants: Elements of an interactive specialization framework. *Child Development, 71,* 75–81.

Johnson, M. H. (2001). Functional brain development in humans. *Nature Review Neuroscience, 2,* 475–483.

Johnson, M. H., de Haan, M., Hatzakis, H., Oliver, A., Smith, W., Tucker, L. A. et al. (2001). Recording and analyzing high density ERPs with infants using the geodesic sensor net. *Developmental Neuropsychology, 19,* 295–323.

Johnson, M. H., Griffin, R., Csibra, G., Halit, H., Farroni, T., de Haan, M. et al. (2005). The emergence of the social brain network: Evidence from typical and atypical development. *Development and Psychopathology, 17,* 599–619.

Johnson, M. H., & Morton, J. (1991). *Biology and cognitive development. The case of face recognition.* Oxford, UK: Blackwell.

Kanwisher, N., McDermott, J., & Chun, M. M. (1997). The fusiform face area: A module in human extrastriate cortex specialized for face perception. *Journal of Neuroscience, 17,* 4302–4311.

Karrer, R., & Ackles, P. K. (1987). Visual event-related potentials of infants during a modified oddball procedure. *Electroencephalography and Clinical Neurophysiology, 49*(Suppl.), 603–608.

Karrer, R., & Monti, L. A. (1995). Event-related potentials of 4–7 week old infants in a visual recognition memory task. *Electroencephalography and Clinical Neurophysiology, 94,* 414–424.

Kutas, M., & Van Petten, C. (1988). ERP studies of language. In P. K. Ackles, J. R. Jennings, & M. G. H. Coles (Eds.), *Advances in psychophysiology.* Greenwich, CT: JAI Press.

Le Grand, R., Mondloch, C. J., Maurer, D., & Brent, H. P. (2001). Neuroperception. Early visual experience and face processing. *Nature, 410,* 890.

Macchi Cassia, V., Kuefner, D., Westerlund, A., & Nelson, C. A. (2006). A behavioural and ERP investigation of 3-month-olds' face preferences. *Neuropsychologia, 44,* 2113–2125.

Maurer, D. (1985). Infants' perception of facedness. In T. M. Field & N. Fox (Eds.), *Social perception in infants* (pp. 73–100). Norwood, NJ: Ablex.

McIsaac, H., & Polich, J. (1992). Comparison of infant and adult P300 from auditory stimuli. *Journal of Experimental Child Psychology, 53,* 115–128.

Mills, D. L., Alvarez, T. D., St. George, M., Appelbaum, L. G., Bellugi, U., & Neville, H. (2000). Electrophysiological studies of face processing in Williams syndrome. *Journal of Cognitive Neuroscience, 12*, 47–64.

Nelson, C. A. (1993). The recognition of facial expressions in infancy: Behavioral and electrophysiological evidence. In B. de Boysson-Bardies, S. de Schonen, P. Jusczyk, & P. MacNeilage (Eds.), *Developmental neurocognition: Speech and face processing in the first year of life* (pp. 187–198). London: Kluwer Academic Press.

Nelson, C. A. (1994). Neural correlates of recognition memory in the first postnatal year of life. In G. Dawson & K. Fischer (Eds.), *Human behavior and the developing brain* (pp. 269–313). New York: Guilford Press.

Nelson, C. A. (1997). Electrophysiological correlates of memory development in the first year of life. In H. W. Reese & M. D. Franzen (Eds.), *Biological and neuropsychological mechanisms. Life-span developmental psychology* (pp. 95–131). Mahwah, NJ: Lawrence Erlbaum Associates Inc.

Nelson, C. A. (2001). The development and neural bases of face recognition. *Infant and Child Development, 10*, 3–18.

Nelson, C. A., & de Haan, M. (1996). Neural correlates of infants' visual responsiveness to facial expressions of emotion. *Developmental Psychobiology, 29*, 577–595.

Nelson, C. A., Thomas, K., de Haan, M., & Wewerka, S. (1998). Delayed recognition memory in infants and adults as revealed by event-related potentials. *International Journal of Psychophysiology, 29*, 145–165.

Nelson, C. A., Wewerka, S., Thomas, K. M., Tribby-Walbridge, S., deRegnier, R., & Georgieff, M. (2000). Neurocognitive sequelae of infants of diabetic mothers. *Behavioral Neuroscience, 114*, 950–956.

Olivares, E. I., Iglesias, J., & Rodriguez-Holquin, S. (2003). Long-latency ERPs and recognition of facial identity. *Journal of Cognitive Neuroscience, 15*, 136–151.

Paller, K. A., Gonsalves, B., Grabowecky, M., Bozic, V. S., & Yamada, S. (2000). Electrophysiological correlates of recollecting faces of known and unknown individuals. *Neuroimage, 11*, 98–110.

Pascalis, O., de Haan, M., & Nelson, C. A. (2002). Is face processing species-specific during the first year of life? *Science, 296*, 1321–1323.

Pascalis, O., de Haan, M., Nelson, C. A., & de Schonen, S. (1998). Long-term recognition memory for faces assessed by visual paired comparison in 3- and 6-month-old infants. *Journal of Experimental Psychology: Learning, Memory and Cognition, 24*, 249–260.

Puce, A., Allison, T., Gore, J. C., & McCarthy, G. (1995). Face-sensitive regions in human extrastriate cortex studied by functional MRI. *Journal of Neurophysiology, 74*, 1192–1199.

Rebai, M., Poiroux, S., Bernard, C., & Lalonde, R. (2001). Event-related potentials for category-specific information during passive viewing of faces and objects. *International Journal of Neuroscience, 106*, 209–226.

Reynolds, G. D., & Richards, J. E. (2005). Familiarization, attention and recognition memory in infancy: An event-related potential and cortical source localization study. *Developmental Psychology, 41*, 598–615.

Rhodes, G., Carey, S., Byatt, G., & Proffitt, F. (1998). Coding spatial variations in faces and simple shapes: A test of two models. *Vision Research, 38*, 2307–2321.

Richards, J. E. (2002). The development of visual attention and the brain. In M. de Haan & M. H. Johnson (Eds.), *The cognitive neuroscience of development* (pp. 73–98). Hove, UK: Psychology Press.

Robinson, A. J. (2002). *The development of memory for contextual and spatial relationships between 6 and 24 months of age.* Unpublished doctoral dissertation.

Rossion, B., Campanella, S., Gomez, C. M., Delinte, A., Debatisse, D., Liard, L. et al. (1999). Task modulation of brain activity related to familiar and unfamiliar face processing: An ERP study. *Clinical Neurophysiology, 110,* 449–462.

Rossion, B., Gauthier, I., Goffaux, V., Tarr, M. J., & Crommelinck, M. (2002). Expertise training with novel objects leads to left-lateralized facelike electrophysiological responses. *Psychological Science, 13,* 250–257.

Rossion, B., Gauthier, I., Tarr, M. J., Despland, P., Bruyer, R., Linotte, S. et al. (2000). The N170 occipito-temporal component is delayed and enhanced to inverted faces but not to inverted objects: An electrophysiological account of face-specific processes in the human brain. *NeuroReport, 11,* 69–74.

Rossion, B., Joyce, C. A., Cottrell, G. W., & Tarr, M. J. (2003). Early lateralization and orientation tuning for face, word and object processing in the visual cortex. *Neuroimage, 20,* 1609–1624.

Rousselet, G. A., Mace, M. J., & Fabre-Thorpe, M. (2004). Animal and human faces in natural scenes: How specific to human face is the N170 ERP component? *Journal of Vision, 4,* 13–21.

Schweinberger, S. R., Pickering, E. C., Burton, A. M., & Kaufmann, J. M. (2002a) Human brain potential correlates of repetition priming in face and name recognition. *Neuropsychologia, 40,* 2057–2073.

Schweinberger, S. R., Pickering, E. C., Jentzsch, I., Burton, A. M., & Kaufmann, J. M. (2002b). Event-related brain potential evidence for a response of inferior temporal cortex to familiar face repetitions. *Brain Research: Cognitive Brain Research, 14,* 398–409.

Schweinberger, S. R., Sommer, W., & Stiller, R. M. (1993). Event-related potentials and models of performance asymmetries in face and word recognition. *Neuropsychologia, 32,* 175–191.

Shibata, T., Nishijo, H., Tamura, R., Miyamoto, K., Eifuku, S., Endo, S. et al. (2002). Generators of visual evoked potentials for faces and eyes in the human brain as determined by dipole localization. *Brain Topography, 15,* 51–63.

Smith, M. E., & Halgren, E. (1987). Event-related potentials elicited by familiar and unfamiliar faces. *Electrophysiology and Clinical Neurophysiology Supplement, 40,* 422–426.

Tarr, M. J., & Gauthier, I. (2000). FFA: A flexible fusiform area for subordinate-level visual processing automatized by expertise. *Nature Neuroscience, 3,* 764–769.

Taylor, M. J. (2002). Non-spatial attentional effects on P1. *Clinical Neurophysiology, 113,* 1903–1908.

Taylor, M. J., Edmonds, G. E., McCarthy, G., & Allison, T. (2001a). Eyes first! Eye processing develops before face processing in children. *Neuroreport, 12,* 1671–1676.

Taylor, M. J., Itier, R. J., Allison, T., & Edmonds, G. E. (2001b). Direction of gaze effects on early face processing: Eyes-only versus full faces. *Brain Research, Cognitive Brain Research, 10,* 333–340.

Taylor, M. J., McCarthy, G., Saliba, E., & Degiovanni, E. (1999). ERP evidence of developmental changes in processing of faces. *Clinical Neurophysiology, 110,* 910–915.

Taylor, M. J., & Pang, E. W. (1999). Developmental changes in early cognitive processes. *Electroencephalography and Clinical Neurophysiology Supplement, 49,* 145–153.

Uhl, F., Lang, W., Spieth, F., & Deecke, L. (1990). Negative cortical potentials when classifying familiar and unfamiliar faces. *Cortex, 26*, 157–161.

Webb, S. J., Long, J. D., & Nelson, C. A. (2005). A longitudinal investigation of visual event-related potentials in the first year of life. *Developmental Science, 8*, 605–616.

Webb, S., Snyder, K., & Nelson, C. A. (2001 April). *Repeated presentations of a familiar stimulus during an infant ERP paradigm*. Poster presented at the Biennial meeting of the Society for Research in Child Development, Minneapolis, MN.

4 Visual attention and recognition memory in infancy

Michelle de Haan
Institute of Child Health,
University College London, UK

The simple observation that infants look longer at familiar than novel stimuli has had a major impact on the study of infant memory (Fantz, 1961). Many investigators have exploited this preference using the "visual paired comparison" procedure to investigate at what age and for how long infants can remember what they see (reviewed in de Haan, 2003). Measurement of infant visual recognition memory has thus been closely tied to visual attention, as the contents of infants' memories are inferred on the basis of their allocation of visual attention (looking time). More recently, event-related potentials (ERPs) have been used to investigate infant recognition memory. ERPs can potentially provide information that behavioural measures cannot, in terms of the precise timing and general spatial pattern of brain activation that occurs when infants see familiar and novel items. The aims of this chapter are to provide an overview of the main ERP components elicited in infant visual recognition memory tasks, a discussion of how these results have influenced theories of infant memory development, and illustrations of the application of ERPs to the study of atypical memory development.

INFANT ERP COMPONENTS RELATED TO RECOGNITION MEMORY

Nc

The Nc (negative central component; see Figure 4.1) is perhaps the most well-studied endogenous component in the infant visual event-related potential. It is a negative deflection that tends to be most prominent over fronto-central electrodes (Ackles & Cook, 1998; Goldman, Shapiro, & Nelson, 2004; Karrer & Monti, 1995; Snyder, Webb, & Nelson, 2002; Webb, Long, & Nelson, 2005; Webb & Nelson, 2001; Wiebe, Cheatham, Lukowski, Haight, Muehleck, & Bauer, 2006). It is believed to be the first endogenous ERP to emerge in development, being present at birth, with peak latency decreasing from 1000–1200 ms in newborns (Nelson, 1996) to about 800 ms in 1-month-olds (Karrer & Monti, 1995), 600 ms in 6-month-olds (Ackles & Cook, 1998) and

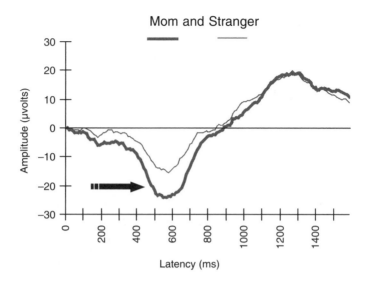

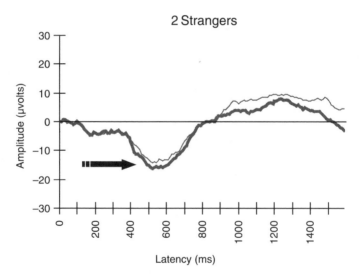

Figure 4.1 Nc elicited by mother's face compared to stranger's face (left side) and two
strangers' faces (right side) in 6-month-old infants. The Nc is indicated by
the arrow. Data are from de Haan and Nelson (1997).

400–500 ms in 1- to 3-year-olds (Goldman et al., 2004; Nelson & deRegnier,
1992; Parker & Nelson, 2005). Its peak amplitude increases with age over the
first year of life (at least between 3 and 12 months in studies that have tested
more than one age with the same procedure; Davis, Karrer, & Walker, 1998;
Richards, 2003; see Webb et al., 2005 for longitudinal results), and then
decreases in the third year of life (Parker & Nelson, 2005). In spite of the fact

that a component of roughly this description has been observed in virtually every visual cognitive ERP study of infants (see Appendix), its functional significance is still a matter of debate. Most investigators would agree that the Nc reflects some aspect of attention, but opinions differ as to whether it reflects an automatic orienting response (e.g., Nelson, 1994; Richards, 2003; Vaughan & Kurtzberg, 1992) or a more controlled deployment of attentional resources (e.g., Ackles & Cook, 1998), and as to whether it reflects primarily attentional processing (e.g., Nelson, 1994; Richards, 2003) or also reflects aspects of memory (e.g., Ackles & Cook, 1998; Courchesne, Ganz, & Norcia, 1981; de Haan & Nelson, 1997).

The Nc has been most often studied using the oddball paradigm, in which one "standard" stimulus is presented frequently and the other "oddball" stimulus is presented infrequently. The results of these studies are quite consistent: by 3 months of age the amplitude of the Nc is larger to the oddball than the standard (Courchesne et al., 1981; Davis et al., 1998; Hill-Karrer, Karrer, Bloom, Chaney, & Davis, 1998; Hunter & Karrer, 1993), and the latency is often longer for the oddball than the standard (Courchesne et al., 1981; Hill-Karrer et al., 1998). The size of the oddball effect does not appear to be influenced by how infrequently the oddball is presented (Ackles & Cook, 1998), so long as the probability is less than 50% (Ackles & Cook, 1998; de Haan & Nelson, 1997; Nelson & Collins, 1991, 1992; Nelson & Salapatek, 1986). Sensitivity to stimulus probability is also observed in infants as young as 1 month, although at this age there is only a latency difference which is in the opposite direction (longer latency Nc to standard than oddball) from that observed in older infants (Karrer & Monti, 1995).

In contrast to the relatively consistent findings of studies using the two-stimulus oddball paradigm, those using the three-stimulus oddball are somewhat conflicting. In the three-stimulus oddball, a standard and oddball are presented, along with an additional low-frequency category of novel, trial-unique stimuli. In a series of experiments, Nelson (Nelson & Collins, 1991, 1992; see also Richards, 2003) first familiarised infants to two female faces by presenting them in alternation over 20 500-ms trials; then infants were tested in a three-stimulus oddball in which one of the two faces was presented frequently (60%), one infrequently (20%), and a unique novel face shown for each of the remaining trials. Neither 4-, 6-, nor 8-month-olds showed any difference in the amplitude or latency of the Nc among the three classes of stimuli. One possible explanation for the null findings is that the familiarisation infants received prior to the three-stimulus oddball prevented the typical pattern of response to the infrequent categories seen in the two-stimulus oddball. To test this hypothesis, Reynolds and Richards (2005) compared 4.5-, 6-, and 7.5-month-old infants' ERPs in the three-stimulus oddball with and without prior familiarisation. Their procedure was somewhat different from that of Nelson and Collins (1991, 1992) in that their stimuli were geometric patterns rather than faces, their familiarisation period was longer (20 seconds cumulated looking to each of the two familiar stimuli), and they presented the stimuli in alternation with a Sesame Street video. Reynolds and Richards found that the Nc was larger to trial-unique novel stimuli compared to other stimuli in the group with prior familiarisation, while Nc amplitude did not differ among the stimuli without prior familiarisation (see Figure 4.2). These findings conflict with those of Nelson and colleagues, but do indicate that the mere presence or absence of a familiarisation period may not be the only factor contributing to the differing results of studies using two- versus three-stimulus oddball paradigms. Another possible explanation for the conflicting results is that the larger number of different stimuli presented to infants in the three- compared to two-stimulus oddball task makes it a more difficult task. In support of this view, infants as young as 3 months show a larger amplitude Nc to the oddball in the two-stimulus task (Davis et al., 1998), while infants do not show a differential response at any latency in the three-stimulus task without familiarisation until 4.5–6 months of age, when they show differential slow-wave activity to the three types of stimuli following the Nc (including a negative slow wave to the trial-unique novel stimuli; Nelson & Collins, 1991, 1992). However, with adequate familiarisation, and as they get older, infants are able to demonstrate a larger Nc to trial-unique novel stimuli. They do so: (a) at 4.5 to 7.5 months when they receive a more extensive exposure during familiarisation (Reynolds & Richards, 2005), (b) at 9 months when they receive repeated real-life exposure (Wiebe et al., 2006), and (c) by 24 months of age even with no familiarisation (Goldman et al., 2004).

The Nc and attention

Looking time

Perhaps the most common interpretation of the Nc is that it reflects allocation of attention to interesting or salient stimuli (Courchesne et al., 1981). This could explain why the Nc is larger for the oddball than standard (reviewed above) and larger for salient faces (e.g., the mother's face; a fearful emotional expression) than comparison faces (de Haan, Belsky, Reid, Volein, & Johnson, 2004; de Haan & Nelson, 1997, 1998, 1999; Nelson, Wewerka, Thomas, Tribby-Wallbridge, deRegnier, & Georgieff, 2000). Researchers have attempted to test this hypothesis by looking for links between the size of the Nc and the length of infants' visual fixations. One approach has been to examine whether oddball stimuli elicit not only larger Ncs but also longer fixations. Infants' fixations during the ERP experiment are measured and then divided according to whether they included only standard stimuli ("standard looks") or at least one oddball ("oddball looks"). Several studies have reported that oddball looks are longer than standard looks (Ackles & Cook, 1998: Hill-Karrer et al., 1998; Karrer & Ackles, 1987), and this holds even when various control analyses are computed (e.g., to disentangle whether oddball looks are in fact longer, or whether the association occurs

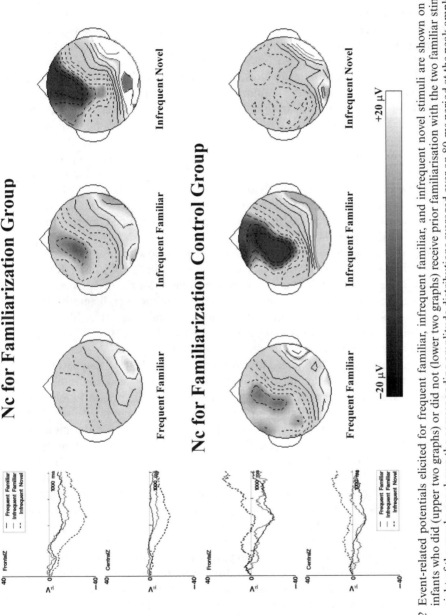

Figure 4.2 Event-related potentials elicited for frequent familiar, infrequent familiar, and infrequent novel stimuli are shown on the left for infants who did (upper two graphs) or did not (lower two graphs) receive prior familiarisation with the two familiar stimuli. To the right of the graphs are shown the corresponding amplitude distributions averaged over an 80-ms period at the peak amplitude of the Nc. Reprinted from Reynolds, G. D., & Richards, J. E. (2005). Familiarization, attention and recognition memory in infancy: An ERP and cortical source localisation study. *Developmental Psychology, 41,* 598–615. Copyright © 2005 by the American Psychological Association. Reprinted with permission. Visit http://www.psypress.co.uk/dehaan to see this figure in colour.

merely because the likelihood of an oddball occurring increases with increasing look length; Ackles & Cook, 1998). While these results suggest that larger Ncs may be related to longer looking times, studies that have related Nc amplitude to looking times recorded in a separate session after the ERP experiment have yielded less positive results. For example: (a) while at 6 months of age the Nc is larger for the mother's face than an unfamiliar face, infants do not look longer at the mother's face (de Haan & Nelson, 1997); (b) while infants show a larger Nc and longer looking times to fearful compared to happy faces (de Haan et al., 2004; de Haan & Nelson, 1998), there is no correlation between the amplitude of the Nc and the length of looking (de Haan et al., 2004); (c) in visual paired comparison tests of novel and standard stimuli given after two-stimulus or three-stimulus oddball tests, there is no consistent evidence that infants look longer at the novel stimuli (Karrer & Monti, 1995; Nelson & Collins, 1991, 1992; but see Quinn, Westerlund, & Nelson, 2006) and no correlation between the Nc and the duration of looking to novelty (Karrer & Monti, 1995); and lastly (d) while both Nc amplitude and the duration of infants' fixations decrease over a study session, the decrease in fixation appears to happen more rapidly (Nikkel & Karrer, 1994).

Together these findings suggest that there is not a close relation between Nc amplitude and length of looking to novel/salient stimuli (Nikkel & Karrer, 1994), at least across individuals. One possible reason for the negative result is that there can be quite large individual differences in the overall amplitude of ERP components; it may be that these more general amplitude differences overwhelm any more subtle modulations related to attentional processes reflected in the Nc, and obscure relations with looking time. A second possible explanation is that a negative slow wave (see below) may often be superimposed on the Nc and confound correlations between Nc amplitude and behavioural measures of attention. A third possible reason is that the Nc reflects a process of orienting or attention allocation, but does not reflect the processes involved in sustaining attention or determining duration of looking. However, this third possibility conflicts with a study showing a correlation between Nc amplitude to oddballs at right frontal (F4, F8) electrodes and performance on the Early Childhood Vigilance Test (essentially a looking-time measure of "time on task" to a 7-minute audio-visual display; Goldman et al., 2004). These authors conclude that the Nc may reflect activation of right frontal brain areas believed to be involved in vigilance/sustained attention (Posner & Petersen, 1990). This latter study may have had more success in finding correlations in part because of the similarity between the Early Childhood Vigilance Task and the stimulus presentation procedure for visual ERPs. Success on both tasks involves being able to maintain attention to a visual display in which interesting visual stimuli are alternated with periods during which the screen is blank. This contrasts with paired comparison measures of novelty preference where stimuli are always present and the measures reflect a choice, switching attention from one to the other.

Heart rate

A link between the Nc and sustained attention has also been observed in studies that have concurrently measured heart rate and ERPs. Infants' heart rates can be used to define different periods of attention, including sustained attention, stimulus orienting, and inattention (Richards, 1997; Richards & Casey, 1991). The results of this research are somewhat mixed. While one study reported that the Nc is larger during periods of sustained attention (as measured by heart rate deceleration) than during periods of inattention, and that age-related increases in Nc amplitude occur only during periods of sustained attention (Richards, 2003), these same findings were not replicated in a subsequent study (Reynolds & Richards, 2005).

Nc and memory

Another hypothesis that has been put forward is that the Nc is related to memory trace strength, such that stimuli with lower trace strengths elicit a larger Nc (Courchesne et al., 1981). This could explain why the Nc is larger for oddball stimuli, as presumably they have a lower trace strength as a consequence of the low frequency with which they occur. However, this hypothesis is difficult to reconcile with findings showing, for example, that for children younger than 24 months the Nc is larger for the mother's face than a stranger's face when the two are present with equal probability (Carver et al., 2003; de Haan & Nelson, 1997, 1999; Nelson et al., 2000; but see Webb et al., 2005). If the memory trace hypothesis were true, a larger Nc for the stranger's face would be expected. At the same time, the fact that the Nc does differ for familiar versus novel stimuli presented with equal probability suggests that at least some aspect of recognition memory must occur at the time of the Nc or preceding it, in order for this differential response to be seen.

Correlational evidence also indirectly supports a link between the Nc, particularly its latency, and infants' memories for familiar items. In these investigations (Bauer et al., 2006; Bauer, Wiebe, Carver, Waters, & Nelson, 2003; Carver, Bauer, & Nelson, 2000), 9- to 10-month-old infants were first familiarised with a series of two-step event sequences by observing experimenters modelling actions leading to an interesting outcome (e.g., "pop up book": 1. open book, 2. pull handle, result is photo of duck popping up); after several exposures over two to three visits, infants were either immediately or after a 1-week delay given an ERP test (in which still photos of the actions from a familiar sequence and of a novel sequence were presented with equal probability) and after 1 month were tested for their recall of the action sequences. These studies report that the latency of the Nc for familiar items is longer than that for novel ones (Bauer et al., 2006, 2003), and that the magnitude of the latency difference predicts the number of items recalled in memory tests 1 month later (Bauer et al., 2006). The authors interpret the longer latency to familiar items as indexing the reintegration of these items into the existing memory trace, a process that presumably facilitates later recall.

Finally, one study has suggested that the Nc is sensitive to repetition priming (Webb & Nelson, 2001). In this study, 6-month-old infants were presented with four blocks of trials, in each of which they first saw 12 unique novel faces and then saw 8 of these repeated intermixed with 4 novel faces. The lag between repetitions varied between 6 and 12 images (15–30 seconds). The results showed that over lateral, but not midline, leads, the Nc was larger in amplitude to primed than novel faces. It is important to note that other studies have observed that Nc amplitude diminishes in response to multiple repeated presentations of a stimulus (Hill-Karrer et al., 1998; Nikkel & Karrer, 1994; Wiebe et al., 2006). It is possible that these findings reflect generalised habituation or fatigue effects rather than responses to repetition of specific stimuli, and/or that there are non-linear changes in Nc amplitude over repeated presentations of the same stimulus. One argument against the general habituation or fatigue interpretation is that the decrease in amplitude from earlier to later blocks of trials occurs only for stimuli that are repeated and not for trial-unique novel stimuli (Wiebe et al., 2006).

Any account of the functional significant of the Nc must be able to explain why the same stimuli elicit different patterns of response at different ages. For example, while several studies have shown that the Nc is larger to the mother's face than a stranger's face in infants of 6 months of age (de Haan & Nelson, 1997, 1999; Nelson et al., 2000), a cross-sectional study of children aged 18–54 months observed that infants aged 18–24 months showed the same effect as the 6-month-olds, while children aged 24–45 months showed no difference between the two faces and children aged 45–54 months showed the opposite pattern with a larger Nc to the stranger's face than the mother's face (Carver et al., 2003). Similarly, in their study examining ERP responses to pictures of toys that were either novel or that infants had previously seen used in demonstrations of action sequences, Bauer et al. (2006) observed that 9-month-olds showed a larger Nc to novel than familiar toys (see also Carver et al., 2000), while 10-month-olds showed a larger Nc to familiar compared to novel toys. This pattern of results is consistent with the view that, while the Nc is clearly influenced by item familiarity, it does not necessarily directly reflect memory trace strength. The results could be seen as consistent with the view that the Nc reflects attention to salient events, but which event is more salient changes with age. The difficulty in this argument is to determine a priori which items are most salient and why, rather than simply using this idea as a post-hoc interpretation. This difficulty in determining why infants sometimes seem to allocate more attention to familiar events and sometimes to novel ones echoes a parallel issue in behavioural studies of infants' novelty preferences in visual paired comparison tests (discussed in Pascalis & de Haan, 2003).

With respect to the Carver et al. (2003) study, it is interesting to note that the response to strangers' faces (novelty) did not change with age, only the response to the mother. This suggests that infants are equally interested in new faces across the age range tested, but that they devote particular resources to the mother's face in the first year and half of life compared to when they are older. The authors argue that these results reflect the fact that infants are forming their attachment to the mother and creating a long-lasting mental representation of her over this period. This interpretation could be seen as consistent with the results of Bauer et al. (2006). In that study, infants at 9 months showed a larger Nc to new than familiar items but showed no evidence of recall 1 month later, while infants at 10 months showed a larger Nc to familiar compared to novel items and did show evidence of recall later. Thus, the 10-month-olds' larger Nc to familiar items could also have reflected their allocation of resources towards forming a lasting mental representation of the action sequences, while the 9-month-olds' greater response to the novel items may have reflected recognition without this further processing.

[It should be noted that the authors themselves reject the notion that the infants were encoding different aspects of the events at different ages, e.g., encoding the actions at 10 months but only perceptual object features at 9 months. They draw an analogy instead to a different study of recognition of the mother's face in which 6-month-olds showed a larger Nc at midline leads to the mother's than a stranger's face only when the two faces were dissimilar (easier task), but showed a larger Nc at lateral leads to a stranger's face than the mother's face when the two faces were similar (harder task; de Haan & Nelson, 1997). They argue that the 10-month-olds found the task easier and thus showed a larger Nc to the familiar item (as the 6-month-olds did to the mother's face in the easy task), while the 9-month-olds showed a larger Nc to the novel item because they found the task harder.]

Is there more than one Nc?

Some authors have noticed a double peak in the Nc component and proposed that it may represent two processes, labelled Nc1 and Nc2 (Hill-Karrer et al., 1998). In infant visual studies, the Nc1 and Nc2 show similar effects in the two-stimulus oddball task, but the Nc2 appears to habituate more quickly as it is more prominent in earlier blocks and disappears in later blocks (Hill-Karrer et al., 1998). This might be why some investigators have not observed the double peak, if they are averaging over a longer session and/or happen to have more "good" trials from later in the recording session. Further support for the suggestion that there are two Ncs comes from a study in which source analysis of the Nc indicated two separate frontal sources with different time courses: a prefrontal activation beginning 250 ms after stimulus onset and a frontal pole activation beginning 500 ms after stimulus onset (Reynolds & Richards, 2005).

The functional distinction between the Nc1 and Nc2 is not clear from visual studies with infants, other than the proposal that the Nc2 reflects "further processing" (Hill-Karrer et al., 1998). However, auditory studies with older children (9–13 years) have also observed a double-peaked Nc in a three-stimulus oddball task using sounds, which is larger in amplitude to oddball or novel sounds (Ceponiene, Lepisto, Soininen, Aronen, Alku, & Naatanen, 2004). The Nc1 occurred between 450 and 800 ms, was largest frontally in mastoid-referenced data, diminished in size with nose-referenced data, and also inverted polarity from anterior to posterior electrodes with nose-referenced data. The Nc2 (800–1000 ms) was also diminished in size in nose- compared to mastoid-referenced data, but showed no anterior to posterior polarity inversion. The authors suggested that the Nc1 reflects the cognitive processing of salient stimuli, while the Nc2 might reflect reorienting after distraction (similar to the "reorienting negativity" that has been reported in adults and children; Schroger, Giard, & Wolff, 2000; Schroger & Wolff, 1998; Wetzel, Berti, Widmann, & Schroger, 2004).

If the Nc does reflect a composite component of two peaks, this has implications for prior infant studies which have tended to focus on a single peak within the Nc time window. If two functionally distinct peaks are present even in infants, then this could possibly contribute to variability between subjects within a study and between studies, if sometimes a peak extraction identified the Nc1 and other times the Nc2 as being the most extreme point in the time window, or if average amplitude measures averaged the two peaks. Future studies in which higher-density electrode arrays are employed may also help to determine whether the Nc1 and Nc2 in infant visual recognition tasks show different topographies.

What are the underlying generators of the Nc?

Although there is some variation across studies, a fairly consistent finding is that the Nc is larger at anterior (Fz, Cz) than posterior (Pz, Oz) electrodes (Davis et al., 1998; Karrer & Monti, 1995; Nelson et al., 2000; Snyder et al., 2002; Webb et al., 2005; Wiebe et al., 2006) and larger at electrodes closer to midline than more lateral electrodes (Webb & Nelson, 2001). Hemispheric differences are not always observed, but when reported tend to favour the right (Carver et al., 2003; Davis et al., 1998; Goldman et al., 2004; Parker & Nelson, 2005; Wiebe et al., 2006). This topographical pattern has led to speculation that the Nc is generated by frontal/anterior brain regions.

A recent study using source analysis (Reynolds & Richards, 2005) is consistent with this speculation. These authors first performed an Independent Component Analysis (ICA; see Chapter 1 for brief description, or Johnson et al., 2001, for more detailed description) on data obtained from 4.5- to 7.5-month-old infants in a three-stimulus oddball paradigm, and then estimated the cortical sources of the ICA weights using an equivalent current dipole procedure. The results of their analyses were interpreted as indicating that the Nc may be generated by areas within the prefrontal and frontal pole regions (see Figure 4.3). The authors noted that the prefrontal source was

Prefrontal ICA Cluster: Medial Frontal Gyrus (25), Inferior Frontal Gyrus (47), Anterior Cingulate Cortex (8)
(Talairach coordinates: 9.4, 42.9, 16.4)

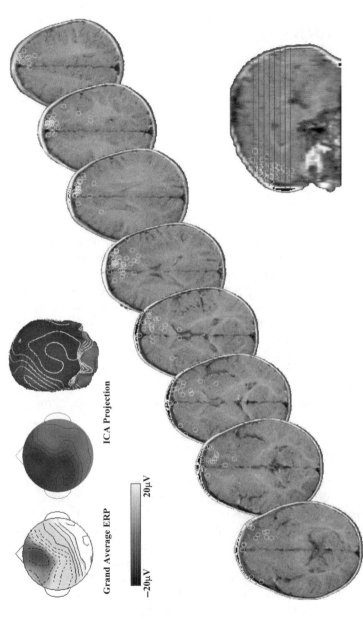

Figure 4.3 ICA component cluster for the prefrontal component. The topographical map average of the ICA loadings is similar to the topographical map of the grand average ERP of the Nc component. The equivalent current dipole locations are displayed on MRI slices, with each location representing an ICA from one individual. Reprinted from Reynolds, G. D., & Richards, J. E. (2005). *Developmental Psychology, 41*, 598–615. Copyright © 2005 by the American Psychological Association. Reprinted with permission. Visit http://www.psypress.co.uk/dehaan to see this figure in colour.

active earlier (by 250 ms) and influenced by familiarisation prior to the oddball procedure, while the frontal polar source was active later (by 500 ms) and was not influenced by familiarisation. They argue that differences across prior studies in the effects of familiarisation on Nc amplitude might be due to differences in activation and/or sensitivity of the ERP procedure to recording activity from the two regions.

Further indirect evidence that can be seen as supporting a link between the Nc and frontal cortex is that the developmental course of changes in Nc amplitude during childhood closely parallels that of cortical synaptogenesis, particularly in the frontal cortex (Courchesne, 1990; Shibasaki & Miyazaki, 1992).

Finally, developmental decreases in the latency of the Nc have also been linked to neuroanatomical development. For example, Courchesne (1990) has argued that these decreases in latency are related to the myelination of the non-specific thalamic radiation that occurs during the first 7 years of life.

Nc: Summary

The Nc is a negative deflection most prominent over midline fronto-central electrodes that peaks about 600 ms in 6-month-olds, and may reflect activation of frontal polar and/or prefrontal cortical sources. The Nc decreases in latency and increases in amplitude over the first year of life. The extent to which this reflects changes in the underlying neural generators and their strength of activation, and/or to which it reflects an increased consistency in the timing of the response over ERP trials, is not clear.

The Nc appears to reflect both aspects of sustained attention and orienting of attention to salient stimuli (which may be salient due to their novelty, or to some other factor, e.g., salience of mother's face to young infants). While some authors have argued that the Nc reflects attentional processes with recognition occurring afterwards (e.g., Nelson, 1994), it seems clear that stimulus recognition must occur on at least some level by the time of the Nc, since its amplitude can differ for stimuli presented with equal probability that differ only in prior familiarity (e.g., de Haan & Nelson, 1997). There is some indication that the latency at which differences between novel and familiar stimuli are observed might decrease with increasing age and/or decreasing task complexity, although this remains to be directly tested.

The Nc may to some extent reflect "automatic" orienting of attention, as it is elicited for virtually all types of visual stimuli. Modulations of its amplitude may reflect more controlled allocation of attentional resources based on memory or other factors. However, it is important to keep in mind that by their design infant visual ERP tasks are essentially tasks of sustained attention (i.e., to obtain sufficient good data infants must show periods of sustained attention to the visual display). This may instead, or in addition, be a factor contributing to its consistent appearance across studies.

Future investigations of the Nc should be aware that it may actually consist of two components, Nc1 and Nc2, and may find it informative to use higher-density arrays to provide a better characterisation of topographies of the Nc in different tasks.

LATE COMPONENTS AND SLOW WAVE ACTIVITY

Various types of ERP activity have been observed following the Nc that are thought to reflect aspects of recognition memory, including positive and negative slow waves and the Pc (see Figure 4.1).

Late slow waves

A pair of late slow waves following the Nc were described by Nelson and colleagues (Nelson & Collins, 1991, 1992; Nelson & deRegnier, 1992): a positive slow wave that was interpreted as reflecting updating of memory representations of partially encoded stimuli, and a negative slow wave that they interpreted as reflecting detection of novelty. A return to baseline was thought to reflect either a response to a fully encoded familiar stimulus or a response to a stimulus that was not encoded at all (for fuller discussion, see Nelson, 1994, 1996). In the three-stimulus oddball, Nelson and colleagues observed no differential activity among the three stimuli at 4 months (Nelson & Collins, 1992); a negative slow wave to novel stimuli, a positive slow wave to the oddball, and a return to baseline for the standard at 6 months (Nelson & Collins, 1991); a negative slow wave to novel stimuli and a return to baseline for oddball and standard at 8 months (Nelson & Collins, 1992). At 12 months of age, the oddball again elicited a positive slow wave, while the novels and standard showed a return to baseline (Nelson & deRegnier, 1992). These results were interpreted as reflecting the increasing memory abilities of infants across the first year of life—by 6 months infants are able to encode even low-frequency stimuli, but these require more updating (positive slow wave) than high-frequency stimuli; by 8 months repeated stimuli are well encoded regardless of frequency (return to baseline for both). With respect to response to novelty, at 6 and 8 months infants were able to detect novelty (negative slow wave) but were not yet able to group the novel stimuli into a category of "novelty". By 12 months of age, however, the return to baseline for the novel stimuli suggests that infants are able to form such a category. This pattern has been generally replicated in other studies using the three-stimulus oddball with infants 4.5–7.5 months of age (Reynolds & Richards, 2005; Richards, 2003).

While this functional interpretation of infant slow wave activity is very useful, one problem is that it can be difficult to predict a priori which stimuli will show positive versus negative slow waves. For example, in one study 3-month-olds were habituated to criterion to one face, and then 2 minutes later ERPs were recorded while they were shown the familiar face and a novel face with equal probabilities (Pascalis, de Haan, Nelson, & de Schonen, 1998). In making predictions with respect to the above model, one might expect several outcomes: (a) no differentiation if the task is too hard; (b) a negative slow wave to novelty; (c) a return to baseline for the familiar since it was encoded to criterion, or a positive slow wave if the memory representation decayed over the 2-minute delay. In fact, the results show a positive slow wave to novel stimuli and a return to baseline for familiar stimuli. While the result for the novel stimuli might not be the most obvious, it is still interpretable in the model—it can be seen as infants' attempts to encode the "novel" stimulus during the course of the experiment.

It is not entirely clear whether the slow waves described above are the same as or independent from two other types of ERP activity that have been reported, an early negative slow wave and the Pc.

Early negative slow wave

The early negative slow wave (eNSW), like the Nc, has a fronto-central maximum and typically begins 100 ms or even earlier after stimulus onset. The time window used to define this slow wave varies across studies and sometimes (e.g., 100–900 ms in Ackles & Cook, 1998) though not always (10–400 ms in Hill-Karrer et al., 1998; 100–500 ms in Davis et al., 1998) overlaps with the start of the typical time window for the negative slow wave described above. Like the Nc, the eNSW is larger to oddball than frequent stimuli (Davis et al., 1998; Hill-Karrer et al., 1998; Karrer & Ackles, 1987; Karrer & Monti, 1995; one exception is Ackles & Cook, 1998 who found no effects, but this may be because they used a much longer time window than the other studies). Unlike the Nc (Courchesne et al., 1981; Nikkel & Karrer, 1994; but see Snyder et al., 2002), the eNSW does not decrease in amplitude over trials (Nikel & Karrer, 1994). The eNSW is believed to represent aspects of attention, such as expectancy regarding when the next stimulus will occur (Karrer & Ackles, 1990) or a processing negativity as has been described in older children and adults (Karrer & Monti, 1995). However, the degree to which this component is separable from the late negative slow wave described above is unclear, as both appear to be larger for novel stimuli. Part of the difficulty is in defining the time window of a slow wave. As illustrated above, time windows for slow waves can vary considerably, and the start of the late NSW is often defined as the end of the Nc time window, even when grand averages suggest that a sustained slow wave has begun before this time (e.g., Nelson & Collins, 1991; Pascalis et al., 1998). In one study the late negative slow wave is described as the result that occurs when the Nc fails to resolve (Nelson et al., 2000), suggesting that the late negative slow wave may be a continuation of processing negativities that have begun at earlier latencies such as the eNSW.

Pc

Instead of a sustained positive slow wave following the Nc, some authors have reported a broader positive peak labelled the Pc. Like the positive slow wave, the Pc is maximal over frontal areas (Courchesne et al., 1981), but unlike the positive slow wave it is not affected by stimulus probability (Ackles & Cook, 1998; Courchesne et al., 1981; Hunter & Karrer, 1993; but see Nelson & Salapatek, 1986). Again, whether the Pc is different from the late positive slow wave described above is unclear. In some prior studies (e.g., de Haan & Nelson, 1997) a broad peak that might be the Pc is observable in the "slow wave" time window, whereas in others this is less obvious (e.g., Pascalis et al., 1998).

An important issue for further studies is the proper definition and interpretation of slow wave activity, as this activity is commonly observed in infants' ERPs. Variations in the definition of slow wave activity, and how such activity might be superimposed on, and influence the analysis and interpretation of, components such as the Nc, has received little attention.

What are the generators of the slow waves?

The slow wave responses can be somewhat variable, but topographical analysis shows they tend to be larger over temporal than midline electrodes (Snyder et al., 2002) and larger over anterior than posterior electrodes (Nelson et al., 2000; Snyder et al., 2002; Webb et al., 2005).

Nelson (1996) has speculated that the positive slow wave may be generated in temporal lobe memory regions. This view is supported by a recent report using source localisation linking the positive slow wave to right temporal regions (Reynolds & Richards, 2005). By contrast the late negative slow wave elicited by novel stimuli may be generated by frontal brain regions (Reynolds & Richards, 2005).

HOW DO INFANT COMPONENTS RELATE TO ADULT COMPONENTS?

The relation of the infant ERP components described above to adult ERP components is not entirely clear. For the Nc, some investigators have argued that it is a developmentally unique component that disappears by adulthood (Courchesne, 1978), while other investigators have suggested that it may be analogous to adult components such as the N2 (Karrer & Monti, 1995; Nelson & Dukette, 1998; Vaughan & Kurtzberg, 1992) or N400 (Friedman, 1991). The same diversity in views applies to the positivities following the Nc. Some investigators have argued that they are independent of the adult P300 (Courchesne et al., 1981), while other authors have suggested that late positive activity may be a precursor to the adult P300 (Nelson, Thomas, de

Haan, & Wewerka, 1998; note that in the auditory domain it has been reported that a P300 may in fact already be evident in infants; McIsaac & Polich, 1992). It is unlikely that these debates can be resolved until there are more studies allowing a direct comparison of ERPs in infants, children, and adults using similar procedures. As can be seen in the Appendix, while some studies have tested infants and adults and used similar procedures, none has used the identical stimuli and task and tested both infants and adults or older children.

INFANT ERP STUDIES AND THEORIES OF MEMORY DEVELOPMENT

In order to appreciate how ERP studies in infants have informed theories of infant memory development, it is necessary to first provide a brief overview of the basic neuroanatomy of visual recognition memory.

Brief neuroanatomy of adult visual recognition memory

The pathway for visual object recognition begins at the retina, where visual input is first received. This information then proceeds to the striate (visual) cortex and on to a ventral/medial-directed chain of cortical visual areas in the temporal lobe that extract information about stimulus quality (e.g., size, colour, and shape) and ultimately synthesise a complete representation of the object (Mishkin & Murray, 1994). Storage occurs each time a representation formed in this way activates relevant memory areas in the medial temporal lobe.

In adults, memory is not a unitary function and can be divided into different components. One such distinction is between explicit and implicit memory (similar distinctions are also meant by declarative versus non-declarative memory and by incidental versus intentional memory). Explicit memory depends on the hippocampus and anatomically related structures in the medial temporal lobe and diencephalons, and is characterised by relatively rapid learning and (at least in adult humans) conscious recollection of previous experiences. Recognition memory is typically considered a test of explicit memory. Implicit memory, by contrast, involves a number of abilities that are independent of the medial temporal lobe and are expressed as skills or habits, some of which are characterised by relatively slow learning over repeated experiences. Implicit memory is typically measured by changes in performance (e.g., decreased reaction time or increased perceptual fluency).

The distinction between explicit and implicit memory arose from studies of patients with damage to the medial temporal region of the brain (Squire, 1992). The first of these patients whose memory was studied quantitatively was the famous case HM, who showed a profound anterograde amnesia (difficulty in remembering things that occurred after the brain injury) following bilateral removal of the medial temporal regions for treatment of epilepsy (Milner, Corkin, & Teuber, 1968; Scoville & Milner, 1957). HM and other patients with similar or more circumscribed medial temporal damage show deficits in explicit memory. For example, HM could neither remember his new address nor be trusted to find his way home alone even 1 year after moving house (Milner, 1966). However, such patients retain some other learning abilities, collectively called implicit memory, such as priming, simple conditioning, and motor learning (Squire & Knowlton, 1995). For example, HM was able to learn to trace a drawing when looking in a mirror, and retained this learning over days (Milner, 1965).

Explicit memory has also been further divided into episodic and semantic memory. Recall of items from episodic memory is by definition associated with retrieval of contextual details related to the encoding, whereas recall of items from semantic memory is not (Tulving, 1972). A similar distinction applies to recognition, whereby it can occur with retrieval of contextual details related to encoding ("recollection-based recognition") or without these additional details ("familiarity-based recognition"; Tulving, 1985; Yonelinas, 1994). There is consensus that the medial temporal lobe-cortical (MTL) circuit, involving the hippocampus and the perirhinal, entorhinal, and parahippocampal cortices, supports cognitive memory in human adults. According to one view (Mishkin, Suzuki, Gadian, & Vargha-Khadem, 1997), structures within the medial temporal lobe function in a hierarchy, wherein perceptual information first enters the parahippocampal regions mediating semantic memory (and familiarity-based recognition), and only then passes to hippocampal regions necessary for episodic memory (and recollection-based recognition).

Theories of infant memory

Theories of infant memory differ as to whether they emphasise continuities or differences in memory processes across the lifespan. Results from behavioural studies of the development of recognition memory demonstrate many similarities in the characteristics of infant and adult recognition memory, suggesting that there is a remarkable continuity in this ability (reviewed in de Haan, 2003). For example, the fact that recognition memory is present from birth and that infants' recognition abilities are related to measures of their intellectual function later in life (Rose & Feldman, 1997) suggests that it may present a basic aspect of cognition that is continuous from infancy into adulthood. This has led some investigators to conclude that ". . . there seems to be considerable invariance in memory development, at least at the level of basic processes and mechanisms. That is, whatever these 'basics' necessary for storage and retrieval of information are, they are clearly present and operating in the first year of life" (Howe & Courage, 1997, p. 157).

By contrast, theories of the neural bases of development of recognition memory have tended to focus on differences between infants and older children and adults, and on seeming discontinuities in memory such as infant-ile amnesia (e.g., Nelson, 1995). For example, some authors have suggested that, while implicit memory is present from early in infancy, explicit memory does not begin to emerge until approximately 8–12 months of age (Schacter & Moscovitch, 1984). In other words, recognition memory is fundamentally different in the first months of life compared to the end of the first year. Other investigators suggest that an immature form of explicit memory, labelled "pre-explicit", is operational from birth (Nelson, 1995; Nelson & Webb, 2003). This form differs from true explicit memory in that it relies primarily on the hippocampus and is driven by response to novelty. According to this view, true explicit recognition memory does not emerge until other structures in the memory circuit (e.g., temporal cortical areas surrounding the hippo-campus, frontal cortex) and their connections with the hippocampus mature. Still others have suggested the opposite view, that early memory is primarily mediated by cortical regions surrounding the hippocampus (perirhinal cortex) that in adults are important for familiarity-based recognition, whereas the hippocampus itself only becomes involved in recognition more slowly as it progressively develops (Bachevalier & Vargha-Khadem, 2005).

ERPs and theories of infant memory

ERPs can potentially provide an important source of evidence regarding the nature of early memory development, as any major change in the brain areas supporting memory would be expected to be reflected in the ERPs. For example, if in the first half-year of life recognition relies mainly on the hippo-campus and later comes to rely on a more complex brain circuit involving additional cortical areas, one would predict changes in the type and/or topography of ERP components elicited in recognition tasks over this time.

Some authors have argued that ERP studies do provide evidence that there is a transition in the developing memory system at about 8–10 months of age. One piece of evidence comes from the studies using the three-stimulus odd-ball (Nelson & Collins, 1991, 1992). In those studies, it was reported that only at 8 months of age are infants able to process a familiar stimulus in the same way regardless of its frequency of occurrence during the memory test (Nelson & Collins, 1992). This was evident in the return-to-baseline for both the frequently occurring and infrequently occurring familiar faces. Before 8 months, infants either do not show evidence of recognition at all (4 months; Nelson & Collins, 1992), or treat the infrequently presented familiar faces differently from the frequently presented familiar ones (6 months; Nelson & Collins, 1991). These results were interpreted as evidence that infants are capable of "true" recognition only at 8 months; prior to this time, infants' responses are driven more by the frequency of occurrence or novelty of stimuli, and thus reflect the pre-explicit form of recognition.

There are some difficulties with this interpretation of the results. For example, it is not clear how the results reported for 12-month-olds fit with this explanation. Why should 12-month-olds show a positive slow wave for the infrequently presented familiar faces, as the 6-month-olds did? In addition, it is not clear that the pattern of results could only be explained by a qualitative change in the neural circuits underlying recognition. For example, the results for 4- to 8-month-olds might also be expected if younger babies simply forget more quickly than older babies. In this interpretation, the 6-month-olds treat the infrequently occurring familiar face differently from the frequently occurring one because their memories for the infrequently occurring face decay more quickly, as they see it less often during the test. If 4-month-olds have more rapidly decaying memories they may not be able to remember the stimuli at all, and if 8-month-olds have less rapid forgetting then they will be able to remember both stimuli equally well. Thus, the same pattern could be accounted for by a more continuous change in rate of forgetting.

Another series of studies involving ERPs has also implicated the period around 9 months of age as a time of potential change in the developing memory system. For example, one study found that only infants who showed ERP evidence of recognising the props they had seen used to model events 1 week earlier were able to recall the order of the steps in the events 1 month later (Carver et al., 2000; see also Bauer et al., 2006, 2003). Specifically, about half of the 9-month-olds were able to recall the order, and these infants showed a larger Nc to novel than familiar items, as well as a positive slow wave to familiar items and a negative slow wave to novel items, during the ERP test. Importantly, a subsequent study demonstrated that this was not simply because the other half of the infants failed to encode the events at all (Bauer et al., 2003). The authors argue that the results indicate that '. . . the memory system that is involved in recognition and recall memory undergoes significant developmental change near the end of the first year of life' (p. 244).

There is thus some indication from ERP studies which might support the view that there is a developmental transition in memory during the second half of the first year of life. However, these data are by no means conclusive and at present do not differentiate among the theories proposing different neuroanatomical bases for the transition. Further investigations using higher-density recording montages will be useful in better characterising the nature of the changes in the neural systems underlying memory during the first year.

USING ERPs TO ASSESS INFANT MEMORY IN SPECIAL POPULATIONS

ERPs during infant visual recognition tasks have been used to examine development in infants with global developmental delay (e.g. Downs syndrome; Hill-Karrer et al., 1998) as well as those believed to be generally at risk for cognitive impairment (deRegnier, Georgieff, & Nelson, 1997) or at particular risk for memory disorders (Nelson et al., 2000; see deRegnier, 2005, for a general review of neurophysiologic investigations of cognitive development in high-risk infants). There are many important factors to consider when using ERPs to compare typically developing and at-risk or atypical groups. As discussed above for the Nc, various aspects of the ERP procedure and data processing can affect the amplitude or latency of components other than true differences in cognitive processing between groups. For example, one study showed that the amplitude of the Nc differed for infants who saw a different total number of trials in the recording procedure (even when there were no differences in number of trials used to create averages; Snyder et al., 2002). Thus, if typical and atypical groups see different total numbers of trials (which can happen as the length of sessions is often determined by the extent of infants' cooperation), differences may be detected that are related to this procedural difference but might be interpreted as reflecting delayed or deviant development in the atypical group.

In spite of these difficulties ERPs, if used carefully, can potentially provide a very useful tool for assessing early cognitive processing. For example, one study examined infants of diabetic mothers, as they may be at risk for memory disorders due to the adverse foetal environment that occurs in this condition, including chronic hypoxia, reactive hypoglycaemia, and iron deficiency. All of these factors may particularly affect a structure known to be critical for normal memory, the hippocampus (see discussion in Nelson et al., 2000, or deRegnier, Chapter 5, this volume, for further discussion). In this study, 6-month-old infants who had been born to diabetic mothers, as well as control infants, were tested with the mother's face and a stranger's face. The results with the control infants largely replicated prior findings showing a larger Nc to the mother's face over right hemisphere electrodes and a larger positive slow wave to the stranger's face (Nelson et al., 2000). By contrast, the infants of diabetic mothers did show an Nc and positive slow wave[1] but did not show differentiation between the two faces. In spite of these differences detected with ERPs, the two groups did not differ on a test of general ability level (Bayley Scales of Infant Development) or in a behavioural test of memory using the visual paired comparison procedure. These results illustrate the potential sensitivity of ERPs in detecting atypical development at the group level. The findings that the slow wave response was atypical is consistent with the idea that hippocampal development was affected in the infants of diabetic mothers, as there is evidence that this response is generated in the temporal lobe (Reynolds & Richards, 2005). However, the extent to which the results can be interpreted as reflecting specifically hippocampal abnormality in this

---

1 Nelson et al. (2000) state that the positive slow wave was "absent or diminished" in the infants of diabetic mothers, but there was no main effect of group on amplitude and they report no other direct statistical comparison of amplitude between groups.

population is unclear. For example, infants of diabetic mothers performed normally on the visual paired comparison test, which is also believed to assess hippocampal function (reviewed in Nelson, 1995; Pascalis & de Haan, 2003; but see Bachevalier & Vargha-Khadem, 2005) and these infants also showed an abnormal Nc, a response thought to be generated in the frontal lobes (Reynolds & Richards, 2005).

While this and a few other studies cited above indicate that ERPs in visual cognitive tasks are potentially sensitive to atypical cognitive processing in young infants at risk, many questions and issues remain regarding their clinical utility, and this area is less developed in the visual compared to the auditory domain (see Molfese et al., Chapter 7 this volume for predictive studies using auditory ERPs). For example, none of these visual studies has as yet provided follow-up information to determine whether and how these early differences relate to later cognitive impairments—thus the specificity and sensitivity of these early measures for predicting later difficulties remains unknown.

SUMMARY AND FUTURE DIRECTIONS

Studies of infant visual recognition memory using ERPs have found that infants show differential brain wave activity to novel compared to familiar visual stimuli as young as 1 month of age (Karrer & Monti, 1995). Generally, novel stimuli elicit more negative-going waveforms while familiar stimuli elicit more positive-going waveforms, although the latency at which these effects are observed can vary across studies. There are important exceptions to this general statement, in that familiar stimuli that are particularly salient to infants of a given age (e.g., their mother's faces) can elicit a more negative-going waveform than novel stimuli. Generally speaking, while visual stimuli typically elicited a robust perceptual response over occipital areas (see McCulloch, Chapter 2 this volume), the components and slow waves that are affected by familiarity are often described as having a more anterior distribution.

Although there is an increasing body of literature describing the development of ERP components related to infant visual recognition and memory (see Appendix), and application of ERP methods to address questions regarding theories of memory development and the nature of atypical early memory development, in many ways this area is still in its beginnings. Further investigations using high-density electrode arrays to study developmental changes at frequent intervals over infancy are needed in order to better characterise normative development. Such data will help to address debates regarding the degree of continuity of memory processes from infancy to childhood. They will also likely prove very useful in understanding results obtained in at-risk populations, such as in evaluating whether development is deviant, or typical but delayed.

ACKNOWLEDGEMENTS

Many thanks to Dr J. E. Richards and Dr G. Reynolds for kindly providing Figures 4.2 and 4.3.

APPENDIX

Authors	Age and number of subjects	Attrition	Stimuli (duration)	Paradigm	Montage (reference)	Time window of Nc	Results
Schulman-Galambos & Galambos, 1978	*Adults* 18–25 years, $n = 20$ *Infants* aged 7 weeks–12 months, $n = 10$ to 21 depending on stimulus condition	*Adults*: 20% *Infants*: 34–68%	Photos of real world scenes, Disneyland, children's drawings, etc. (2000 ms; stimulus set differed for different ages/ subjects)	A variety of images presented in or out of focus	C3, C4, Lower EOG (linked ears)	All recordings "dominated by a large negative deflection peaking between 500–650 ms for most subjects"	No statistical analyses reported
Courchesne et al., 1981	4–7.2 months, $n = 10$	62%	2 female faces (100 ms)	Oddball with 88/12 probability	Fz, Pz EOG (right mastoid)	300–1200	Amplitude is larger to oddball than standard at all electrodes, and latency is 200 ms slower to oddball
Nelson & Salapatek, 1986	6 months, $n = 15$ to 16 in each of 3 experiments	54%	Male and female faces (100 ms)	Familiarisation to one face, and then familiar and novel shown 80/20 (*Expt 1*) or 50/50 (*Expt 2*) Two faces shown 50/50 without familiarisation (Expt 3)	Oz, Pz, Fz, EOG (right mastoid)	300–700	*Expt 1*: Area larger to frequent than oddball at Cz in the 551–700 ms window *Expt 2*: Area larger to during the familiarisation trials than to the novel during test at Cz in the 551–700 ms window *Expt 3*: No differences *(Continued overleaf)*

Authors	Age and number of subjects	Attrition	Stimuli (duration)	Paradigm	Montage (reference)	Time window of Nc	Results
Nelson & Collins, 1991	6 months, n = 12	84%	Female faces (500)	Familiarisation with two faces shown in alternation for 20 trials, then immediately a test with one familiar face shown 60%, the other 20%, and trial unique faces for 20%	Oz, Pz, Cz, Fz (linked ears)	400–800	No differences
Nelson & Collins, 1992	4 months, n = 14 and 8 months, n = 17	4 months: 54% 8 months: 58%	Female faces (500)	Same as Nelson & Collins (1991)	Oz, Pz, Cz, Fz (linked ears)	Not reported (appears ~400–800 ms in graphs)	Not analysed
Hunter & Karrer, 1993	6 months, n = 36	n/a	n/a	Oddball with 80/20 probability, varying stimulus duration (100, 500, or 1000)	Oz, midline and hemispheric	n/a	Amplitude larger for oddballs Stimulus duration affects latency, with longer latency for 500 ms duration than for shorter or longer presentations
Nikkel & Karrer, 1994	6 months, n = 28		2 female faces	Oddball with 80/20, but here examine only response to frequent and how it changes over the first, second, and last third of the session	Fz, Cz, Pz, Oz, C3/4 EOG (linked ears)	400–900	Amplitude decreases from second to third blocks at Cz

Study	Age, n	Stimuli	Probability	Electrodes	Latency window	Results
	included depending on analysis					Latency is longer to frequent than oddball at Fz, Cz, C3/4
Nelson & de Haan, 1996	7 months, n = 19 per experiment	Happy, fearful, and angry faces (500 ms)	Expt 1: Happy and fearful face presented 50/50 Expt 2: Fearful and angry face presented 50/50 Expt 1: 55% Expt 2: 64%	Oz, Pz, Cz, Fz, T3/4 (linked ears)	370–680	Expt 1: Amplitude larger for fearful than happy faces Expt 2: No difference in amplitude or latency for fearful compared to angry faces
de Haan & Nelson, 1997	6 months, n = 22 per experiment	Expt 1: Mother's and dissimilar stranger's face Expt 2: Two dissimilar strangers' faces Expt 3: Mother's and similar stranger's face Expt 4: Two similar strangers' faces Expt 1: 64% Expt 2: 65% Expt 3: 64% Expt 4: 61%	Two faces presented with equal probability	Oz, Pz, Cz, Fz, T3/4: T5/6, EOG (linked ears)	Midlines: 400–800 Lateral: 250–700	Across all experiments amplitude was negative at T3/4 and positive at T5/6 In experiments 2 and 4 latency was increased from anterior to posterior midline leads Larger amplitude for mother's face compared to dissimilar stranger at Pz, Cz, Fz, and T4 Larger amplitude for similar stranger than mother's face at T6 and T5 (with strongest effect at T5) No difference in Nc amplitude or latency between two strangers' faces

(Continued overleaf)

Authors	Age and number of subjects	Attrition	Stimuli (duration)	Paradigm	Montage (reference)	Time window of Nc	Results
deRegnier et al., 1997	4 months, $n = 16$ (an additional 16 infants who had experienced medical problems at birth were also tested)	Not reported	Red cross and red corkscrew shapes (500 ms)	Familiarisation to red cross, then familiar red cross shown 80% and novel red corkscrew shown 20%	Oz, Cz, Pz, Fz, EOG (linked ears)	500–1000	No effects
Ackles & Cook, 1998	6 months, $n = 96$ (16 per stimulus condition)	36%	Female faces	Oddball with 90/10, 80/20, 70/30, or 60/40 probabilities, or 50/50 with random or alternating sequence	Oz, Pz, Cz, Fz, EOG (right ear)	350–900	Amplitude biggest centrally and latency decreases from anterior to posterior Amplitude significantly bigger to oddball for 90/10 and 60/40 conditions and similar trend for 70/30, but not significant for 80/20 or 50/50 conditions. No effect of probability on Nc latency Local probability effects also reported (e.g., no bigger for oddball and standard preceding oddball than standard after oddball)
Hill-Karrer et al., 1998	6 months, $n = 10$ [also tested 10 infants with Downs syndrome]	19%	2 female faces	Oddball with 2 female faces 80/20	Oz, Cz, Pz, Fz, C3/4 EOG (left ear)	Nc1: 400–800 Nc2: 800–1200	Nc1 peak is larger to oddball at all electrodes and area larger to oddball at all but C4

Study	Participants		Stimuli	Design	Leads	Time range	Findings
Nelson et al., 1998	Adults 17–40 yrs, $n = 48$ 8 months, $n = 20$	Adults: 39% Babies: 73%	Female faces (500 ms)	Babies: Habituation-to-criterion to one face, then either 1 or 5 min delay and ERP test with familiar and novel faces presented 50/50 condition. Adults tested under similar but not identical conditions.	Oz, Pz, Cz, Fz, C3/4, T3/4, T5/6, EOG (linked mastoids)	300–703	Nc2 area is larger to oddball at Fz and Cz and peak latency is longer to oddball at Fz, Pz, and C3/4 Nc1 and Nc2 amplitude/area decrease across blocks of trials for both oddball and standard Nc1 latency decreases over first 2 blocks then increases. Amplitude larger over anterior compared to posterior leads Amplitude to familiar stimuli larger over left than right hemisphere Over right hemisphere only, amplitude larger to familiar than novel stimuli For 5-min delay only, latency longer to familiar than novel.

(Continued overleaf)

Authors	Age and number of subjects	Attrition	Stimuli (duration)	Paradigm	Montage (reference)	Time window of Nc	Results
Pascalis et al., 1998	3 months, $n = 15$	75%	Female faces (500 ms)	Habituation to criterion to one face shown in different poses, then ERP test with familiar and novel face shown 50/50	Oz, Pz, Cz, Fz, C3/4, T3/4, T5/6, EOG (linked mastoids)	750–1200	Amplitude larger to familiar face at lateral and midline leads
de Haan & Nelson, 1999	6 months, $n = 44$	50%	Mothers' and strangers' faces and familiar and unfamiliar toys (500 ms)	Mother's and dissimilar stranger's face presented 50/50 or familiar and unfamiliar toy presented 50/50	Oz, Pz, Cz, Fz, T3/4, T5/6, EOG	250–800	Amplitude larger to mother's face than stranger's face at Pz, Cz, Fz, and T4 Amplitude larger to familiar toy than novel toy at Pz, Cz, Fz, and lateral leads
Carver, Bauer, & Nelson, 2000	9 months, $n = 20$	57%	Slides of 2-step action sequences plus end state, one of a new event, and one of a familiar sequence observed over 3 real-life exposure sessions (500 ms)	Familiarisation to action sequence in 3 distributed, real life demonstrations of the sequence, then one week after last exposure ERP test with still images of familiar and novel sequences presented 50/50	Pz, Cz, Fz, T3/4, T5/6 (linked ears)	260–870	Amplitude larger to novel than familiar images at midline but not lateral leads Planned comparisons show this effect is significant only for infants who were able to recall (imitate) complete event sequences one month after the ERP test

Nelson et al., 2000	6 months, n = 34 [also tested 26 infants of diabetic mothers]	30% (for entire study)	Mothers' and dissimilar strangers' faces (500 ms)	Mother's and dissimilar stranger's face presented 50/50	Oz, Pz, Cz, Fz, T3/4, T5/6, C3/4, EOG (average reference)	400–800	Amplitude larger over anterior leads and latency increased from anterior to posterior leads Amplitude larger to mother and stranger over C4 (and over right hemisphere generally when leads were collapsed by within hemisphere)
Webb & Nelson, 2001	Adults 17–28 yrs, n = 30 Babies 6 months, n = 24	Adults: 21% Babies: 44%	Female faces presented upright and inverted (500)	Phase 1: A set of trial-unique faces Phase 2: Some of Phase 1 faces repeated intermixed with some new faces (time between repeated images was 15–30 seconds) Adults tested with similar but not identical paradigm	Pz, Cz, Fz, T3/4, T5/6, F3/4, C3/4 EOG (linked ears)	300–800	At lateral leads amplitude larger at fronto/central than temporal leads Amplitude for upright faces larger than inverted faces At lateral leads larger amplitude for novel than primed faces regardless of orientation
Snyder et al., 2002	6 months, n = 94 (re-analysis of data from Nelson et al., 2000; Webb & Nelson, 2001; Stolarova et al., 2003)	(See individual studies)	Mothers' and dissimilar strangers' faces (500 ms)	Mother's and dissimilar stranger's face presented 50/50 Expt 1: Examined how responses changed over the first compared to second block of 30 trials	Oz, Pz, Cz, Fz, T3/4/5/6, C3/4 (linked ears)	280–730	Expt 1: Amplitude largest anteriorly, and trend for largest amplitude to be for familiar faces over the right hemisphere No difference between first and second blocks

(Continued overleaf)

Authors	Age and number of subjects	Attrition	Stimuli (duration)	Paradigm	Montage (reference)	Time window of Nc	Results
				Expt 2: Examined how response differed depending on the number of total trials viewed (<60, 61–80, 81–100)			*Expt 2:* Amplitude larger and latency shorter for the 61–80 trials group than the group who saw fewer trials The latency to the novel face decreased with increasing number of trials included The latency was faster to the novel face only in the group who saw the most trials
Bauer et al., 2003	9.5 months, $n = 57$	39%	Same as Carver et al., 2000	Familiarisation to event sequence in 3 distributed, real-life demonstrations of the event, then both immediately and one week after last exposure ERP test with still images of familiar and novel events presented 50/50	Oz Cz Pz Fz, T3/4, T5/6 C3/4 (linked ears)	260–870	At immediate test, Nc amplitude larger for novel for all groups At delay test no amplitude differences, but for children who were able to recall the events in the deferred imitation test, the latency is longer for old than new events

| Carver et al., 2003 | 18–24 months, 24–45 months, and 45–54 months $n = 14$ per age group | 44% | Mother's and strangers' faces and familiar and unfamiliar toys (500 ms) | Mother's and dissimilar stranger's face presented 50/50 in a separate session familiar and unfamiliar toy presented 50/50 | 64 electrodes (average reference) | 360–920 | Also only for the infants who recalled the events, latency was longer for old events at delayed than immediate test

The difference in peak amplitude between old and new events predicted the number events recalled in correct order

Faces: Younger group showed larger amplitude to mother than stranger; middle group showed no difference, and older group showed larger amplitude to stranger than mother

Toys: Amplitude larger over right than left hemisphere. Amplitude larger for unfamiliar than familiar toys |

(*Continued overleaf*)

Authors	Age and number of subjects	Attrition	Stimuli (duration)	Paradigm	Montage (reference)	Time window of Nc	Results
Richards, 2003	4.5, 6, and 7.5 months n = 16 per age group	*4.5 months*: 12.5% *6 months*: 25% *7.5 months*: 25%	Video 'Follow that Bird', and 16 computer generated geometric patterns overlaid on the video (500 ms)	Familiarisation to two patterns (20 sec accumulated looking time trials then brief alternating presentations 5 times each) followed by ERP with one familiar 60%, one 20% and trial unique images for the remaining 20% Also measured heart rate to define different phases of attention	20 electrodes (averaged mastoids)	450–550 [analysed 250–750]	No differences between stimulus conditions Amplitude at fronto-central and frontal lateral leads larger during orienting and sustained attention than inattention Amplitude increased with age during periods of attention but not inattention
Stolarova et al., 2003	6 months, 4 months, and preterm corrected age 4 months n = 20 per group	*Fullterms*: 59% *Preterms*: 66%	Female faces (500)	62 different faces were presented, with 20 repeated immediately after the first presentation, another 20 repeated	Fz, Cz, Pz, Oz, F3/4, C3/4, T3/4, T5/6, P3/4, EOG (linked mastoids)	400–770	Amplitude larger over fronto-central than parietal sites Latency longer for 4-month-olds and preterms than 6-month-olds (by

Study	Age, n		Stimuli	Electrodes	Time window	Findings
						about 60 ms) over fronto-central but not parietal sites
			after 4 intervening faces, and 22 not repeated			Only for 6-month-olds latency longer for delayed repetitions than for novel or immediate repetition
de Haan et al., 2004	7 months, $n = 40$	63%	Female faces posing happy, fearful, or neutral expressions (500 ms)	Happy, fearful, and neutral faces shown with equal probability	62 electrodes (average reference)	400–600	Amplitude larger anteriorly; larger over right than left side at temporal electrodes, but opposite pattern at parietal sites
						Amplitude larger to fearful than happy faces (responses to neutral note reported)
						Amplitude was affected by infant temperament and maternal personality
Goldman et al., 2004	27 months, $n = 14$	46%	Stuffed animals	Oddball with one stuffed animal presented frequently (70%) and additional, trial-unique stuffed animals presented the remaining 30%	Fz, Cz, Pz, F3/4, F7/8, P3/4, O1/2, EOG (linked mastoids)	400–800	Amplitude larger anteriorly
						Amplitude larger for novel than familiar at midline and lateral sites
						Latency shorter over left than right hemisphere for familiar only

(Continued overleaf)

Authors	Age and number of subjects	Attrition	Stimuli (duration)	Paradigm	Montage (reference)	Time window of Nc	Results
							Amplitude for novel over right, frontal sites correlated with behavioural test of attention
Lukowski et al., 2005	9.5 months, $n = 79$	64%	Same as Carver et al. (2000), (500 ms)	Familiarisation by watching real-life 2-step action sequences in 2 separate sessions. Half the infants allowed to imitate after watching, half not allowed. Immediately and one week after last familiarisation session ERPs recorded to still images of the familiar action sequence and a novel action sequence presented with equal probability	25 electrodes (average reference)	260–700	Larger amplitude for novel sequences at immediate test Larger amplitude for imitate group than watch only group for familiar sequences at one-week delay

Reference	Participants		Stimuli	Electrodes	Time window (ms)	Findings
Parker & Nelson, 2005	8- to 32-month-olds, $n = 33$ [also tested institutionalised children]	57%	Female faces posing happy, sad, angry, or fearful expressions (500 ms)	Cz, Pz, Fz, O1/2m T7/8, P3/4, C3/4, F3/4, EOG (average mastoids)	325–650	Happy, sad, angry, and fearful faces shown with equal probability — Amplitude larger for younger than older infants but no age-related changes in latency. Peak latency for fearful faces was quicker over the left than right hemispheres
Reynolds & Richards, 2005	4.5, 6, and 7.5 months, $n = 22$ at each age	15%	Video 'Follow that Bird', and 16 computer-generated geometric patterns overlaid on the video (500 ms)	124 electrodes (average reference)	400–800	*Familiarisation group:* Familiarisation to two patterns (20 sec accumulated looking time trials then brief alternating presentations 5 times each) followed by ERP with one familiar 60%, one 20%, and trial unique images for the remaining 20%. *No familiarisation group:* As above only without familiarisation. Also measured heart rate to define different phases of attention — Amplitude largest to novel, intermediate to infrequent familiar and smallest to frequent familiar at frontal and central leads, and this pattern occurred primarily for the infants who received familiarisation. Amplitude was larger during inattention than attention for 4.5-month-olds at frontal and central electrodes; no difference by attention for other ages

(Continued overleaf)

Authors	Age and number of subjects	Attrition	Stimuli (duration)	Paradigm	Montage (reference)	Time window of Nc	Results
Webb et al., 2005	4, 6, 8, 10, and 12 months longitudinal, n's range from 16 to 28	4% (96% had at least one good data point across the 5 ages & 2 stimulus conditions)	*Task 1:* Mother's face and dissimilar-looking stranger's face (500) *Task 2:* Familiar toy and unfamiliar toy (500)	Familiar and unfamiliar images presented 50/50 in separate sessions for faces and toys	Oz, Pz, Cz, T3/4, T5/6, C3/4, EOG (linked mastoids)	*4 and 6 months:* 350–750 *8, 10 and 12 months:* 300–700	Larger amplitude at anterior than posterior electrodes and at right than left electrodes Larger amplitude for objects than faces Linear and cubic trends for change in amplitude with age: increases [i.e., becomes more negative] most marked between 4–6 months and 10–12 months, relatively flat 6–10 months Latency faster for faces than objects Linear and quadratic trends for change in amplitude with age: decrease most prominent 4–8 months

Study	Age, n	%	Stimuli	Procedure	Electrodes	Time window	Results
Quinn et al., 2006	6.5 months, n = 10	68%	Images of familiarised cats, novel cats, and novel dogs (500 ms)	Familiarisation with 36 images of cats followed by 20 novel cats intermixed with 20 novel dogs	62 electrodes (average reference)	350–750 ms	Larger amplitude for novel dogs than familiar or novel cats
Wiebe et al., 2006	9 months, n = 42	11%	Images of a familiar 2-step action sequences plus end state observed over 2 real-life exposure sessions, images of a new 2-step sequence and trial-unique images of other unseen events (500 ms)	Familiarisation to action sequence in 2 distributed, real-life demonstrations of the sequence, then immediately after last exposure ERP test with still images of familiar sequence, novel sequence, and trial-unique images of other novel sequences presented with 33.3/33.3/33.3 probability	29 electrodes (averaged mastoids)	350–750 ms	Amplitude larger and latency slower at anterior compared to posterior midline electrodes Larger amplitude in early versus later trials and midline ($p < .06$) and lateral ($p < .05$) leads At lateral leads, larger amplitude for trial unique novel than familiar, with novel repeated intermediate between the two
Bauer et al., in press	9.5 months at entry n = 11 for Phase 1 and n = 14 for Phase 2	65%	Similar to Carver et al. 2001 except had only two exposure sessions, then given ERP test for immediate recognition and imitation test for recall one month later	Familiarisation to event sequence in 2 distributed, real-life demonstrations of the event, then immediately after last exposure ERP test with still images of familiar and novel events presented 50/50	25 electrodes (average reference)	260–700	Latency tended to be longer for familiar than novel at midlines Amplitude tend to be larger for novel than familiar images at 9 months but larger for familiar than novel images at 10 months at midlines

(Continued overleaf)

Authors	Age and number of subjects	Attrition	Stimuli (duration)	Paradigm	Montage (reference)	Time window of Nc	Results
			Participants given same procedure but with different event sequences at 9 and 10 months				At 10 months the difference in latency between novel and familiar events at Cz predicted the number of actions recalled one month later; the same also for area scores at T5/6 and for peak amplitude at T6 with recall of order
Davis, Karrer & Walker, unpublished ms 1998	1 month, $n = 20$ 3 months, $n = 21$ 6 months, $n = 18$	1 month: 43% 3 months: 37% 6 months: 70%	Geometric shapes (1 month and 3 months) or faces (3 months and 6 months)	Oddball with 80/20 probability within stimulus type	Fz, Cz, Pz, Oz, C3/4, EOG (linked ears)	1 month: 500–1000 3 months: 500–1100 6 months: 400–800	*Shapes:* Area and amplitude bigger at 3 than 1 month over Fz and Cz and area the same at C3/4 Area larger for oddball than frequent and trend for latency to be longer for oddball than frequent Area larger for C4 than C3 *Faces:* Area and amplitude bigger for rare than frequent Latency shorter at 6 than 3 months Overall, is indication that Nc for older infants viewing faces is larger and faster than for younger infants viewing

REFERENCES

Ackles, P. K., & Cook, K. G. (1998). Stimulus probability and event-related potentials of the brain in 6-month-old human infants: A parametric study. *International Journal of Psychophysiology, 29*, 115–143.

Bachevalier, J., & Vargha-Khadem, F. (2005). The primate hippocampus: Ontogeny, early insult and memory. *Current Opinion in Neurobiology, 15*, 168–174.

Bauer, P. J., Wiebe, S. A., Carver, L. J., Lukowski, A. F., Haight, J. C., Waters, J. M. et al. (2006). Electrophysiological indices of encoding and behavioural indices of recall: Examining relations and developmental change in the first year of life. *Developmental Neuropsychology, 29*, 293–320.

Bauer, P. J., Wiebe, S. A., Carver, L. G., Waters, J. M., & Nelson, C. A. (2003). Developments in long-term explicit memory late in the first year of life: Behavioral and electrophysiological indices. *Psychological Science, 14*, 629–635.

Carver, L. J., Bauer, P. J., & Nelson, C. A. (2000). Associations between infant brain activity and recall memory. *Developmental Science, 3*, 234–246.

Carver, L. J., Dawson, G., Panagiotides, H., Meltzoff, A. N., McPartland, J., Gray, J. et al. (2003). Age-related differences in neural correlates of face recognition during the toddler and preschool years. *Developmental Psychobiology, 42*, 148–159.

Ceponiene, R., Lepisto, T., Soininen, M., Aronen, E., Alku, P., & Naatanen, R. (2004). Event-related potentials associated with sound discrimination versus novelty detection in children. *Psychophysiology, 41*, 130–141.

Courchesne, E. (1978). Neurophysiological correlates of cognitive development: Changes in long-latency event-related potentials from childhood to adulthood. *EEG & Clinical Neurophysiology, 45*, 468–482.

Courchesne, E. (1990). Chronology of postnatal human brain development: Event related potential, positron emission tomography, myelinogenesis and synaptogenesis studies. In J. W. Rohrbaugh, R. Parasuraman, & R. Johnson Jr. (Eds.), *Event related brain potentials: Basic issues and applications* (pp. 210–241). New York: Oxford University Press.

Courchesne, E., Ganz, L., & Norcia, A. M. (1981). Event-related brain potentials to human faces in infants. *Child Development, 52*, 804–811.

Davis, M., Karrer, R., & Walker, M. (1998). *Event-related potentials from a visual oddball task using age-appropriate stimuli: A comparison across ages one, three and six months.* Unpublished manuscript.

de Haan, M. (2003). Development and neural bases of infant visual recognition memory. In B. Hopkins & S. P. Johnson (Eds.), *Neurobiology of infant vision* (pp. 148–179). Westport, CT: Praeger Publishers.

de Haan, M., Belsky, J., Reid, V., Volein, A., & Johnson, M. H. (2004). Maternal personality and infants' neural and visual responsivity to facial expressions of emotion. *Journal of Child Psychology and Psychiatry, 45*, 1209–1218.

de Haan, M., & Nelson, C. A. (1997). Recognition of the mother's face by 6-month-old infants: A neurobehavioral study. *Child Development, 68*, 187–210.

de Haan, M., & Nelson, C. A. (1998). Discrimination and categorization of facial expressions of emotion during infancy. In A. Slater (Ed.), *Perceptual development* (pp. 247–286). Hove, UK: Psychology Press.

de Haan, M., & Nelson, C. A. (1999). Brain activity differentiates face and object processing by 6-month-old infants. *Developmental Psychology, 34*, 1114–1121.

deRegnier, R.-A. (2005). Neurophysiologic evaluation of early cognitive development in high-risk infants and toddlers. *Mental Retardation and Developmental Disabilities Research Reviews, 11*, 317–324.

deRegnier, R.-A., Georgieff, M. K., & Nelson, C. A. (1997). Visual event-related brain potentials in 4-month-old infants at risk for neurodevelopmental impairments. *Developmental Psychobiology, 30*, 11–28.

Fantz, R. (1961). The origins of form perception. *Scientific American, 204*, 66–72.

Friedman, D. (1991). The endogenous scalp-recorded brain potentials and their relationship to cognitive development. In J. R. Jennings & M. G. H. Coles (Eds.), *Handbook of cognitive psychophysiology: Central and autonomic nervous system approaches* (pp. 621–656). Chichester, UK: John Wiley.

Goldman, D. Z., Shapiro, E. G., & Nelson, C. A. (2004). Measurement of vigilance in 2-year-old children. *Developmental Neuropsychology, 25*, 227–250.

Hill-Karrer, J., Karrer, R., Bloom, D., Chaney, L., & Davis, R. (1998). Event-related brain potentials during an extended visual recognition memory task depict delayed development of cerebral inhibitory processes among 6-month-old infants with Downs syndrome. *International Journal of Psychophysiology, 29*, 167–200.

Howe, M. L., & Courage, M. L. (1997). Independent paths in the development of infant learning and forgetting. *Journal of Experimental Child Psychology, 67*, 131–163.

Hunter, S., & Karrer, R. (1993). ERPs indicate event duration effects on infants' visual attention and recognition memory. *EEG & Clinical Neurophysiology, 87*, S38.

Johnson, M. H., de Haan, M., Hatzakis, H., Oliver, A., Smith, W., Tucker, L. A. et al. (2001). Recording and analyzing high density event-related potentials with infants using the Geodesic Sensor Net. *Developmental Neuropsychology, 19*, 295–323.

Karrer, R., & Ackles, P. (1987). Visual event-related potentials of infants during a modified oddball procedure. In R. Johnson, J. W. Rohrbaugh, & R. Parasuraman (Eds.), *Current trends in event-related potential research* (pp. 603–608). Amsterdam: Elsevier Science Publishers.

Karrer, R., & Ackles, P. (1990). ERP evidence for expectancy in six-month-old infants. In C. H. M. Brunia, A. W. K. Gaillard, & A. Kok (Eds.), *Psychophysiological brain research* (pp. 157–160). Tilburg: University Press.

Karrer, R., & Monti, L. A. (1995). Event-related potentials of 4–7-week-old infants in a visual recognition memory task. *EEG & Clinical Neurophysiology, 94*, 414–424.

Lukowski, A. F., Wiebe, S. A., Haight, J. C., DeBoer, T., Nelson, C. A., & Bauer, P. J. (2005). Forming a stable memory representation in the first year of life: Why imitation is more than child's play. *Developmental Science, 8*, 279–298.

McIsaac, H., & Polich, J. (1992). Comparison of infant and adult P300 from auditory stimuli. *Journal of Experimental Child Psychology, 53*, 115–128.

Milner, B. (1965). Visually-guided maze learning in man: Effects of bilateral hippocampal, bilateral frontal and unilateral cerebral lesions. *Neuropsychologia, 3*, 317–338.

Milner, B. (1966). Amnesia following operations on the temporal lobes. In C. W. M. Whitty & O. I. Zangwill (Eds.), *Amnesia* (pp. 109–133). London: Butterworth.

Milner, B., Corkin, S., & Teuber, H.-L. (1968). Further analysis of the hippocampal amnesia syndrome: 14 year follow-up of HM. *Neuropsychologia, 6*, 215–234.

Mishkin, M., & Murray, E. A. (1994). Stimulus recognition. *Current Opinion in Neurobiology, 4*, 200–206.

Mishkin, M., Suzuki, W. A., Gadian, D. G., & Vargha-Khadem, F. (1997). Hierarchical organization of cognitive memory. *Philosophical Transactions of the Royal Society of London B, Biological Sciences, 352*, 1461–1467.

Nelson, C. A. (1994). Neural correlates of recognition memory in the first postnatal year of life. In G. Dawson & K. Fischer (Eds)., *Human behaviour and the developing brain* (pp. 269–313). New York: Guilford Press.

Nelson, C. A. (1995). The ontogeny of human memory: A cognitive neuroscience perspective. *Developmental Psychology, 31*, 723–738.

Nelson, C. A. (1996). Electrophysiological correlates of memory development in the first year of life. In H. Reese & M. Franzen (Eds.), *Biological and neuropsychological mechanisms: Life span developmental psychology* (pp. 95–131). Hillsdale, NJ: Lawrence Erlbaum Associates Inc.

Nelson, C. A., & Collins, P. F. (1991). Event-related potentials and looking-time analysis of infants' responses to familiar and novel events: Implications for recognition memory. *Developmental Psychology, 27*, 50–58.

Nelson, C. A., & Collins, P. F. (1992). Neural and behavioural correlates of recognition memory in 4- and 8-month-old infants. *Brain & Cognition, 19*, 105–121.

Nelson, C. A., & de Haan, M. (1996). Neural correlates of infants' visual responsiveness to facial expressions of emotion. *Developmental Psychobiology, 29*, 577–595.

Nelson, C. A., & deRegnier, R.-A. (1992). Neural correlates of attention and memory in the first year of life. *Developmental Neuropsychology, 8*, 119–134.

Nelson, C. A., & Dukette, D. (1998). Development of attention and memory. In J. E. Richards (Ed.), *Cognitive neuroscience of attention: A developmental perspective* (pp. 327–362). Hillsdale, NJ: Lawrence Erlbaum Associates Inc.

Nelson, C. A., & Salapatek, P. (1986). Electrophysiological correlates of infant recognition memory. *Child Development, 57*, 1483–1487.

Nelson, C. A., Thomas, K. M., de Haan, M., & Wewerka, S. S. (1998). Delayed recognition memory in infants and adults as revealed by event-related potentials. *International Journal of Psychophysiology, 29*, 145–165.

Nelson, C. A., & Webb, S. J. (2003). A cognitive neuroscience perspective on early memory development. In M. de Haan & M. H. Johnson (Eds.), *The cognitive neuroscience of development* (pp. 99–125). Hove, UK: Psychology Press.

Nelson, C. A., Wewerka, S., Thomas, K. M., Tribby-Wallbridge, S., deRegnier, R., & Georgieff, M. (2000). Neurocognitive sequelae of infants of diabetic mothers. *Behavioural Neuroscience, 114*, 950–956.

Nikkel, L., & Karrer, R. (1994). Differential effects of experience on the ERP and behaviour of 6-month-old infants: Trend during repeated stimulus presentations. *Developmental Neuropsychology, 10*, 1–11.

Parker, S. W., & Nelson, C. A. (2005). The impact of early institutional rearing on the ability to discriminate facial expressions of emotion: An event-related potential study. *Child Development, 76*, 54–72.

Pascalis, O., & de Haan, M. (2003). Recognition memory and novelty preference: Which model? In H. Hayne & J. W. Fagen (Eds.), *Progress in infancy research, Vol. 3* (pp. 95–119). Mahwah, NJ: Lawrence Erlbaum Associates Inc.

Pascalis, O., de Haan, M., Nelson, C. A., & de Schonen, S. (1998). Long-term recognition memory assessed by visual paired comparison in 3- and 6-month-old infants. *Journal of Experimental Psychology: Learning, Memory and Cognition, 24*, 249–260.

Posner, M. I., & Petersen, S. E. (1990). The attention system of the human brain. *Annual Review of Neuroscience, 13*, 25–42.

Quinn, P. C., Westerlund, A., & Nelson, C. A. (2006). Neural markers of categorization in 6-month-old infants. *Psychological Science, 17*, 59–66.

Reynolds, G. D., & Richards, J. E. (2005). Familiarization, attention and recognition memory in infancy: An ERP and cortical source localisation study. *Developmental Psychology, 41*, 598–615.

Richards, J. E. (1997). Effects of attention on infants' preference for briefly exposed visual stimuli in the paired-comparison recognition-memory paradigm. *Developmental Psychology, 33*, 27–31.

Richards, J. E. (2003). Attention affects the recognition of briefly presented visual stimuli in infants: An ERP study. *Developmental Science, 6*, 312–328.

Richards, J. E., & Casey, B. J. (1991). Heart rate variability during attention phases in young infants. *Psychophysiology, 28*, 43–53.

Rose, S. A., & Feldman, J. F. (1997). Memory and speed: Their role in the relation of infant information processing to later IQ. *Child Development, 68*, 630–641.

Schacter, D. L., & Moscovitch, M. (1984). Infants, amnesics and dissociable memory systems. In M. Moscovitch (Ed.), *Infant memory* (pp. 173–216). New York: Plenum Press.

Schroger, E., Giard, M.-H., & Wolff, C. (2000). Auditory distraction: Event-related potential and behavioural indices. *Clinical Neurophysiology, 111*, 1450–1460.

Schroger, E., & Wolff, C. (1998). Attentional orienting and reorienting is indicated by human event-related brain potentials. *Neuroreport, 9*, 3355–3358.

Schulman-Galambos, C., & Galambos, R. (1978). Cortical responses from adults and infants to complex visual stimuli. *EEG & Clinical Neurophysiology, 45*, 425–435.

Scoville, W. B., & Milner, B. (1957). Loss of recent memory after bilateral hippocampal lesions. *Journal of Neurology, Neurosurgery & Psychiatry, 20*, 11–21.

Shibasaki, H., & Miyazaki, M. (1992). Event-related potential studies in infants and children. *Journal of Clinical Neurophysiology, 9*, 408–418.

Snyder, K., Webb, S. J., & Nelson, C. A. (2002). Theoretical and methodological implications of variability in infant brain response during a recognition memory paradigm. *Infant Behavior and Development, 25*, 466–494.

Squire, L. R. (1992). Declarative and nondeclarative memory: Multiple brain systems supporting learning and memory. *Journal of Cognitive Neuroscience, 4*, 232–243.

Squire, L. R., & Knowlton, B. J. (1995). Memory, hippocampus and brain systems. In M. Gazzaniga (Ed.), *The cognitive neurosciences* (pp. 825–837). Cambridge, MA: MIT Press.

Stolarova, M., Whitney, H., Webb, S. J., deRegnier, R., Georgieff, M. K., & Nelson, C. A. (2003). Electrophysiological brain responses of six-month-old low risk premature infants. *Infancy, 4*, 437–450.

Tulving, E. (1972). Episodic and semantic memory. In E. Tulving & W. Donaldson (Eds.), *Organization of memory* (pp. 381–403). New York: Plenum Press.

Tulving, E. (1985). Memory and consciousness. *Canadian Psychologist, 262*, 1–12.

Vaughan, H. G. Jr., & Kurtzberg, D. (1992). Electrophysiologic indices of human brain maturation and cognitive development. In M. Gunnar & C. A. Nelson (Eds.), *Developmental behavioural neuroscience* (pp. 1–36). Hillsdale, NJ: Lawrence Erlbaum Associates Inc.

Webb, S. J., Long, J. D., & Nelson, C. A. (2005). A longitudinal investigation of visual event-related potentials in the first year of life. *Developmental Science, 8*, 605–616.

Webb, S. J., & Nelson, C. A. (2001). Perceptual priming for upright and inverted faces in infants and adults. *Journal of Experimental Child Psychology*, *79*, 1–22.

Wetzel, M., Berti, S., Widmann, A., & Schroger, E. (2004) Distraction and reorientation in children: A behavioural and event-related potential study. *Neuroreport*, *15*, 1355–1358.

Wiebe, S. A., Cheatham, C. L., Lukowski, A. F., Haight, J. C., Muehleck, A. J., & Bauer, P. J. (2006). Infants' ERP responses to novel and familiar stimuli change over time: Implications for novelty detection and memory. *Infancy*, *9*, 21–44.

Yonelinas, A. (1994). Receiver-operating characteristics in recognition memory: Evidence for a dual-process model. *Journal of Experimental Psychology: Learning, Memory & Cognition*, *20*, 1341–1354.

5   Auditory recognition memory in infancy

Raye-Ann deRegnier
Northwestern University Feinberg School of Medicine, Chicago, USA

In the adult brain, memory is a complex function that is subserved by several neural networks. Recognition memory is a function of the explicit memory or declarative memory network that is known to be dependent upon medial temporal lobe structures such as the hippocampus and the entorhinal cortex (Broadbent, Clark, Zola, & Squire, 2002; Clark, Broadbent, Zola, & Squire, 2002; Reed & Squire, 1997) and it is one of the earliest types of explicit memory to develop (Fagan, 1990; Nelson, 1995). As such, the evaluation of the development of recognition memory in the infant offers the opportunity to understand the evolution of the explicit memory network from the "ground up" and enhance our understanding of the role of memory in overall cognitive development. Understanding the memory abilities of the youngest infants also allows the researcher the opportunity to document perinatal brain injury to memory networks and to further evaluate the role of plasticity in neural development.

It is important to recognize that the immature memory network of the newborn infant is accompanied by immature sensory systems and limited experience. Thus, prerequisites to the study of memory in the newborn include sufficient maturity of the sensory organs and sensory brain pathways leading into the memory circuits themselves. Experiences to be remembered must be appropriate for the processing abilities of the infant, and methodology for testing must take all these factors into account.

Although most studies of infant recognition memory have focused on visual memory, there is evidence that the memory networks of the brain are amodal (Broadbent et al., 2002) and are connected to each of the sensory pathways (also see Squire, Schmolck, & Stark, 2001). Although visual recognition memory is most commonly studied, in the newborn infant visual acuity is poor (Volpe, 2001) and visual experience is very limited. In contrast, hearing begins during the fetal period and by term gestation, the newborn has relatively good auditory acuity (Lary, Briassoulis, de Vries, Dubowitz, & Dubowitz, 1985; Starr, Amlie, Martin, & Sanders, 1977) as well as several months of prenatal auditory experience (Lecaunet & Schaal, 1996). Both of these features facilitate the study of auditory recognition memory.

This chapter will describe the development of the sensory and neural networks that are thought to underlie the neurobehavioral manifestations of auditory recognition memory. Although auditory discrimination is likely required for recognition memory, it will not be discussed here as it is the focus of Dr Cheour's chapter of this book (Chapter 6). The use of event-related potentials (ERPs) in the evaluation of auditory recognition memory in the newborn infant will be discussed, and behavioral, psychophysiological, and event-related potential evidence of early auditory recognition memory will be reviewed.

THE NEURAL PATHWAY FOR AUDITORY RECOGNITION MEMORY

Although many parts of the neural pathway for auditory recognition memory have been elucidated, the complete neural pathway for auditory recognition memory has not been described in either the adult or the infant. Through decades of work, the pathway for perception of environmental sounds from the ear to the primary auditory cortex has been established, and the development of this pathway has been studied using histological, behavioral, and neurophysiologic techniques. There is much less information regarding the central auditory processing leading into and including the memory network that is responsible for auditory recognition memory in the infant. Recent studies have detailed pathways linking perception and memory in animal models (Suzuki & Amaral, 1994) and in human adults, using functional magnetic resonance scanning (fMRI) (Daseleer, Veltman, & Witter, 2004; Dolan & Fletcher, 1999; Lepage, Habib, & Tulving, 1998; Shah et al., 2001). The development of central auditory processing and recognition memory have not been as well described, but both ERPs and neuroimaging procedures have augmented the traditional procedures to improve our understanding of both anatomic and functional development.

A pathway of neural structures likely to be involved in auditory recognition memory is seen in Figure 5.1. The first part of the pathway (Hudspeth, 2000) involves the transformation of sound to neural impulses. Sound is transmitted to the outer ear via amniotic fluid, bone, or air, and transmitted through the external ear canal through the middle ear to the cochlea where the vibration of the middle ear ossicles is converted into neural impulses by vibration of the frequency-specific hair cells in the organ of corti. These hair cells are innervated by bipolar neurons of the spiral ganglia which make up the auditory nerve. The auditory nerve terminates in the dorsal and ventral cochlear nuclei of the brainstem. At this point, the neural pathway divides into ipsilateral and contralateral tracts that ascend further through the superior olivary nucleus to the lateral lemniscus (where further crossing may occur), to the inferior colliculus and medial geniculate body of the thalamus, to the primary auditory cortex found in the superior temporal gyrus where perception presumably begins.

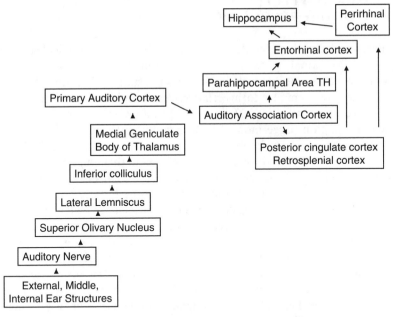

Figure 5.1 Neural structures likely to be involved in auditory recognition memory. (Broadbent et al., 2002; Hudspeth, 2000; Squire et al., 2001; Suzuki & Amaral, 1994).

The pathway from perception to auditory recognition memory is not as well known and is more complex, likely involving a network of brain areas that are variably activated, depending on the exact nature of the memory task. However, it is known that the primary auditory cortex connects to higher-order auditory association areas and ultimately projects to the hippocampus and rhinal cortex through projections to area TH of the para-hippocampal cortex (Squire et al., 2001; Suzuki & Amaral, 1994). Recognition of voices in the adult is also associated with activation of the posterior cingulate cortex and retrosplenial cortex of the limbic system (which also project to the perirhinal, parahippocampal, and entorhinal cortex) (Shah et al., 2001).

From this discussion it should be apparent that evaluation of recognition memory in the infant requires that the entire neural pathway is sufficiently mature before testing can be accomplished. In adults and older children this can be assumed. However, when discussing memory in the very young infant, it becomes important to understand what is known about the histological and functional development of these pathways during gestation and early infancy. This knowledge is helpful in preparing paradigms to be used to study this age group, and in understanding the variability that may be seen in ERP studies at these young ages.

ANATOMIC DEVELOPMENT OF THE NEURAL PATHWAY
FOR AUDITORY RECOGNITION MEMORY

All parts of the ear begin to develop in the embryo, with the cochlea appearing to be functional by 18–20 weeks gestation. Inner ear function overall appears to be at mature levels by 36 weeks gestation (Lecaunet & Schaal, 1996). The brainstem also forms relatively early and has a short time course of myelination starting near 23–24 weeks gestation and completing at about 37 weeks gestation (Eggermont, 1988). In contrast, the cerebral cortex has a prolonged period of development. Neurons destined for the cerebral cortex proliferate from 7 weeks through midgestation and then migrate to their final destinations in one of the six layers of the cerebral cortex. Neurons migrate in the neocortex in an "inside-out" pattern, with the deepest layers (5–6) developing first and the more superficial layers developing later. By 32 weeks gestation, all six layers of the cerebral cortex can be observed. Once the neurons have formed and migrated, they extend axons and dendrites, form synapses, and undergo further differentiation and apoptosis (Nelson, 2002).

Synaptogenesis is critical in order for neural impulses to be transmitted throughout the nervous system. Although most synapses form after birth, Huttenlocher and Dabholkar (1997) demonstrated early synapse formation in all six layers of the auditory cortex beginning by 28 weeks gestation. Synaptic density was maximal in this area at 3 months of age, with synapse elimination appearing to be complete by 12 years of age. Thus, synaptic connections are known to exist from the auditory nerve through primary auditory cortex by mid to late gestation in the fetus.

There is less information regarding early histologic development in the auditory association areas or within the memory networks of the human brain. A notable exception to this is the development of the hippocampus, reviewed in detail by Dr László Seress of Hungary (Seress, 2001). The human hippocampus begins to develop during fetal life, with development continuing to adulthood. Most of the neurons in the hippocampal formation are formed in the first half of gestation, the exception being the dentate gyrus, where the neurons develop later. An "inside-out" pattern of neural migration is noted that is similar to that seen in the neocortical regions, except for the neurons of the dentate gyrus that migrate throughout the first postnatal year and develop from the outside in. Entorhinal-hippocampal projections are noted during midgestation (Hevnar & Kinney, 1996). These connections appear to be among the first cortico-cortical connections in the human brain. Although the human hippocampus is quite immature at birth, it appears that sufficient synaptic connections are present to support at least rudimentary recognition memory at term gestation.

Medial temporal lobe development has also been described in early infancy using magnetic resonance imaging (MRI). In one study of children from 3 weeks to 14 years of age (Utsunomiya, Takano, Okazaki, & Mitsudome, 1999), it was noted that the basic morphology of the hippocampal formation was similar to that seen in adults. The volume of the hippocampal formation increased rapidly through age 2 and more slowly thereafter. The hippocampal formation composed a larger percentage of the temporal lobe in younger infants compared with older children. The right hippocampal formation was larger than the left in 91% of the children, beginning in early infancy. Early myelination was noted in the parahippocampal gyrus from age 3 months continuing through 2–5 years for the limbic system and related structures. These MRI data show a disproportionately large size for the hippocampus within the temporal lobe in very young infants, supporting a central role for this brain structure in early cognition.

Taken altogether, these anatomic studies show sufficient histologic development to support hearing and auditory perception by 28 weeks gestation. The hippocampus appears to have sufficient synaptic connections to support functional abilities by term gestation, if not earlier. Neurophysiologic and behavioral studies support these basic timetables and will be reviewed next.

BEHAVIORAL AND EVOKED POTENTIAL MEASURES OF AUDITORY PROCESSING

Fetal hearing has been tested using a variety of methods (reviewed in Lecanuet & Schaal, 1996), with the most common responses being fetal cardiac responses or motor responses. By 23–24 weeks gestation, some fetuses show an increase in heart rate or motor activity in response to sound, becoming more uniformly present over the next month of gestation (Hepper & Shahidullah, 1994; Lecanuet & Schaal, 1996). These behavioral studies are consistent with developmental studies of the auditory processing pathway through primary cortex and suggest that efferent pathways controlling heart rate and motor activity must be sufficiently developed as well. Further information about the development of hearing later in gestation can be gained through neurophysiologic assessment of premature infants, who are able to survive outside of the womb by about 23–24 weeks gestation (deRegnier, 2002). The auditory brainstem response (ABR) methodology has been used in a number of studies to evaluate the maturation of the auditory nerve through the brainstem. In an averaged ABR, a series of well-described, numbered peaks track the transmission of neural impulses from the auditory nerve (wave I) through the medial geniculate body of the thalamus (wave VI) (Counter, 2002). Although very young premature infants typically do not display all of these peaks in their ABR, even infants as young as 24 weeks gestation have shown reproducible waveforms indicating transmission of neural impulses through the brainstem (Amin, Orlando, Dalzell, Merle, & Guillet, 1999; Starr, et al., 1977). Similar to fetal behavioral studies, auditory brainstem responses become more robust by 27–28 weeks gestation. A great deal of maturation occurs in this part of the neural pathway, continuing through gestation and the first year of life (Salamy & McKean, 1976). Hearing thresholds improve from 40 dB nHL at 28–34 weeks gestation to less than 20 dB nHL by 2 weeks post term (Adelman, Levi, Linder, & Sohmer, 1990; Lary et al., 1985). Additionally, conduction time within the brainstem (assessed using the wave I–V latency difference) improves dramatically between 24 weeks gestation and term (Amin et al., 1999; Starr et al., 1977). This is thought to be reflective of increases in both synaptic density and early myelination (Eggermont, 1988). Lastly, the use of the ABR has also demonstrated that the brainstem has a slight but significant right ear advantage for auditory processing (Eldredge & Salamy, 1996).

Moving past the brainstem to cortical processing, long-latency ERP responses to sounds have also been generated as early as 23 weeks gestation (Weitzman & Graziani, 1968). In these extremely premature infants, a simple negativity with a long latency (180–270 ms) has been demonstrated over the midline and lateral electrode sites (denoted as N1 by these authors). Interestingly, at this very young age, these responses are more robust than those potentials arising from the brainstem (the ABR). With maturation, the latency of the N1 wave decreases over the posterior scalp, and a subsequent positive wave develops that becomes predominant over the midline. This positive component has been denoted as P2, and with further maturation the positive component also begins to predominate the lateral waveforms (Kurtzberg, Hilpert, Kreuzer, & Vaughan, 1984; Novak, Kurtzberg, Kreuzer, & Vaughan, 1989). It has been speculated that this change from a predominant negative polarity to a predominant positive polarity may reflect development of specific laminae of the cerebral cortex. Initially, the thalamocortical innervation is limited to lamina IV. In the animal, this innervation generates a surface negative potential. As lamina III becomes innervated, this may result in a shift to a surface positive potential (Novak et al., 1989).

The Einstein group developed a scoring system to assess the maturity of the auditory cortical responses (Kurtzberg et al., 1984). In this system, level I is the most immature response, with predominantly negative responses over both midline and lateral scalp sites (Figure 5.2), level III indicates a positive midline but negative lateral response, and level V showing positive waveforms over both midline and lateral scalp sites from 100 to 400 ms post-stimulus. Using this classification scheme, most term newborns are in maturity level III, but all levels from I to V are commonly seen at this age (deRegnier, Nelson, Thomas, Wewerka, & Georgieff, 2000; deRegnier, Wewerka, Georgieff, Mattia, & Nelson, 2002; Novak et al., 1989). Further dramatic maturational changes have been described over the first year of life (Kushnerenko, Ceponiene, Balan, Fellman, Huotilainen, & Näätänen, 2002), with increases in amplitude and shortening of latencies noted, although the time course for these processes appeared to differ for the different peaks noted in the waveforms. These changes in morphology occurring over a relatively short time period have been described by several authors and are important to note because they can introduce large amounts of variability into ERP waveforms obtained from very young infants.

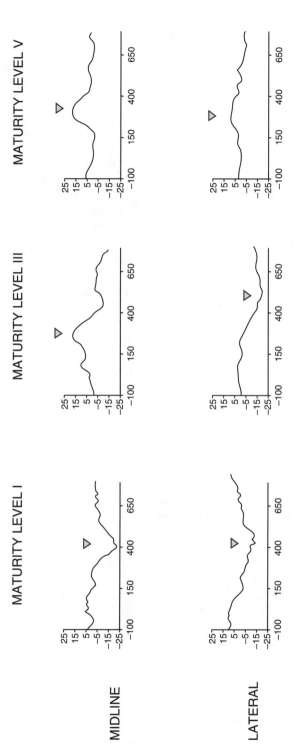

Figure 5.2 ERPS from three individual infants illustrating maturity levels I, III, and V in response to a computer chime (400 ms, 80 dB SPL). Reprinted with permission from deRegnier et al. (2000).

Interestingly, functional MRI studies of hearing in the fetus and newborn also demonstrate variable responses to auditory stimuli. The fMRI response is assessed through evaluation of the blood oxygenation level dependent (BOLD) imaging, which is a measure of blood oxygenation that is presumed to increase with increased neuronal activity (Casey, Davidson, & Rosen, 2002). Hykin and colleagues (1999) studied fetal MRI in response to the maternal voice. The four fetuses were studied at 38–39 weeks gestation, with the fetal head engaged in the maternal pelvis to reduce motion artifact. Of the three subjects with technically satisfactory scans, two showed significant activation of the temporal lobe that was also seen in the adult control subjects. In a study of 14 unsedated term newborn infants, Anderson and colleagues (2001) reported fMRI results using pure tone stimuli, compared with four adult control subjects. All of the adults, but only 5/14 neonates showed a positive increase in the MRI BOLD signal in the superior temporal region. In contrast, the majority of infants showed a negative BOLD signal in the same area of the brain. The significance of these variable responses in BOLD signaling is not well understood, but may be due to differences in methodology or as part of a developmental pattern that will emerge with more research. In support of this, Dehaene-Lambertz, Dehaene, and Hertz-Pannier (2002) studied unsedated infants using speech stimuli. The task did not require recognition memory. At 2–3 months of age, this group reported activations (with no significant inversions in polarity) in a large area of the left temporal lobe, with non-significant activation in the right temporal lobe. Thus, by 2–3 months of age, no negative inversions of BOLD polarity were noted. More research is needed regarding this topic, but it appears that fMRI may be a valuable method to study the development of regional specialization of brain functions, including infant memory.

In summary, the sensory organs and central nervous system of the fetus are prepared to receive auditory input in the mid to latter part of gestation, and the hippocampus appears to be sufficiently developed to support memory abilities by term. It is important to consider the types of sounds that the fetus is exposed to in utero as these sounds may be encoded into memory during the latter part of pregnancy. The fetal sound environment includes noises associated with the mother (speech, heart sounds, placental blood flow, and digestive sounds) as well as external noises that are transmitted through the uterus. The uterus acts as a low-pass filter for airborne extrauterine sounds, with moderate attenuation of sound levels from 400 to 1000 Hz and further attenuation (up to 35 dB SPL) at 10 kHz (Lecanuet & Schaal, 1996). Environmental voices near the uterus are therefore audible to the fetus, but since the higher frequencies are attenuated, voices are muffled, though prosody is preserved. Querleu, Renard, Versyp, Paris-Delrue, and Vervoort (1988) estimated that up to 30% of extrauterine speech is intelligible in utero. The maternal voice is transmitted to the fetus through the airborne route, but it is also transmitted through body tissue and bone, which results in less filtering of higher frequencies (Lecanuet & Schaal, 1996). The net result of this is that the maternal voice is louder in utero than ex utero and less subject to distortion of the acoustic properties than are the airborne voices of others. Since the maternal voice is heard by the fetus whenever the mother speaks, the fetus has many weeks of experience of it by the time of birth. Although the duration of experience required for encoding in the newborn is not known, the fetal experience with the maternal voice should result in encoding if the neural mechanisms are sufficiently developed.

AUDITORY RECOGNITION MEMORY IN THE FETUS AND NEWBORN

Psychophysiologic and behavioral studies

Although the maternal voice has been used in a number of studies of the fetus, it has often been used to evaluate the infant for hearing and sound discrimination rather than memory (see Fifer & Moon, 1995, for a review). For any comparisons of the maternal voice and a stranger's voice, it is important to utilize recordings of the maternal voice that can played back ex utero to contrast with the stranger's voice. Otherwise, as previously mentioned, the maternal voice will be louder than the stranger's voice and will have different acoustic properties due to tissue and bone conduction. Kisilevsky's group (2003) tested term fetuses with 2-minute tape recordings of the maternal voice, a stranger's voice, and silence. The voice of the previous mother served as the stranger. They reported an increase in the fetal heart rate for the maternal voice for the 90 seconds post stimulus onset, whereas the stranger's voice led to a fetal heart rate deceleration. No differences in body movements were noted for the two voices. These data show that, at term, the fetus is able to respond differently to the maternal voice than to a stranger's voice, and this is suggestive of recognition memory.

After birth, recognition of the maternal voice and other fetal experiences has been tested by several authors. Querleu, Lefebvre, Titran, Renard, Morillion, and Crepin (1984) videotaped 25 newborn infants (< 2 hours of age) with no prior postnatal exposure to the maternal voice. Each infant listed to recordings of five voices, including that of the mother. The videotapes were scored by blinded observers who documented orienting movements to the maternal voice more often than to the strangers' voices. DeCasper and Fifer (1980) tested 2-day-old infants with an operant sucking procedure and noted that the infants could learn to suck at a specific rate that would produce a recording of the maternal voice rather than a stranger's voice. In this study it was unclear whether the results of the study reflected fetal or neonatal learning. However, DeCasper and Spence (1986) later showed that prenatal stimulation with specific speech sounds was associated with changes in newborns' perceptions of those sounds. Fifer and Moon (1995) also tested newborn infants with a filtered version of the maternal voice created to mimic conditions in utero compared with an unfiltered version. The newborns sucked preferentially to elicit the filtered version, providing additional evidence that intrauterine experience is encoded. Therefore, current psychobiologic and behavioral evidence supports the concept that the late gestation fetus and newborn is capable of encoding auditory stimuli and shows behavioral evidence of recognition memory.

Evaluation of auditory recognition memory using event-related potentials

There are a number of favorable attributes supporting the use of ERPs in the study of auditory recognition memory in the newborn. Compared with assessments such as MRI scanning, ERPs are relatively inexpensive. Furthermore, they are non-invasive, sedation is not needed, and behavioral responses are not required. ERPs are also known to have excellent temporal resolution. Lastly, sleeping newborns can be studied with minimal attrition. Because of these attributes, we have used ERPs to study recognition of the maternal voice in newborn infants.

There are several points of methodology that are important in testing auditory ERPs in the newborn infant. The first concerns the stimuli chosen. Although the fetal and behavioral studies use long segments of speech as stimuli, it is difficult to synchronize neural activity to a long segment of speech in an ERP study, and shorter segments are preferable. One-word utterances make up a significant part of the natural sound environment of young infants and are suitable for study (Korman & Lewis, 2002). Second, it is important to control sleep state. Although it would be optimal to study awake infants, the quiet awake state is unusual in a newborn (Thoman, 1990) and cannot be produced reliably in the laboratory. We have therefore studied newborns in the behavioral stage of active sleep, as cortical evoked potentials are similar in active sleep as in awake infants (Ellingson, Danahy, Nelson, & Lathrop, 1974). Furthermore, active sleep is abundant in the newborn, occurring about 50% of the time (Thoman, 1990).

To evaluate long-term memory abilities of the newborn, a paradigm was developed with no familiarization period. The maternal voice served as the familiar stimulus, with a stranger's voice serving as the novel stimulus. The stranger was the previous mother. This means that in the course of the study, each voice was heard in both the mother and stranger conditions. The word "baby" was used as the stimulus, with the mother instructed to use prosody in the recording. Stimuli were digitized and then edited to 750 ms and 80 dB SPL. The maternal and stranger's voices were presented with equal frequencies so that there would be no differential encoding of one of the voices during the study. The interstimulus interval was varied randomly from 3900 to 4900 ms to prevent infants from anticipating the onset of the subsequent voice, and to allow evaluation of the long latency activity. Stimuli were presented to the right ear with an insert earphone to utilize the right ear advantage for language processing (Ahonniska, Cantell, Tolvanen, & Lyytinen, 1993) and to prevent compression obstruction of the ear, which can be seen with external earphones. The ERPs were recorded from Pz, Cz, Fz, T3, and T4 (Jasper, 1958) in a behavioral state of active sleep.

The first study (deRegnier et al., 2000) tested the development of auditory recognition memory for the maternal voice in 28 normal hearing newborn infants born at term and tested at a mean age of 10.7 (± 2) days. In this group of infants (Figure 5.3), the maternal and stranger's voices evinced positive components in the window from 150 to 400 ms, denoted as "P2". Review of the waveform reveals that a negative slow wave (NSW) is also present in the ERP derived from the stranger's voice. The negative slow wave begins early in the recording and results in a smaller amplitude P2 peak for the stranger's voice and a more negative area under the curve for the entire recording. Additionally, the latency to the P2 peak at the Cz electrode site was shorter for the stranger's voice than for the maternal voice.

Negative slow waves have been described in studies of visual recognition memory in early infancy (see Chapter 4, this volume, for further discussion). In a previous neonatal study, deRegnier (1993) reported that infrequent novel tones inserted into a train of frequent familiar tones elicited a negative slow wave, but only when a sequence of five or more repeated familiar tones preceded the novel tone. Additionally, deRegnier, Georgieff, and Nelson (1997) noted a negative slow wave in response to a novel visual stimulus in 4-month-old infants. Nelson and Collins (1991) similarly described a negative slow wave in response to unique novel faces (presented only once) in an ERP study of 6-month-old full term infants. Nelson has postulated that the negative slow wave is indicative of novelty detection, a function of the hippocampus (Dolan & Strange, 2002; Nelson, 1994; Nelson & deRegnier, 1992). If this speculation is correct, that means that even after hearing the stranger's voice 60 times during the ERP testing session, the stranger's voice remained a novel stimulus, corroborating behavioral evidence of very slow visual encoding in young infants.

In another experiment designed to further evaluate the role of experience and postmenstrual age on memory development, three groups of normal hearing infants were tested using the paradigm described above (deRegnier et al., 2002). To evaluate the effects of maturity and experience, minimally preterm infants (35–38 weeks gestation) were tested during the first postnatal week (mean age: 1.6 days at test) and compared with a group of full term newborn infants (mean gestation 40.1 weeks) tested at 2 days of age. This group was more mature, but still had little postnatal experience. The third comparison group also consisted of full term infants (tested at 40.9 weeks postmenstrual age) who had 2 weeks of postnatal experience. Thus, the minimally preterm group was immature and inexperienced; the full term newborn group was more mature but with little postnatal experience, and the experienced group was of similar postmenstrual age, but had more postnatal experience.

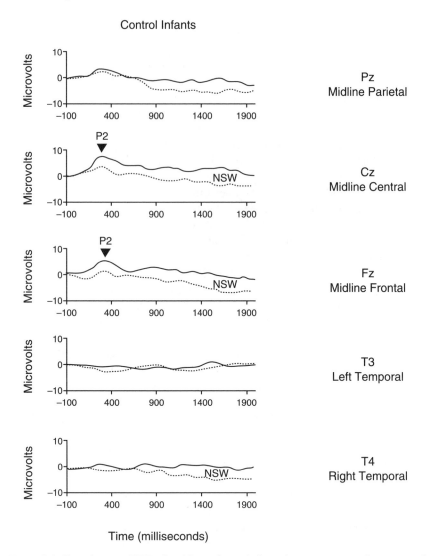

Figure 5.3 Grand mean ERPs for 28 newborn infants in response to the maternal (solid line) and stranger's (dotted line) voices. Areas of significant difference between mother and stranger ERP areas under the curve are denoted NSW (negative slow wave). Reprinted with permission from deRegnier et al. (2000).

In this study, both the full term newborn group and the experienced group showed positive waves for the maternal voice and negative slow waves for the stranger's voice, whereas the minimally preterm group did not show significant differences between the stimuli (Figure 5.4). The minimally preterm infants' maternal and stranger ERPs were similar to the stranger ERPs in the full term newborn and experienced groups. Hypothesizing that the negative slow waves are associated with novelty detection, the fact that the preterm infants' maternal ERPs showed predominantly negative waveforms may indicate that these less mature infants have not fully encoded the maternal voice to the same degree as the older infants. Since we know that infants born at 35–38 weeks gestation have many weeks of prenatal experience with the maternal voice, experience would not be the limiting factor for these younger infants. Rather the results are consistent with immaturity of the memory network itself until close to term gestation. Thus brain immaturity (indexed here by postmenstrual age) appears to be an important determinant of recognition memory.

The study showed that postnatal experience was also important in maternal voice recognition. For the full term groups, the group with more postnatal experience showed a longer latency for the maternal voice than to the stranger's voice. The latency to the stranger's voice in the experienced group was similar to the latencies for the maternal and stranger's voices in the newborn infants tested at 2 days of age. Thus, the effect of experience was to prolong the latency to the maternal voice. The grand mean figures (Figure 5.4) also show that the waveform in this group was more complex, with new peaks surfacing in the mid portion of the ERP. This may indicate a separate but overlaid response to the second syllable of the word "baby" in this group, and appears to be consistent with a greater depth of processing associated with postnatal experience.

Overall, this study showed that both maturation and postnatal experience have effects on neonatal auditory recognition memory. It is known from behavioral studies of visual recognition memory that newborns encode novel stimuli very slowly and that the speed of encoding improves dramatically over the first 6 months of life (Fagan, 1990). We speculated that immature encoding abilities might be overcome by additional familiarization with the stimulus, facilitating recognition memory. In a third study (Therien, Worwa, Mattia, & deRegnier, 2004), 40 full term newborns (2 days old at test) were studied using the basic paradigm described previously. However, half of the infants received a familiarization period with 60 trials of the maternal voice prior to the test phase in which the maternal voice alternated with a stranger's voice. The additional familiarization did not produce any significant effects on the peak amplitudes, latency measurements, or areas under the curve of the ERP. In this study, the auditory cortical maturity level also did not correlate with the performance on the recognition memory task. These data, as well as the previously described study of minimally preterm infants, suggest that although neonates do show evidence of recognition memory, this seems to require very intensive exposure to a stimulus, such as occurs on a daily basis during the last trimester of pregnancy. This is substantiated by the behavioral studies of DeCasper and Prescott (1984), who demonstrated that newborn infants did not show behavioral evidence of recognition memory for the paternal voice, even with 4–10 hours of postnatal measured voice exposure prior to the testing.

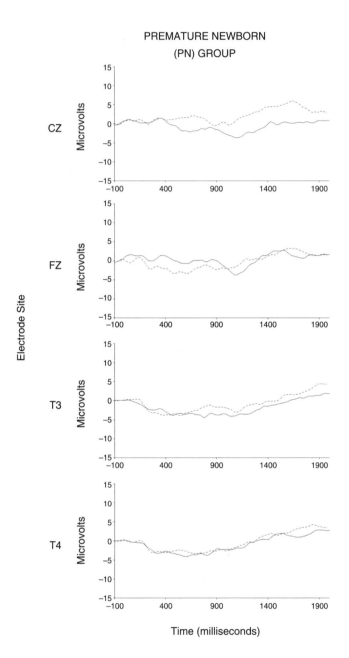

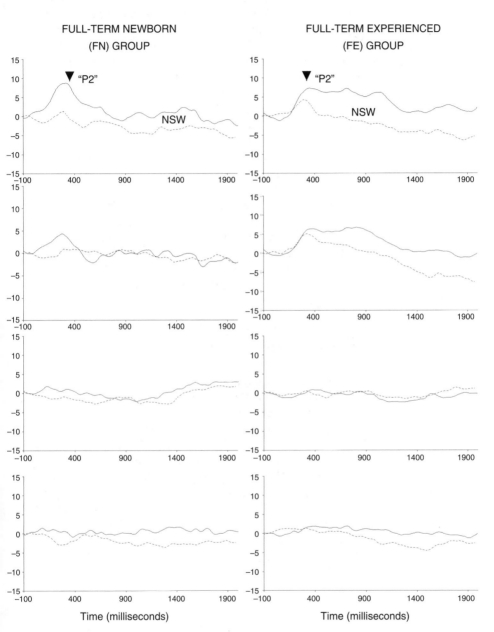

Figure 5.4 Grand mean ERPs in response to the maternal (solid line) and stranger's (dashed line) voices recorded from premature newborn infants, full term newborn infants, and full term experienced infants with 2 weeks postnatal experience. NSW indicates the area of the negative slow wave. Reprinted with permission from deRegnier et al. (2002).

ERP studies of recognition memory corroborate behavioral studies indicating neonatal recognition memory for the maternal voice at term. The ERP studies also indicate that recognition memory abilities in the newborn are the product of both maturation of the neural circuitry and experience, and that a great deal of experience appears to be necessary to demonstrate long-term memory in the immediate perinatal period. Further research is required to determine the neural structures responsible for this response, although neurohistologic and MRI studies implicate the hippocampus as an important structure in the development of cognitive function during infancy. The hippocampus and parahippocampal region both appear to be involved in encoding and retrieval of memory in adults (Daseleer et al., 2004; Dolan & Fletcher, 1999), and further investigation is needed to determine if these structures are also responsible for these functions in the newborn as well. It is speculated that the negative waveforms seen on the infant ERP in response to novel stimuli may be due to the detection and subsequent encoding of novel stimuli, and that as the hippocampus matures, encoding also matures, and these waves will evolve into the positive slow waves seen in older infants in response to partially encoded stimuli in the older infant (Nelson, 1994; Nelson & deRegnier, 1992; see Chapter 4, this volume, for further discussion of positive slow waves).

STUDIES OF HIGH-RISK POPULATIONS

One advantage of developing techniques to study the development of memory in newborn infants is that these methods can be used to evaluate perinatal brain injury and plasticity. It is now known that infants with prematurity (Curtis, Lindeke, Georgieff, & Nelson, 2002; de Haan, Bauer, Georgieff, & Nelson, 2000; Isaacs et al., 2000; Rose, 1983; Rose, Feldman, & Jankowski, 2001, 2002), perinatal hypoxia-ischemia (Maneru et al., 2003; Nyakas, Buwalda, & Luidten, 1996), and poorly controlled maternal diabetes (deRegnier et al., 2000; Nelson, Wewerka, Borscheid, deRegnier, & Georgieff, 2003; Nelson, Wewerka, Thomas, Tribby-Walbridge, deRegnier, & Georgieff, 2000; Sidappa, Georgieff, Wewerka, Worwa, Nelson, & deRegnier, 2004) are at increased risk for difficulties with memory. ERPs have been used to evaluate memory development in premature infants and infants of diabetic mothers.

Premature infants

Premature infants may experience multiple episodes of perinatal hypoxia-ischemia due to complications of labor and delivery, respiratory disorders, or recurrent episodes of apnea and bradycardia (Mattia & deRegnier, 1998). It is known that the hippocampus is vulnerable to hypoxia (Nyakas et al., 1996) and indeed, the increasing use of MRI scanning and the availability of volumetric studies have demonstrated that premature children often have evidence of hippocampal injury and atrophy (Isaacs et al., 2000; Vargha-Khadem, Gadian, & Mishkin, 2001; Vargha-Khadem, Salmond, Watkins, Friston, Gadian, & Mishkin, 2003) as well as patterns of explicit memory deficits. Volumetric MRI studies have shown that significant memory impairments appear to be associated with a 20–30% reduction of bilateral hippocampal volumes (Isaacs, Vargha-Khadem, Watkins, Lucas, Mishkin, & Gadian, 2003). Interestingly, long before this was described, Susan Rose's group demonstrated early and persistent deficits in visual recognition memory as well as cross-modal memory in premature infants (Rose, 1983; Rose, Feldman, McCarton, & Wolfson, 1988). De Haan and colleagues (2000) also described deficits in explicit memory, including ordered recall in 27–34-week preterm children at a mean of 19 months adjusted age. Premature preteen and teenage children also have been shown to have deficits in spatial memory span length and more forgetting errors on a spatial working memory task (Curtis et al., 2002), with some improvements noted with further development in adolescence.

We have studied auditory recognition memory in a group of premature newborns born at less than 32 weeks gestation (Therien et al., 2004). All underwent at least two cranial ultrasounds during the neonatal period and all had normal hearing. ERPs were recorded at 40 weeks postmenstrual age in a counterbalanced paradigm that included an auditory change paradigm as well as the maternal voice recognition paradigm. Compared with healthy term controls, the preterm infants demonstrated several differences in their ERPs. First, although they did show significant differences between the frequent and infrequent speech sounds in the auditory change paradigm, it was in the opposite direction from that seen in the control infants. Whereas control infants showed a positive wave for the infrequent stimulus, the preterm infants showed a negative wave that was similar to a mismatch negativity response. The preterm infants' responses also were more widely distributed over the scalp than the control infants. In the recognition memory paradigm, preterm infants also did not show any differences between the maternal voice and a stranger's voice, even when a familiarization period was provided at the beginning of the maternal voice recognition paradigm. The preterm infants had been discharged to home a mean of 17.5 days prior to the ERP study and also had weeks of postnatal exposure to the maternal voice that should have facilitated recognition providing that their neural substrate was intact and sufficiently mature. Evaluation of the maturity levels for the "P2" peak did not elucidate any significant differences between the control and preterm infants in maturity of the auditory cortex. Maturity levels also did not correlate with the presence of the negative slow wave. Thus, the alterations in auditory discrimination and memory noted in this study did not appear to be a simple function of maturity of the auditory cortex. Although further investigation is clearly required, these findings may be consistent with the memory deficits described in premature children by other authors.

The aforementioned data and the recent data of Fellman, Kushnerenko, Mikkola, Ceponiene, Leipälä, and Näätänen (2004) both indicate that auditory processing in premature children is altered compared with controls. Although the patients described by Vargha-Khadem and colleagues have shown isolated hippocampal atrophy (Vargha-Khadem et al., 2001), preterm infants are more typically at risk for a variety of brain abnormalities including intracranial hemorrhage, ischemic changes in the white matter, and decreased growth of gray matter (Maalouf et al., 1999; Peterson et al., 2000). It is most likely that the differences in auditory processing and recognition memory in preterm infants are due to overlapping problems of widespread brain injury or maldevelopment, and further investigation is required to elucidate both the types of insults that cause difficulties with recognition memory and the complex interactions between auditory processing and discrimination and recognition memory.

Infants of diabetic mothers

It has been known for many years that infants of poorly controlled diabetic mothers have lower scores on standardized tests of cognitive function (Ornoy, Wolf, Ratzon, Greenbaum, & Dulitzky, 1999; Rizzo, Metzger, Dooley, & Cho, 1997). Poorly controlled maternal diabetes is associated with a number of fetal metabolic derangements including fetal hyper- and hypoglycemia, ketonemia, increased oxygen consumption, and chronic fetal hypoxia, as well as iron deficiency (Nold & Georgieff, 2004). Hypoxia and brain iron depletion both may target the hippocampus and other parts of the explicit memory pathway (Jorgenson, Wobken, & Georgieff, 2003; Rao, Tkac, Townsend, Gruetteer, & Georgieff, 2003; deUngria, Rao, Wobken, Luciana, & Georgieff, 2000), potentially resulting in difficulties with memory development in infants of diabetic mothers.

We have studied newborn infants of diabetic mothers (IDMs) using the maternal voice/stranger's voice paradigm described above. In the first study (deRegnier et al., 2000), all infants of diabetic mothers were included, regardless of the degree of control of diabetes during pregnancy. The IDMs showed attenuation of the negative slow wave seen in the control infants (Figure 5.5). Additionally, the area of the negative slow wave was correlated to the 1-year Mental Developmental Index Score on the Bayley Scales of Infant Development in IDMs and control newborns. This study did not assess the role of fetal risk factors, and in a subsequent study (Sidappa et al., 2004), we demonstrated that infants with low brain iron stores showed near obliteration of the negative slow wave and no significant differences between the maternal and stranger ERP (Figure 5.6), whereas IDMs who were brain iron sufficient showed a normal appearance of the ERP. The degree of the brain iron deficiency, as assessed by neonatal ferritin levels, was associated with attenuation of the right temporal (T4) activity on the ERP.

These infants have been studied longitudinally, and showed abnormal

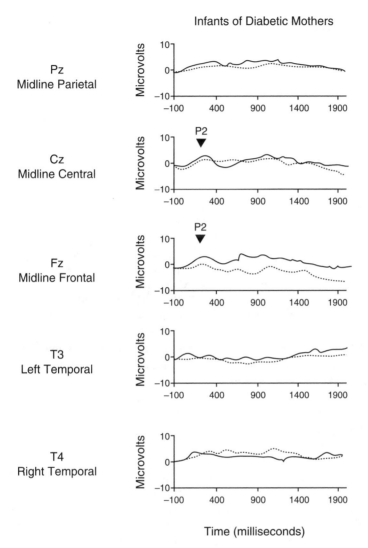

Figure 5.5 Grand mean ERPs for 22 newborn infants of diabetic mothers in response to the maternal (solid line) and stranger's (dotted line) voices. Note attenuation of NSW (negative slow wave) compared with control infants in Figure 5.3. Reprinted with permission from deRegnier et al. (2000).

ERPs for visual recognition memory at 6 months of age and abnormal ERPs for cross-modal memory at 8 months of age (Nelson et al., 2003, 2000). Preliminary reports using elicited imitation paradigms have shown the emergence of behavioral evidence of deficits in delayed recall abilities at 1 year of age (DeBoer, Wewerka, Bauer, Georgieff, & Nelson, 2005). These children are currently in long-term follow-up to determine if they are at significant risk for

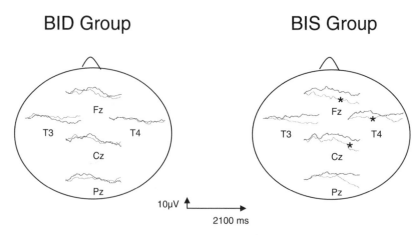

Figure 5.6 Grand mean ERPs for newborn infants of diabetic mothers in response to the maternal (thick line) and stranger's (thin line) voices for the brain iron deficient (BID) and (BIS) groups. Areas of significant difference between maternal and stranger's ERPs are denoted by*. Note near complete obliteration of the negative slow wave in the BID group. Reprinted with permission from Sidappa et al. (2004).

behavioral manifestations of memory deficits, as this is not yet known. These longitudinal data will be helpful in establishing the role of plasticity in recovery from perinatal brain injury.

SUMMARY

In summary, recognition memory is one of the first cognitive functions to develop in the newborn. Auditory recognition memory becomes possible during pregnancy through sufficient maturation of the auditory perception pathways, auditory experiences are provided to the infant in utero, and early histologic and MRI data suggest that the hippocampus is sufficiently developed to begin to encode these auditory experiences by late gestation, if not earlier. ERP and behavioral data suggest that encoding is poor in the newborn, and intensive exposure to a stimulus may be required, such as the weeks of experience with the maternal voice that occur during late gestation.

ERPs have been useful in neonatal evaluation of high-risk newborns. Pre-term infants are known to be at risk for memory deficits, and early ERP evidence suggests that this may be manifested in impairments of auditory recognition memory as early as term postmenstrual age. Infants of poorly controlled diabetic mothers have a well-studied pattern of perinatal brain injury that would theoretically lead to memory impairments. Early ERP studies appear to verify this, showing that early auditory, visual, and cross-modal recognition memory are impaired in these infants, possibly due to deficiencies of hippocampal iron stores that occur as a result of the metabolic derangements.

REFERENCES

Adelman, C., Levi, H., Linder, N., & Sohmer, H. (1990). Neonatal auditory brain-stem response threshold and latency: 1 hour to 5 months. *Electroencephalography and Clinical Neurophysiology, 77*, 77–80.
Ahonniska, J., Cantell, M., Tolvanen, A., & Lyytinen, H. (1993). Speech perception and brain laterality: The effect of ear advantage on auditory event-related potentials. *Brain and Language, 45*, 127–146.
Amin, S. B., Orlando, M. S., Dalzell, L. E., Merle, K. S., & Guillet, R. (1999). Morphological changes in serial auditory brain stem responses in 24–32 weeks' gestational age infants during the first week of life. *Ear and Hearing, 20*, 410–418.
Anderson A. W., Marois, R., Colson, E. R., Peterson, B. S., Duncan, C. C., Ehrenkrantz, R. A. et al. (2001). Neonatal auditory activation detected by functional magnetic resonance imaging. *Magnetic Resonance Imaging, 19*, 1–5.
Broadbent, N. J., Clark, R. E., Zola, S., & Squire, L. R. (2002). The medial temporal lobe and memory. In L. R. Squire & D. L. Schacter (Eds.), *Neuropsychology of memory, third edition* (pp. 3–23). New York: Guilford Press.
Casey, B. J., Davidson, M., & Rosen, B. (2002). Functional magnetic resonance imaging: Basic principles of and application to developmental science. *Developmental Science, 5*, 301–309.
Clark, R. E., Broadbent, N. J., Zola, S. M., & Squire, L. R. (2002). Anterograde amnesia and temporally graded retrograde amnesia for a nonspatial memory task after lesions of hippocampus and subiculum. *Journal of Neuroscience, 22*, 4663–4669.
Counter, S. A. (2002). Fetal and neonatal development of the auditory system. In H. Lagencrantz, M. Hanson, P. Evrard, & C. Rodeck (Eds.), *The newborn brain: Neuroscience and clinical applications* (pp. 226–251). Cambridge, UK: Cambridge University Press.
Curtis, W. J., Lindeke, L. L., Georgieff, M. K., & Nelson, C. A. (2002). Neurobehavioral functioning in neonatal intensive care unit graduates in late childhood and early adolescence. *Brain, 125*, 1646–1659.
Daseleer, S. M., Veltman, D. J., & Witter, M. P. (2004). Common pathway in the medial temporal lobe for storage and recovery of words as revealed by event-related functional MRI. *Hippocampus, 2004*, 163–169.
DeBoer, T., Wewerka, S., Bauer, P. J., Georgieff, M. K., & Nelson, C. A. (2005). Explicit memory performance in infants of diabetic mothers at 1 year of age. *Developmental Medicine and Child Neurology, 47*, 525–531.
DeCasper, A. J., & Fifer, W. P. (1980). Of human bonding: Newborns prefer their mothers' voices. *Science, 208*, 1174–1176.
DeCasper, A. J., & Prescott, P. A. (1984). Human newborns' perception of male voices: Preference, discrimination, and reinforcing value. *Developmental Psychobiology, 17*, 481–491.
DeCasper, A. J., & Spence, M. J. (1986). Prenatal maternal speech influences newborns' perception of speech sounds. *Infant Behavioral and Development, 6*, 19–25.

de Haan, M., Bauer, P. J., Georgieff, M. K., & Nelson, C. A. (2000). Explicit memory in low risk infants aged 19 months born between 27 and 42 weeks of gestation. *Developmental Medicine and Child Neurology, 42*, 304–312.

Dehaene-Lambertz, G., Dehaene, S., & Hertz-Pannier, L., (2002). Functional neuroimaging of speech perception in infants. *Science, 298*, 2013–2015.

deRegnier R. (1993). *Auditory event-related potentials (ERPs) in newborn infants: The effects of stimulus sequence.* Presented at the 1993 meeting of the Society for Research in Child Development.

deRegnier, R. (2002). Mortality and morbidity of the extremely preterm infant. In L. G. Keith & I. Blickstein (Eds.), *Triplet pregnancies and their consequences* (pp. 307–318). Boca Raton, FL: Parthenon Publishing Group.

deRegnier, R. O., Georgieff, M. K., & Nelson, C. A. (1997). Visual event-related brain potentials in 4-month-old infants at risk for neurodevelopmental impairments. *Developmental Psychobiology, 30*, 11–28.

deRegnier, R. A., Nelson, C. A., Thomas, K., Wewerka, S., & Georgieff, M. K. (2000). Neurophysiologic evaluation of auditory recognition memory in healthy newborn infants and infants of diabetic mothers. *Journal of Pediatrics, 137*, 777–784.

deRegnier, R., Wewerka, S., Georgieff, M. K., Mattia, F., & Nelson, C. A. (2002). Influences of post-conceptional age and postnatal experience on the development of auditory recognition memory in the newborn infant. *Developmental Psychobiology, 41*, 216–225.

deUngria, M., Rao, R., Wobken, J. D., Luciana, M., & Georgieff, M. K. (2000). Perinatal iron deficiency decreases cytochrome c oxidase activity in selective regions of the brain. *Pediatric Research, 48*, 169–176.

Dolan, R. J., & Fletcher, P. F. (1999). Encoding and retrieval in human medial temporal lobes: An empirical investigation using functional magnetic imaging (fMRI). *Hippocampus, 9*, 25–34.

Dolan, R. J., & Stranger, B. A. (2002). Hippocampal novelty responses studied with functional neuroimaging. In L. R. Squire & D. L. Schacter (Eds.), *Neuropsychology of memory, third edition* (pp. 204–214). New York: Guilford Press.

Eggermont, J. J. (1988). On the rate of maturation of sensory evoked potentials. *Electroencephalography and Clinical Neurophysiology, 70*, 293–305.

Eldredge, L., & Salamy, A. (1996). Functional auditory development in preterm and full term infants. *Early Human Development, 45*, 215–228.

Ellingson, R. J., Danahy, T., Nelson, B., & Lathrop, G. H. (1974). Variability of auditory evoked potentials in human newborns. *Electroencephalography and Clinical Neurophysiology, 36*, 155–162.

Fagan, J. F. III (1990). The paired-comparison paradigm and infant intelligence. *Annals of the New York Academy of Sciences, 608*, 337–364.

Fellman, V., Kushnerenko, E., Mikkola, K., Ceponiene, R., Leipälä, J., & Näätänen, R. (2004). Atypical auditory event-related potentials in preterm infants during the first year of life: A possible sign of cognitive dysfunction? *Pediatric Research, 56*, 291–297.

Fifer, W. P., & Moon, C. M. (1995). The effects of fetal experience with sound. In J. P. Lecanuet, W. P. Fifer, N. A. Krasnegor, & W. P. Smotherman (Eds.), *Fetal development: A psychobiologic perspective* (pp. 351–356). Hillsdale NJ: Lawrence Erlbaum Associates Inc.

Hepper, P. G., & Shahidullah, B. S. (1994). Development of fetal hearing. *Archives of Diseases in Childhood, 71*, F81–F87.

Hevnar, R. F., & Kinney, H. C. (1996). Reciprocal entorhinal-hippocampal connections established by human fetal mid-gestation. *Journal of Comparative Neurology*, *372*, 384–394.

Hudspeth, A. J. (2000). Hearing. In E. R. Kandel, J. H. Schwartz, & T. M. Jessell (Eds.), *Principles of neural science, fourth edition* (pp. 590–613). New York: McGraw-Hill.

Huttenlocher, P. R., & Dabholkar, A. S. (1997). Regional differences in synaptogenesis in human cerebral cortex. *Journal of Comparative Neurology*, *387*, 167–178.

Hykin, J., Moore, R., Duncan, K., Clare, S., Baker, P., Johnson, C. L. et al. (1999). Fetal brain activity demonstrated by functional magnetic resonance imaging. *The Lancet*, *354*, 645–646.

Isaacs, E. B., Lucas, A., Chong, W. K., Wood, S. J., Johnson, C. L., Marshall, C. et al. (2000). Hippocampal volumes and everyday memory in children of very low birthweight. *Pediatric Research*, *47*, 713–720.

Isaacs, E. B., Vargha-Khadem, F., Watkins, K. E., Lucas, A., Mishkin, M., & Gadian, D. G. (2003). Developmental amnesia and its relationship to degree of hippocampal atrophy. *Proceedings of the Academy of National Sciences of the United States of America*, *100*, 13060–13063.

Jasper, H. H. (1958). The ten–twenty electrode system of the international federation. *Electroencephalography and Clinical Neurophysiology*, *10*, 371–375.

Jorgenson, L. A., Wobken, J. D., & Georgieff, M. K. (2003). Perinatal iron deficiency alters apical dendritic growth in hippocampal CA1 pyramidal neurons. *Developmental Neuroscience*, *25*, 412–420.

Kisilevsky, B. S., Hains, S. M. J., Lee, K., Xie, X., Huang, H., Ye, H. H. et al. (2003). Effects of experience on fetal voice recognition. *Psychological Science*, *14*, 220–224.

Korman, M., & Lewis, C. (2002). *Changes in caregiver speech to prelinguistic infants over time. Is there a significant shift between 6 & 16 weeks?* Poster presented at the meeting of the International Society for Infant Studies.

Kurtzberg, D., Hilpert, P. L., Kreuzer, J. A., & Vaughan, H. G. Jr. (1984). Differential maturation of cortical auditory evoked potentials to speech sounds in normal full term and very low-birthweight infants. *Developmental Medicine and Child Neurology*, *26*, 466–475.

Kushnerenko, E., Ceponiene, R., Balan, P., Fellman, V., Huotilainen, M., & Näätänen, R. (2002). Maturation of the auditory event-related potentials during the first year of life. *NeuroReport*, *13*, 47–51.

Lary, S., Briassoulis, G., de Vries, L., Dubowitz, L. M. S., & Dubowitz, V. (1985). Hearing threshold in preterm and term infants by auditory brainstem response. *Journal of Pediatrics*, *107*, 593–599.

Lecaunet, J.-P., & Schaal, B. (1996). Fetal sensory competencies. *European Journal of Obstetrics and Gynecology*, *68*, 1–23.

Lepage, M., Habib, R., & Tulving, E. (1998). Hippocampal PET activations of memory encoding and retrieval: The HIPER model. *Hippocampus*, *8*, 313–322.

Maalouf, E. F., Duggan, P. J., Rutherford, M. A., Counsell, S. J., Fletcher, A. M., Battin, M. et al. (1999). Magnetic resonance imaging of the brain in a cohort of extremely preterm infants. *Journal of Pediatrics*, *135*, 351–357.

Maneru, C., Serra-Grabulosa, J. M., Junque, C., Salgado-Pineda, P., Bargallo, N., Olondo, M. et al. (2003). Residual hippocampal atrophy in asphyxiated term neonates. *Journal of Neuroimaging*, *13*, 68–74.

Mattia, F. R., & deRegnier, R. A. O. (1998). Chronic physiologic instability is associated with neurodevelopmental morbidity at one and two years in extremely premature infants. *Pediatrics Electronic Pages, 102*, e35.

Nelson, C. A. (1994). Neural correlates of recognition memory in the first postnatal year of life. In G. Dawson & K. Fischer (Eds.), *Human behavior and the developing brain* (pp. 269–313). New York: Guilford Press.

Nelson, C. A. (1995). The ontogeny of human memory: A cognitive neuroscience perspective. *Developmental Psychology, 31*, 723–738.

Nelson, C. A. (2002). Neural development and life-long plasticity. In R. M. Lerner, F. Jacobs, & D. Wetlieb (Eds.), *Promoting positive child, adolescent, and family development: Handbook of program and policy interventions* (pp. 31–60). Thousand Oaks, CA: Sage Publications.

Nelson, C. A., & Collins, P. F. (1991). An event-related potential and looking time analysis of infants' responses to familiar and novel events: Implications for visual recognition memory. *Developmental Psychology, 27*, 50–58.

Nelson, C. A., & deRegnier, R. (1992). Neural correlates of attention and memory in the first year of life. *Developmental Neuropsychology, 8*, 119–134.

Nelson, C. A., Wewerka, S. S., Borscheid, A. J., deRegnier, R., & Georgieff, M. K. (2003). Electrophysiologic evidence of impaired cross-modal recognition memory in 8-month-old infants of diabetic mothers. *Journal of Pediatrics, 142*, 575–582.

Nelson, C. A., Wewerka, S., Thomas, K. M., Tribby-Walbridge, S., deRegnier, R., & Georgieff, M. K. (2000). Neurocognitive sequelae of infants of diabetic mothers. *Behavioral Neuroscience, 114*, 950–956.

Nold, J., & Georgieff, M. (2004). Infants of diabetic mothers. *Pediatric Clinics of North America, 51*, 619–637.

Novak, G. P., Kurtzberg, D., Kreuzer, J. A., & Vaughan, H. G. Jr. (1989). Cortical responses to speech sounds and their formants in normal infants: Maturational sequence and spatiotemporal analysis. *Electroencphalography and Clinical Neurophysiology, 73*, 295–305.

Nyakas, C., Buwalda, B., & Luidten, P. G. (1996). Hypoxia and brain development. *Progress in Neurobiology, 49*, 1–51.

Ornoy, A., Wolf, A., Ratzon, C., Greenbaum, C. & Dulitzky, M. (1999). Neurodevelopmental outcome at early school age of children born to mothers with gestational diabetes. *Archives of Diseases in Childhood Fetal and Neonatal Edition, 81*, F10–14.

Peterson, B. S., Vohr, B., Staib, L. H., Cannistraci, C. J., Dolberg, A., Schnieder, K. C. et al. (2000). Regional brain volume abnormalities and long-term cognitive outcome in preterm infants. *JAMA, 284*, 1939–1947.

Querleu, D., Lefebvre, C., Titran, M., Renard, X., Morillion, M., & Crepin, G. (1984). Reaction of the newborn infant less than 2 hours after birth to the maternal voice. *Journal de gynécologie, obstetrique et biologie de la reproduction* (Paris), *13*, 125–134.

Querleu, D., Renard, X., Versyp, F., Paris-Delrue, L., & Vervoort, P. (1988). Intra-amniotic transmission of the human voice. *Revue française de gynécologie et d'obstetrique, 83*, 43–50.

Rao, R., Tkac, I., Townsend, E. L., Gruetteer, R., & Georgieff, M. K. (2003). Perinatal iron deficiency alters the neurochemical profile of the developing rat hippocampus. *Journal of Nutrition, 133*, 3215–3221.

Reed, J. M., & Squire, L. R. (1997). Impaired recognition memory in patients with lesions limited to the hippocampal formation. *Behavioral Neuroscience, 111*, 667–675.

Rizzo, T. A., Metzger, B. E., Dooley, S. L., & Cho, N. H. (1997). Early malnutrition and child neurobehavioral development: Insights from the study of children of diabetic mothers. *Child Development, 68,* 26–38.

Rose, S. A. (1983). Differential rates of visual information processing in full-term and preterm infants. *Child Development, 54,* 1189–1198.

Rose, S. A., Feldman, J. F., & Jankowski, J. J. (2001). Attention and recognition memory in the 1st year of life: A longitudinal study of preterm and full-term infants. *Developmental Psychology, 37,* 135–151.

Rose, S. A., Feldman, J. F., & Jankowski, J. J. (2002). Processing speed in the 1st year of life: A longitudinal study of preterm and full-term infants. *Developmental Psychology, 38,* 895–902.

Rose, S. A., Feldman, J. F., McCarton, C. M., & Wolfson, J. (1988). Information processing in seven-month-old infants as a function of risk status. *Child Development, 59,* 589–603.

Salamy, A., & McKean, C. M. (1976). Postnatal development of human brainstem potentials during the first year of life. *Electroencephalograpy and Clinical Neurophysiology, 40,* 418–426.

Seress, L. (2001). Morphological changes of the human hippocampal formation from midgestation to early childhood. In C. A. Nelson & M. Luciana (Eds.), *Handbook of developmental cognitive neuroscience* (pp. 45–58). Cambridge, MA: MIT Press.

Shah, N. J., Marshall, J. C., Zafiris, O., Schwab, A., Zilles, K., Markowitsch, H. J. et al. (2001). The neural correlates of person familiarity: A functional magnetic resonance imaging study with clinical implications. *Brain, 124,* 804–815.

Sidappa, A., Georgieff, M. K., Wewerka, S., Worwa, C., Nelson, C. A., & deRegnier, R. (2004). Iron deficiency alters auditory recognition memory in newborn infants of diabetic mothers. *Pediatric Research, 55,* 1034–1041.

Squire, L. R., Schmolck, H., & Stark, S. M. (2001). Impaired auditory recognition memory in amnesic patients with medial temporal lobe lesions. *Learning and Memory, 8,* 252–256.

Starr, A., Amlie, R. N., Martin, W. H., & Sanders, S. (1977). Development of auditory function in newborn infants revealed by auditory brainstem potentials. *Pediatrics, 60,* 831–839.

Suzuki, W. A., & Amaral, D. G. (1994). Perirhinal and parahippocampal cortices of the Macaque monkey: Cortical afferents. *Journal of Comparative Neurology, 350,* 497–533.

Therien, J. M., Worwa, C. T., Mattia, F. R., & deRegnier, R. O. (2004). Altered pathways for auditory discrimination and recognition memory in premature newborns. *Developmental Medicine and Child Neurology, 46,* 816–824.

Thoman, E. B. (1990). Sleeping and waking states in infants: A functional perspective. *Neuroscience and Biobehavioral Reviews, 14,* 93–107.

Utsunomiya, H., Takano, K., Okazaki, M., & Mitsudome, A. (1999). Development of the temporal lobe in infants and children: Analysis by MR-based volumetry. *American Journal of Neuroradiology, 20,* 717–723.

Vargha-Khadem, F., Gadian, D. G., & Mishkin, M. (2001). Dissociations in cognitive memory: The syndrome of developmental amnesia. *Philosophical Transactions of the Royal Society of London, Series B, Biological Sciences, 356,* 1435–1440.

Vargha-Khadem, F., Salmond, C. H., Watkins, K. E., Friston, K. J., Gadian, D. G., & Mishkin, M. (2003). Developmental amnesia: Effect of age at injury. *Proceedings of the National Academy of Sciences, 100,* 10055–10060.

Volpe, J. J. (2001). *Neurology of the newborn, fourth edition* (p. 109). Philadelphia: W. B. Saunders Company.

Weitzman, E. D., & Graziani, L. J. (1968). Maturation and topography of the auditory evoked response of the prematurely born infant. *Developmental Psychobiology, 1,* 79–89.

6 Development of mismatch negativity (MMN) during infancy

Marie Cheour
University of Miami, USA

Mismatch negativity (MMN) is an electrophysiological manifestation of pre-attentive processing in response to oddball stimuli (Kraus & Näätänen, 1995; Näätänen & Escera, 2000). Although MMN has been extensively studied through the use of auditory stimuli, there are some reports suggesting that it can be elicited in other modalities (e.g., Alho, Woods, Algazi, & Näätänen, 1992; Kekoni, Hämäläinen, McCloud, Reinikainen, & Näätänen, 1996; Krauel, Schott, Sojka, Pause, & Ferstl, 1999; Shinozaki, Yabe, Sutoh, Hiruma, & Kaneko, 1998; Tales, Newton, Troscianko, & Butler, 1999; Woods, Alho, & Algazi, 1992; for a review, see Näätänen & Alho, 1995; for animal studies see Astikainen, Ruusuvirta, & Korhonen, 2000). MMN is usually elicited using an oddball paradigm, whereby different types of occasional changes (in an otherwise recurrent stimulus sequence) are presented outside the focus of attention, and is regarded as an automatic change-detection response (Näätänen, Gaillard, & Mäntysalo, 1978). In a typical MMN odd-ball paradigm, a "deviant" auditory stimulus is sporadically distributed within a sequence of "standard" auditory stimuli. The MMN is evident in the difference waveform obtained by subtracting the ERP elicited by the standard stimulus from that evoked by the deviant stimulus. The difference-waveform in adults is characterized by a negative-going component with a typical latency peaking between 100 and 250 ms from the onset of the deviant stimulus, and with an amplitude that depends on the magnitude of the deviance. MMN has been demonstrated by manipulating basic physical features of pure and harmonic tones, e.g., frequency, intensity, duration, inter-stimulus interval (ISI), and location (for a review, see Näätänen, 1992), as well as by more complex dimensions such as phonetic information, temporal order, or an abstract relation between pairs of tones (for a review, see Kraus & Cheour, 2000; Näätänen & Tiitinen, 1998; Näätänen & Winkler, 1999). Although other theoretical explanations exist (e.g., Winkler, Karmos, & Näätänen, 1996), MMN is generally viewed as an outcome of an alleged mechanism that compares current auditory input to memory traces formed by previous auditory inputs and signals at an incongruent occurrence (Cowan, Winkler, Teder, & Näätänen, 1993; Näätänen, 1990, 1992; Ritter, Deacon, Gomes, Javitt, & Vaughan, 1995).

The cognitive mechanisms associated with MMN are thought to be pre-attentive, and they are not thought to draw on attentional resources (e.g., Näätänen, 1992; Näätänen, Paavilainen, Tiitinen, Jiang, & Alho, 1993). In fact, in its conventional form, MMN is elicited when a subject is instructed to disregard the auditory stimuli while engaging in another task. A subject may be reading a book, watching a silent movie, or engrossed in a cognitively demanding non-auditory task (e.g., Alho et al., 1992; Lyytinen, Blomberg, & Näätänen, 1992). Recent studies have carried MMN from the laboratory environment into more ecological settings (e.g., Winkler, 2000). These studies feature ambient noise (e.g., Winkler, 2000) and soundtrack movies (e.g., Kraus, McGee, Carrell, Zecker, Nicol, & Koch, 1996), and report that MMN is successfully educed even when background sound is present concomitantly with the auditory stimuli.

MMN responses have also been elicited in laboratory animals (e.g., Csépe, Karmos, & Molnár, 1987; King, McGee, Rubel, Nicol, & Kraus, 1995; Ruusuvirta, Penttonen, & Korhonen, 1998) and comatosed human patients (e.g., Fischer & Luaute, 2005; Fischer, Morlet, & Giard, 2000; Kane et al., 1996). The bulk of these studies support the automatic, bottom-up nature of MMN, and is consistent with the hypothesis that attention is not needed to invoke MMN response. Indeed, MMN is commonly regarded as an index for a pre-attentive mechanism, and not just a non-attentive mechanism, because the detection of the mismatch appears to trigger an involuntary shift of attention (Alho, Escera, Diaz, Yago, & Serra, 1997; Escera, Alho, Winkler, & Näätänen, 1998; Näätänen, 1990, 1992; Novak, Ritter, & Vaughan, 1992; Schröger, 1996; Schröger & Wolff, 1998; see, however, Woldorff, Hackley, & Hillyard, 1991). Thus, MMN is a passively elicited and involuntary response reflecting the detection of a change when deviant stimuli are incorporated intermittently into a stream of standards. This naturally makes MMN an especially promising tool for studying pediatric populations that are not always willing or able to pay attention to the auditory stimuli presented to them.

MMN IN ADULTS AND CHILDREN

It is not always easy to compare pediatric and adult ERPs because they generally change throughout development. The ERP waveform complexity may increase with maturation and new constituents may emerge while other components may fade, or disappear completely. In general ERP latencies tend to be short, and amplitudes are apt to increase over the course of development (Thomas & Crow, 1994). Although the neurobiological bases for these maturational changes in ERPs are poorly understood, it has been proposed that these alterations result from an increase in neural signal conduction due to myelination (Eggermont, 1988, 1992), and especially an increase from a synaptic density in the auditory cortex (Eggermont, 1988; Huttenlocher, 1979; Huttenlocher, De Courten, Garey, & van der Loos, 1982).

MMN goes through many developmental changes as well. In contrast to many other ERP components (e.g., Anderer, Semlitsch, & Saletu, 1997), MMN can be obtained very early in infancy (Cheour, Alho, Saino, Reinikainen, Renlund, & Aaltonen, 1997a; Kurtzberg, Vaughan, Kreuzer, & Flieger, 1995; Leppänen, Eklund, & Lyytinen, 1997), and is observable in preterm infants (Cheour-Luhtanen et al., 1996), and even in fetuses (Draganova, Eswaran, Murphy, Huotilainen, Lowery, & Preissl, 2005; Huotilainen et al., 2003).

There are many differences between adult and infant MMN responses, however. One difference can be seen in MMN scalp distributions (Gomot, Giard, Roux, Barthelemy, & Bruneau, 2000; Martin, Shafer, Morr, Kreuzer, & Kurtzberg, 2003). In adults MMN is a fronto-centrally dominant response (e.g., Alho, 1995), whereas in infants MMN often displays a broader scalp distribution (Cheour et al., 1997a, 1998a; Cheour-Luhtanen et al., 1995, 1996; Jing & Benasich, 2006: cf. Leppänen et al., 1997). The reason for these distribution dissimilarities may emanate from the physical distance between brain areas and differences in skull thickness, as well as bone conductance among these age groups. It is also possible that the infant brain is not as specialized as the adult brain, and due to this, information is processed in a larger area.

Sleep and fatigue foster yet another difference between pediatric and adult MMNs. Whereas numerous studies demonstrate that a discernible MMN is obtainable from young infants throughout all sleep states as well as wakefulness (Cheour et al., 2002; Cheour-Luhtanen et al., 1995; Hirasawa, Kurihara, & Konishi, 2002; Martynova, Kirjavainen, & Cheour, 2003), in adults MMN tends to decline during drowsiness and before falling asleep (e.g., Doran, 1999; Nakagome et al., 1998; Raz, 1999; Sallinen & Lyytinen, 1997; Winter, Kok, Kenemans, & Elton, 1995) as a result of prolonged wakefulness, total sleep deprivation (Raz, 1999), and when exposed to anesthetic gas (Pang & Fowler, 1999). Although some earlier studies suggest that MMN response disappears completely when adults are asleep (e.g., Paavilainen, Cammann, Alho, Reinikainen, Sams, & Näätänen, 1987), more recent work has reported that MMN can be elicited during adult REM (Atienza, 2000; Atienza, Cantero, & Comez, 1997; Doran, 1999). However, data from investigations of NREM sleep have been inconsistent (for stage-2 sleep, see Campbell, Bell, & Bastien, 1991; Sallinen, Kaartinen, & Lyytinen, 1994). Thus, whether or not MMN persists into all adult sleep stages is still contestable (cf. Doran 1999; Loewy, Campbell, & Bastien, 1996; Näätänen & Lyytinen, 1996; Sallinen et al., 1994, 1996, 1997). MMN studies of sleep and fatigue in intermediate ages (i.e., gradually ranging from infants to mature adults and the elderly) have yet to be performed.

Sleep literature (e.g., Acebo et al., 1999; Sadeh, Raviv, & Gruber, 2000; cf. Gruber, Sadeh, & Raviv, 2000), as well as MMN studies (e.g., Cheour, Leppänen, & Kraus, 2000; Näätänen & Lyytinen, 1996), acknowledge the different role that sleep assumes in adult and pediatric groups. Infants spend far more time than adults in REM sleep, and these REM periods differ from their adult forms. It has been suggested that the relatively disproportionate amount of time infants spend sleeping, particularly the period of REM sleep, is essential for the maturation of the central nervous system (Sheldon, 1996).

The midbrain may be viewed as a railway station through which innumerable neural circuits from different parts of the brain and body travel en route to other areas. The adult midbrain is capable of switching these connections on and off. The more thalamo-cortical and cortico-cortical circuits the midbrain disconnects, the less conscious we become, and vice versa. While awake, adult neural circuitry is largely switched on. However, during sleep, the midbrain halts connections from the cortex to the rest of the body leaving the other cortical circuitry active (Sheldon, 1996). The sleeping infant thalamus, however, is incapable of efficiently inhibiting information before the second or third month of life. Therefore it is reasonable to expect MMNs to be elicited in different states of infant sleep as well as during wakefulness, whereas in adults, probably due to a different function that sleep subserves, subcortical control dampens the cortical activation. Recent MMN study even shows that neonates are able to learn to discriminate speech sounds while sleeping (Cheour et al., 2002; see Figure 6.1).

On the other hand, both infants and young children possess higher auditory awakening threshold (AAT) when asleep, and a louder acoustic signal is required to awaken them (e.g., Busby, Mercier, & Pivik, 1994; Nozza, 1995; cf. Franco, Pardou, Hassid, Lurquin, Groswasser, & Kahn, 1998). Also, infant motor behavior during REM is not as inhibited as in older children and adults (e.g., Vaal, van Soest, & Hopkins, 2000). Although infant elevated AAT and lack of REM atonia may be correlated, and thus provide means to theorize about both infant sleep and developmental MMN, no substantial work has attempted to piece these matters into a cohesive whole to date.

Numerous studies have reported that MMN is stable over a developmental timeline in terms of latency (Csépe, 1995; Kraus, McGee, Carrell, Sharma, Micco, & Nicol, 1993a; Kraus, McGee, Sharma, Carrell, & Nicol, 1992). MMN latency tends to be slightly longer in infants and young children than in adults (Cheour et al., 1997a, 1998a, 1998b; Cheour-Luhtanen et al., 1996; Kurtzberg et al., 1995). In contrast, the MMN amplitude is more susceptible to developmental changes. In fact, it has been shown in many studies that besides traditional negative MMN response peaking between 100 and 300 ms (Cheour et al., 1997a, 1998a, 1998b; Hirasawa et al., 2002; Kushnerenko et al., 2001, 2002; Martynova et al., 2003; Weber, Hahne, Friedrich, & Friederici, 2004), a positive discriminative response peaking between 300 and 400 ms can also be obtained from young infants (Dehaene-Lambertz & Dehaene, 1994; Friederici, Friedrich, & Weber, 2002; Jing & Benasich, 2006; Leppänen, Guttorm, Pihko, Takkinen, Eklund, & Lyytinen, 2006; Morr, Shafer, Kreuzer, & Kurtzberg, 2002; Pihko, Leppänen, Eklund, Cheour, Guttorm, & Lyytinen,

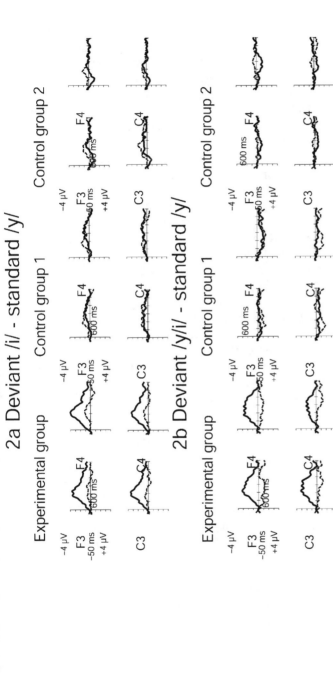

2a Deviant /i/ - standard /y/

Experimental group Control group 1 Control group 2

2b Deviant /y/i/ - standard /y/

Experimental group Control group 1 Control group 2

----- Session 1   ——— Session 2

Figure 6.1 The MMN (grand-averaged "deviant minus standard" difference waveforms) educed by the first and second MMN recording sessions. The significant difference between the pre- and post-training sessions suggests that following auditory exposure, sleeping newborns are better able to discriminate the speech sounds /y/ and /i/ (2a) as well as /y/ and /y/i/ (2b). On the other hand, MMN responses obtained from a control group exposed to no "training" and a control group trained to discriminate other speech sounds reveal an insignificant difference between the two sessions. (Figure adapted from Cheour et al., 2002.)

1999). It seems that both negative and positive responses are fairly commonly observed in infants since very few studies have reported that only negative or positive response has been obtained from all subjects. Some scientists have suggested that this early discriminative response is negative only in young infants such as pre-terms and neonates and it later becomes positive (Leppanen et al., 2004; Vaughan & Kurtzberg, 1991), but there are many studies that have shown negative discriminitive responses in older infants (Cheour et al., 1998b; Trainor, Samuel, Desjardins, & Sonnadara, 2001; Weber et al., 2004). It has also been suggested that the early positive discriminative response could arise from an obligatory nonrefractory response to a new stimulus, or possibly represent an infant response analogous to P3a (Ceponiene, Kushnerenko, Fellman, Renlund, Suominen, & Näätänen, 2002; Kushnerenko et al., 2002). Although some studies show that this response cannot be found in young infants, some authors have also stated that MMN could be masked by preponderant slow wave activity in infants (Morr et al., 2002).

It is very challenging to compare the results of different infant oddball studies because the paradigms vary so much between studies. For example, filtering has differed greatly in these studies and it is very likely to affect the results significantly. It seems that in many studies that have reported positivities there has been no high pass filtering, or the filtering has been approximately 0.5 or less (Dehaene-Lambertz & Dehaene, 1994; Dehaene-Lambertz, Dupoux, & Gout, 2000; Guttorm, Leppanen, Tolvanen, & Lyytinen, 2003; Leppänen et al., 1997, 2006; Pihko et al., 1999; Weber et al., 2004). On the other hand, in many studies that have reported negativities, the filtering has been at least 0.5 and typically more (Ceponiene et al., 2002; Cheour et al., 1997a, 1998a, 1998b; Kushnerenko et al., 2002, Martynova et al., 2003; Weber et al., 2004). Infant EEGs contain considerable amounts of slow wave activity during all sleep and awake states. Therefore it is possible that this slow wave activity could be related to the positive discriminative responses.

It is also possible that instead of having one single response that changes in polarity as children mature, for example, infants could have two discriminative responses that reflect different functions. It is clear that more longitudinal studies are needed in order to fully solve this puzzle. It would also be beneficial to see different filterings reported in a single study in order to see how much they affect the results (as an example see Weber et al., 2004).

Even when it comes to the negative discriminative response, it is still not fully understood whether the early-life MMN is indeed isomorphic to the adult MMN. More specifically, not enough is known about the possible differences in the locus and orientation of the MMN generators. Also, since it has been suggested that there is less specificity and more redundancy in the connections between different cortical areas in infancy (e.g., Neville, 1995), the pediatric MMN may reflect the activity of much larger parts of the brain, compared to that of the adult MMN.

SPEECH-PROCESSING MMN STUDIES IN HEALTHY
INFANTS AND CHILDREN

During recent years, one of the most active areas of infant and adult MMN study has been the investigation of plastic changes associated with learning of a language. Studies have demonstrated that training, or the experience of a certain language environment, can change the MMN amplitude, latency, or duration (Kraus, McGee, Carrell, King, Tremblay, & Nicol, 1995b; Näätänen et al., 1997; Winkler et al., 1999). Importantly, behavioral studies yielded results consistent with those of MMN studies. Many studies show that the MMN amplitude reflects a categorical effect in discriminating phonemes (Cheour et al., 1998b; Dehaene-Lambertz & Baillet, 1998; Maiste, Wiens, Hunt, Scherg, & Picton, 1995; Näätänen et al., 1997; Winkler et al., 1999). These studies also show that the MMN amplitude is larger for a speech sound that served as a prototype in one's native language than for non-native speech sounds. This is so even when the acoustical difference from the standard stimulus was larger for the non-native deviant than for the native deviant. Interestingly, it has been shown that the MMN amplitude parallels the perceptual magnetic effect (see Kuhl, 1993; Kuhl et al., 1991; see, however, Sharma & Dorman, 1998; Sharma et al., 1993).

Dehaene-Lambertz and Baillet (1998) were among the first to study the existence of language-specific memory traces in infants by employing ERPs. These authors presented four synthesized syllables to infants. One of these served as a standard and the others as deviants. Two of these were perceived by French and English adults as belonging to the same phoneme category and one to a different category. Interestingly, although the acoustical change was of similar magnitude for the two deviants, the MMN response was larger for a phonological change than an acoustic change. Thus, at the age of 3 months, French infants displayed phonological processing devices analogous to those found in adults. This study can be regarded as providing evidence for the existence of language-specific memory traces in infants.

Furthermore, Cheour et al. (1998b) demonstrated in Finnish and Estonian infants how the language-specific memory traces develop. These two languages were chosen because they are closely related to each other and have very similar vowel structures. In this study, all the stimuli were vowel prototypes in both languages, except for one that was a prototype only in the Estonian language. It was found that at the age of 6 months, the MMN amplitude in Finnish infants reflected only the acoustical difference between the deviant and standard stimuli, being larger for the Estonian than Finnish prototype. However, by 1 year of age, the MMN was attenuated in Finnish infants in response to the Estonian vowel, i.e., Finnish non-prototype, relative to the MMN elicited by the Finnish vowel. In contrast, Estonian 1-year-olds showed almost equally large MMNs to both vowels, both of which are Estonian prototypes. Importantly, these results also showed that the MMN amplitude for Finnish vowels increased in Finnish infants between 6 months and 1 year of age. Thus by 1 year, not only has a child's ability to perceive non-native vowels diminished, but the perception of native vowels has also improved.

The results of these two studies seem to yield somewhat different time estimates for the emergence of language-specific memory traces. The results of Dehaene-Lambertz and Baillet (1998) suggest that they are developed by the age of 3 months, whereas the study by Cheour et al. (1998b) suggests that they are developed by the age of 12 months. Recently Rivera-Gaxiola, Lara-Ayala, Cadena, and Kuhl (2004) showed that these language-specific memory traces had developed in 11-month-old American infants for American–English contrasts but not in Mexican infants for Spanish contrasts. Also, previous studies using behavioral methods have yielded very different estimates with regard to the age by which the child's language environment has affected the way they perceive native and non-native speech. For example, the results of Kuhl, Williams, Lacerda, Stevens, and Lindblom (1992) suggest that this happens by the age of 6 months, whereas according to Werker and Tees (1984), and Polka and Werker (1994), this happens by the age of 9–10 months. It seems that the results of these kinds of experiments depend on, for example, the child's language environment, the nature of the stimuli used (synthesized or natural, vowels or consonants), and on whether the child is brought up in a monolingual or bilingual environment.

Recently, Csépe, Honbolygó, Ragó, Róna, and Beke (2004) as well as Weber et al. (2004, 2005) have shown that not only the way we discriminate phonemes, but also the way we perceive stress patterns of our native and non-native languages, changes during the first year of life. Csépe et al. (2004) employed the oddball paradigm to investigate sub- and suprasegmental speech contrasts in adults and in infants. Voice onset time (VOT) and stress pattern changes of bisyllabic Hungarian words were used in a passive oddball paradigm. Csépe and colleagues showed that the MMN latency was time-locked both to the stressed and the unstressed syllables. Notably, the MMN had larger amplitude when the second syllable changed from unstressed to stressed. This is interesting because in Hungarian it is the first syllable that is always stressed. Both types of the MMN could be recorded in all 3- to 10-month-old infants, including pre-term infants, except those with low birth weight. Thus, very young infants have already learned the typical stressed patterns of their language environment.

According to Weber et al. (2004), at least in German infants the language environment begins to affect the way infants perceive stressed patterns somewhat later. Weber et al. recorded ERPs to varying stress patterns of two-syllable items in adults as well as in 4- and 5-month-old infants using the oddball paradigm. Adults displayed MMN to the stress on the first syllable as well as to the stress on the second syllable item. At the age of 4 months no reliable discrimination response was seen. However, at the age of 5 months a significant MMN was observed, but only when the stress was on the first syllable, the most common stress pattern in German.

MMN STUDIES IN CLINICAL PEDIATRIC POPULATIONS

Although some preliminary attempts are currently under way, MMN has not been used as a diagnostic or prognostic tool in clinical practice to date. Nonetheless, MMN has been extensively harnessed to investigate numerous clinical populations. Most of these studies have been conducted in adults (for a review, see Morlet, Bouchet, & Fischer, 2000; Näätänen & Escera, 2000), and include psychiatric patients (in particular, people with schizophrenia) along with patients suffering from depression and obsessive-compulsive disorder. Normal and abnormal geriatric groups, Parkinsonian patients, as well as populations with brain injury, such as cerebral lesions, unilateral lesions of the dorsolateral frontal cortex, closed head injuries, unilateral neglect, and aphasia, have also been investigated. Furthermore, MMN has been studied in alcoholics, in subjects under the influence of various drugs, and in comatose patients, cochlear-implant users, HIV carriers, and blind subjects. Although recent work (Csépe & Molnar, 1997; Näätänen & Escera, 2000) grappled with the general relevance of MMN to clinical applications, emphasis to date has been primarily given to adult studies. Only a few reviews have particularly focused on MMN in a clinical pediatric setting (Csépe, 1995; Kurtzberg et al., 1995; Lang, Eerola, Korpilahti, Holopainen, Salo, & Aaltonen, 1995; Leppänen & Lyytinen, 1997).

The study of MMN in children with attentional difficulties is an emerging trend. Although these populations have been increasingly acknowledged in recent research, too few imaging studies have investigated the underlying brain bases of such disorders as autism (e.g., Chiron et al., 1995; Filipek, 1995; Ring et al., 1999), Attention Deficit Hyperactivity Disorder (ADHD) (e.g., Casey et al., 1997; Giedd et al., 1994; Rubia, Taylor, Taylor, & Sergeant, 1999; Vaidya et al., 1998), and dyslexia (e.g., Rumsey, Nace, Donohue, Wise, Maisog, & Andreason, 1997; Semelin, Service, Kiesila, Uutela, & Salonen, 1996; Shaywitz, Shaywitz, Pugh, & Skudlarski, 1996; Simos et al., 2000a, 2000b; Tuchman, 1999). MMN data comparing such groups to normal sets are also scarce (e.g., Kemner, Verbaten, Cuperus, Camfferman, & van Engeland, 1995). Although earlier work suggests that autistic children show aberrant ERP components (e.g., Lincoln, Courchesne, Harms, & Allen, 1993; Oades et al., 1988), attempts to replicate these results have not always been successful. Autistic children offer an interesting group because ERP studies in this population have been so contradictory. Some studies suggest that the MMN and N1 amplitudes are larger in this population than in healthy controls (Ferri, Elia, Agarwal, Lanuzza, & Musumeci, 2003), whereas other studies say that autistic children show normal MMN and N1 amplitudes (Ceponiene et al., 2003). There are also other ERPs such as the P3 component that have been reported to be either larger (Ceponiene et al., 2003) or smaller (Novick, Kurtzberg, & Vaughan, 1979) in autistic children than in healthy controls (e.g., Kemner et al., 1995). It has also been reported (Gomot, Giard, Adrien, Barthelemy, & Bruneau, 2002) that the

MMN latency is shortened in autistic children as compared to healthy controls.

ADHD is the most prevalent psychiatric disorder of childhood in the United States. Inconsistent diagnostic criteria used in Europe (see "hyperkinetic disorder" [HKD] in the International Classification of Diseases [ICD], 1992, 1993) and North America (see the Diagnostic and Statistical Manual [DSM-IV], 1994) have obscured precise classification of the disorder, and the situation has been recently remedied (Swanson, 1997; Swanson et al., 1998a, 1998b). In a pivotal longitudinal study comparing ADHD and control boys, Satterfield, Schell, Nicholas, Satterfield, and Frees (1990) reported developmental abnormalities in ERPs associated with selective attention. More recently, general, reduced-amplitude MMN has been reported in distractible children, particularly as part of its later, frontally mediated component (e.g., Kilpeläinen et al., 1999). Currently an estimated 2–5% of school-age children are suffering from the disorder, which is known to have a familial basis. Whereas most MMN studies of ADHD children found small P3 peaks in response to targets, Kemner et al. (1996) showed that the MMN obtained in response to changes in speech stimuli was significantly smaller in amplitude in ADHD children than in healthy controls. Winsberg, Javitt, Silipo, and Doneshka (1993) examined MMN in ADHD children who were clinical responders to methylphenidate (MP) therapy. Their initial data suggest that in addition to MP significantly decreasing hyperkinetic behavior, information-processing abnormalities may also be sensitive to MP treatment. Although in their later study Winsberg, Javitt, and Silipo (1997) did not find significant MMN differences between experimental conditions, this may have resulted from an insufficient sample size (six ADHD and five control; see below). Nonetheless, an enhanced P3 in MP-treated hyperactive children, as compared to placebo administration, was discernible. This augmented P3 was comparable to that obtained in a normal control group. These findings, in addition to further irregularities in P3, suggest that MP has an influence on attentional processes. Jonkman et al. (2000) recently reported similar findings, and specifically they found that MP had ameliorating effects on performance and ERPs, but not on capacity allocation. Thus, the bulk of the evidence suggests that ADHD children display some anomalous ERP components as well as irregular MMNs.

Research associating the neurotransmitter dopamine with normal attention (e.g., Posner & Raichle, 1994) as well as with abnormal attention (e.g., Barkley, 1998; Cook et al., 1995) has recently been extended to ADHD (e.g., LaHoste et al., 1996; Paterson, Sunohara, & Kennedy, 1999; Swanson et al., 2000). These assays may illuminate some MMN trends among dopamine-related disorders. For example, comparing ADHD and Tourette syndrome children with a normal group, Oades, Dittmann-Balcar, Schepker, Eggers, and Zerbin (1996) found that shorter MMN latencies were evident in ADHD as early as 100 ms accompanied with an anteriorly shifted enhanced P2. These results were complemented by data suggesting that ADHD children exhibit irregular laterality for both MMN and P3. Oades et al. (1996) interpreted the results as being congruent with difficulties in sustained attention that both ADHD and Tourette patients are known to possess.

Recently, MMN has been employed to investigate many pediatric psychiatric populations such as children who are socially withdrawn (Bar-Haim, Marshall, Fox, Schorr, & Gordon-Salant, 2003) or depressed (Lepisto, Soininen, Ceponiene, Almqvist, Näätänen, & Aronen, 2004). According to these studies, socially withdrawn children had attenuated MMN amplitude whereas depressed children showed shorter MMN latency, but no difference in the MMN amplitude as compared with the healthy controls.

Although it has been reported that cancer survivors commonly display late cognitive effects (Meister & Meadows, 1993), Lähteenmäki et al. (Lähteenmaki, Holopainen, Krause, Helenius, Salmi, & Heikki, 2001; Lähteenmäki, Krause, Salmi, & Lang, in press) found that MMNs of equal amplitude and area were obtained from healthy teenagers as compared to survivors of childhood leukemia and solid tumors. Interestingly, a significant difference between the study and control groups was detected in the P3 latency.

Adult data suggest that MMN may provide objective information about the cochlear-implant (CI) function (Kraus et al., 1993b; Ponton & Don, 1995; Ponton, Eggermont, Don, & Kwong, 2000a; Ponton, Eggermont, Don, Waring, Kwong, & Cunningham, 2000b). About 0.3% of children younger than 5 years of age suffer profound deafness induced by the impairment of hair cell function (Blanchfield, Dunbar, Feldman, & Gardner, 1999; Reis, 1991). Although CIs affect the rehabilitation of individuals who fail to benefit from conventional hearing aids, rising health care costs have discouraged the use of CI technology (e.g., Steiner, Powe, Anderson, & Das, 1996). However, a recent cost-utility analysis of CIs in children (Cheng, Rubin, Powe, Mellon, Francis, & Niparko, 2000; cf. Summerfield & Marshall, 1995; Summerfield, Marshall, & Archbold, 1997; O'Neill, O'Donoghue, Archbold, & Normand, 2000) reports that in profoundly deaf children CIs have a positive effect on the quality of life at reasonable direct cost, and result in net savings to society. These deaf children provide a unique opportunity to investigate auditory development.

Ponton et al. (2002) compared the ERPs of 5- to 20-year-old subjects with CIs and those of healthy controls. Surprisingly, it was found that the integrated MMN magnitude for individual implanted children and teenagers was much larger than those of healthy controls. Moreover, unlike healthy controls, children with CIs showed a prominent MMN in the absence of N1. Ponton et al. (2000a, 2000b) also reported that the maturation of MMN was not affected by age of implantation, but rather by factors such as post-implantation training and mode of education.

Clinical MMN studies conducted in children have mainly focused on investigating reading (dyslexic), learning, or language-impaired (dysphasic) children. In a pioneering study, Korpilahti and Lang (1994) showed that the peak amplitude of the frequency-change MMN was attenuated in 7- to

13-year-old children with developmental dysphasia, relative to healthy controls. However, when the duration-change MMN was used, a significant difference between the groups was found only when the standard–deviant difference was large (50 versus 500 ms). The authors also reported that the MMN latency was shortened as a function of age in controls, but not in children with dysphasia. Also, the same research team showed later that the frequency-change MMN was attenuated in 3- to 7-year-old children with developmental dysphasia (Holopainen, Korpilahti, Juottonen, Lang, & Sillanpää, 1997) as well as in 5- to 8-year-old mentally retarded children with delayed language and speech development (Holopainen et al., 1998). More recently Uwer, Albrecht, and von Suchodoletz (2002) demonstrated in 5- to 10-year-old children with specific language impairement (SLI), and in their healthy controls, that SLI children had attenuated MMN amplitudes to CV syllable changes but not to changes in tones.

However, language and speech deficits, as well as learning problems, are not limited to dyslexic and dysphasic patients. In fact, there is literature reporting a similar phenomenology in children with Velo Cardio Facial (VCF) syndrome. In addition to suffering from learning disabilities, these children often possess cleft palate and cardiac anomalies as a result of a micro-deletion of chromosome 22 (Haapanen & Somer, 1993; Kok & Solman, 1995). Through the use of frequency-change MMNs, Cheour et al. (1997b) demonstrated that these problems are not only due to the dysmorphology of the articulatory system, but are also the result of CNS dysfunction. Later it was shown that MMN is attenuated not only in children with the VCF syndrome, but also in children with non-syndromic cleft palate (Cheour et al., 1998c). More recently Ceponiene et al. (1999), using the same paradigm, investigated children with non-syndromic oral cleft palate. It was reported that when the longest ISI was used, only children with the cleft lip did not significantly differ in MMN amplitude from healthy controls. Among the isolated palatal clefts, it was found that the more posteriorly delimited the cleft, the smaller was the MMN amplitude. The MMNs of smallest amplitude were obtained from the subgroup with the complete unilateral cleft of the lip and palate.

Cheour et al. (1999) have also shown that the MMN amplitude in response to changes in frequency was reduced in cleft palate newborns, and that this dysfunction of the auditory cortex was still present at 6 months of age (Ceponiene et al., 2000). Thus MMN might reflect learning difficulties long before they surface behaviorally.

Most of the studies mentioned so far have used tones as stimuli for investigating children with learning disabilities. Interestingly, Schulte-Korne, Deimel, Bartling, and Remschmidt, (1998) showed that the MMN amplitude in dyslexic males (mean age of 12.5 years) was attenuated for speech stimuli, but not for tones. More recently, Uwer et al. (2002) reported the same results in 5- to 10-year-old children with specific language impairment (SLI). Dysphasic children often find it difficult to discriminate rapid changes in speech (e.g., Merzenich, Jenkins, Johnston, Schreiner, Miller, & Tallal, 1996; Tallal, 1981). Kraus et al. (1996) investigated how 6- to 15-year-old children with learning disabilities discriminate rapid spectro-temporal changes in speech stimuli. The children were divided into groups of "good" and "poor" perceivers based on their behavioral discrimination of the stimuli. A major finding was that the diminished ability to discriminate the speech stimuli was associated with a reduced MMN magnitude. It was concluded that discrimination deficits in some children originated in the auditory pathway before conscious perception. Bradlow et al. (1999) have also investigated children with learning disorders by using rapid changes in speech stimuli. Their data suggest that, relative to controls, the MMN was diminished in the experimental group when 40-ms formant–transition duration was used. The difference between controls and learning-disabled children decreased, however, with the use of a longer, 80-ms formant–transition duration. Surprisingly, lengthening the formant–transition duration did not result in improved discrimination thresholds for the subjects relative to the control group.

The majority of clinical pediatric MMN studies have been conducted in older children, and MMN studies in clinical infant populations are still very rare. Yet MMN has been employed to examine the cognitive consequences associated with a predisposition for certain learning disabilities. Dyslexia, for example, is known to have a genetic basis (e.g., Fisher, Stein, & Monaco, 1999; Nothen et al., 1999; Pennington & Smith, 1997). Leppänen, Richardson, and Lyytinen (1996) investigated awake, 6-month-old infants of families with at least one dyslexic parent as well as a familial background of reading difficulties. Pseudo-words of various durations were used as stimuli. In both the predisposed and control groups, deviant stimuli elicited a negative response, albeit different scalp distributions were evident between the two groups. The MMN amplitude was significantly smaller over the left hemisphere in the predisposed group relative to the control one. In another study by the same research group (Leppänen & Lyytinen, 1997), the authors used the same subjects and stimuli, and showed that in the predisposed group the MMN scalp distribution had a clear right hemisphere dominance, whereas in the control group the MMN was either bilateral or slightly left-hemisphere dominant (see also Guttorm et al., 2003). MMN has also been shown to be attenuated in infants with oral clefts (Ceponiene et al., 2000; Cheour et al., 1999).

CONCLUSIONS AND FUTURE DIRECTIONS

The studies reviewed in the present chapter clearly suggest that MMN has already been proven to be a prominent tool in studying auditory discrimination and learning in healthy infants and possibly even in clinical groups. Before MMN can reliably be obtained and interpreted at the individual level, there are several problems that need to be solved. It is quite clear that not enough normative data have been collected from infants, or young children, to settle the limits of the so-called normal variation. Moreover, very few studies have tried to determine so-called optimal MMN paradigms for infant studies, even though studies like this are quite common in adults.

Optimal MMN paradigm studies aim at finding the best parameters with respect to signal-to-noise ratio (SNR) and reliability. In these studies, such topics as sound characteristics, deviant probability, and data analysis are studied (e.g., McGee, Kraus, & Nicol, 1997; Sinkkonen & Tervaniemi, 2000). Studies examining sound characteristics have shown that if the difference between the standard and deviant is too big, MMN can easily be contaminated by other components such as N1 or P3a (Näätänen, 1992). Yet the large difference between the standard and deviant usually elicits high-amplitude MMN responses (Tiitinen, May, Reinikainen, & Näätänen, 1994). Hence, studies strive to compromise between a pronounced MMN and its corruption by other components. According to most studies, pristine MMNs are elicited when deviances up to 10% are used (e.g., Lang et al., 1990; Näätänen, 1995). Early MMN studies commonly used pure tones, but recent studies show that complex stimuli produce higher-amplitude MMNs (Tervaniemi et al., 2000a, 2000b). Among the different kinds of stimuli that have been reported and compared in the literature, it appears that changes in duration (e.g., Kathmann, Frodl-Bauch, & Hegerl, 1999) usually elicits MMN with the largest and most replicable amplitude (Pekkonen, Rinne, & Näätänen, 1995; Sinkkonen & Tervaniemi, 2000; Tervaniemi et al., 1999, 2000b; Uwer & Schodoletz, 2000).

It has been shown that the size of the MMN response is directly proportional to the logarithm of the stimulus' probability (Sinkkonen, 1999; Sinkkonen & Tervaniemi, 2000; Sinkkonen et al., 1996). Hence if deviants are rare, large MMNs can be obtained. Unfortunately, a small number of deviants result in a poor SNR, and therefore one needs to optimize these two factors. Most studies report that if the number of deviants is kept between 10% and 15%, the MMN amplitude and SNR are usually optimal (Sinkkonen & Tervaniemi, 2000).

As stated previously, there are many differences between pediatric and adult MMNs, and the optimal parameters for clinical MMN studies in adults and children are not likely to be identical. Furthermore, in adult studies it is not uncommon for the experiment to last well over an hour (e.g., May, Tiitinen, Sinkkonen, & Näätänen, 1994). However, in young children and infants, it is recommended that recordings do not exceed 30 minutes. If longer sessions are needed the child should be scheduled for multiple visits. Another difference concerns interludes and planned rests throughout the MMN experiment. Whereas breaks are commonly neglected in adult studies, they are of crucial importance when working with children. According to McGee et al. (1997) the MMN magnitude drops significantly as early as 10 minutes into an experiment. More importantly, this result was obtained not only for children but also for adults. On the other hand, a recent study in infants shows that MMN amplitude drops less dramatically in infants (Cheour et al., 2006). These studies demonstrate that conducting long experiments and collecting large volumes of data may not be the ideal way to run MMN experiments in children. Instead, one should aim for shorter sessions with copious breaks. Nevertheless, in both adults and children about 100 accepted deviants should be collected (Reinikainen et al., unpublished data).

Lastly, another difference between adults and children that needs to be taken into account while planning the experiments is that the hearing of these groups is not identical. Children, for example, achieve adult low-frequency threshold at about the age of 10–18 years (Elliot & Katz, 1980; Trehub, Schneider, Morrongiello, & Thorpe, 1980). Moreover, it has been demonstrated that some measures of temporal processing do not mature before late childhood (Hall & Grose, 1994; Irwin, Ball, Kay, Stillman, & Bosser, 1985; Grose, Hall, & Gibbs, 1993). Contrary to these differences in auditory perception, it is important to note that whereas intensity is a vital parameter that can enhance MMN elicitation, the normal infant ear has more hair cells than the adult ear, and infants are therefore at least as sensitive to auditory sounds as adults. Stimuli intensity in infants and young children should therefore not exceed those levels used in adult studies (up to 70 dB).

Although in the majority of children a prominent MMN can be obtained even when the ideal MMN parameters are not fully known, there are some healthy infants in whom no kind of MMN response can be seen in the particular experimental paradigm used. It has been reported that there was no evidence of MMN in about 25% to 30% (Ceponiene et al., 2000; Cheour et al., 1998a; Kurtzberg et al., 1995) or 50% (Leppänen et al., 1997) of the newborns studied. Most of these infants had a positive response in the latency range where MMN is typically obtained. More studies should be conducted in order to find out whether this is due to maturational factors (Kurtzberg et al., 1995; Leppänen et al., 2006), filtering settings (Weber et al., 2004), or perhaps slow-wave activity in spontaneous EEG. It is also possible that this positivity reflects another discriminative response, or that several of these options contribute to whether a negative or positive response can be seen in infants. Further studies are obviously needed to solve this issue.

REFERENCES

Acebo, C., Sadeh, A., Seifer, R., Tzischinsky, O., Wolfson, A. R., Hafer, A. et al. (1999). Estimating sleep patterns with activity monitoring in children and adolescents: How many nights are necessary for reliable measures? *Sleep*, *22*, 95–103.

Alho, K. (1995). Cerebral generator of mismatch negativity (MMN) and its magnetic counterpart (MMNm) elicited by sound changes. *Ear & Hearing*, *16*, 38–51.

Alho, K., Escera, C., Díaz, R., Yago, E., & Serra, J. M. (1997). Effects of involuntary auditory attention on visual task performance and brain activity. *NeuroReport*, *8*, 3233–3237.

Alho, K., Woods, D. L., Algazi, A., & Näätänen, R. (1992). Intermodal selective attention II: Effects of attentional load on processing auditory and visual stimuli in central space. *Electroencephalography and Clinical Neurophysiology, 82*, 356–368.

American Psychiatric Association. (1994). *Diagnostic and Statistical Manual of Mental Disorders* (4th ed.). Washington, DC: APA.

Anderer, P., Semlitsch, H., & Saletu, B. (1997). Multichannel auditory event-related brain potentials: Effects of normal aging on the scalp distribution of N1, P2, N2, and P300 latencies and amplitudes. *Electroencephalography and Clinical Neurophysiology, 99*, 458–472.

Astikainen, P., Ruusuvirta, T., & Korhonen, T. (2000). Cortical and subcortical visual event-related potentials to oddball stimuli in rabbits. *NeuroReport, 11*, 1515–1517.

Atienza, M. (2000, June). *REM sleep precessing of auditory perceptual information learned in previous wakefulness*. Talk presented at the meeting of MMN2000, Barcelona.

Atienza, M., Cantero, J. L., & Gomez, C. M. (1997). The mismatch negativity component reveals the sensory memory during REM sleep in humans. *Neuroscience Letters, 237*, 21–24.

Bar-Haim, Y., Marshall, P. J., Fox, N. A., Schorr, E. A., & Gordon-Salant, S. (2003). Mismatch negativity in socially withdrawn children. *Biological Psychiatry, 1*, 17–24.

Barkley, R. A. (1998). Attention-deficit hyperactivity disorder. *Scientific American, 279*, 66–71.

Blanchfield, B., Dunbar, J., Feldman, J., & Gardner, E. (1999). *The severely to profoundly hearing impaired population in United States: Prevalence and demographics*. Bethesda, MD: Project HOPE Center for Health Affairs.

Bradlow, A. R., Kraus, N., Nicol, T. G., McGee, T. J., Cunningham, J., Zecker, S. G. et al. (1999). Effects of lengthened formant transition duration on discrimination and neural representation of synthetic CV syllables by normal and learning-disabled children. *Journal of the Acoustical Society of America, 106*, 2086–2096.

Busby, K. A., Mercier, L., & Pivik, R. T. (1994). Ontogenetic variations in auditory arousal threshold during sleep. *Psychophysiology, 31*, 182–188.

Campbell, K., Bell, I., & Bastien, C. (1991). Evoked potential measures of information processing during natural sleep. In R. Broughton & R. Ogilvie (Eds.), *Sleep, arousal and performance* (pp. 88–116). Cambridge, MA: Birkhauser, Boston.

Casey, B. J., Castellanos, F. X., Giedd, J. N., Marsh, W. L., Hamburger, S. D., Schubert, A. B. et al. (1997). Implication of right frontostriatal circuitry in response inhibition and attention-deficit/hyperactivity disorder. *Journal of the American Academy of Child and Adolescent Psychiatry, 36*, 374–383.

Ceponiene, R., Hukki, J., Cheour, M., Haapanen, M. L., Koskinen, M., Alho, K. et al. (2000). Dysfunction of the auditory cortex persists in infants with cleft types. *Developmental Medicine and Child Neurology, 42*, 258–265.

Ceponiene, R., Hukki, J., Cheour, M., Haapanen, M. L., Ranta, R., & Näätänen, R. (1999). Cortical auditory dysfunction in children with oral clefts: Relation with cleft type. *Clinical Neurophysiology, 110*, 1921–1926.

Ceponiene, R., Kushnerenko, E., Fellman, V., Renlund, M., Suominen, K., & Näätänen, R. (2002). Event-related potential features indexing central auditory discrimination by newborns. *Brain Research: Cognitive Brain Research, 13*, 101–113.

Ceponiene, R., Lepisto, T., Shestakova, A., Vanhala, R., Alku, P., Naatanen, R. et al. (2003). Speech-sound-selective auditory impairment in children with autism: They can perceive but do not attend. *Proceedings of the National Academy of Science USA, 29*, 5567–5572.

Cheng, A. K., Rubin, H. R., Powe, N. R., Mellon, N. K., Francis, H. W., & Niparko, J. K. (2000). Cost-utility analysis of cochlear implant in children. *Journal of the American Medical Association, 284*, 850–856.

Cheour, M., Alho, K., Ceponiene, R., Reinikainen, K., Sainio, K., Pohjavuori, M. et al. (1998a). Maturation of mismatch negativity in infants. *International Journal of Psychophysiology, 29*, 217–226.

Cheour, M., Alho, K., Saino, K., Reinikainen, K., Renlund, M., & Aaltonen, O. (1997a). The mismatch negativity to changes in speech sounds at the age of three months. *Developmental Neuropsychology, 13*, 167–174.

Cheour, M., Ceponiene, R., Hukki, J., Haapanen, M.-L., Näätänen, R., & Alho, K. (1999). Brain dysfunction in neonates with cleft-palate revealed by the mismatch negativity (MMN). *Electroencephalogrphy and Clinical Neurophysiology, 110*, 324–328.

Cheour, M., Ceponiene, R., Lehtokoski, A., Luuk, A., Allik, J., Alho, K. et al. (1998b). Development of language-specific phoneme representations in the infant brain. *Nature Neuroscience, 1*, 351–353.

Cheour, M., Haapanen, M.-L., Ceponiene, R., Hukki, J., Ranta, R., & Näätänen, R. (1998c). Mismatch negativity (MMN) as an index of auditory sensory memory deficit in cleft-palate and CATCH-syndrome children. *NeuroReport, 9*, 2709–2712.

Cheour, M., Haapanen, M.-L., Hukki, J., Ceponiene, R., Kurjenluoma, S., Alho, K. et al. (1997b). The first neurophysiological evidence for cognitive brain dysfunctions in CATCH children. *NeuroReport, 8*, 1785–1787.

Cheour, M., Leppänen, P., & Kraus, N. (2000). Mismatch negativity (MMN) as a tool for investigating auditory discrimination and auditory sensory memory in infants and children: A review. *Electroencephalography and Clinical Neurophysiology, 117*, 4–16.

Cheour, M., Martynova, O., Näätänen, R., Erkkola, R., Sillanpää, M., Kero, P. et al. (2002). Sleep can be used for on-line training of speech sound discrimination in human newborns. *Nature, 7*, 599–600.

Cheour, M., Martynova, O., Wang, T., & Näätänen R. (2006). *The effect of session duration on neonatal ERPs.* Manuscript in preparation.

Cheour-Luhtanen, M., Alho, K., Kujala, T., Saino, K., Reinikainen, K., Renlund, M. et al. (1995). Mismatch negativity indicates vowel discrimination in newborns. *Hearing Research, 82*, 53–58.

Cheour-Luhtanen, M., Alho, K., Sainio, K., Rinne, T., Reinikainen, K., Pohjavuori, M. et al. (1996). The ontogenetically earliest discriminative response of the human brain. *Psychophysiology, 33*, 478–481.

Chiron, C., Leboyer, M., Leon, F., Jambaque, I., Nultin, C., & Syrota, A. (1995). SPECT of the brain in childhood autism: Evidence for a lack of normal hemispheric asymmetry. *Developmental Medicine and Child Neurology, 37*, 849–860.

Cook, E. H. Jr., Stein, M. A., Krasowski, M. D., Cox, N. J., Olkon, D. M., Kieffer, J. E. et al. (1995). Association of attention-deficit disorder and the dopamine transporter gene. *American Journal of Human Genetics, 56*, 993–998.

Cowan, N., Winkler, I., Teder, W., & Näätänen, R. (1993). Memory prerequisites of mismatch negativity in the auditory event-related potential (ERP). *Journal of Experimental Psychology: Learning, Memory & Cognition, 19*, 909–921.

Csépe, V. (1995). On the origin and development of the mismatch negativity. *Ear and Hearing, 16*, 90–103.

Csépe, V., Honbolygó, F., Ragó, A., Róna, Z., & Beke. (2004, March). *MMN to suprasegmental cues.* Talk given at the meeting of EPIC XIV, Leipzig, Germany.

Csépe, V., Karmos, G., & Molnár, M. (1987). Evoked potential correlates of stimulus deviance during wakefulness and sleep in cat-animal model of mismatch negativity. *Electroencephalography and Clinical Neurophysiology, 66*, 571–578.

Csépe, V., & Molnár, M. (1997). Towards the possible clinical application of the mismatch negativity component of event-related potentials. *Audiology & Neuro-otology, 2*, 354–369.

Dehaene-Lambertz, G., & Baillet, S. (1998). A phonological representation in the infant brain. *NeuroReport, 9*, 1885–1888.

Dehaene-Lambertz, G., & Dehaene, S. (1994). Speed and cerebral correlates of syllable discrimination in infants. *Nature, 370*, 292–351.

Dehaene-Lambertz, G., Dupoux, E., & Gout, A. (2000). Electrophysiological correlates of phonological processing: A cross-linguistic study. *Journal of Cognitive Neuroscience, 12*, 635–647.

Doran, S. (1999). *Context effects on target detection during wake and sleep.* Doctoral dissertation, Department of Psychology, University of Oregon, Eugene, OR, USA.

Draganova, R., Eswaran, H., Murphy, P., Huotilainen, M., Lowery, C., & Preissl, H. (2005). Sound frequency change detection in fetuses and newborns, a magnetoencephalographic study. *Neuroimage, 28*, 354–361.

Eggermont, J. J. (1988). On the rate of maturation of sensory evoked potentials. *Acta Otolaryngologica (Stockholm), 70*, 293–305.

Eggermont, J. J. (1992). Development of auditory evoked potentials. *Electroencephalography and Clinical Neurophysiology, 112*, 197–200.

Elliot, L. L., & Katz, D. R. (1980). Children's pure tone detection. *Journal of the Acoustical Society of America, 67*, 343–344.

Escera, C., Alho, K., Winkler, I., & Näätänen, R. (1998). Neural mechanisms of involuntary attention to acoustic novelty and change. *Journal of Cognitive Neuroscience, 10*, 590–604.

Ferri, R., Elia, M., Agarwal, N., Lanuzza, B., & Musumeci, S. A. (2003). The mismatch negativity and the P3a components of the auditory event-related potentials in autistic low-functioning subjects. *Clinical Neurophysiology, 111*, 1671–1680.

Filipek, P. A. (1995). Quantitative magnetic resonance imaging in autism: The cerebellar vermis. *Current Opinion in Neurology, 8*, 134–138.

Fischer, C., & Luaute, J. (2005). Evoked potentials for the prediction of vegetative state in the acute stage of coma. *Neuropsychological Rehabilitation, 15*, 372–380.

Fischer, C., Morlet, D., & Giard, M. H. (2000). Mismatch negativity and N100 in comatose patients. *Audiology & Neuro-otology, 5*, 192–197.

Fisher, S. E., Stein, J. F., & Monaco, A. P. (1999). A genome-wide search strategy for identifying quantitative trait loci involved in reading and spelling disability (developmental dyslexia). *European Child & Adolescent Psychiatry, 8*(Suppl. 3), 47–51.

Franco, P., Pardou, A., Hassid, S., Lurquin, P., Groswasser, J., & Kahn, A. (1998). Auditory arousal thresholds are higher when infants sleep in the prone position. *Journal of Pediatrics, 132*, 240–243.

Friederici, A. D., Friedrich, M., & Weber, C. (2002). Neural manifestation of cognitive and precognitive mismatch detection in early infancy. *NeuroReport, 13*, 1251–1254.

Giedd, J. N., Castellanos, F. X., Casey, B. J., Kozuch, P., King, A. C., Hamburger, S. D.

et al. (1994). Quantitative morphology of the corpus callosum in attention deficit hyperactivity disorder. *American Journal of Psychiatry, 151*, 665–669.

Gomot, M., Giard, M. H., Adrien, J. L., Barthelemy, C., & Bruneau, N. (2002). Hypersensitivity to acoustic change in children with autism: Electrophysiological evidence of left frontal cortex dysfunctioning. *Psychophysiology, 39*, 577–584.

Gomot, M., Giard, M. H., Roux, S., Barthelemy, C., & Bruneau, N. (2000). Maturation of frontal and temporal components of mismatch negativity (MMN) in children. *NeuroReport, 28*(11), 3109–3112.

Grose, J. H., Hall, J. W., & Gibbs, C. (1993). Temporal analysis in children. *Journal of Speech and Hearing Research, 36*, 351–356.

Gruber, R., Sadeh, A., & Raviv, A. (2000). Instability of sleep patterns in children with attention-deficit/hyperactivity disorder. *Journal of the American Academy of Child and Adolescent Psychiatry, 39*, 495–501.

Guttorm, T. K., Leppanen, P. H., Tolvanen, A., & Lyytinen, H. (2003). Event-related potentials in newborns with and without familial risk for dyslexia: Principal component analysis reveals differences between the groups. *Journal of Neural Transmission, 110*, 1059–1074.

Haapanen, M.-L., & Somer, M. (1993). Velocardiofacial syndrome analysis of phoniatric and other clinical findings. *Folia Phoniatrica, 45*, 239–246.

Hall, J. W. III, & Grose, J. H. (1994). Development of temporal resolution in children as measured by the temporal modulation transfer function. *Journal of the Acoustical Society of America, 96*, 351–356.

Hirasawa, K., Kurihara, M., & Konishi, Y. (2002). The relationship between mismatch negativity and arousal level: Can mismatch negativity be an index for evaluating the arousal level in infants? *Sleep Medicine, 3*(Suppl. 2), S45–48.

Holopainen, I. E., Korpilahti, P., Juottonen, K., Lang, H., & Sillanpää, M. (1997). Attenuated auditory event-related potential mismatch negativity in children with developmental dysphasia. *Neuropediatrics, 28*, 253–256.

Holopainen, I. E., Korpilahti, P., Juottonen, K., Lang, H., & Sillanpää, M. (1998). Abnormal frequency mismatch negativity in mentally retarded children and in children with developmental dysphasia. *Journal of Child Neurology, 13*, 178–183.

Huotilainen, M., Kujala, A., Hotakainen, M., Shestakova, A., Kushnerenko, E., Parkkonen, L. et al. (2003). Auditory magnetic responses of healthy newborns. *Neuroreport, 6*(14), 1871–1875.

Huttenlocher, P. R. (1979). Synaptic density in human frontal cortex: Developmental changes and effects of aging. *Brain Research, 163*, 195–205.

Huttenlocher, P. R., De Courten, C., Garey, L. G., & van der Loos, H. (1982). The synaptogenesis in human visual cortex—evidence for synapse elimination during normal development. *Neuroscience Letters, 33*, 247–252.

Irwin, R. J., Ball, A. K. R., Kay, N., Stillman, J. A., & Bosser, J. (1985). The development of auditory temporal acquity in children. *Child Development, 56*, 614–620.

Jing, H., & Benasich, A. A. (2006). Brain responses to tonal changes in the first two years of life. *Brain Development, 28*, 247–256.

Jonkman, L. M., Kemner, C., Verbaten, M. N., van Engeland, H., Camfferman, G., Buitelaar, J. K. et al. (2000). Attention capacity, a probe ERP study: Differences between children with attention-deficit hyperactivity disorder and normal control children and effects of methylphenidate. *Psychophysiology, 37*, 334–336.

Kane, N. M., Curry, S. H., Rowlands, C. A., Manara, A. R., Lewis, T., Moss, T. et al. (1996). Event-related potentials: Neurophysiological tools for predicting emergency and early outcome for traumatic coma. *Intensive Care Medicine, 22,* 39–46.

Kathmann, N., Frodl-Bauch, T., & Hegerl, U. (1999). Stability of the mismatch negativity under different stimulus and attention conditions. *Clinical Neurophysiology, 110,* 317–323.

Kekoni, J., Hämäläinen, H., McCloud, V., Reinikainen, K., & Näätänen, R. (1996). Is the somatosensory N250 related to deviance discrimination or conscious target detection? *Electroencephalography and Clinical Neurophysiology, 100,* 115–125.

Kemner, C., Verbaten, M. N., Cuperus, J. M., Camfferman, G., & van Engeland, H. (1995). Auditory event-related brain potentials in autistic children and three different control groups. *Biological Psychiatry, 38,* 150–165.

Kemner, C., Verbaten, M. N., Koelega, H. S., Buitelaar, J. K., van der Gaag, R. J., Camfferman, G. et al. (1996). Event-related brain potentials in children with attention-deficit and hyperactivity disorders: Effects of stimulus deviancy and task relevancy in the visual and auditory modality. *Biological Psychiatry, 40,* 522–534.

Kilpeläinen, R., Luoma, L., Herrgård, E., Sipilä, P., Yppärilä, H., Partanen, J. et al. (1999). Distractible children show abnormal orienting to non-attended auditory stimuli. *NeuroReport, 10,* 1869–1874.

King, C., McGee, T. J., Rubel, E. W., Nicol, T. G., & Kraus, N. (1995). Acoustic features and acoustic changes are represented by different central pathways. *Hearing Research, 85,* 45–52.

Kok, L. L., & Solman, R. T. (1995). Velocardiofacial syndrome: Learning difficulties and intervention. *Journal of Medical Genetics, 32,* 612–618.

Korpilahti, P., & Lang, H. (1994). Auditory ERP components and mismatch negativity in dysphasic children. *Electroencephalography and Clinical Neurophysiology, 91,* 256–264.

Krauel, K., Schott, P., Sojka, B., Pause, B. M., & Ferstl, R. (1999). Is there a mismatch negativity analogue in the olfactory event-related potential? *Journal of Psychophysiology, 13,* 49–55.

Kraus, N., & Cheour, M. (2000). Speech sound representation in the brain. *Audiology and Neuro-otology, 5,* 140–150.

Kraus, N., McGee, T. J., Carrell, T. D., King, C., Tremblay, K., & Nicol, T. G. (1995b). Central auditory plasticity associated with speech discrimination training. *Journal of Cognitive Neuroscience, 7,* 25–32.

Kraus, N., McGee, T., Carrell, T. D., Sharma, A., Micco, A., & Nicol, T. (1993a). Speech-evoked cortical potentials in children. *Journal of the American Academy of Audiology, 4,* 238–248.

Kraus, N., McGee, T. J., Carrell, T. D., Zecker, S. G., Nicol, T. G., & Koch, D. B. (1996). Auditory neurophysiologic responses and discrimination deficits in children with learning problems. *Science, 273,* 971–973.

Kraus, N., McGee, T., Sharma, A., Carrell, T., & Nicol, T. (1992). Mismatch negativity event-related potential to speech stimuli. *Ear and Hearing, 13,* 158–164.

Kraus, N., Micco, A. G., Koch, D. B., McGee, T. J., Carrel, T. D., & Sharma, A. (1993b). The mismatch negativity cortical evoked potential elicited by speech in cochlear-implant users. *Hearing Research, 65,* 118–124.

Kraus, N., & Näätänen, R. (Eds.). (1995). Mismatch negativity as an index of central auditory function. *Ear Hear, Special Issue, 16,* 38–51.

Kuhl, P. (1993). Developmental speech perception: Implications for models of language impairment. *Annals of the New York Academy of Sciences, 682,* 248–263.

Kuhl, P. K., Williams, K. A., Lacerda, W. F., Stevens, K. N., & Lindblom, B. (1992). Linguistic experiences alter phonetic perception in infants by 6 months of age. *Science*, *255*, 606–608.

Kuhl, P., Williams, K. A., & Meltzoff, A. N. (1991). Cross-modal speech perception in adults and infants using nonspeech auditory stimuli. *Journal of Experimental Psychology: Human Perception and Performance*, *17*, 829–840.

Kurtzberg, D., Vaughan, H. G. Jr., Kreuzer, J. A., & Fliegler, K. Z. (1995). Developmental studies and clinical applications of mismatch negativity: Problems and prospects. *Ear and Hearing*, *16*, 105–117.

Kushnerenko, E., Ceponiene, R., Balan, P., Fellman, V., Huotilainen, M., & Näätänen, R. (2002). Maturation of the auditory event-related potentials during the first year of life. *NeuroReport*, *13*, 47–51.

Kushnerenko, E., Cheour, M., Ceponiene, R., Fellman, V., Renlund, M., Soinen, K. et al. (2001). Central auditory processing of durational changes in complex speech patterns by newborns: An event-related brain potential study. *Developmental Neuropsychology*, *19*, 83–97.

LaHoste, G. J., Swanson, J. M., Wigal, S. B., Glabe, C., Wigal, T., King, N. et al. (1996). Dopamine D4 receptor gene polymorphism is associated with attention deficit hyperactivity disorder. *Molecular Psychiatry*, *1*, 121–124.

Lähteenmäki, P. M., Holopainen, I., Krause, C. M., Helenius, H., Salmi, T. T., & Heikki, L. A. (2001). Cognitive functions of adolescent childhood cancer survivors assessed by event-related potentials. *Medical and Pediatric Oncology*, *36*, 442–450.

Lähteenmäki, P. M., Krause, C. M., Salmi, T. T., & Lang, A. H. (in press). Event-related synchronization as a psycho-physiological correlate of impaired attention and memory function after the treatment of childhood cancer. *Clinical Neurophysiology*.

Lang, A. H., Eerola, O., Korpilahti, P., Holopainen, I., Salo, S., & Aaltonen, O. (1995). Practical issues in the clinical application of mismatch negativity. *Ear and Hearing*, *16*, 117–129.

Lang, A. H., Nyrke, T., Ek, M., Aaltonen, O., Raimo, I., & Näätänen, R. (1990). Pitch discrimination performance and auditory event-related potentials. In C. H. M. Brunia, A. W. K. Gaillard, & A. Kok (Eds.), *Psychophysiological brain research* Vol. 1 (pp. 294–298). Tilburg, The Netherlands: Tilburg University Press.

Lepisto, T., Soininen, M., Ceponiene, R., Almqvist, F., Näätänen, R., & Aronen, E. T. (2004). Auditory event-related potential indices of increased distractibility in children with major depression. *Clinical Neurophysiology*, *115*, 620–627.

Leppänen, P. H., Eklund, K. M., & Lyytinen, H. (1997). Event-related potentials to change in vowels in newborns. *Developmental Neuropsychology*, *13*, 175–204.

Leppänen, P. H., Guttorm, T. K., Pihko, E., Takkinen, S., Eklund, K. M., & Lyytinen, H. (2004). Maturational effects on newborn ERPs measured in the mismatch negativity paradigm. *Experimental Neurology*, *190*, S91-S101.

Leppänen, P. H. T., Guttorm, T. K., Pihko, E., Takkinen, S., Eklund, K. M., & Lyytinen, H. (2006). *Maturational effects on newborn ERPs measured in the mismatch negativity (MMN) paradigm*. Manuscript submitted for publication.

Leppänen, P. H. T., & Lyytinen, H. (1997). Auditory event-related potentials in the study of developmental language-related disorders. *Audiology & Neuro-otology*, *2*, 308–340.

Leppänen, P. H. T., Richardson, U., & Lyytinen, H. (1996, April). *Brain event-related potentials as a measure of quantity discrimination in six-month-old infants*. Poster session presented at the 10th Biennial International Conference on Infants Studies, Providence, Rhode Island.

Lincoln, A. J., Courchesne, E., Harms, L., & Allen, M. (1993). Contextual probability evaluation in autistic, receptive developmental language disorder, and control children: Event-related brain potential evidence. *Journal of Autism and Developmental Disorders, 23*, 37–58.

Loewy, D. H., Campbell, K. B., & Bastien, C. (1996). The mismatch negativity to frequency deviant stimuli during natural sleep. *Electroencephalography and Clinical Neurophysiology, 98*, 493–501.

Lyytinen, H., Blomberg, A. P., & Näätänen, R. (1992). Event-related potentials and autonomic responses to a change in unattended stimuli. *Psychophysiology, 29*, 523–534.

Maiste, A. C., Wiens, A. S., Hunt, M. J., Scherg, M., & Picton, T. W. (1995). Event-related potentials and the categorical perception of speech sounds. *Ear and Hearing, 16*, 38–51.

Martin, B. A., Shafer, V. L, Morr, M. L., Kreuzer, J. A., & Kurtzberg, D. (2003). Maturation of mismatch negativity: A scalp current density analysis. *Ear and Hearing, 24*, 463–471.

Martynova, O., Kirjavainen, J., & Cheour, M. (2003). Mismatch negativity and late discriminative negativity in sleeping human newborns. *Neuroscience Letters, 10*(340), 75–78.

May, P., Tiitinen, H., Sinkkonen, J., & Näätänen, R. (1994). Long-term stimulation attenuates the transient 40-Hz response. *NeuroReport, 5*, 1918–1920.

McGee, T., Kraus, N., & Nicol, T. (1997). Is it really a mismatch negativity? An assessment of methods for determining response validity in individual subjects. *Electroencephalography and Clinical Neurophysiology, 104*, 359–368.

Meister, L. A., & Meadows, A. T. (1993). Late effects on childhood cancer therapy. *Current Problems in Pediatrics, 23*, 102–131.

Merzenich, M. M., Jenkins, W. M., Johnston, P., Schreiner, C., Miller, S. L., & Tallal, P. (1996). Temporal processing deficits of language-learning impaired children ameliorated by training. *Science, 271*, 77–81.

Morlet, D., Bouchet, P., & Fischer, C. (2000). Mismatch negativity and N100 monitoring: Potential clinical value and methodological advances. *Audiology and Neuro-otology, 5*, 198–206.

Morr, M. L., Shafer, V. L., Kreuzer, J. A., & Kurtzberg, D. (2002). Maturation of mismatch negativity in typically developing infants and preschool children. *Ear and Hearing, 23*, 118–136.

Näätänen, R. (1990). The role of attention in auditory information processing as revealed by event-related potentials and other brain measures of cognitive function. *Behavioral Brain Science, 13*, 201–288.

Näätänen, R. (1992). *Attention and brain function*. Hillsdale, NJ: Lawrence Erlbaum Associates Inc.

Näätänen, R. (1995). The mismatch negativity: A powerful tool for cognitive neuroscience. *Ear and Hearing, 16*, 6–18.

Näätänen, R., & Alho, K. (1995). Mismatch negativity—a unique measure of sensory processing in audition. *International Journal of Neuroscience, 80*, 317–337.

Näätänen, R., & Escera, C. (2000). Mismatch negativity: Clinical and other applications. *Audiology and Neuro-ontology, 5*, 105–110.

Näätänen, R., Gaillard, A. W. K., & Mäntysalo, S. (1978). Early selective attention effect on evoked potential reinterpreted. *Acta Psychologica, 42*, 313–329.

Näätänen, R., Lehtokoski, A., Lennes, M. M., Cheour, M., Huotilainen, M., Livonen,

A. et al. (1997). Language-specific phoneme representations revealed by electric and magnetic brain responses. *Nature*, *385*, 432–434.

Näätänen, R., & Lyytinen, H. (1996). Mismatch negativity in sleep. In J. Harsh & R. Ogulvie (Eds.), *Sleep onset normal and abnormal process* (pp. 339–350). Washington, DC: American Psychological Association.

Näätänen, R., Paavilainen, P., Tiitinen, H., Jiang, D., & Alho, K. (1993). Attention and mismatch negativity. *Psychophysiology*, *30*, 436–450.

Näätänen, R., & Tiitinen, H. (1998). Auditory information processing as indexed by the mismatch negativity. In M. Sabourin, F. I. M. Craik, & M. Robert (Eds.), *Advances in psychological science: Biological and cognitive aspects* (pp. 145–170). Hove, UK: Psychology Press.

Näätänen, R., & Winkler, I. (1999). The concept of auditory stimulus representation in cognitive neuroscience. *Psychological Bulletin*, *125*, 826–859.

Nakagome, K., Ichikawa, I., Kanno, O., Akaho, R., Suzuki, M., Takazawa, S. et al. (1998). Overnight effects of triazolam on cognitive function: An event-related potentials study. *Neuropsychobiology*, *38*, 232–240.

Neville, H. (1995). Developmental specificity in neurocognitive development in humans. In M. S. Gazzaniga (Ed.), *The cognitive neurosciences* (pp. 219–232). Cambridge, MA: Bradford Books.

Nothen, M. M., Schulte-Korne, G., Grimm, T., Chichon, S., Vogt, I. R., Muller-Myhsok, B. et al. (1999). Genetic linkage analysis with dyslexia: Evidence for linkage of spelling disability to chromosome 15. *European Child and Adolescent Psychiatry*, *8*(Suppl. 3), 56–59.

Novak, G., Ritter, W., & Vaughan, H. G. Jr. (1992). Mismatch detection and the latency of temporal judgements. *Psychophysiology*, *29*, 398–411.

Novick, B., Kurtzberg, D., & Vaughan, H. G. (1979). An electrophysiologic indication of defective information storage in childhood autism. *Psychiatry Research*, *1*, 101–108.

Nozza, R. J. (1995). Estimating the contribution of non-sensory factors to infant–adult differences in behavioral thresholds. *Hearing Research*, *91*, 72–78.

Oades, R. D., Dittmann-Balcar, A., Schepker, R., Eggers, C., & Zerbin, D. (1996). Auditory event-related potentials (ERPs) and mismatch negativity (MMN) in healthy children and those with attention-deficit or tourettic symptoms. *Biological Psychology*, *43*, 163–185.

Oades, R. D., Walker, M. K., Geffen, L. B., & Stern, L. M. (1988). Event-related potentials in autistic and healthy children on an auditory choice reaction time task. *International Journal of Psychophysiology*, *6*, 25–37.

O'Neill, C., O'Donoghue, G. M., Archbold, S. M., & Normand, C. (2000). A cost-utility analysis of pediatric cochlear implantation. *Laryngoscope*, *110*, 156–160.

Paavilainen, P., Cammann, R., Alho, K., Reinikainen, K., Sams, M., & Näätänen, R. (1987). Event-related potentials to pitch change in an auditory stimulus sequence during sleep. In R. Johnson, R. Parasuraman Jr., & J. W. Rohrbaugh (Eds.), *Current trends in event-related potential research* (pp. 246–255). Amsterdam: Elsevier.

Pang, E. W., & Fowler, B. (1999). Dissociation of the mismatch negativity and processing negativity attentional waveforms with nitrous oxide. *Psychophysiology*, *36*, 552–558.

Paterson, A. D., Sunohara, G. A., & Kennedy, J. L. (1999). Dopamine D4 receptor gene: Novelty or nonsense? *Neuropsychopharmacology*, *21*, 3–16.

Pekkonen, E., Rinne, T., & Näätänen, R. (1995). Variability and replicability of the mismatch negativity. *Electroencephalography and Clinical Neurophysiology, 96,* 546–554.

Pennington, B. F., & Smith, S. D. (1997). Genetic analysis of dyslexia and other complex behavioral phenotypes. *Current Opinion in Pediatrics, 9,* 636–641.

Pihko, E., Leppänen, P., Eklund, K. M., Cheour, M., Guttorm, T. K., & Lyytinen, H. (1999). Cortical responses of infant with and without risk for dyslexia: I. Age effects. *NeuroReport, 10,* 901–905.

Polka, L., & Werker, J. F. (1994). Developmental changes in perception of nonnative vowel contrasts. *Journal of Experimental Psychology: Human Perception & Performance, 20,* 421–435.

Ponton, C. W., & Don, M. (1995). The mismatch negativity in cochlear implant users. *Ear and Hearing, 16,* 131–146.

Ponton, C. W., Eggermont, J. J., Don, M., & Kwong, B. (2000a). Maturation of human central auditory system activity: Evidence from multi-channel evoked potentials. *Clinical Neurophysiology, 5,* 167–185.

Ponton, C. W., Eggermont, J. J., Don, M., Waring, M. D., Kwong, B., & Cunninghan, J. (2000b). Maturation of the mismatch negativity: Effects of profound deafness and cochlear implant use. *Audiology and Neuro-otology, 5,* 167–185.

Ponton, C., Eggermont, J. J., Khosla, D., Kwong, B., & Don, M. (2002). Maturation of human central auditory system activity: Separating auditory evoked potentials by dipole source modeling. *Clinical Neurophysiology, 113*(3), 407–420.

Posner, M. I., & Raichle, M. E. (1994). *Images of mind.* New York: Scientific American Library.

Raz, A. (1999). *Effects of total sleep deprivation on the spotlight of visual attention and on pre-attentional processing.* Doctoral dissertation, Department of Psychology and Interdisciplinary Center for Neural Computation, Hebrew University of Jerusalem, Israel.

Reis, R. (1991). Prevalence and characteristics of persons with hearing trouble: United States, 1990–1991. *Vital Health Statistics, 10,* 1.

Ring, H. A., Baron-Cohen, S., Wheelwright, S., Williams, S. C., Brammer, M., Andrew, C. et al. (1999). Cerebral correlates of preserved cognitive skills in autism: A functional MRI study of embedded figures task performance. *Brain, 122,* 1305–1315.

Ritter, W., Deacon, D., Gomes, H., Javitt, D. C., & Vaughan, H. G. Jr. (1995). The mismatch negativity of event-related potentials as a probe of transient auditory memory: A review. *Ear and Hearing, 16,* 52–67.

Rivera-Gaxiola, M., Lara-Ayala, L., Cadena, C., & Kuhl, P. K. (2004, April). *Discrimination of voice-onset time speech contrasts in Mexican and American 11 month-old infants: An event-related potential study.* Poster session presented at the annual meeting of the CNS, San Francisco, CA.

Rubia, K., Taylor, A., Taylor, E., & Sergeant, J. A. (1999). Synchronization, anticipation, and consistency in motor timing of children with dimensionally defined attention deficit hyperactivity behaviour. *Perceptual and Motor Skills, 89,* 1237–1258.

Rumsey, J. M., Nace, K., Donohue, B., Wise, D., Maisog, J. M., & Andreason, P. (1997). A positron emission tomography study of impaired word recognition and phonological processing in dyslexic men. *Archives of Neurology, 54,* 562–573.

Ruusuvirta, T., Penttonen, M., & Korhonen, T. (1998). Auditory cortical event-related potentials to pitch deviances in rats. *Neuroscience Letters, 248,* 45–48.

Sadeh, A., Raviv, A., & Gruber, R. (2000). Sleep patterns and sleep disruptions in school-age children. *Developmental Psychology, 36,* 291–301.

Sallinen, M., Kaartinen, J., & Lyytinen, H. (1994). Is the appearance of mismatch negativity during stage 2 sleep related to the elicitation of K-komplex? *Electroencephalography and Clinical Neurophysiology, 91*, 140–148.

Sallinen, M., Kaartinen, J., & Lyytinen, H. (1996). Processing of auditory stimuli during tonic and phasic periods of REM sleep as revealed by event-related brain potentials. *Journal of Sleep Research, 5*, 220–228.

Sallinen, M., Kaartinen, J., & Lyytinen, H. (1997). Precursors of the evoked K-complex in event related brain potentials in stage 2 sleep. *Electroencephalography and Clinical Neurophysiology, 102*, 363–373.

Sallinen, M., & Lyytinen, H. (1997). Mismatch negativity during objective and subjective sleepiness. *Psychophysiology, 34*, 694–702.

Satterfield, J. H., Schell, A. M., Nicholas, T. W., Satterfield, B. T., & Frees, T. E. (1990). Ontogeny of selective attention effects on event-related potentials in attention-deficit hyperactivity disorder and normal boys. *Biological Psychiatry, 28*, 879–903.

Schröger, E. (1996). The influence of stimulus intensity and inter-stimulus interval on the detection of pitch and loudness changes. *Electroencephalography and Clinical Neurophysiology, 100*, 517–526.

Schröger, E., & Wolff, C. (1998). Attentional orienting and reorienting is indicated by human event-related brain potentials. *NeuroReport, 9*, 3355–3358.

Schulte-Korne, G., Deimel, W., Bartling, J., & Remschmidt, H. (1998). Auditory processing and dyslexia: Evidence for a specific speech processing deficit. *NeuroReport, 26*, 337–340.

Semelin, R., Service, E., Kiesila, P., Uutela, K., & Salonen, O. (1996). Impaired visual word processing in dyslexia revealed with magneto-encephalography. *Annals of Neurology, 40*, 157–162.

Sharma, A., & Dorman, M. F. (1998). Exploration of the perceptual magnet effect using the mismatch negativity auditory evoked potential. *Journal of the Acoustical Society of America, 104*, 511–517.

Sharma, A., Kraus, N., McGee, T., Carrell, T., & Nicol, T. (1993). Acoustic versus phonetic representation of speech as reflected by the mismatch negativity event-related potential. *Electroencephalography & Clinical Neurophysiology, 88*, 64–71.

Shaywitz, B. A., Shaywitz, S. E., Pugh, K. R., & Skudlarski, P. (1996). Functional magnetic resonance imaging as a tool to understand reading and reading disability. In R. W. Thatcher & G. R. Lyon (Eds.), *Developmental neuroimaging: Mapping the development of brain and behavior* (pp. 157–167). San Diego, CA: Academic Press.

Sheldon, S. H. (1996). *Evaluating sleep in infants and children.* Philadelphia, PA: Lippincott-Raven.

Shinozaki, N., Yabe, H., Sutoh, T., Hiruma, T., & Kaneko, S. (1998). Somatosensory automatic responses to deviant stimuli. *Brain Research: Cognitive Brain Research, 7*, 165–171.

Simos, P. G., Breier, J. I., Fletcher, J. M., Bergman, E., & Papanicolaou, A. C. et al. (2000a). Cerebral mechanisms involved in word reading in dyslexic children: A magnetic source imaging approach. *Cerebral Cortex, 10*, 809–816.

Simos, P. G., Breier, J. I., Fletcher, J. M., Foorman, B. R., Bergman, E., Fishbeck, K. et al. (2000b). Brain activation profiles in dyslexic children during non-word reading: A magnetic source imaging study. *Neuroscience Letters, 290*, 61–65.

Sinkkonen, J. (1999). Information and resource allocation. In R. Baddley, P. Hancock,

& P. Foldiak (Eds.), *Information theory and the brain* (pp. 241–254). Cambridge, UK: Cambridge University Press.

Sinkkonen, J., Kaski, S., Huotilainen, M., Ilmoniemi, R. J., Näätänen, R., & Kaila, K. (1996). Optimal resource allocation for novelty detection in a human auditory memory. *NeuroReport*, *7*, 2479–2482.

Sinkkonen, J., & Tervaniemi, M. (2000). Towards optimal recording and analysis of the mismatch negativity. *Audiology and Neuro-otology*, *5*, 235–246.

Steiner, C. A., Powe, N. R., Anderson, G. F., & Das, A. (1996). The review process used by US health care plans to evaluate new medical technology for coverage. *Journal of General Internal Medicine*, *11*, 294–302.

Summerfield, A. Q., & Marshall, D. H. (1995). *Cochlear implantation in the UK 1990–1994*. London: MRC-INR, HMSO.

Summerfield, A. Q., Marshall, D. H., & Archbold, S. (1997). Cost-effectiveness considerations in pediatric cochlear implantation. *The American Journal of Otology*, *18*, S166–S168.

Swanson, J., Castellanos, F. X., Murias, M., LaHoste, G., & Kennedy, J. (1998a). Cognitive neuroscience of attention deficit hyperactivity disorder and hyperkinetic disorder. *Current Opinion in Neurobiology*, *10*, 263–271.

Swanson, J., Flodman, P., Kennedy, J., Spence, M. A., Moyzis, R., Schuck, S. et al. (2000). Dopamine, genes and ADHD. *Neuroscience and Biobehavioral Reviews*, *24*, 21–25.

Swanson, J. M. (1997). Hyperkinetic disorders and attention deficit hyperactivity disorders. *Current Opinion in Psychiatry*, *10*, 300–305.

Swanson, J. M., Sergeant, A., Taylor, E., Sonuga-Barke, E. J. S., Jensen, P. S., & Cantwell, D. P. (1998b) Attention-deficit hyperactivity disorder and hyperkinetic disorder. *Lancet*, *351*, 429–433.

Tales, A., Newton, P., Troscianko, T., & Butler, S. (1999). Mismatch negativity in the visual modality. *NeuroReport*, *10*, 3363–3367.

Tallal, P. (1981). Language disabilities in children: Perceptual correlates. *International Journal of Pediatric Otorhinolaryngology*, *3*, 1–13.

Tervaniemi, M., Ilvonen, T., Sinkkonen, J., Kujala, A., Alho, K., Huotilainen, M. et al. (2000a). Harmonic partials facilitate pitch discrimination in humans: Electrophysiological and behavioral evidence. *Neuroscience Letters*, *279*, 29–32.

Tervaniemi, M., Lehtokoski, A., Sinkonen, J., Virtanen, J., & Ilmoniemi, R. J. (1999). Test–retest reliability of mismatch negativity for duration, frequency and intensity changes. *Clinical Neurophysiology*, *110*, 1388–1393.

Tervaniemi, M., Schröger, E., Saher, M., & Näätänen, R. (2000b). Effects of spectral complexity and sound duration on automatic complex-sound pitch processing in humans: A mismatch negativity study. *Neuroscience Letters*, *290*, 66–70.

Thomas, D. G., & Crow, C. D. (1994). Development of evoked electrical brain activity in infancy. In G. Dawson & K. W. Fischer (Eds.), *Human behavior and the developing brain* (pp. 207–231). New York: Guilford Press.

Tiitinen, H., May, P., Reinikainen, K., & Näätänen, R. (1994). Attention and novelty detection in humans is governed by pre-attentive sensory memory. *Nature*, *372*, 90–92.

Trainor, L. J., Samuel, S. S., Desjardins, R. N., & Sonnadara, R. R. (2001). Measuring temporal resolution in infants using mismatch negativity. *NeuroReport*, *8*, 2443–2448.

Trehub, S. E., Schneider, B. A., Morrongiello, B. A., & Thorpe, L. A. (1980). Auditory sensitivity in school-age children. *Journal of Experimental Child Psychology*, *29*, 281–293.

Tuchman, R. F. (1999). Neuroanatomical, neuroradiological and functional magnetic resonance imaging correlates of developmental dyslexia. *Revisita de Neurologica*, *29*, 322–326.

Uwer, R., Albrecht, R., & von Suchodoletz, W. (2002). Automatic processing of tones and speech stimuli in children with specific language impairment. *Developmental Medicine and Child Neurology*, *44*, 527–532.

Uwer, R., & von Suchodoletz, W. (2000). Stability of mismatch negativities in children. *Clinical Neurophysiology*, *111*, 45–52.

Vaal, J., van Soest, A. J., & Hopkins, B. (2000). Spontaneous kicking behavior in infants: Age-related effects of unilateral weighting. *Developmental Psychobiology*, *36*, 111–122.

Vaidya, C. J., Austin, G., Kirkorian, G., Ridlehuber, H. W., Desmond, J. E., Glover, G. H. et al. (1998). Selective effects of methylphenidate in attention deficit hyperactivity disorder: A functional magnetic resonance study. *Proceedings of the National Academy of Sciences USA*, *95*, 14494–14499.

Vaughan, H. G. J., & Kurtzberg, D. (1991). Electrophysiologic indices of brain maturation and cognitive development. In M. R. Guunar & C. A. Nelson (Eds.), *Minnesota Symposia on Child Psychology, Vol. 24* (pp. 1–36). Hillsdale, NJ: Lawrence Erlbaum Associates Inc.

Weber, C., Hahne, A., Friedrich, M., & Friederici, A. D. (2004). Discrimination of word stress in early infant perception: Electrophysiological evidence. *Brain Research: Cognitive Brain Research*, *18*, 149–161.

Weber, C., Hahne, A., Friedrich, M., & Friederici, A. D. (2005). Reduced stress pattern discrimination in 5-month-olds as a marker of risk for later language impairment: Neurophysiologial evidence. *Brain Research: Cognitive Brain Research*, *25*, 180–187.

Werker, J. F., & Tees, R.C. (1984). Cross-language speech perception: Evidence for perceptual reorganization during the first year of life. *Infant Behavior and Development*, *7*, 49–63.

Winkler, I. (2000, June). *Change detection in natural auditory environments*. Talk presented at meeting of MMN2000, Barcelona.

Winkler, I., Karmos, G., & Näätänen, R. (1996). Adaptive modeling of the unattended acoustic environment reflected in the mismatch negativity event-related potential. *Brain Research*, *742*, 239–252.

Winkler, I., Lehtokoski, A., Alku, P., Vainio, M., Czigler, I., Csepe, V. et al. (1999). Pre-attentive detection of vowel contrasts utilizes both phonetic and auditory memory representations. *Brain Research: Cognitive Brain Research*, *7*, 357–369.

Winsberg, B. G., Javitt, D. C., & Silipo, G. S. (1997). Electrophysiological indices of information processing in methylphenidate responders. *Biological Psychiatry*, *42*, 434–445.

Winsberg, B. G., Javitt, D. G., Silipo, G. S., & Doneshka, P. (1993). Mismatch negativity in hyperactive children: Effects of methylphenidate. *Psychopharmacology Bulletin*, *29*, 229–233.

Winter, O., Kok, A., Kenemans, J. L., & Elton, M. (1995). Auditory event-related potentials to deviant stimuli during drowsiness and stage 2 sleep. *Electroencephalography and Clinical Neurophysiology*, *96*, 398–412.

Woldorff, M. G., Hackley, S. A., & Hillyard, S. A. (1991). The effects of channel-selective attention on the mismatch negativity wave elicited by deviant tones. *Psychophysiology, 28*, 30–42.

Woods, D. L., Alho, K., & Algazi, A. (1992). Intermodal selective attention I: Effects on event-related potentials to lateralized auditory and visual stimuli. *Electroencephalography and Clinical Neurophysiology, 82*, 341–355.

7 The use of event-related evoked potentials to predict developmental outcomes

Dennis L. Molfese, Victoria J. Molfese and Nikki L. Pratt
University of Louisville, Kentucky, USA

There is great interest by researchers, clinicians, educators, and parents in understanding brain functioning and cognitive skill development. This interest has been heightened by the development of methodologies for measuring brain responses that have revealed differences between typically developing and at-risk or disabled children. Some useful and relatively new techniques for studying the cognitive skills include event-related potentials (ERPs) that use scalp electrodes to detect electrical activity generated by neurons in the brain. These brain responses, in turn, can be related to behavioral measures to look for reliable commonalities useful for understanding how brain mechanisms correspond to behavior. The purpose of this chapter is to review the use of ERP techniques in research to better understand how brain-based responses can be systematically related to developmental changes in specific cognitive skills. From this review it should be clear that the ERP technique provides insights into brain–behavior development that complements and supplements information obtained through more traditional behavioral measures.

ERPs INDEX SPEECH PERCEPTION

Early studies using ERP measures focused on the more general issue of whether brain responses reflected discriminations of speech compared to non-speech sounds and whether such discriminations were accompanied by differences in the responding of the two brain hemispheres to these stimuli (Cohn, 1971; Friedman, Simson, Ritters, & Rapin, 1975; Galambos, Benson, Smith, Schulman-Galambos, & Osier, 1975; Jaramillo, Ilvonen, Kujala, Alku, Tervaniemi, & Alho, 2001; Kayser, Tenke, & Bruder, 1998; Molfese, Freeman, & Palermo, 1975; Morrell & Salamy, 1971; Neville, 1974). However, this line of research focusing on discrimination of gross differences between auditory stimuli soon came to an end. As Molfese (1978b) noted, speech sounds differ from non-speech sounds on many acoustical dimensions (e.g., frequency, formant structure and duration, number of formants, frequency transitions, rise and decay times) thereby making the ultimate goal of the early research difficult if not impossible to attain because of the many co-varying and confounding variables.

As researchers began to examine more specific dimensions of auditory stimuli, variations were found in ERP components or waveform peaks that occurred in response to changes in stimulus dimensions in adults (Molfese, 1978b, 1980a, 1980b) as well as in infants and children (Cheour et al., 1998a, 1998b, 2002; Cheour-Luhtanen et al., 1995, 1996; Dehaene-Lambertz & Pena, 2001; Dehaene-Lambertz, Pena, Christophe, & Landrieu, 2004; Martynova, Kirjavainen, & Cheour, 2003). As researchers pursued these investigations, some questioned whether there might be a link between the abilities to discriminate auditory stimuli as evidenced by changes in the ERP and concurrent or later cognitive skills, particularly in infants (Butler & Engel, 1969; Engel & Fay, 1972; Engel & Henderson, 1973; Henderson & Engel, 1974; Jensen & Engel, 1971). This interest in developmental changes in brain responses and the meaning of the changes in terms of predicting later outcomes opened what has become a robust area of research interest.

THE USE OF ERPs TO PREDICT LANGUAGE OUTCOMES

The earliest studies attempting to relate brain responses to later behavioral measures used ERPs recorded from infants in response to a simple flash of light. A series of studies using visual ERPs with infants and children found an early peak in the brainwave (with the latency of the N1 component occurring at approximately 146 ms) that correlated with several behavioral measures. For example, Butler and Engel (1969) reported the first success in finding correlations between the visual ERP latencies obtained from neonates and later measures of intelligence obtained in infancy. In this study, a sample of 433 children was obtained from the Collaborative Project on Cerebral Palsy, Mental Retardation and Other Neurological and Sensory Disorders of Infancy and Childhood. Performance measures on the Bayley Infant Scales at 8 months were obtained and used as the criterion measures. Although the correlations between the behavioral measures and photic latency were significant, the effects were small and accounted for little of the variance (r ranged from .23 to .33). These correlations were similar in magnitude to those obtained using gestational age and the same developmental scores, although the correlations between birth weight and developmental scores were somewhat lower. While photic latency was found to contribute to the correlations with developmental scores independent of gestational age and birth weight, the amount of variance accounted for by photic latency alone was little better than that accounted for by gestational age alone. Jensen and Engel (1971) reported correlations between neonatal photic latencies and developmental scores (i.e., age of walking) at 1 year of age. In this study photic responses were obtained from 1074 neonates. When photic latency responses were divided into three regions it was found that those infants with the shortest photic latencies were the earliest walkers.

Studies that attempted to extend the period of predictivity beyond the first year of life and into the second and third years of life (and beyond) have reported less success. Engel and Fay (1972) investigated the relationship between visual ERPs recorded in 852 neonates and later performance on tests of articulation obtained at age 3 years and on the Stanford-Binet obtained at age 4 years. They found that those infants with faster photic latencies (less than 146 ms) performed better at 3 years of age on the initial and final consonant articulation task than did slow reactors. Photic latency, however, was not predictive of differences in performance on the Stanford-Binet at 4 years. The authors concluded that while photic latency may be predictive of motor development, such as that involved in articulation, it is not predictive of symbolic/intellectual development. Engel and Henderson (1973) and Henderson and Engel (1974) conducted subsequent studies with somewhat older populations of children. These studies failed to find a relationship between five peaks identified in neonatal visual ERPs and any of a variety of scores on WISC-R subtests and scores on the Bender Gestalt test obtained at 7–8 years of age from a sample of 122 children. The authors concluded that neonatal photic latency responses in neurologically normal children are not related to later intelligence test performance. Henderson and Engel (1974) reached a similar conclusion in their subsequent study. In that study they assessed whether the neonatal visual ERPs could be used to predict total WISC-R IQ and subtest scores, sensorimotor, perceptual-motor, and achievement test scores at 7 years of age. The photic latency data from 809 infants did not significantly correlate with any of the performance scores.

In general, studies conducted during the late 1960s and early 1970s report some early relationship between one component of the visual ERP, the latency or length of the interval between stimulus onset and the first negative waveform peak, and subsequent motor, cognitive-motor, or language-related abilities during the first year of life. However, further research comparing neonatal ERPs with later intelligence score measured after the first year failed to demonstrate that such a relationship continued into the toddler, preschool, and early elementary school years (see Appendix).

Although it might appear discouraging based on these early studies that ERP measures could be used as predictors of later cognitive functioning, more recent studies suggest that such relationships do in fact exist (Molfese & Molfese, 1985; Molfese & Searock, 1986). The differences in success between such studies reflect a number of differences in both methodology and experimental design. First, Molfese and his associates focused their attention on the analysis of the entire evoked potential waveform, while earlier investigators typically confined their analysis to a single peak in the waveform. Molfese argued that an approach that analyzed all data collected instead of only a small subset increases the likelihood of identifying a relationship between early brain responses and later developmental outcomes, if such relationships exist. Second, the frequency range of the ERPs studied by Molfese included a lower range of frequencies (below 2 Hz) than those employed by earlier investigators. Given that the brain wave frequencies characterizing the evoked potentials of very young infants are concentrated in the frequency range below 1–2 Hz, earlier investigations omitted a significant portion of the ERP signal from their data. However, the inclusion of lower-frequency signals through a change in the filtering of the brain responses enables much more of the response to be assessed, increasing the possibility of finding relationships between an enhanced and more comprehensive brain response and other behavioral indicators. Third, these later studies employed language-related stimuli, usually speech sounds, as the evoking stimuli rather than the photic flashes used by the researchers cited above. The relationship of photic flashes to the types of cognitive processing reflected in language skills and in the various cognitive skills tapped by intelligence tests is not known. However, data are available indicating that speech perception abilities are specifically related to language and that verbal skills of young children play an important part in their performance on intelligence tests (Molfese, Yaple, Helwig, Harris, & Connell, 1992). Since predictors of successful performance are generally better if they measure factors more directly related to the predicted skills, the inclusion of more language-relevant materials as the evoking stimuli should increase the likelihood for predicting later language-related skills. These methodological changes could be responsible for the better success found in the studies described at more length below in using auditory evoked responses recorded at birth to predict later language functioning and language-related cognitive skills, such as reading.

Molfese et al. (1975) were the first to report evidence of functional laterality in young infants to speech. In subsequent work, Molfese charted changes in lateralization patterns into adulthood. The early work is significant because theoreticians had speculated that the absence of hemispheric or lateralized differences in children indicates that the child is at risk for certain cognitive or language disabilities (Travis, 1931). Three decades later, Lenneberg (1967) argued that lateralization is a biological sign of language. Such views advanced the notion that the presence of hemisphere differences per se is predictive of language development. In sharp contrast to this view, Molfese et al. (1975) pointed out that lateralized brain responding was already present in early infancy, a finding subsequently replicated and supported by investigators using a range of different methodologies. A decade later, Molfese and Molfese (1985) argued that lateralization per se was not the effective predictor of later language development. Rather, they argued and reported evidence to support the contention that predictions concerning language performance are effective only when specific speech perception processing capacities are lateralized.

Molfese and Molfese (1985) recorded ERPs in response to different consonant and vowel contrasts from 16 infants using electrodes placed over the left and right temporal areas (T3 and T4 referred to the ipsilateral mastoid and with a bandpass set to 0.1–30 Hz) at birth and again at 6-month intervals until the child's third birthday. Information was also obtained for a variety of prenatal and perinatal events, IQ, language, SES, and child-centered activities in the home.

Analyses indicated that ERPs recorded at birth identified children who performed better or worse on language tasks by 3 years of age. Two ERP components were identified. An initial large negative peak (N230) over left hemisphere (LH) electrodes reliably discriminated children whose McCarthy Verbal Index scores were above 50 (the HIGH group) from those with lower scores (the LOW group). The LOW group displayed no such lateralized discrimination for either the speech or the non-speech sounds. A second component of the ERP with a late negative peak (N664) also discriminated HIGH from LOW groups. Unlike the earlier component, however, the second component occurred across both hemispheres and, consequently, reflected bilateral activity. While the second component discriminated speech from non-speech stimuli, its ability to discriminate between specific consonant sounds depended on which vowel followed the consonant. Hemispheric differences alone in the neonatal ERP responses did not discriminate between infants who varied in their language skills at 3 years of age. Given that ERP components discriminating between the two groups detected differences between speech and non-speech sounds, it appears that the ERPs reflected the infant's sensitivity to specific language-related cues rather than the overall readiness of the brain to respond to any general auditory stimulus.

In subsequent analyses of these data, Molfese and Molfese (1986) employed a stepwise multiple regression model using Peabody Picture Vocabulary Test (PPVT) and McCarthy Verbal Index scores obtained at 3 years of age as dependent variables. The ERP components obtained at birth that best discriminated the different consonant sounds in the previous research were used as the independent variables. This model accounted for 78% of the total variance in predicting McCarthy scores from the brain responses, whereas 69% of the variance was accounted for in predicting Peabody scores (Molfese, 1989). Clearly, a strong relation exists between early ERP discrimination of speech sounds and later language skills. Interestingly, the inclusion of perinatal measures and Brazelton scores improved the amount of variance by less than 3%, reinforcing the notion that the brain responses at this stage of development were more potent than other neonatal measures in predicting later developmental outcomes, at least in the healthy children who participated in the research

In a study with older infants, Molfese and Searock (1986) extended the predictive relationship between early ERP activity and emerging language skills at 3 years to include vowel sound discrimination. ERPs that reflected greater discrimination between vowel sounds at 1 year of age characterized infants who performed better on language tasks at 3 years. Thus, ERPs at birth as well as at 1 year successfully predict language performance at 3 years. Molfese (1989) replicated these findings using a different sample of infants, different electrode placements, and different statistical approaches. In that study, ERPs were recorded at birth from frontal, temporal, and parietal scalp areas over the left hemisphere (LH) and right hemisphere (RH) of 30 infants in response to the speech syllables /bi, gi/, and their non-speech analogues. The infants were brought back for retesting at their birthdates for behavioral testing on a variety of cognitive tests, including the McCarthy Scales of Children's Abilities. Discriminant function procedures used the ERP regions identified by Molfese and Molfese (1985) to classify each of the 720 averaged ERPs into one of two groups (either resembling LOW or HIGH language performers). Classification accuracy was significantly above chance, accounting for 68.6% of the children in the HIGH group and 69.7% of those in the LOW group. This replication across different populations of children is noteworthy, indicating the stability of specific regions in the brainwaves across samples in correctly classifying infants to predict later language skills.

More recently, Molfese and Molfese (1997) noted that the relationship between early neonatal ERPs and later language performance measures continues into the elementary school years. ERPs were recorded from 71 full term, newborn infants, in response to nine consonant-vowel syllables that combined each of the initial consonants, /b, d, g/ with a following vowel, either /a, i, or u/. Electrode sites and recording procedures were identical to Molfese (1989). Children were retested at 5 years of age using the Stanford-Binet Intelligence Test. These 71 children were divided into two groups based on their Stanford-Binet verbal scores: 62 children with verbal IQ scores above 100 (High Group) and 9 with verbal IQ scores less than 100 (the break-point of 100 was based on the standardized norms for this test in which the average score is 100). No differences were noted between groups in prenatal, perinatal, and SES measures. A discriminant function analysis correctly classified 8 of 9 children belonging to the Low group (88.9%) along with 60 of 62 children (96.8%) belonging to the High group. Thus, analyses indicated a high level of accuracy in using neonatal ERPs recorded in response to speech sound stimuli to classify children's language performance at 5 years of age.

ERPs AS PREDICTORS OF LANGUAGE-RELATED OUTCOMES: READING

The language studies were expanded in a subsequent study by Molfese (2000) to include children's performance on tests of word-level decoding. In these studies, neonatal ERPs were tested to determine whether they could be used to predict reading skills at 8 years of age. Molfese hypothesized that since ERPs were predictive of language skills, and since language skills are correlated with reading skills, it should be possible to predict reading skills using the same types of ERP measures that were predictive of language skills. Thus, auditory ERPs were recorded from LH and RH frontal, temporal, and parietal scalp regions of 48 infants within 36 hours of birth to /bi/ and /gi/, and non-speech homologues of these sounds. All children were subsequently tested within 2 weeks of their 8-year birth date using a range of language and reading measures. The reading measures tapped two different types of reading skills—real word and pseudoword reading. The Word Reading subtest of the WRAT (Wide Range Achievement Test—Revised; Wilkinson, 1993) Reading subscale was used to identify skills in reading words in isolation. The Woodcock-Johnson Word Attack subtest was used to identify skills in reading nonwords. Nonword reading is believed to separate sight word reading skills from skills depending on phonological ability that would be needed for the reading of nonwords. Within this group there were 17 children whose reading skills characterized them as having dyslexia, 7 who were characterized as poor readers, and 24 children who served as controls and were matched on the basis of IQ and SES factors to the other children. Children identified as Dyslexic at 8 years of age had normal full-scale IQ (FSIQ) scores (mean FSIQ = 110.0) as measured by the Wechsler Intelligence Scales for Children–3 (Wechsler, 1991; WISC–3). In contrast, their WRAT reading scores were below average (mean = 80.6). A group identified as Poor Readers had both low reading scores (mean WRAT = 85.4) and lower WISC Full Scale IQ scores (mean FSIQ = 96.9). Although the FSIQ scores of the Poor Readers and Dyslexics differed from each other, their reading scores did not. The Control children were matched to the full-scale IQ scores of the Dyslexic children (mean WISC FSIQ = 111.7), although their WRAT reading scores were higher than those obtained by both the Poor Readers and Dyslexic children (mean WRAT = 103.75).

In the analyses of these data, the peak latencies and amplitudes from the ERP regions earlier identified by Molfese and Molfese (1985) were used as the dependent measures in a discriminant function analysis to classify the children's reading performance at 8 years. In general, results indicated faster latencies for the Control children in comparison to the Dyslexic and Poor Reading groups, as well as larger N1 amplitudes for the Control infants, while the N2 amplitudes were larger in the Dyslexic and Poor Reading groups. The Poor Reading group also generated a larger P2 amplitude response. Two significant canonical discriminant functions correctly classified 81.25% of the entire sample (39 of 48 children) at 8 years of age, that included 6 of 7 children identified as Poor Readers (85.7%), 14 of 17 identified as Dyslexics (82.4%), and 19 of 24 Controls (79.2%). These data extended findings previously reporting strong relationships between neonatal speech discrimination and language performance measures at 3 and 5 years to a similarly strong relation between neonatal ERPs and reading skills at 8 years of age. There is a strong relationship between infant abilities to discriminate speech sounds and later language and reading performance.

A subsequent study by Andrews Espy, Molfese, Molfese, Simos, and Modglin (2004) employed a growth curve analysis to track the development of 109 children (61 females), within 2 weeks of their birthday, at ages 1 through 8 years, to specifically test whether the development of perceptual skills beyond the newborn period were related to subsequent reading abilities. A total of 25 repetitions each of four auditory stimuli (speech and non-speech versions of /bi/ and /gi/) that were earlier used by Molfese (Molfese & Molfese, 1979a, 1985) were presented to each child using different random orderings of the four stimuli with varied intervals and an equal probability of occurrence. Electrode placements were comparable to those employed by Molfese (2000). Baseline-to-peak analyses were carried out for the first negative peak deflection from prestimulus baseline (N1), the large positive peak deflection (P2) that occurred immediately following N1, and the next negative peak (N2) which followed directly after P2. At age 8 years, children were administered two reading tests during yearly testing sessions as part of the longitudinal study. The Word Attack subtest of the Woodcock-Johnson Psychoeducational Battery—Revised (Woodcock & Johnson, 1989) was administered to assess nonsense-word decoding, unconfounded by familiarity. In the Word Attack subtest, children decode single nonsense words, some of which are irregular and some of which can be sounded out by regular phonetic rules. Normative data are available by age and grade level—age-level normative data were used to transform the raw score into the resultant standard score for grouping participants. The Wide Range Achievement Test—Revised (WRAT-R; Jastak & Wilkinson, 1984) Reading subtest was also administered to assess real-word decoding abilities. This instrument provides a time-efficient index of single word reading. Children are presented with an array of 42 words and are instructed to read one word at a time. The number of words read correctly is scored. Normative data are available by age and grade level—age-level normative data were used to transform the raw score into a standard score for the purpose of parsing participants into groups.

A categorical grouping scheme was used to compare growth trajectories between children of different reading abilities. Children were divided into groups by their WJ-R Word Attack scores at age 8 years, where those with average scores (WA-AVG group) were defined as those who obtained a standard score ≤ 90 ($n = 96$) and children in the low-scoring group (WA-LOW group) were defined as those who scored ≤ 89 ($n = 13$). When the WRAT-R Reading standard scores were used to create groups using the same cut-score, there were 79 children in the R-AVG group ($M = 104.79$) and 30 in the WR-LOW group ($M = 80.67$).

Growth curve analysis using hierarchical linear modeling was utilized to analyze the longitudinal data, using a mixed model design and restricted maximum likelihood estimation. For ERP latencies, a cubic model best described change from ages 1 through 8 for the N1 peak, whereas a quadratic model was the best fit for the P2 and N2 waveforms. There was evidence of different rates of growth in the peak latencies during the early period (ages 1 to 4 years) and the later period (ages 4 to 8 years). For WJ-R Word Attack, some growth parameters describing development of the ERP N1 and N2 peaks differed as a function of group, i.e., Word Attack—average (WA-AVG) and Word Attack—low (WA-LOW) groups.

Early change in N1 amplitudes recorded to speech sounds occurred at frontal, temporal, and parietal sites. For frontal and parietal recording sites, the linear changes in N1 amplitudes to speech sounds at age 4 years were more steeply negative in the WA-LOW group relative to the WA-AVG group only during the 1- to 4-year period. Additionally, the N1 amplitudes recorded at the frontal leads in response to speech stimuli were more negative during the early observation period, with steeper changes in amplitude, particularly between ages 2 and 3, and 3 and 4 years. A similar pattern occurred for parietal sites, where there were pronounced differences in N1 amplitudes in response to speech sounds between the WA-AVG and WA-LOW groups, with steeper changes in ERP growth in the WA-LOW group for the speech condition and more attenuated changes for the non-speech condition.

For the WRAT-R Reading group, the group-related differences in the trajectories of ERP development differed substantially from results using the WJ-R Word Attack. Group-related differences in N2 growth were evident only from age 4 through 8 years. There were no group-related differences in N2 amplitude growth in the early observation period, or in the maturation of N1 or P2 amplitudes. However, the expected amplitude at age 4 years was more negative for the WR-LOW group by -3.12 μV. In addition, the linear rate of change in N2 amplitude at age 4 years for the WR-LOW group was more steeply positive relative to that of the WR-LOW group.

Overall, the relations between ERP responses to speech stimuli and reading scores were most evident for the early processing component, the N1 ERP waveform. This relationship between N1 and nonsense single pseudoword reading is consistent with previously observed relations between the N1 from newborn ERPs and language abilities at age 3 and 5 years (Molfese & Molfese, 2000), and the identification of reading in disabled readers at age 8 (Molfese, 2000; Molfese, Molfese, & Modglin, 2001). The present findings suggest that it is not just biologically based differences in the processing of auditory information in the newborn brain that underlie later cognitive proficiencies. Rather, it is the early *development* (between the ages of 1 and 4 years) of these brain-based perceptual skills, manifested by changes in ERP N1 amplitudes, that provides a dynamic platform for the later development of language-related abilities, such as reading skills. In less proficient readers, the N1 amplitudes were consistently larger, with a more rapid rate of change in the early observation period. Because ERPs likely reflect the maturation of neuronal activation patterns in the auditory cortex, both in neuronal circuitry (i.e., anatomy), as well as neuronal signaling (i.e., function) (Nunez, 1981; Molfese, Molfese, & Modglin, 2001), these amplitude differences suggest that less proficient readers must recruit greater cortical surface or volume than average readers to perceive auditory information that is critical for reading. Support for this hypothesis is provided by recent findings using high-density array ERP techniques in which greater amplitude responses distributed over broader brain regions is observed in dyslexic/poor readers compared to average readers (Molfese et al., 2003).

MISMATCH NEGATIVITY AND PREDICTION OF LANGUAGE OUTCOMES

A series of related studies assessed the relationship between ERPs and language-related events using a different technique—the mismatch negativity (MMN) paradigm. Näätänen et al. (1997) first described MMN as a negative deflection in the brain waveform that has a typical latency of 100–250 ms in adults. The amplitude of the negative component is largest at frontal and central electrode sites (Fabiani, Gratton, & Coles, 2000; Liebenthal, Ellingson, Spanaki, Prieto, Ropella, & Binder, 2003). The MMN is elicited using an odd-ball paradigm where an infrequently occurring deviant stimulus is presented in a stream of a more frequent standard stimulus. Because MMN paradigms typically do not require attention to the stimuli, they have been widely used in developmental research (Csépe, 1995; Csépe, Pantev, Hoke, Hampson, & Ross, 1992; Kraus, McGee, Micco, Sharma, Carrell, & Nicol, 1993). In the auditory modality, the MMN can be evoked by any perceivable physical deviance from the standard stimulus, such as changes in tone duration, frequency, intensity, and interstimulus interval (Rosburg, 2003). MMN is thought to be an index of the early, pre-attentive sensory memory, most likely only echoic memory (Näätänen, 1990, 1992). MMN has been used as a measure of the participant's ability to discriminate linguistic stimuli (e.g., speech sounds with different voice onset time or place of articulation; Näätänen, 1992). In this method, ERPs elicited by the standard stimuli are subtracted from the ERPs for the deviants to determine whether the presence of a deviant stimulus has been detected. The subtracted component generally displays onset latency as short as 50 ms and a peak latency of 100–200 ms (Näätänen, 1992).

A number of investigators have applied this paradigm to their investigations into links between infant brain responses and dyslexia. In an early application, Leppänen, Pihko, Eklund, and Lyytinen (1999) recorded MMN during a oddball paradigm from 23 newborn infants to a series of two speech syllables, /kaa/ and /ka/, that varied in stimulus duration from 250 ms for /kaa/ to 110 ms for /ka/. The babies were divided into two groups, a High Risk group of 12 babies who had a familial background of dyslexia, and a Low Risk group of 11 babies. Classification into the High Risk group was based on parent self-report or report about a close relative with dyslexia, or a diagnosis of dyslexia that included a performance one standard deviation below the norm on accuracy or speed of oral reading or accuracy of written spelling plus a minimum of two single-word measures (e.g., word recognition, pseudo-word decoding, lexical decision). Parents of both groups had full-scale IQ scores equal or greater than 85 based on the Raven Matrices B,C,D. The Low Risk group that included 11 babies matched the High Risk group on a variety of factors including SES and parent education. The Low Risk group generated larger-amplitude ERP responses to the slow vs. the fast stimuli over the F4 electrode site at both the 130–225 ms and 225–400 ms regions, while the High Risk group exhibited no such differences. In general, larger-amplitude

ERPs were noted across frontal sites for the High Risk group for shorter stimuli and over right hemisphere sites for the longer stimuli.

In a subsequent study with 6-month-old infants, Leppanen et al. (2002) tested 76 healthy infants that included a Risk group of 37 infants (20 males) from families with a history of dyslexia using criteria comparable to Leppanen et al. (1999). Infants attended to naturally produced pseudowords that included a vowel-consonant-vowel syllable /ata/ in which the stop consonant varied from 95 ms (ata) to 195 ms (atta) to 255 ms (attta). The syllables were presented at 75 dB SPL, using an oddball design (80/10/10) and difference waves were then calculated by subtracting the short /ata/ from the long /attta/. The intermediate stimulus was not analyzed. A Main Effect for groups was found in which the Risk group exhibited less differentiation between the standard and target stimuli between 590–625 ms and 715–755 ms. Overall, the researchers failed to find a MMN-like response in the at-risk group for changes in consonant duration, suggesting less sensitivity to temporal processing information for those with a familial risk of dyslexia.

Richardson, Leppanen, Leiwo, and Lyytinen (2003) studied infants from families at risk for dyslexia and from families not at risk. The familial risk group had one or both parents who identified themselves as dyslexic through self-report, scored at 1 SD below the norm in an assessment of oral reading/ spelling skills, and showed similar deviations on at least two measures of: pseudoword reading (speed/accuracy), word recognition speed, lexical decision (speed and accuracy from written items), and syllabic segmentation. In addition, in the at-risk families at least one first- or second-degree relative was reported to have reading problems. The study compared the auditory discrimination skills in at-risk and control infants as well as the perception of their parents in a series of behavioral tasks. While this study did not report ERP effects, the results are important for considering the mechanisms responsible as identified by the Jyväskylä group as well as the findings reported by Molfese and his associates.

The study involved two experiments, the first with infants and the second their parents. A total of 105 (out of 187) 6-month-old infants were conditioned (*M* age = 6 months, 5 days) of whom 54 were at risk (33 boys) and 51 were controls (29 boys). All were healthy, with normal hearing. The infants' categorization ability was assessed using a head-turn procedure (correct head turns were visually reinforced using an animated toy). One stimulus, ata, was the repeated stimulus with change trials using a longer t sounds (atta). Speech stimuli were presented with offset-to-onset interstimulus intervals of 1000 ms. For Experiment 2, 133 parents of the infants in Experiment 1 were tested. This included 57 (24 males) with dyslexia and 76 (36 males) who exhibited no problems in reading or writing.

Experiment 1 found that the at-risk and control infants responded differently to stimuli at or near the category boundary, with 57% of the controls responding with a head turn vs. 32% of the at-risk infants. In Experiment 2 with the parents of these infants, stimulus effects were significant between adults with and without dyslexia. As with the infants, adults with dyslexia needed longer-duration stimuli to distinguish ata from atta. In other words, the category boundary differed between the group with dyslexia compared to the group without dyslexia. This study showed that differences in categorizing speech sounds according to duration of the sound, a factor that is crucial to intelligibility in Finnish, is associated with familial risk for dyslexia early in infancy. This difference in speech sound categorization persists into adulthood and characterizes those adults suffering from dyslexia. Richardson et al. concluded that dyslexia may involve a deficiency in processing of speech sound duration early in development.

Using ERP measures, Pihko, Leppänen, Eklund, Cheour, Guttorm, and Lyytinen (1999) recorded auditory ERP from newborns and 6-month-old infants, about half of whom had a familial risk for dyslexia. The infants tested at 1 week included 73 babies: 42 at high familial risk for dyslexia and 31 controls. A follow-up test was conducted at 6 months that included 51 babies: 28 at high risk and 23 controls. Newborn ERPs were recorded from F3, F4, C3, C4, P3, P4, and an electrode cap was used to test 6-month-olds. An oddball paradigm was used to test infants that involved a frequent CV-Syllable (/kaa/ duration 250 ms, probability at 88%) and a deviant stimulus (/ka/ duration 110 ms, probability at 12%). The /kaa/ was digitized from natural speech and shortened to form /ka/, but all speech tokens had equal rise and fall times, differing only in duration of the vowel. Significant group differences occurred only at 6 months of age in response to /kaa/ with right hemispheric differences in late latencies occurring for the at-risk group, while effects occurred over the left hemisphere for controls. In both groups, the responses to the deviant /ka/ were more positive than those to the standard /kaa/ stimuli, contrary to the findings of adult ERPs to duration changes. The results also suggested differences in brain activation patterns between groups.

In a follow-up to this work, Lyytinen et al. (2004; see also Lyytinen et al. 2001) describe the long-term follow-up of children at familial risk for dyslexia ($N = 107$) and their controls ($N = 93$) from birth to school entry in skill areas generally considered relevant to reading. Gestational age, birth weight, and Apgar scores were equivalent between groups. At school entry, the at-risk children exhibited a significant difference in verbal IQ from the control children. Lyytinen et al. noted that group differences in speech processing in infancy predicted a link between the first steps in reading and ERPs. Lyytinen recorded ERPs during first days of life that differed for vowel duration change (/kaa/ deviant—/ka/—ISI = 855 ms) in an oddball/MMN paradigm. The at-risk infants generated larger and positive ERPs to shorter-duration and deviant stimuli. In addition, following Molfese and Molfese (1985, 1997; see also Molfese, 2000), at-risk and control newborns responded differently to stimulus features in speech sounds /ba/ /da/ /ga/. Using this task, the at-risk infants generated larger ERP responses and with larger differences over the right hemisphere electrode sites, whereas more marked differences were noted over the left hemisphere sites for control infants. In addition, responses to the speech syllable /ga/ were more positive in amplitude and longer duration over right hemisphere electrode sites for at-risk infants. Various measures of early language skills, including pronunciation accuracy, and phonological and morphological skills, discriminated between both groups and correlated with later reading outcomes. The majority of these measures became stronger with age, suggesting an increased reliability of the measures with age. Lyytinen and colleagues viewed these results as promising for increasing our understanding of the early identification dyslexia. These researchers view the at-risk children as less efficient at representing temporal speech signals, a deficit they believe can be seen at a pre-attentive level (as noted in the MMN responses) and that is related to poor categorical speech perception.

WHY ARE ERPs PREDICTIVE OF LANGUAGE DEVELOPMENT?

Researchers continue to raise questions regarding the consequence of speech perception processes present so early in development that relate to the emergence of development of language and language-related skills. Clearly, some phonological skills that are important for analyzing and discriminating sound patterns in spoken words are present at or near birth. One such example is the ability of young infants to discriminate between place of articulation cues such as a /b/ sound from a /g/ consonant sound (Molfese & Molfese, 1979a). The perception of other speech cues appears to develop later in infancy, such as the discrimination of voice onset time (Lisker & Abramson, 1970) that enables voiced consonants (e.g., /b,d,b/) to be discriminated from voiceless consonants (e.g., /p,t,k/). This ability appears to be present as early as 1 month of age (Eimas, Siqueland, Jusczyk, & Vigorito, 1971; Molfese & Molfese, 1986). There are also changes in the discrimination skills of young infants that arise from repeated exposures to the phonetic contrasts that are characteristic of their language environments (Eilers, Wilson, & Moore, 1977; Eimas et al., 1971; Molfese, 2000; Molfese and Molfese, 1979a, 1979b). These changes in the infant's sensitivity to the unique characteristics of the language environment appear to facilitate language acquisition. Infants who are better able to discriminate between /b/ and /p/, for example, would be able to more readily discriminate between words such big and pig, as phonetic contrasts are mapped to word differences. This basic link between the ability to rapidly and effectively discriminate between phonetic contrasts, and the later ability to process these differences phonemically to discriminate between words and map from the phonemes onto the letter orthography, we believe is the reason why differences in newborn ERP responses to speech sounds link with subsequent differences in children's language and reading skills.

In the preschool period, further language skills become evident. Children develop the ability to segment spoken monosyllable words into onsets and rimes, and thus to play nursery rhyme games (Vellutino & Scanlon, 1987). As they approach kindergarten age, children can segment polysyllabic words into syllables, and around first grade are able to segment monosyllabic words into phonemes (Liberman, Cooper, Shankweiler, & Studdert-Kennedy, 1967). The ability to attend to and manipulate the sound structure of words is referred to as "phonological awareness" and phonological awareness skills are funda-mental to language development and to subsequent reading abilities (Brady, 1991; Catts, Fey, Zhang, & Tomblin, 1999; Wagner, Torgesen, & Rashotte, 1994). Researchers report that skills in phonological awareness, phonological processing (the process of identifying sounds and the words that the sounds combine to make), and phonological memory (the ability to keep phono-logical information, such as phonemes or words, in short-term or long-term memory) are all important for the development of reading skills, and these skills become evident as children begin the elementary school grades.

A strong link between phonological processing skills and reading has been established through behavior and brain studies (e.g., Eden & Zeffiro, 1998; Molfese, 2000; Simos, Breier, Fletcher, Bergman, & Papanicolaou, 2000). Recent advances in event-related potentials (ERP) technology involving high-density electrode arrays provide an effective means to map topographically the flow of electrical currents across the scalp. Molfese et al. (2006) studied brain processing while 9- to 11-year-olds performed word-reading tasks. Children were classified using standardized reading assessments as dyslexic (reading 2 years below grade level), average, or proficient (reading 2 years beyond their grade level). ERPs were recorded using 128-electrode high-density arrays while children discriminated visually presented words (sat), pronounceable pseudo-words (kat), and nonwords (dak), and listened to speech sounds. All chil-dren differentiated words from pseudowords and from nonwords, although accuracy was highest for the advanced readers. ERP measures reflected clear group differences in brain processing. Advanced readers processed reading information markedly faster than did average and below-average readers, and left hemisphere amplitudes significantly differed between groups. ERP amplitudes in the region of P2 decreased linearly in size as reading skills increased. We believe that these amplitude differences reflect processing effort. Additionally, dyslexic readers responded with the slowest P2 latencies while average readers responded more quickly, and the advanced readers faster still.

Using a different technique (PEPSI, proton echo-planar spectroscopic imaging), Richards et al. (1999) studied dyslexic and non-dyslexic boys (8–13 years old) during an auditory task. The boys with dyslexia showed a larger distribution of activation in the left anterior lobe compared to typical readers during the phonological processing task where they compared pairs of words and nonwords. Compared to typical readers, the children with dyslexia acti-vated over four times as much brain area. Richards et al. (2002) replicated this finding with boys and girls 9–12 years of age. In both of these studies it was evident that brain-processing differences were seen between the different reading groups, and that the extent of activation in the brains of children with dyslexia involved greater processing effort even with a relatively simple task involving reading words in isolation, rather than the more complex task for isolating individual words in a text passage.

SUMMARY AND CONCLUSIONS

Studies of brain processing provide another avenue to study the development of cognitive skills in infancy and early childhood. The studies described in this chapter are examples of how event-related potentials (ERPs) could be used in combination with behavioral measures to address developmental questions. Recent advances in techniques available to study brain processing allow new research questions to be addressed. For example, the use of high-density-array electrode technology allows brain processing to be measured across many different scalp regions while children are engaged in tasks. Because of the number of electrodes employed and dispersed across the scalp, these procedures can provide information from activation patterns across the scalp that can be used to infer the neural and temporal substrates for cognitive and behavioral processes. The high-density-array technique has been applied to children where differences in brain activity are seen across ages, as a function of intervention/training, and between groups differing in skills and experience (Molfese, Molfese, Modglin, Kelly, & Terrell, 2002). ERP techniques have also been used with a variety of different paradigms in which brain processing is measured during different types of auditory discrimination tasks or during problem-solving tasks, such as reading tasks where real words must be differentiated from nonwords. Such studies that include both brain and behavior measures offer unique opportunities to identify individual as well as group differences using converging data methods.

Across these studies, commonalities in the timing of brain waveform components, the brain regions showing the greatest responsiveness, and the temporal sequencing of brain responses across regions, need to be linked with behavioral outcome measures to better understand the intricate relationships that exist between brain and behavior. As with any methods, there are possibilities for wide differences in findings reported across studies. Differences can arise due to variations in the evoking stimuli, scalp recording sites, recording procedures, and the analysis techniques. However, as research progresses in identifying commonalities across studies using increasingly sophisticated techniques, we are drawing closer to an understanding of where in the brain differences in processing are located that are useful for understanding behaviors. While localizing the sources of the ERP within the brain is not an easy process because such sources are not isomorphic with the scalp recording location, due to the signal propagation patterns within the brain and across the scalp of different densities and skull thicknesses, new source analysis techniques (e.g., BESA; Scherg & Berg, 1996) and research combining different brain-imaging techniques, such as MEG and fMRI in combination with ERPs, are opening both old and new vistas to investigation.

ACKNOWLEDGMENTS

This work was supported in part by grants from the National Institute of Child Health and Human Development (R01-HD17860), and the US Department of Education (R215K000023, R215R990011).

APPENDIX

Studies Using Neonatal ERPs to Predict Later Language Development

Study	Subjects	Electrodes	Task	Results
Butler & Engel (1969)	ERPs recorded within first 5 days after birth Retested 8 months of age on Bayley Scales n = 433	Six electrodes per hemisphere (no specific sites identified)	Visual ERPs to light flashes Three variables: photic latency, gestational age, birth weight Modified version of Bayley Scales at 8 months of age (Mental, Gross Motor, Fine Motor)	Correlations involving photic response latency and gestational age higher than the correlations involving birthweight Mental test score had higher correlations with neonatal measures than fine motor or gross motor scores
Engel & Fay (1972)	Tested at birth, 3 years, 4 years n = 828	Placed over the inion of both occipital areas	Visual ERPs to light flashes at birth Separated into three Reactor groups: Fast, Average, Slow Three measures of speech and language (pronunciation of initial consonants, pronunciation of final consonants, verbal comprehension) at 3 years of age Stanford-Binet at 4 years of age	Articulation of initial and final consonants at 3 years of age significantly greater in the fast reactors No significant correlation found between neonatal VER and verbal comprehension at 3 years or with IQ at 4 years

Study	Subjects	Electrodes	Task	Results
Engel & Henderson (1973)	7- to 8-year-old children $n = 119$	14 electrodes positioned symmetrically over both hemispheres; 15th electrode over inion	Visual ERPs to light flashes WISC (Information, Comprehension, Vocabulary, Digit Span, Picture Arrangement, Block Design, Coding) Bender Visual Motor Gestalt	Latency of the VERP peaks did not contribute to prediction of IQ No VERPs correlated significantly with behavioral measures alone at 7–8 years
Henderson & Engel (1974)	Tested within first week after birth Tested again at 7 years of age $n = 809$	Oz referred to C3, Oz referred to C4, or O1 referred to C3, O2 referred to C4	Visual ERPs to light flashes at birth WISC (Information, Comprehension, Vocabulary, Digit Span, Picture Arrangement, Block Design, Coding) Bender Gestalt Test using the Koppitz system Tactile Finger Recognition Test (from Reitan Neuro-psychological Battery for Children) WRAT (Spelling, Arithmetic, Reading)	No relation found between neonatal VERPs and IQ, perceptual measures, or achievement measures
Molfese & Molfese (1985)	Infants studied longitudinally from birth through 3 years $n = 16$	T3, T4 referenced to linked ears	ERPs recorded to speech and nonspeech consonant-vowel sounds at birth McCarthy Scales of Children's Abilities administered at 3 years	Newborn ERPs identified children performing better or worse on language tasks 3 years later

(Continued overleaf)

Study	Subjects	Electrodes	Task	Results
				ERPs 88–240 ms discriminated High vs. Low Groups on McCarthy Verbal Index at 3 years
				ERP component at 664 ms discriminated High vs. Low Groups at 3 years
Molfese & Searock (1986)	1-year-old infants retested at 3 years $n = 16$	T3, T4 referenced to linked ears	At 1 year, ERPs recorded to speech and nonspeech vowel sounds McCarthy test administered at 3 years	Children with above-average language skills at 3 years exhibited ERPs at 1 year that discriminated different vowel sounds
Andrews Espy et al. (2004)	109 children (48 males and 61 females) tested annually within 2 weeks of their birthday, at ages 1–8 years	FL, FR, T3, T4, PL, PR referenced to linked ears	Each year, ERPs recorded to speech and nonspeech consonant-vowel syllables Baseline-to-peak analyses conducted Word Attack subtest of the Woodcock-Johnson Psychoeducational Battery—Revised (WJ-R) Wide Range Achievement Test—Revised (WRAT-R)	Growth curve analysis using hierarchical linear modeling utilized to analyze longitudinal data Change in amplitude in the N1 waveform from ages 1–4 and N2 amplitude from 4–8 years differed between average and poorer readers defined by the WJ-R

Study	Subjects	Electrodes	Task	Results
Molfese (1989)	Newborns retested at 3 years $n = 30$ 15 with McCarthy scores below 50 and 15 with scores above 50	T3, T4 referenced to linked ears	At birth, ERPs to speech and nonspeech consonant-vowel sounds were recorded McCarthy test administered at 3 years	Discriminant function correctly classified 68.6% of ERPs recorded from High group and 69.7% of ERPs recorded from Low group
Molfese & Molfese (1993)	Newborns retested at 3 years $n = 54$ 27 with McCarthy scores below 50 and 27 with McCarthy scores above 54	FL, FR, T3, T4, PL, PR referenced to linked ears	At birth ERPs recorded to speech and nonspeech consonant-vowel sounds McCarthy test administered at 3 years	Positive peak of neonatal LH responses 70–210 ms discriminated consonant sounds for High group at age 3 Positive peak of neonatal parietal response between 470 and 670 ms discriminated consonants for High group at 3 years
Molfese, Gill, Simos, & Tan (1995)	Newborns tested again at 5 years $n = 79$	FL, FR, T3, T4, PL, PR referenced to linked ears	At birth, ERPs collected to nine consonant-vowel syllables Stanford-Binet administered at 5 years of age	PCA-discriminant function analysis performed Three groups established based on Stanford-Binet Verbal reasoning subtest scores at 5 years Two discriminant functions classified children with 81% accuracy

(Continued overleaf)

Study	Subjects	Electrodes	Task	Results
Molfese (1995)	Newborns tested again at 3 years of age n = 79	FL, FR, T3, T4, PL, PR referenced to linked ears	At birth, ERPs collected to nine consonant-vowel syllables Stanford-Binet administered at 3 years of age	PCA-discriminant function analysis Three groups based on Stanford-Binet Verbal reasoning subtest scores at 3 years Two discriminant functions classified children with 100% accuracy
Molfese & Molfese (1997)	Newborns tested again at 5 years of age n = 71	FL, FR, T3, T4, PL, PR referenced to linked ears	At birth, ERPs collected to nine consonant-vowel syllables Stanford-Binet administered at 5 years of age	Two groups based on Stanford-Binet Verbal reasoning subtest scores at 5 years: 62 > 100 VIQ, 9 < 100 VIQ Three discriminant functions classified children with 78.9%, 91.6%, and 95.8% accuracy using three, six, and seven variables
Molfese (2000)	Newborns also tested at 8 years: 17 dyslexic, 7 have lower FSIQ & poor reading, 24 controls n = 48	FL, FR, T3, T4, PL, PR referenced to linked ears	At birth, ERPs collected to nine consonant-vowel syllables WRAT3 administered at 8 years of age	Three groups based on WRAT3 Reading scores at 8 years Two discriminant functions classified 82.1% children

Study	Subjects	Electrodes	Task	Results
Leppänen et al. (1999)	23 newborns, GA = 38–40 weeks High Risk group: 12 with familial background of dyslexia Low Risk group: 11 babies matched to High Risk group	F3, F4, C3, C4, P3, P4 referenced to ipsilateral mastoid	Stimuli presented using oddball paradigm CV syllables: /kaa/ with vowel duration of 250 ms, presented 88% of trials (standard); /ka/ vowel duration short (110 ms), presented 12% of trials	Low Risk group: frequent standard slow > fast @ F4 at latencies of 130–225 ms and 225–400 ms. No effects for High Risk group Low Risk: /ka/ vs. /kaa/ was more positive @ P3 in 155–200 ms and more negative @ F3 in 430–475 ms (all left hemisphere) High Risk: /ka/ deviant more positive @ C4 in 280–350 ms and @ P4 in 380–425 ms (all right hemisphere effects)
Pihko et al. (1999)	ERPs recorded at 1 week *n* = 73 (42 high risk, 31 controls) ERPs recorded at 6 months *n* = 51 (28 high risk, 23 controls)	F3, F4, C3, C4, P3, P4 reference to the ipsilateral mastoid EOG referred to left mastoid	Recorded ERPs from consonant-vowel syllables /ka/ and /kaa/	6 months begin to show differences between groups At-risk group more effects in right hemisphere
Guttorm, Leppänen, Richardson, & Lyytinen (2001)	Newborns tested from 1 to 7 days after birth *n* = 49	F3, F4, T3, T4, C3, C4, P3, P4 referenced to ipsilateral mastoid except for T3— referenced to T4	At birth, ERPs collected to /ba/ /da/ and /ga/	Discriminant Function Analysis (composite scores of 540–630 ms) averaging responses for /ga/ in right hemisphere. Accuracy of 69.4%

(Continued overleaf)

Study	Subjects	Electrodes	Task	Results
Guttorm, Leppänen, Tolvanen, & Lyytinen (2003)	Newborns tested from 1 to 7 days after birth $n = 49$	F3, F4, T3, T4, C3, C4, P3, P4 referenced to ipsilateral mastoid except for T3—referenced to T4	At birth, ERPs collected to /ba/ /da/ and /ga/ And natural consonant-vowel syllables /paa/ /taa/ and /kaa/	Discriminant Function Analysis (composite for factors 4 and 3 /ga/ over right hemisphere; and composite for Factor 2 /da/ over parietal channels) Accuracy of 73.5%
				Compared PCA factors to original averaged ERP data Showed slightly lower accuracy rate: 67.3%
Leppänen et al. (2002)	76 infants, mean age = 6 months 5 days Risk group: 37 infants (20 males) from families with history of dyslexia Control: 39 infants (21 males) from families without history of dyslexia	F3, F4, T3, T4, C3, C4, P3, P4 referenced to ipsilateral mastoid	Naturally produced pseudowords: short /ata/ (95 ms silence for consonant), 133 ms; intermediate /ata/ (195 ms silence), long /atta/ (255 ms silence) 75 dB SPL, oddball design: 80%/10%/10% short /ata/ deviant = 12 at-risk and 12 control infants; long /atta/ deviant = 25 at-risk and 27 control infants	At risk: less differentiation between standard and target stimuli in 590–625 ms and 715–755 ms No group differences noted for RH F3, C3, T3, P3: P470 larger for at risk than for controls For short /ata/ deviants: N550 at F, C, P sites resembled MMN in controls only

REFERENCES

Andrews Espy, K., Molfese, D., Molfese, V., Simos, P., & Modglin, A. (2004). Development of auditory event-related potentials in young children and relations to word-level reading abilities at age 8 years. *Annals of Dyslexia, 54*, 9–38.

Brady, S. (1991). The role of working memory in reading disability. In S. A. Brady & D. P. Shankweiler (Eds.), *Phonological processes in literacy: A tribute to Isabelle Y. Liberman* (pp. 129–161). Hillsdale, NJ: Lawrence Erlbaum Associates Inc.

Butler, B., & Engel, R. (1969). Mental and motor scores at 8 months in relation to neonatal photic responses. *Developmental Medicine and Child Neurology, 11*, 77–82.

Catts, H., Fey, M., Zhang, X., & Tomblin, J. (1999). Language basis of reading and reading disabilities: Evidence from a longitudinal investigation. *Scientific Study of Reading, 3*, 331–361.

Cheour, M., Alho, K., Ceponiene, R., Reinikainen, K., Sainio, K., Pohjavuori, M. et al. (1998a). Maturation of mismatch negativity in infants. *International Journal of Psychophysiology, 29*, 217–226.

Cheour, M., Ceponiene, R., Lehtokoski, A., Luuk, A., Allik, J., Alho, K. et al. (1998b). Development of language-specific phoneme representations in the infant brain. *Nature Neuroscience, 1*, 351–353.

Cheour, M., Martynova, O., Näätänen, R., Erkkola, R., Sillanpää, M., Kero, P. et al. (2002). Speech sounds learned by sleeping newborns. *Nature*, 415, 599–600.

Cheour-Luhtanen, M., Alho, K., Kujala, T., Sainio, K., Reinikainen, K., Renlund, M. et al. (1995). Mismatch negativity indicates vowel discrimination in newborns. *Hearing Research, 82*, 53–58.

Cheour-Luhtanen, M., Alho, K., Sainio, K., Rinne, T., Reinikainen, K., Pohjavuori, M. et al. (1996). The ontogenetically earliest discriminative response of the human brain. *Psychophysiology, 33*, 478–481.

Cohn, R. (1971). Differential cerebral processing of noise and verbal stimuli. *Science, 172*, 599–601.

Csépe, V. (1995). On the origin and development of the mismatch negativity. *Ear and Hearing, 16*, 91–104.

Csépe, V., Pantev, C., Hoke, M., Hampson, S., & Ross, B. (1992). Evoked magnetic responses of the human auditory cortex to minor pitch changes: Localization of the mismatch field. *Journal of Electroencephalography and Clinical Neurophysiology, 84*, 538–548.

Dehaene-Lambertz, G., & Pena, M. (2001). Electrophysiological evidence for automatic phonetic processing in neonates. *NeuroReport, 12*, 3155–3158.

Dehaene-Lambertz, G., Pena, M., Christophe, A., & Landrieu, P. (2004). Phoneme perception in a neonate with a left sylvian infarct. *Brain and Language, 88*, 26–38.

Eden, G., & Zeffiro, T. (1998). Neural systems affected in developmental dyslexia revealed by functional neuroimaging. *Neuron, 21*, 279–282.

Eilers, R., Wilson, W., & Moore, J. (1977). Developmental changes in speech discrimination in infants. *Journal of Speech and Hearing Research, 20*, 766–780.

Eimas, P., Siqueland, E., Jusczyk, P., & Vigorito, J. (1971). Speech perception in infants. *Science, 171*, 303–306.

Engel, R., & Fay, W. (1972). Visual evoked responses at birth, verbal scores at three years, and IQ at four years. *Developmental Medicine and Child Neurology, 14*, 283–289.

Engel, R., & Henderson, N. (1973). Visual evoked responses and IQ scores at school age. *Developmental Medicine and Child Neurology*, *15*, 136–145.

Fabiani, M., Gratton, G., & Coles, M. G. H. (2000). Event-related brain potentials: Methods, theory, and applications. In J. T. Cacioppo, L. G. Tassinary, & G. G. Berntson (Eds.), *Handbook of psychophysiology* (2nd ed., pp. 53–84). Cambridge, UK: Cambridge University Press.

Friedman, D., Simson, R., Ritters, W., & Rapin, I. (1975). Cortical evoked potentials elicited by real speech words and human sounds. *Journal of Electroencephalography and Clinical Neurophysiology*, *38*, 13–19.

Galambos, R., Benson, P., Smith, T. S., Schulman-Galambos, C., & Osier H. (1975). On hemispheric differences in evoked potentials to speech stimuli. *Journal of Electroencephalography and Clinical Neurophysiology*, *39*, 279–283.

Guttorm, T. K., Leppänen, P. H. T., Richardson, U., & Lyytinen, H. (2001). Event-related potentials and consonant differentiation in newborns with familial risk for dyslexia. *Journal of Learning Disabilities*, *34*, 534–544.

Guttorm, T. K., Leppänen, P. H. T., Tolvanen, A., & Lyytinen, H. (2003). Event-related potential in newborns with and without familial risk for dyslexia: Principal component analysis reveals differences between the groups. *Journal of Neural Transmission*, *110*, 1059–1074.

Henderson, N., & Engel, R. (1974). Neonatal visual evoked potentials as predictors of psychoeducational testing at age seven. *Developmental Psychology*, *10*, 269–276.

Jaramillo, M., Ilvonen, T., Kujala, T., Alku, P., Tervaniemi, M., & Alho, K. (2001). Are different kinds of acoustic features processed differently for speech and non-speech sounds? *Cognitive Brain Research*, *12*, 459–466.

Jastak, S., & Wilkinson, G. (1984). *The Wide Range Achievement Test—revised.* Wilmington, CA: Jastak Associates

Jensen, D. R., & Engel, R. (1971). Statistical procedures for relating dichotomous responses to maturation and EEG measurements. *Electroencephalography and Clinical Neurophysiology*, *30*, 437–443.

Kayser, J., Tenke, C., & Bruder, G. E. (1998). Dissociation of brain ERP topographies for tonal and phonetic oddball tasks. *Psychophysiology*, *35*, 576–590.

Kraus, N., McGee, T. J., Micco, A., Sharma, A., Carrell, T. D., & Nicol, T. G. (1993). Mismatch negativity in school-age children to speech stimuli that are just perceptually different. *Journal of Electroencephalography and Clinical Neurophysiology*, *88*, 123–130.

Lenneberg, E. (1967). *Biological foundations of language.* New York: Wiley.

Leppänen, P. H., Pihko, E., Eklund, K. M., & Lyytinen, H. (1999). Cortical responses of infants with and without a genetic risk for dyslexia: II. Group effects. *NeuroReport*, *10*, 969–973.

Leppänen, P. H., Richardson, U., Pihko, E., Eklund, K. M., Guttorm, T. K., Aro, M. et al. (2002). Brain responses to changes in speech sound durations differ between infants with and without familial risk for dyslexia. *Developmental Neuropsychology*, *22*, 407–422.

Liberman, A., Cooper, F., Shankweiler, D., & Studdert-Kennedy, M. (1967). Perception of the speech code. *Psychological Review*, *74*, 431–461.

Liebenthal, E., Ellingson, M. L., Spanaki, M. V., Prieto, T. E., Ropella, K. M., & Binder, J. R. (2003). Simultaneous ERP and fMRI of the auditory cortex in a passive oddball paradigm. *Neuroimage*, *19*, 1395–1404.

Lisker, L., & Abramson, A. S. (1970). The voicing dimension: Some experiments in comparative phonetics. In *Proceedings of the 6th International Congress of Phonetic Sciences* (pp. 563–567). Prague: Academia.

Lyytinen, H., Ahonen, T., Eklund, K., Guttorm, T., Kulju, P., Laakso, M. L. et al. (2004). Early development of children at familial risk for dyslexia—follow-up from birth to school age. *Dyslexia, 10*, 146–178.

Lyytinen, H., Ahonen, T., Eklund, K., Guttorm, T. K., Laakso, M. L., Leinonen, S. et al. (2001). Developmental pathways of children with and without familial risk for dyslexia during the first years of life. *Developmental Neuropsychology, 20*, 535–554.

Martynova, O., Kirjavainen, J., & Cheour, M. (2003). Mismatch negativity and late discriminative negativity in sleeping human newborns. *Neuroscience Letters, 340*, 75–78.

Molfese, D., Fonaryova Key, A., Kelly, S., Cunningham, N., Terrell, S., Ferguson, M. et al. (2006). Below-average, average, and above-average readers engage different and similar brain regions while reading. *Journal of Learning Disabilities, 39*, 352–363.

Molfese, D., Molfese, V., & Kelly, S. (2001). The use of brain electrophysiology techniques to study language: A basic guide for the beginning consumer of electrophysiology information. *Learning Disability Quarterly, 24*, 177–188.

Molfese, D. L. (1978a). Left and right hemispheric involvement in speech perception: Electrophysiological correlates. *Perception & Psychophysics, 23*, 237–243.

Molfese, D. L. (1978b). Neuroelectrical correlates of categorical speech perception in adults. *Brain and Language, 5*, 25–35.

Molfese, D. L. (1980a). Hemispheric specialization for temporal information: Implications for the processing of voicing cues during speech perception. *Brain and Language, 11*, 285–299.

Molfese, D. L. (1980b). The phoneme and the engram: Electrophysiological evidence for the acoustic invariant in stop consonants. *Brain and Language, 10*, 372–376.

Molfese, D. L. (1989). The use of auditory evoked responses recorded from newborns to predict later language skills. In N. Paul (Ed.), *Research in infant assessment.* (pp. 68–81). White Plains, NY: March of Dimes.

Molfese, D. L. (1995). Electrophysiological responses obtained during infancy and their relation to later language development: Further findings. In M. G. Tramontana & S. R. Hooper (Eds.), *Advances in child neuropsychology, Vol. 3* (pp. 1–11). New York: Springer-Verlag.

Molfese, D. L. (2000). Predicting dyslexia at 8 years using neonatal brain responses. *Brain and Language, 72*, 238–245.

Molfese, D. L., Fonaryova Key, A., Molfese, V., Kelly, S., Cunningham, N., Rumage, C. et al. (2003, February). *Brain response differences between dyslexic, average, and advanced readers.* Paper presented at the 31st Annual Meeting of the International Neuropsychological Society, Honolulu, Hawaii.

Molfese, D. L., Freeman, R., & Palermo, D. (1975). The ontogeny of lateralization for speech and nonspeech stimuli. *Brain and Language, 2*, 356–368.

Molfese, D. L., Gill, L. A., Simos, P. G., & Tan, A. (1995). Implications of biological mechanisms for assessing and modifying development. In L. DiLalla & S. Clancy (Eds.), *The assessment of biological mechanisms across the life span* (pp. 173–190). Mahwah, NJ: Lawrence Erlbaum & Associates Inc.

Molfese, D. L., & Molfese, V. J. (1979a). Hemisphere and stimulus differences as reflected in the cortical responses of newborn infants to speech stimuli. *Developmental Psychology, 15,* 505–511.

Molfese, D. L., & Molfese, V. J. (1979b). VOT distinctions in infants: Learned or innate? In H. Whitaker & H. Whitaker (Eds.), *Advances in neurolinguistics: Vol. 4.* New York: Academic Press.

Molfese, D. L., & Molfese, V. J. (1985). Electrophysiological indices of auditory discrimination in newborn infants: The bases for predicting later language development. *Infant Behavior and Development, 8,* 197–211.

Molfese, D. L., & Molfese, V. J. (1986). Psychophysical indices of early cognitive processes and their relationship to language. In J. E. Obrzut & G. W. Hynd (Eds.), *Child neuropsychology: Vol 1. Theory and research.* New York: Academic Press.

Molfese, D. L., & Molfese, V. J. (1993). Predicting long-term development from electrophysiological measures taken at birth. In G. Dawson & K. Fischer (Eds.), *Human behavior and brain development* (pp. 493–517). New York: Guilford Press.

Molfese, D. L., & Molfese, V. J. (1997). Discrimination of language skills at five years of age using event related potentials recorded at birth. *Developmental Neuropsychology, 13,* 135–156.

Molfese, D. L., & Molfese, V. J. (2000). The continuum of language development during infancy and early childhood: Electrophysiological correlates. In C. Rovee-Collier, L. P. Lipsitt, & H. Hayne (Eds.), *Progress in infancy research, Vol. 1* (pp. 251–287). Mahwah, NJ: Lawrence Erlbaum Associates Inc.

Molfese, D. L., Molfese, V., Modglin, A., Kelly, S., & Terrell, S. (2002). Reading and cognitive abilities: Longitudinal studies of brain and behavior changes in young children. *Annals of Dyslexia, 52,* 99–119.

Molfese, D. L., & Searock, K. (1986). The use of auditory evoked responses at one year of age to predict language skills at 3 years. *Australian Journal of Communication Disorders, 14,* 35–46.

Molfese, V., Yaple, K., Helwig, S., Harris, L., & Connell, S. (1992). Stanford-Binet Intelligence Scale (4th edition): Factor structure and verbal subscale scores for three year olds. *Journal of Psychoeducational Assessment, 10,* 47–58.

Molfese, V. J., Molfese, D. L., & Modglin, A. (2001). Newborn and preschool predictors of second grade reading scores: An evaluation of categorical and continuous scores. *Journal of Learning Disabilities, 34,* 545–554.

Morrell, L. K., & Salamy, J. G. (1971). Hemispheric asymmetry of electrocortical responses to speech stimuli. *Science, 174,* 164–166.

Näätänen, R. (1990). The role of attention in auditory information processing as revealed by event-related potentials and other brain measures of cognitive function. *Behavioral Brain Sciences, 13,* 201–233.

Näätänen, R. (1992). *Attention and brain function.* Hillsdale, NJ: Lawrence Erlbaum Associates Inc.

Näätänen, R., Lehtokoski, A., Lennes, M., Cheour, M., Huotilainen, M., Iivonen, A. et al. (1997). Language-specific phoneme representations revealed by electric and magnetic brain responses. *Nature, 385,* 432–434.

Neville, H. (1974). Electrographic correlates of lateral asymmetry in the processing of verbal and nonverbal auditory stimuli. *Journal of Psycholinguistic Research, 3,* 151–163.

Nunez, P. (1981). *Electric fields in the brain: The neurophysics of EEG.* New York: Oxford University Press.

Pihko, E., Leppanen, P. H., Eklund, K. M., Cheour, M., Guttorm, T. K., & Lyytinen, H. (1999). Cortical responses of infants with and without a genetic risk for dyslexia: I. Age effects. *NeuroReport, 10*, 901–905.

Richards, T., Berninger, V., Aylward, E., Richards, A., Thomson, J., Nagy, W. et al. (2002). Reproducibility of Proton MR Spectroscopic Imaging (PEPSI): Comparison of dyslexic and normal reading children and effects of treatment on brain lactate levels during language tasks. *American Journal of Neuroradiology, 23*, 1678–1685.

Richards, T., Dager, S., Corina, D., Serafini, S., Heide, A., Steury, K. et al. (1999). Dyslexic children have abnormal brain lactate response to reading-related language tasks. *American Journal of Neuroradiology, 20*, 1393–1398.

Richardson, U., Leppänen, P. H., Leiwo, M., & Lyytinen, H. (2003). Speech perception of infants with high familial risk for dyslexia differs at the age of 6 months. *Developmental Neuropsychology, 23*, 385–397.

Rosburg, T. (2003). Left hemispheric dipole locations of the neuromagnetic mismatch negativity to frequency, intensity and duration deviants. *Cognitive Brain Research, 16*, 83–90.

Scherg, M., & Berg, P. (1996). *Brain Electromagnetic Source Analysis (BESA) user manual*. Munich: MEGIS.

Simos, P. G., Breier, J. I., Fletcher, J. M., Bergman, E., & Papanicolaou, A. C. (2000). Cerebral mechanisms involved in word reading in dyslexic children: A magnetic source imaging approach. *Cerebral Cortex, 10*, 809–816.

Travis, L. (1931). *Speech pathology*. New York: Appleton-Century.

Vellutino, F., & Scanlon, D. (1987). Phonological coding: Phonological awareness, and reading ability: Evidence from a longitudinal and experimental study. *Merrill-Palmer Quarterly, 33*, 321–363.

Wagner, R., Torgesen, J., & Raschotte, C. (1994). Development of reading-related phonological processing abilities: New evidence of bidirectional causality from a latent variable longitudinal study. *Developmental Psychology, 30*, 73–87.

Wechsler, D. (1991). *Wechsler Intelligence Scales for Children*. New York: The Psychological Corporation.

Wilkinson, G. S. (1993). *Wide Range Achievement Test*. Wilmington, CA: Wide Range.

Woodcock, R. W., & Johnson, M. B. (1989). *Woodcock-Johnson Revised Tests of Achievement*. Itasca, IL: Riverside.

8 Infant EEG and ERP in relation to social and emotional development

Peter J. Marshall
Temple University, Philadelphia, USA

Nathan A. Fox
University of Maryland, USA

In this chapter we aim to introduce the reader to some current directions in the use of electroencephalography (EEG) and event-related potential (ERPs) in the study of social and emotional development in infancy, with a particular emphasis on temperament. In the first section, we focus on the use of EEG power and EEG asymmetry indices across a variety of frequency bands. As part of this section, we discuss the development of the EEG in children exposed to the adverse social environment of institutional life. We also cover work describing the relation of infant temperament to measures of EEG power and asymmetry. Specifically, we will describe our work on temperamentally reactive infants who tend to respond with strong affective valence (positive or negative) to novel stimuli. In the second section, we outline recent work and future possibilities for using ERPs to assess reactivity to novel stimuli and sensory gating in temperamentally different infants.

EEG BAND POWER

There is a rich history of examining the development of EEG power in infants and young children (for reviews, see Bell, 1998; Schmidt & Fox, 1998; see also Chapter 9, this volume). In a number of early studies (e.g., Henry, 1944), changes in band power were linked to the development of motor skills and intelligence. Others have linked developmental data on changes in EEG band power over the period of early childhood (e.g., Matousek & Petersen, 1973) to Piagetian stages of development. However, at the time that these studies were being carried out, there were virtually no similar studies examining relations between EEG power and social and emotional development in infants and young children. In contrast, the past 30 years have seen a spate of studies linking social and emotional development in infants and children to changes in the EEG. For the most part, these studies have focused on the alpha band, since activity in this band is prominent from early infancy onwards, and its magnitude is assumed to be inversely proportional to cortical activity.

Alpha power is maximally pronounced at posterior recording sites, but can be recorded in a lower-amplitude form at other locations on the scalp. It is stronger when the eyes are closed and is desynchronized (blocked) when the eyes are opened. There is some debate over the precise boundaries of the alpha band and how it changes over infancy and early childhood. Given clear developmental changes in alpha peak frequency, it is likely that alternative frequency bands are needed for developmental work (Marshall, Bar-Haim, & Fox, 2002). Early studies such as those of Smith (1938), Lindsley (1938), and Henry (1944) focused on the development of the occipital alpha rhythm over infancy and childhood. These authors noted the emergence of a 3–5 Hz occipital rhythm at around 3 months of age, which increased in terms of its dominant frequency to around 6–7 Hz by the end of the first year of life. The oscillations in early infancy were labeled as "alpha" by these authors because of a visual resemblance to the classical adult alpha rhythm. Another notable early finding was that the infant alpha rhythm was blocked by visual stimulation even in infants a few months old, suggesting a functional as well as a visual similarity between infant alpha at posterior sites and the adult alpha rhythm (Lindsley, 1938). Drawing on this early work and that of others (see Stroganova & Orekhova, Chapter 9, this volume), we found that the 6–9 Hz band appears to be a suitable alpha-range frequency band for use from the end of the first year of life into early childhood (Marshall et al., 2002). Other research groups have used similar frequency bands. For instance, Orekhova and colleagues used a frequency band of 6.4–10.0 Hz as the "alpha range" in infants aged 7–12 months. They conceptualized this band as encompassing both posterior alpha rhythms (the classical alpha rhythm) and sensorimotor rhythms such as mu, which is an alpha-range rhythm prominent at central electrode sites in infants (Orekhova, Stroganova, & Posikera, 2001).

Alpha-range rhythms

The use of alpha rhythms in the study of early social and emotional development has mainly involved relating hemispheric asymmetries in alpha power to individual differences in temperament (see below). However, band power in the alpha range (not asymmetry) has also shown some interesting relations with early temperament. Calkins, Fox, and Marshall (1996) found that high levels of behavioral inhibition to the unfamiliar, which is operationalized in infancy as long latencies to approach and interact with unfamiliar people and objects, were associated with lower alpha band power at frontal electrode sites at 14 months of age. Given the inverse relation between alpha band power and cortical activation, this finding was interpreted as reflecting increased cortical arousal in the inhibited infants. Henderson, Marshall, Fox, and Rubin (2004) report a similar relation between low alpha power and higher levels of reticent, anxious behavior in social situations in preschoolers. In this study, alpha power was suppressed across the entire scalp relative to two other groups of children: a group of more outgoing, socially exuberant children, and a third group of withdrawn children who showed solitary behaviors that were less indicative of anxiety. This finding was interpreted as reflecting elevated tonic arousal levels in reticent, anxious children, an interpretation that is consistent with Eysenck's model of adult personality in which individual differences in introversion were associated with lowered thresholds for cortical arousal in response to signals from the limbic system (Eysenck & Eysenck, 1985).

As mentioned above, the alpha frequency range includes not only the classical posterior alpha rhythm, but also the sensorimotor mu rhythm (Niedermeyer, 1997). The mu rhythm itself has become the focus of recent research on social processes (Pineda, 2005), although developmental aspects of this work have not been addressed. The emergence of the mu rhythm in infancy and early childhood has been documented in a longitudinal sample of typically developing infants and young children (Marshall et al., 2002). This study showed that the mu rhythm is particularly strong in early development, appearing in the first year of life at a peak frequency of 6–9 Hz in the EEG signal over central electrode sites.

Theta rhythms

Theta rhythms have been examined from a variety of developmental perspectives, including learning disorders (Chabot, di Michele, Prichep, & John, 2001), joint attention (Mundy, Card, & Fox, 2000), voluntary attention (Orekhova, Stroganova, & Posikera, 1999), and working memory processes (Bell, 2002). In infants, phasic increases in theta activity during visual attention have been found to be positively correlated with positive affect (Orekhova, Stroganova, Posikera, & Malykh, 2003), while high levels of tonic theta activity have been associated with developmental disorders of learning and attention in older children (Barry, Clarke, & Johnstone, 2003). Regarding the latter association, there have been two primary explanations for the association of high theta power with learning disorders. Since the amount of slow power (e.g., delta and theta power) in the EEG decreases with age, and the amount of higher-frequency power (e.g., alpha and beta) increases with age (Matousek & Petersen, 1973), an excess of theta power has been taken to indicate a maturational lag in the development of the EEG (Matsuura et al., 1993). A competing model states that an excess of low-frequency power and a deficit in high-frequency power is a marker of chronic underarousal (Satterfield, Cantwell, & Satterfield, 1974). Although both models have been subject to criticism, recent work using these approaches has shown some promise in clarifying EEG patterns in disorders of learning and attention (Barry et al., 2003).

Findings of an association between increased theta activity and learning disorders have primarily been described in older children. However, a recent study of infants and young children living in institutions in Bucharest, Romania, provides evidence of increased theta activity under conditions of environmental deprivation. Using data from the Bucharest Early Intervention Project (BEIP), Marshall, Fox, and the BEIP Core Group (2004b) reported EEG findings for both absolute power and relative power across a variety of frequency bands from a group of institutionalized infants who were between 9 and 30 months of age. Given the association of an excess of theta power with a variety of learning and behavior disorders in children (Chabot et al., 2001) and with exposure to adverse rearing environments (Harmony et al., 1988), it was hypothesized that this pattern would be seen in the instutional-ized children, relative to a comparison group of never-institutionalized children from the surrounding community who were matched to the insti-tutionalized group on age. In agreement with this hypothesis, the insti-tutionalized group had significantly higher theta (3–5 Hz) absolute power at occipital sites than the community comparison group. However, the most striking group differences concerned relative power in the theta band, par-ticularly at frontal, parietal, and occipital electrode sites. The institutional-ized group showed significantly higher relative theta power in these regions, compared with the community comparison group. The interpretation of these findings was related to the cognitive deficits associated with institutionaliza-tion, which in turn are likely to be the product of the aberrant social environment that characterizes institutional life. Further work is currently being carried out to determine the relations of EEG band power in this sample to various measures of emotion expression and social attachment, as well as finer measures of the quality of the caregiving environment. In addi-tion, the effect of family care on the development of the EEG in previously institutionalized infants and children is also being assessed.

Other frequency bands

Frequency bands higher or lower than theta or alpha have rarely been con-sidered in infant work. Very low-frequency activity in the delta band has only generally been approached from the clinical perspective of neurology and has not been studied in terms of its psychological correlates. In terms of higher-frequency bands, a notable set of studies has examined infant gamma band activity in relation to visual processing in both typically developing and developmentally disordered populations (Csibra, Davis, Spratling, & Johnson, 2000; Grice et al., 2001; see Chapter 10, this volume).

EEG ASYMMETRY

Rather than focus on band power per se, a larger number of research studies have focused on hemispheric asymmetry in EEG power, especially in the alpha band. The rationale for this approach in studying social and emotional development comes from various sources across the neuropsychological literature. For instance, a variety of data has implicated the anterior regions of the left and right cerebral hemispheres in the expression and/or experience of different emotions (Fox, 1994). Evidence suggests that the left frontal region of the cortex is associated with the expression and experience of positive affect, while the right frontal region is associated with the expression and experience of negative affect (Silberman & Weingartner, 1986). Studies of unilateral injection of sodium amytal have reported the production of severe emotional reactions, with striking differences in the nature of these reactions depending on the side of injection (e.g., Lee, Loring, Meader, & Brooks, 1990; Perria, Rosadini, & Rossi, 1961). Following injection into the left carotid artery, descriptions of individual patients' behaviors included crying, pessimistic statements, feelings of nothingness, indignity, or despair, and an inability to hold back fears or negative thoughts. Unilateral injection into the right carotid artery elicited an opposite response characterized by a euphoric reaction, including smiling, optimism, and an overall sense of well-being. Related findings come from a retrospective study by Sackeim and colleagues (Sackeim, Greenberg, Weiman, Gur, Hungerbuhler, & Geschwind, 1982), who found that pathological over-expression of positive affect was associated with predominantly right-sided brain damage, whereas pathological over-expression of negative affect was mainly associated with left-sided damage.

A second, complementary conceptualization of the functional significance of hemispheric asymmetry is the possible relation to underlying motivational systems of approach and withdrawal. For many years, comparative psychologists, animal behaviorists, and ethologists have noted that across many species, behavior is organized around the motivation to approach (obtain food, sex, fight) or withdraw (flee, escape predators and danger). A number of researchers have speculated that these two motivational systems are subsumed by different neural circuitry. For instance, Fox and Davidson (1984) proposed a model that stressed the primacy of approach and withdrawal tendencies in the development of emotional behaviors. This model is based on the association of asymmetries in the frontal cortical region with the regulation of motivational responses to appetitive or aversive stimuli (Fox, 1991). In this perspective, the left frontal region promotes appetitive, approach-directed emotional responses, while the right frontal region promotes withdrawal-directed responses to perceived aversive stimuli. At the present time, the precise neurophysiological basis of frontal EEG asymmetry has not been ascertained: Asymmetries in frontal EEG activation may be a function of asymmetries in projections from subcortical structures, or may be generated within the cortex itself (Davidson, 1998).

One method of assessing hemispheric asymmetry is via the recording of EEG from homologous sites over the left and right hemispheres and the computation of an index of asymmetry based on EEG band power. Typically, studies of hemispheric asymmetries and emotional development have examined asymmetries in alpha power. Such studies have utilized either a laterality ratio score or a difference score between left and right homologous scalp leads. Bearing in mind that the relation between alpha power and cortical activation is inverse, decreased alpha power in the EEG recorded from the left scalp electrode relative to power from the right scalp electrode has been taken as indicating increased activation in that particular left frontal scalp region. If such a pattern were found for two frontal scalp leads it would be referred to as "left frontal asymmetry". Conversely, "right frontal asymmetry" refers to a pattern where activation in the right frontal region is greater than activation in the left frontal region, with alpha power from the right frontal electrode being lower relative to that from the left frontal electrode.

Conceptually, the laterality index has been utilized as both a state and trait marker. As a state marker, Davidson and colleagues (Davidson, Ekman, Saron, Senulis, & Friesen, 1990; Wheeler, Davidson, & Tomarken, 1993) have shown a relation between frontal asymmetry and the pattern of emotion expression elicited in adults to various types of stimuli. In these studies, right frontal asymmetry was associated with negative emotions and right frontal asymmetry with positive emotions. A set of programmatic studies by Fox and Davidson first provided evidence for the relation between patterns of EEG recorded over left and right prefrontal regions and the development of social and emotional behavior. For example, Davidson and Fox (1982) reported that 10-month-old infants watching a video of an actress crying or smiling displayed differential EEG patterns, with greater right frontal EEG activation during the crying segments. While viewing the positive segment, infants exhibited relatively greater left frontal EEG activation relative to right frontal activation. A further study found this asymmetry in frontal EEG activity to be present also in infants' response to sweet and sour tastes (Fox & Davidson, 1986). Fox and Davidson (1988) also isolated instances of disgust and joy expressions in infants and found that frontal EEG asymmetry coincident with these expressions differed as a function of the type of expression. During the expression of positive affect infants exhibited left frontal EEG asymmetry, while during the expression of negative affect infants displayed right frontal EEG asymmetry. In a separate study, Fox and Davidson (1987) found that 10-month-old infants exposed to the approach of an unfamiliar adult and to maternal separation displayed right frontal EEG asymmetry, while to the approach of their own mother they displayed left frontal EEG asymmetry. Thus, with regard to the validity of the use of frontal EEG asymmetry as a state marker reflecting either positive or negative emotion or approach–withdrawal tendencies there are data from both adult and developmental studies.

Frontal EEG asymmetry has also been presented in the literature as reflecting a trait marker, either for the disposition to express positive or negative affect or for the predisposition towards approach or withdrawal tendencies. In the adult literature, Davidson and colleagues have shown that right frontal EEG asymmetry (recorded during a baseline session, often at a different time from a subsequent emotion assessment) is associated with negative ratings of mildly evocative video clips, with depressive symptomatology, and with lower self-ratings of approach (Sutton & Davidson, 1997). Likewise, Davidson and colleagues recently found that baseline left frontal EEG asymmetry was related to a more positive, optimistic outlook (Urry et al., 2004).

Several studies have related individual differences in approach or withdrawal behaviors in infancy and childhood to patterns of asymmetrical alpha activity over frontal electrode sites. For example, Davidson and Fox (1989) reported that infants' baseline EEG patterns at 10 months of age predicted their subsequent response to maternal separation. Infants displaying right frontal EEG asymmetry were more likely to cry to maternal separation than those displaying left frontal EEG asymmetry. Fox and colleagues have expanded on this work to examine the association between frontal EEG asymmetry and infant and child temperament. This research has focused on the electrophysiological correlates of behavioral inhibition to the unfamiliar, which has mainly been assessed in laboratory paradigms that expose an infant or toddler to unfamiliar people, objects, and contexts. Infants who displayed a pattern of stable right frontal EEG asymmetry during a visual baseline across the first 2 years of life tended to be more inhibited at both 14 and 24 months of age compared with infants who exhibited a pattern of stable left frontal EEG (Fox, Calkins, & Bell, 1994). A related study found that infants who went on to be consistently inhibited up to 4 years of age exhibited stronger right frontal EEG asymmetry at 9 and 14 months of age than infants who were to become less inhibited (Fox, Henderson, Rubin, Calkins, & Schmidt, 2001b). The latter group of infants exhibited weak right frontal EEG at 9 months of age and left frontal EEG asymmetry at 14 months of age.

Studies have also shown relations between high levels of negative reactivity in early infancy, right frontal EEG asymmetry, and behavioral inhibition in later infancy. Infants who were selected at 4 months of age for high frequencies of motor behavior and negative affect tended to show right frontal EEG asymmetry at 9 months of age, and were more behaviorally inhibited at 14 months of age compared with infants who showed either high positive affect or low levels of positive and negative reactivity at 4 months of age (Calkins et al., 1996). As well, Henderson, Fox, and Rubin (2001) found that the combination of infant negative temperament and right frontal EEG asymmetry was the best predictor of social reticence in preschool children. Infants whose mothers reported them to have negative temperament but who displayed left frontal EEG asymmetry during an attention task were less likely to show social reticence at 4 years of age. Other recent work has provided more insights into the correlates of frontal EEG asymmetry in infants. In 6-month-olds, higher cortisol levels were associated with right EEG asymmetry, and infants showing such right frontal asymmetry showed higher levels of sadness during the approach of a stranger (Buss, Schumacher, Dolski, Kalin, Goldsmith, & Davidson, 2003).

Much of the work described above has focused on individual differences in EEG asymmetry in relation to temperamental variation in approach and withdrawal behaviors in infancy and childhood. Work from Geraldine Dawson's laboratory showing right frontal asymmetry in infants of depressed mothers also suggests a role for the influence of the social environment as well as temperament in EEG asymmetry (Dawson et al., 1999). Relatedly, Hagemann and colleagues have carried out a state-trait analysis of EEG asymmetry in adults (Hagemann, Naumann, Thayer, & Bartussek, 2002) and found that for most scalp regions, about 60% of the variance of the asymmetry measure was due to individual differences (i.e., a temporally stable latent trait), and around 40% was due to state-specific fluctuations. Another key aspect of frontal asymmetry research is the need to discern whether the observed asymmetry is a mediator, moderator, or correlate of the behavior (Cacioppo, 2004; Coan & Allen, 2004; Davidson, 2004). Specifically, frontal EEG asymmetry may be a mediator when the asymmetrical neural activation produces tonic approach or withdrawal tendencies, or it may be a moderator when it dampens or augments the processes that produce the state changes in approach or withdrawal. These kinds of considerations are important to apply to temperament research, and may take us beyond the level of reporting correlations to a more thorough interpretation and discussion of mechanisms.

Although the work reviewed above has typically focused on the behavioral correlates of individual differences in frontal EEG asymmetries, it is important to note that hemispheric asymmetries occur as part of the typical development of the EEG. We have a variety of unpublished data that demonstrate a tendency for typically developing infants and young children to show left frontal asymmetry in infancy and early childhood, and slight right frontal asymmetry in middle childhood. Figure 8.1 shows some of these data from a longitudinal sample from 9 months to 7 years of age. In the same sample, other scalp regions (e.g., central, parietal, occipital) show little change in asymmetry scores over the same time frame. While further investigations should reveal whether we can generalize from these findings to other populations, they suggest that in early development, individual differences in frontal EEG asymmetry may be superimposed on these more general maturational patterns. In addition, the absence of EEG asymmetries across various scalp regions has also been associated with developmental disorders or environmental adversity: There is some evidence of reduced hemispheric asymmetries in the EEG in autism (Dawson, Klinger, Panagiotides, Lewy, & Castelloe, 1995) and young children living in institutions (Marshall et al., 2004b).

EVENT-RELATED POTENTIALS AND AFFECTIVE DEVELOPMENT

Event-related potentials (ERPs) are averaged EEG responses that are time-locked to specific events, such as the onset of discrete stimuli or a participant's

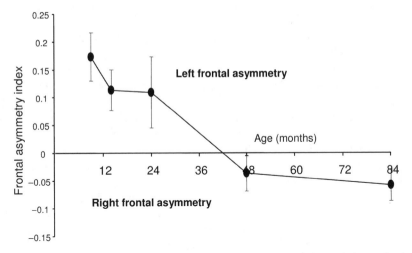

Figure 8.1 Hemispheric asymmetry in alpha band power over frontal electrode sites from 9 to 84 months of age in a longitudinal sample (*N* = 29). Error bars indicate ± 1 Standard Error.

reaction to a task demand. In ERP analysis, the variables that are typically of interest are amplitude and latency of specific components in the ERP waveform (see Chapter 1, this volume, for more details about recording and analysing ERPs). Approaches to interpretation of ERP data (e.g., amplitude or latency differences between trial types) typically come from the perspective of cognitive neuroscience (Fabiani, Gratton, & Coles, 2000). However, in recent years there has been increasing interest in applying such models to the study of affect and the interaction between cognition, emotion, and sensory processing. Developmental aspects of this approach are being explored, and this promises to be a very fertile intersection of cognitive neuroscience with affective development. In the following section we will describe some recent work carried out with ERPs in the domain of early social and emotional development.

Temperament and auditory novelty processing

In the literature on neurobiological models of behavioral inhibition to the unfamiliar, one potentially important but relatively uninvestigated area is the relation of individual differences in early stages of sensory processing to the expression of inhibited behavior in childhood (Marshall & Stevenson-Hinde, 2001). Links between early stages of sensory processing and temperamental individual differences have not been well explored. In fact, the literature relating infant temperament to auditory ERP responses is very sparse. One exception is the study of Woodward et al. (2001), who found that children previously classified as highly negatively reactive as infants showed larger amplitudes on a specific component of the auditory brainstem response when tested in middle childhood.

One useful measure of early sensory processing in the auditory modality is the mismatch negativity (MMN; see Chapter 6, this volume, for further discussion of the MMN). The MMN indexes a change-detection mechanism in primary auditory cortex, and it is elicited using auditory "oddball" paradigms without specific task demands (Picton, Alain, Otten, Ritter, & Achim, 2000). In such paradigms, the presentation of a frequent, repetitive stimulus (the "standard" stimulus) is interspersed with the occasional presentation of a less frequent "deviant" stimulus which differs from the standard in its physical make-up, e.g., the deviant may have a different duration or frequency from the standard. The MMN is usually derived from a comparison of the ERPs to the deviant and standard stimuli, specifically by the computation of a difference waveform in which the ERP to the standard stimulus is subtracted from the ERP to the deviant stimulus. The MMN is often taken as the most negative point in this difference waveform within a given latency range, although its characteristics in terms of morphology and latency vary over infancy and childhood (Cheour et al., 1998; Gomot, Giard, Roux, Barthelemy, & Bruneau, 2000; Morr, Shafer, Kreuzer, & Kurtzberg, 2002; Shafer, Morr, Kreuzer, & Kurtzberg, 2000).

Bar-Haim and colleagues examined the mismatch negativity (MMN) in the auditory ERP of socially withdrawn and control children aged 7–12 years (Bar-Haim, Marshall, Fox, Schorr, & Gordon-Salant, 2003). They found that socially withdrawn children have reduced MMN amplitude compared with the more outgoing control children. In some ways, this finding echoes the results of Gunnar and Nelson (1994), who found that infants rated by their parents as being high in positive emotionality had larger ERP responses to novelty in a visual oddball paradigm, and infants rated high in fearfulness had smaller amplitude responses. We have continued this line of research with infants, using an auditory oddball paradigm at 9 months of age to assess whether temperamentally different infants show corresponding variability in the processing of discrete changes in the auditory environment (Marshall, Hardin, & Fox, 2006). We were particularly interested in using different levels of novelty in order to investigate the possibility of differential responses to varying degrees of stimulus novelty according to infant temperament. Specifically, we examined ERP responses using an auditory oddball paradigm in a sample of infants who had been selected for high or low levels of motor activity and affect in a screening procedure at 4 months of age. The rationale for this was that behavioral reactivity to novel or intense stimuli in the first half-year of life has been identified as a precursor of approach and withdrawal tendencies to novelty in later infancy and toddlerhood. Specifically, the combination of high levels of negative affect and motor activity in response to a battery of novel sensory stimuli at 4 months of age has been related to behavioral inhibition to the unfamiliar in later infancy and early childhood (Calkins & Fox, 1992; Calkins et al., 1996; Kagan &

Snidman, 1991). In addition, Fox and colleagues (2001b) focused interest on infants who also showed high levels of motor activity in response to sensory stimulation at 4 months of age, but who showed high levels of positively valenced behaviors such as smiling during the presentation of the novel stimuli. These infants tend to show more "exuberant", outgoing behavior in later infancy and early childhood, and as a group show more consistency in this behavioral style over time than high negatively reactive infants, who tend to become less inhibited with time (Fox et al., 2001b). The positive and negative responses of these groups of infants to novelty have been conceptualized as temperamental biases towards the expression of approach or withdrawal behaviors, which may in turn affect later cognitive and social styles (Fox, Henderson, & Marshall, 2001a).

The MMN has been elicited quite consistently in studies of school-age children (e.g., Bar-Haim et al., 2003; Cheour, Korpilahti, Martynova, & Lang, 2001; Gomes, Molholm, Ritter, Kurtzberg, Cowan, & Vaughan, 2000; Gomot et al., 2000), but there is some debate as to the morphology of this ERP component in infancy. While some researchers have reported the infant mismatch response to resemble that seen in older children and adults, with a more negative-going response to the deviant than to the standard stimulus in the normal latency range of the MMN (e.g., Ceponiene, Lepisto, Soininen, Aronen, Alku, & Näätänen, 2004), a number of researchers have found the reverse, especially in infants under 1 year of age. While part of this diversity of findings may be explained by differences in stimulus characteristics and methodology, it is also possible that individual differences in temperament may influence components such as the MMN. In part, this was our premise for using an auditory oddball design in a sample of infants that had been subjected to stringent selection at 4 months of age in order to obtain groups of infants that were extreme on emotional reactivity.

In addition to the standard and deviant stimuli such as those used in MMN paradigms, we also employed a third category of widely deviant, complex novel stimuli. Such stimuli, when used in oddball paradigms in adults, tend to elicit specific ERP components that are associated with aspects of an orienting response (Escera, Alho, Winkler, & Näätänen, 1998). One such component is the "novelty P3", which can be elicited when the novel sounds are interspersed among simpler standard and deviant tones to which the participant is attending or responding (e.g., Gaeta, Friedman, Ritter, & Cheng, 1998). A novelty P3 has also been observed in children for attended tasks (e.g., Cycowicz, Friedman, & Rothstein, 1996; Gumenyuk et al., 2001). Various theoretical accounts have been proposed for the novelty P3, although the approach summarized by Friedman, Cycowicz, and Gaeta (2001) seems to hold much promise. The premise of these authors is that the novelty P3 consists of two subcomponents: (1) the P3a, which has a frontal scalp distribution, is elicited by large deviance levels, and reflects orienting or involuntary capture of attention, and (2) the P3b, which has a more posterior scalp distribution, and is larger during paradigms in which participants have been instructed to attend and/or respond to other changes in a stimulus train. Concerning work with infants, the paradigms outlined above are subject to the obvious constraint that infants cannot be instructed to attend to the deviant stimuli. However, an unattended variant of the three-stimulus odd-ball paradigm lends itself quite readily to application with infants and young children. In this task with adults, participants are instructed to ignore all the auditory stimuli and focus their attention on an unrelated activity such as reading (e.g., Friedman, Kazmerski, & Cycowicz, 1998). ERP analyses from such tasks have shown that deviant tones tend to elicit an MMN response, while the complex novel sounds elicit a novelty P3 that is generally smaller than that seen in similar attended tasks (Friedman et al., 1998). Despite the fact that the passive nature of this paradigm is ideal for use with infants, no previous study has a similar three-stimulus auditory oddball paradigm with infants. Kushnerenko, Ceponiene, Balan, Fellman, and Näätänen (2002) used a two-stimulus oddball to elicit a possible analog of the P3a in newborns and 2-year-olds using complex novel sounds interspersed among frequent standard tones.

The results of our study of 9-month-olds showed that groups of infants differing in temperamental reactivity to novel and moderately intense sensory stimuli at 4 months of age showed different patterns of ERP responses to the two levels of auditory change at 9 months of age. Interestingly, over the sample as a whole we did not find clear evidence of a more negative ERP response to the deviant tone compared with the standard tone. As shown in Figure 8.2, we confirmed the finding seen in certain other studies in this age range that the infant response to the deviant stimulus tends to be more positive-going than that to the standard (e.g., Morr et al., 2002). When analyzed by temperament group, the magnitude of this positive-going component was particularly strong for the high negative temperament group. Given the similar morphology and latency of this positivity with the response to the complex novel stimulus (see below), it is possible that high negative infants showed an orienting response or attention switch to the deviant tone.

As in older children and adults, we found that the complex novel stimuli elicited a strong positive-going response in the infants, with a prominent frontal component (Ceponiene et al., 2004; Friedman et al., 2001). The peak amplitude of this component also varied with scalp region and temperament group in an interactive fashion. In particular, the amplitude at frontal sites was largest for the high positive group compared with the other two groups. If indeed there is an association of this component with the frontal P3a as observed in adults, this would suggest that the high positive group showed a greater degree of orienting or attention switching to the large degree of change between the standard and complex novel stimuli. In contrast, a lower level of novelty (i.e., the deviant tone) was sufficient to elicit an orienting response or involuntary attention switch in the high negative temperament group. Given this finding that the ERP responses in this oddball paradigm seem to vary with infant temperament, it would be helpful for infant

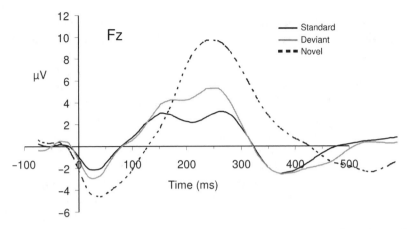

Figure 8.2 ERP responses at Fz to standard and deviant tonal stimuli, and complex novel auditory stimuli across a sample of 9-month-old infants.

researchers to try to assess or account for individual variations in temperamental reactivity in their samples, in order to better understand the individual variability seen in the auditory ERP in infancy (see Kurtzberg, Vaughan, Kreuzer, & Fliegler, 1995).

A particularly interesting question concerning the results outlined above is whether individual differences in sensory processing related to infant temperament are a consequence of "top-down" influences by higher affective centers, or whether they reflect "bottom-up" differences in early processing that may feed forward to affect the later processing and evaluation of sensory information. Although it is difficult to distinguish between these alternatives in our current data, more work is clearly required to explore this question further.

Temperament, sensory gating, and P50 suppression

Sensory gating represents the nervous system's ability to inhibit responding to irrelevant environmental stimuli. The middle latency response (MLR) of the human auditory event-related potential (ERP) spans the time period between 10 and 80 milliseconds after stimulus onset, and is characterized by a specific series of components, which are labeled as No, Po, Na, Pa, Nb, and P50. The P50 component (which is also labeled as Pb or P1) occurs with a latency of around 50 ms in adults, and it has been the subject of research from audiological, psychological, and psychiatric perspectives. In the audiological literature, research on the P50 has examined its clinical utility as a measure of low-frequency hearing and as a measure of the function of the higher auditory pathways (Kraus & McGee, 1990). In the psychological and psychiatric literatures, research has examined the role of the P50 in early sensory processing in relation to the gating of irrelevant or repetitive stimulus information ("sensory gating"). In non-psychiatric adults, the P50 to the second stimulus in a paired-click paradigm is reduced in amplitude compared with the P50 response to the first click. In schizophrenic patients, this suppression of P50 to the second click is impaired (Adler, Pachtman, Franks, Pecevich, Waldo, & Freedman, 1982; Clementz, Geyer, & Braff, 1997). Although the bulk of P50 suppression research has been carried out in relation to P50 suppression deficits in schizophrenia, researchers have recently begun to study its relation to a variety of other conditions, including head injury (Arciniegas et al., 2000), recreational drug use (Patrick & Struve, 2000), post-traumatic stress disorder (Neylan et al., 1999), and Alzheimer's disease (Jessen et al., 2001). The basic model of P50 suppression assumes that impaired suppression to the second click reflects poor sensory gating, which in turn is proposed to be associated with an influx of irrelevant or distracting information that can cause perceptual or attentional deficits (Braff & Geyer, 1990).

While there is little developmental research on P50 gating, a recent report showed that significant P50 suppression to the second click was found in healthy infants aged between 1 and 4 months (Kisley, Polk, Ross, Levisohn, & Freedman, 2003). These results demonstrate that the neural circuits underlying sensory gating are functional very early in postnatal development. There are very few other developmental studies of P50 gating. Two studies are by Freedman and colleagues, who examined P50 suppression in cross-sectional samples using a range of age groups. The first study used six age groups from infancy to 65 years of age, including groups of children 1–8 years, 9–11 years, and 11–19 years of age (Freedman et al., 1987). P50 gating was found to be highly variable during childhood, and adult levels of P50 suppression were not found until late adolescence. The second study employed a different range of age groups up to 40 years of age, with the youngest group spanning 10–14 years of age (Myles-Worsley, Coon, Byerley, Waldo, Young, & Freedman, 1996). Compared to the previous study, P50 suppression showed greater stability and a different developmental time course: In the 10- to 14-year-old age group, P50 suppression was at the same level of adults tested in the same study. The third study of P50 suppression in children found no differences in P50 suppression between autistic children and normal controls in a sample of children aged 7–14 years (Kemner, Oranje, Verbaten, & van Engeland, 2002). Finally, socially withdrawn and more outgoing control children did not differ on P50 gating (Marshall, Bar-Haim, & Fox, 2004a).

Despite the very small number of studies in infants and young children, P50 suppression may be particularly meaningful from the perspective of developmental cognitive neuroscience. The maturational course of the capacity to inhibit irrelevant stimuli is an important part of developmental theories of attention (van der Molen, 2000). A developmental increase in the ability to gate irrelevant stimuli may be expected, since it may parallel the development of certain inhibitory capacities that are known to be dependent on the frontal lobes (Bunge, Dudukovic, Thomason, Vaidya, & Gabrieli, 2002; Casey et al., 1997). While the dominant model of the mechanism underlying P50 suppression deficits in schizophrenia proposes a failure of GABA-mediated inhibition of pyramidal cells in the hippocampus (Freedman et al., 1996), there is increasing evidence suggesting that the frontal cortex may also play an important role in mediating P50 suppression. Patients with damage to the prefrontal cortex show augmentation of the Pa and P50 components (Knight, Scabini, & Woods 1989) and show problems with suppression of the P50 to the second stimulus in a paired-click paradigm (Knight, Staines, Swick, & Chao, 1999). Furthermore, a recent source analysis found a secondary P50 generator in the frontal lobe (Weisser, Weisbrod, Roehrig, Rupp, Schroeder, & Scherg, 2001), in addition to a bilateral generator in auditory cortex that is thought to be the primary source of the P50 component (Liegeois-Chauvel, Musolino, Badier, Marquis, & Chauvel, 1994; Yoshiura, Ueno, Iramina, & Masuda, 1995).

Studies of P50 suppression in infants and children may potentially provide important information about the development of sensory gating. However, such studies must take into consideration the development of the MLR, which has a relatively long maturational time course. The P50 is clearly present from infancy and early childhood as a longer-latency P50 component that becomes shorter in latency with increasing age, until by middle childhood it dominates the MLR response (McGee & Kraus, 1996; Ponton, Don, Eggermont, Waring, & Masuda, 1996). In contrast, the detectability and saliency of the Pa component increases more slowly through childhood and into early adolescence (Kraus & McGee, 1995; Kraus, Smith, Reed, Stein, & Cartee, 1985; Suzuki & Hirabayashi, 1987; Tucker & Ruth, 1996). How the presence or absence of the Pa affects the P50 (and suppression of the P50 in a paired-click paradigm) has not been explored. The amplitude of the P50 is usually assessed in relation to the amplitude of the Nb, which is the negativity that precedes the P50 in the MLR. The properties of the Nb may in turn be influenced by the presence or absence of the Pa, which precedes it in the MLR. An understanding of these developmental issues is of critical importance for the quantification and interpretation of the P50 in infants and young children. A further issue that needs to be incorporated into models of P50 suppression is whether MLR components earlier than the P50 are also subject to suppression in a paired-click paradigm. Such components (e.g., the Pa) have not routinely been examined in studies of P50 suppression, although suppression of the Pa to the second click in a paired-click paradigm in adults has been reported by some authors (Muller, Keil, Kissler, & Gruber, 2001).

Despite a theoretical link between variations in sensory gating and normative variation in behavioral traits, very little work has examined individual differences in P50 suppression outside the clinical literature. However, it is conceivable that variation in sensory gating may also be associated with individual differences in temperament. Individual differences in reactivity to sensory stimuli are an important component of models of both infant temperament and adult personality (Strelau, 1998). For instance, introverts may find noisy social situations aversive due to their low threshold of arousal and their difficulty in filtering out extraneous noise (Eysenck & Eysenck, 1985; Weinstein, 1978). Given that P50 suppression deficits have been theoretically associated with a perceptually disturbing influx of irrelevant or distracting information, there may be a link between deficits in P50 suppression and certain temperamental tendencies. The existence of P50 suppression in infants raises various questions about the development of sensory gating and its relation to infant temperament, an area that is clearly open for investigation.

CONCLUSIONS

There are at least three domains in which electrophysiology has contributed and will continue to contribute to our understanding of the neural correlates of social and emotional development in infants and young children. The first is with regard to the findings on EEG alpha power in behavioral inhibition, as well as to the relation of theta power to the cognitive deficits resulting from early social deprivation. The second is the literature on frontal EEG asymmetry and social behavior. The widely replicated findings relating right frontal EEG asymmetry to temperamental behavioral inhibition and withdrawal-related behaviors suggest that frontal EEG asymmetry reflects a fundamental aspect of social behavior. Future work is needed to uncover the neural bases of this asymmetry. In the absence of such work these findings, though of great interest to the developmental and psychological communities, will continue to be at most curiosities to the neuroscience community. It is therefore imperative in the next wave of work for this fundamental research to occur.

The third domain that has contributed to our understanding of the neural correlates or substrates of both cognitive and social behavior in infancy is the use of event-related potentials. ERP methods continue to provide the neuroscience and developmental communities with important information about the processing of information, from basic sensory processing levels to more complex levels of perception and cognition, by the pre-verbal infant and young child. While functional neuroimaging technologies provide more accurate spatial resolution of sources of neural activity, the barriers to the use of this technology with infants and young children will stay in place for the foreseeable future. ERP studies can elucidate aspects of the temporal response of the young brain and as such provide important windows into sensation, perception, and cognition. Although methodologically difficult, the inclusion of individual differences into this work opens up a range of possibilities for studying brain–behavior relations in social and emotional development.

REFERENCES

Adler, L. E., Pachtman, E., Franks, R. D., Pecevich, M., Waldo, M. C., & Freedman, R. (1982). Neurophysiological evidence for a defect in neuronal mechanisms involved in sensory gating in schizophrenia. *Biological Psychiatry, 17*, 639–654.

Arciniegas, D., Olincy, A., Topkoff, J., McRae, K., Cawthra, E., Filley, C. M. et al. (2000). Impaired auditory gating and P50 nonsuppression following traumatic brain injury. *Journal of Neuropsychiatry and Clinical Neurosciences, 12*, 77–85.

Bar-Haim, Y., Marshall, P. J., Fox, N. A., Schorr, E. A., & Gordon-Salant, S. (2003). Mismatch negativity in socially withdrawn children. *Biological Psychiatry, 54*, 17–24.

Barry, R. J., Clarke, A. R., & Johnstone, S. J. (2003). A review of electrophysiology in attention-deficit/hyperactivity disorder: 1. Qualitative and quantitative electro-encephalography. *Clinical Neurophysiology, 114*, 171–183.

Bell, M. A. (1998). The ontogeny of the EEG during infancy and childhood: Implications for cognitive development. In B. Barreau (Ed.), *Neuroimaging in child developmental disorders* (pp. 97–111). Berlin: Springer.

Bell, M. A. (2002). Power changes in infant EEG frequency bands during a spatial working memory task. *Psychophysiology, 39*, 450–458.

Braff, D. L., & Geyer, M. A. (1990). Sensorimotor gating and schizophrenia. Human and animal model studies. *Archives of General Psychiatry, 47*, 181–188.

Bunge, S. A., Dudukovic, N. M., Thomason, M. E., Vaidya, C. J., & Gabrieli, J. D. (2002). Immature frontal lobe contributions to cognitive control in children: Evidence from fMRI. *Neuron, 33*, 301–311.

Buss, K. A., Schumacher, J. R., Dolski, I., Kalin, N. H., Goldsmith, H. H., & Davidson, R. J. (2003). Right frontal brain activity, cortisol, and withdrawal behavior in 6-month-old infants. *Behavioral Neuroscience, 117*, 11–20.

Cacioppo, J. T. (2004). Feelings and emotions: Roles for electrophysiological markers. *Biological Psychology, 67*, 235–243.

Calkins, S. D., & Fox, N. A. (1992). The relations among infant temperament, security of attachment, and behavioral inhibition at twenty-four months. *Child Development, 63*, 1456–1472.

Calkins, S. D., Fox, N. A., & Marshall, T. R. (1996). Behavioral and physiological antecedents of inhibited and uninhibited behavior. *Child Development, 67*, 523–540.

Casey, B. J., Trainor, R., Giedd, J., Vauss, Y., Vaituzis, C. K., Hamburger, S. et al. (1997). The role of the anterior cingulate in automatic and controlled processes: A developmental neuroanatomical study. *Developmental Psychobiology, 30*, 61–69.

Ceponiene, R., Lepisto, T., Soininen, M., Aronen, E., Alku, P., & Näätänen, R. (2004). Event-related potentials associated with sound discrimination versus novelty detection in children. *Psychophysiology, 41*, 130–141.

Chabot, R. J., di Michele, F., Prichep, L., & John, E. R. (2001). The clinical role of computerized EEG in the evaluation and treatment of learning and attention disorders in children and adolescents. *Journal of Neuropsychiatry and Clinical Neuroscience, 13*, 171–186.

Cheour, M., Alho, K., Ceponiene, R., Reinikainen, K., Sainio, K., Pohjavuori, M. et al. (1998). Maturation of mismatch negativity in infants. *International Journal of Psychophysiology, 29*, 217–226.

Cheour, M., Korpilahti, P., Martynova, O., & Lang, A. H. (2001). Mismatch negativity and late discriminative negativity in investigating speech perception and learning in children and infants. *Audiology and Neuro-otology, 6*, 2–11.

Clementz, B. A., Geyer, M. A., & Braff, D. L. (1997). P50 suppression among schizophrenia and normal comparison subjects: A methodological analysis. *Biological Psychiatry, 41*, 1035–1044.

Coan, J. A., & Allen, J. J. (2004). Frontal EEG asymmetry as a moderator and mediator of emotion. *Biological Psychology, 67*, 7–49.

Csibra, G., Davis, G., Spratling, M. W., & Johnson, M. H. (2000). Gamma oscillations and object processing in the infant brain. *Science, 290*, 1582–1585.

Cycowicz, Y. M., Friedman, D., & Rothstein, M. (1996). An ERP developmental study of repetition priming by auditory novel stimuli. *Psychophysiology, 33*, 680–690.

Davidson, R. J. (1998). Anterior electrophysiological asymmetries, emotion, and depression: Conceptual and methodological conundrums. *Psychophysiology, 35*, 607–614.

Davidson, R. J. (2004). What does the prefrontal cortex "do" in affect: Perspectives on frontal EEG asymmetry research. *Biological Psychology, 67*, 219–233.

Davidson, R. J., Ekman, P., Saron, C. D., Senulis, J. A., & Friesen, W. V. (1990). Approach–withdrawal and cerebral asymmetry: Emotion expression and brain physiology. *Journal of Personality and Social Psychology, 58*, 330–341.

Davidson, R. J., & Fox, N. A. (1982). Asymmetrical brain activity discriminates between positive and negative affective stimuli in human infants. *Science, 218*, 1235–1237.

Davidson, R. J., & Fox, N. A. (1989). Frontal brain asymmetry predicts infants' response to maternal separation. *Journal of Abnormal Psychology, 98*, 127–131.

Dawson, G., Frey, K., Self, J., Panagiotides, H., Hessl, D., Yamada, E. et al. (1999). Frontal brain electrical activity in infants of depressed and nondepressed mothers: Relation to variations in infant behavior. *Development and Psychopathology, 11*, 589–605.

Dawson, G., Klinger, L. G., Panagiotides, H., Lewy, A., & Castelloe, P. (1995). Subgroups of autistic children based on social behavior display distinct patterns of brain activity. *Journal of Abnormal Child Psychology, 23*, 569–583.

Escera, C., Alho, K., Winkler, I., & Näätänen, R. (1998). Neural mechanisms of involuntary attention to acoustic novelty and change. *Journal of Cognitive Neuroscience, 10*, 590–604.

Eysenck, H. J., & Eysenck, M. W. (1985). *Personality and individual differences: A natural science approach.* New York: Plenum Press.

Fabiani, M., Gratton, G., & Coles, M. G. (2000). Event-related brain potentials. In J. T. Cacioppo, L. G. Tassinary, & G. G. Bernston (Eds.), *Handbook of psychophysiology* (2nd ed., pp. 53–84). New York: Cambridge University Press.

Fox, N. A. (1991). If it's not left, it's right: Electroencephalograph asymmetry and the development of emotion. *American Psychologist, 46*, 863–872.

Fox, N. A. (1994). Dynamic cerebral processes underlying emotion regulation. In N. A. Fox (Ed.), "The development of emotion regulation: Behavioral and biological considerations". *Monographs of the Society for Research in Child Development, 59* (2–3), 152–166.

Fox, N. A., Calkins, S. D., & Bell, M. A. (1994). Neural plasticity and development in the first two years of life: Evidence from cognitive and socioemotional domains of research. *Development and Psychopathology, 6*, 677–696.

Fox, N. A., & Davidson, R. J. (1984). Hemispheric substates of affect: A developmental approach. In N. A. Fox & R. J. Davidson (Eds.), *The psychobiology of affective development* (pp. 353–381). Hillsdale, NJ: Lawrence Erlbaum Associates Inc.

Fox, N. A., & Davidson, R. J. (1986). Psychophysiological measures of emotion: New directions in developmental research. In C. E. Izard & P. B. Read (Eds.), *Measuring emotions in infants and children, Vol. 2* (pp. 13–47). New York: Cambridge University Press.

Fox, N. A., & Davidson, R. J. (1987). Electroencephalogram asymmetry in response to the approach of a stranger and maternal separation in 10-month-old infants. *Developmental Psychology, 23,* 233–240.

Fox, N. A., & Davidson, R. J. (1988). Patterns of brain electrical activity during facial signs of emotion in 10-month-old infants. *Developmental Psychology, 24,* 230–236.

Fox, N. A., Henderson, H. A., & Marshall, P. J. (2001a). The biology of temperament: An integrative approach. In C. A. Nelson & M. Luciana (Eds.), *Handbook of developmental cognitive neuroscience* (pp. 631–646). Cambridge, MA: MIT Press.

Fox, N. A., Henderson, H. A., Rubin, K. H., Calkins, S. D., & Schmidt, L. A. (2001b). Continuity and discontinuity of behavioral inhibition and exuberance: Psychophysiological and behavioral influences across the first four years of life. *Child Development, 72,* 1–21.

Freedman, R., Adler, L. E., Gerhardt, G. A., Waldo, M., Baker, N., Rose, G. M. et al. (1987). Neurobiological studies of sensory gating in schizophrenia. *Schizophrenia Bulletin, 13,* 669–678.

Freedman, R., Adler, L. E., Myles-Worsley, M., Nagamoto, H. T., Miller, C., Kisley, M. et al. (1996). Inhibitory gating of an evoked response to repeated auditory stimuli in schizophrenic and normal subjects. Human recordings, computer simulation, and an animal model. *Archives of General Psychiatry, 53,* 1114–1121.

Friedman, D., Cycowicz, Y. M., & Gaeta, H. (2001). The novelty P3: An event-related brain potential (ERP) sign of the brain's evaluation of novelty. *Neuroscience and Biobehavioral Reviews, 25,* 355–373.

Friedman, D., Kazmerski, V. A., & Cycowicz, Y. M. (1998). Effects of aging on the novelty P3 during attend and ignore oddball tasks. *Psychophysiology, 35,* 508–520.

Gaeta, H., Friedman, D., Ritter, W., & Cheng, J. (1998). An event-related potential study of age-related changes in sensitivity to stimulus deviance. *Neurobiology of Aging, 19,* 447–459.

Gomes, H., Molholm, S., Ritter, W., Kurtzberg, D., Cowan, N., & Vaughan, H. G. Jr. (2000). Mismatch negativity in children and adults, and effects of an attended task. *Psychophysiology, 37,* 807–816.

Gomot, M., Giard, M. H., Roux, S., Barthelemy, C., & Bruneau, N. (2000). Maturation of frontal and temporal components of mismatch negativity (MMN) in children. *NeuroReport, 11,* 3109–3112.

Grice, S. J., Spratling, M. W., Karmiloff-Smith, A., Halit, H., Csibra, G., de Haan, M. et al. (2001). Disordered visual processing and oscillatory brain activity in autism and Williams syndrome. *NeuroReport, 12,* 2697–2700.

Gumenyuk, V., Korzyukov, O., Alho, K., Escera, C., Schroger, E., Ilmoniemi, R. J. et al. (2001). Brain activity index of distractibility in normal school-age children. *Neuroscience Letters, 314,* 147–150.

Gunnar, M. R., & Nelson, C. A. (1994). Event-related potentials in year-old infants: Relations with emotionality and cortisol. *Child Development, 65,* 80–94.

Hagemann, D., Naumann, E., Thayer, J. F., & Bartussek, D. (2002). Does resting electroencephalograph asymmetry reflect a trait? An application of latent state-trait theory. *Journal of Personality and Social Psychology, 82*, 619–641.

Harmony, T., Alvarez, A., Pascual, R., Ramos, A., Marosi, E., Diaz de Leon, A. E. et al. (1988). EEG maturation on children with different economic and psychosocial characteristics. *International Journal of Neuroscience, 41*, 103–113.

Henderson, H. A., Fox, N. A., & Rubin, K. H. (2001). Temperamental contributions to social behavior: The moderating roles of frontal EEG asymmetry and gender. *Journal of the American Academy of Child and Adolescent Psychiatry, 40*, 68–74.

Henderson, H. A., Marshall, P. J., Fox, N. A., & Rubin, K. H. (2004). Psychophysiological and behavioral evidence for varying forms and functions of nonsocial behavior in preschoolers. *Child Development, 75*, 251–263.

Henry, J. R. (1944). Electroencephalograms of normal children. *Monographs of the Society for Research in Child Development, 9.*

Jessen, F., Kucharski, C., Fries, T., Papassotiropoulos, A., Hoenig, K., Maier, W. et al. (2001). Sensory gating deficit expressed by a disturbed suppression of the P50 event-related potential in patients with Alzheimer's disease. *American Journal of Psychiatry, 158*, 1319–1321.

Kagan, J., & Snidman, N. (1991). Temperamental factors in human development. *American Psychologist, 46*, 856–862.

Kemner, C., Oranje, B., Verbaten, M. N., & van Engeland, H. (2002). Normal P50 gating in children with autism. *Journal of Clinical Psychiatry, 63*, 214–217.

Kisley, M. A., Polk, S. D., Ross, R. G., Levisohn, P. M., & Freedman, R. (2003). Early postnatal development of sensory gating. *NeuroReport, 14*, 693–697.

Knight, R. T., Scabini, D., & Woods, D. L. (1989). Prefrontal cortex gating of auditory transmission in humans. *Brain Research, 504*, 338–342.

Knight, R. T., Staines, W. R., Swick, D., & Chao, L. L. (1999). Prefrontal cortex regulates inhibition and excitation in distributed neural networks. *Acta Psychologica, 101*, 159–178.

Kraus, N., & McGee, T. (1990). Clinical applications of the middle latency response. *Journal of the American Academy of Audiology, 1*, 130–133.

Kraus, N., & McGee, T. (1995). The middle latency response generating system. *Electroencephalography and Clinical Neurophysiology, 44*, 93–101.

Kraus, N., Smith, D. I., Reed, N. L., Stein, L. K., & Cartee, C. (1985). Auditory middle latency responses in children: Effects of age and diagnostic category. *Electroencephalography and Clinical Neurophysiology, 62*, 343–351.

Kurtzberg, D., Vaughan, H. G. Jr., Kreuzer, J. A., & Fliegler, K. Z. (1995). Developmental studies and clinical application of mismatch negativity: Problems and prospects. *Ear and Hearing, 16*, 105–117.

Kushnerenko, E., Ceponiene, R., Balan, P., Fellman, V., & Näätänen, R. (2002). Maturation of the auditory change detection response in infants: A longitudinal ERP study. *NeuroReport, 13*, 1843–1848.

Lee, G. P., Loring, D. W., Meader, K. J., & Brooks, B. B. (1990). Hemispheric specialization for emotional expression: A reexamination of results from intracarotid administration of sodium amobarbital. *Brain and Cognition, 12*, 267–280.

Liegeois-Chauvel, C., Musolino, A., Badier, J. M., Marquis, P., & Chauvel, P. (1994). Evoked potentials recorded from the auditory cortex in man: Evaluation and topography of the middle latency components. *Electroencephalography and Clinical Neurophysiology, 92*, 204–214.

Lindsley, D. B. (1938). Electrical potentials of the brain in children and adults. *Journal of Genetic Psychology, 19*, 285–306.

Marshall, P. J., Bar-Haim, Y., & Fox, N. A. (2002). Development of the EEG from 5 months to 4 years of age. *Clinical Neurophysiology, 113*, 1199–1208.

Marshall, P. J., Bar-Haim, Y., & Fox, N. A. (2004a). The development of P50 suppression in the auditory event-related potential. *International Journal of Psychophysiology, 51*, 135–141.

Marshall, P. J., Fox, N. A., & the BEIP Core Group (2004b). A comparison of the electroencephalogram (EEG) between institutionalized and community children in Romania. *Journal of Cognitive Neuroscience, 16*, 1327–1338.

Marshall, P. J., Hardin, M. G., & Fox, N. A. (2006). *Electrophysiological responses to auditory novelty in temperamentally different 9-month-old infants.* Manuscript in preparation.

Marshall, P. J., & Stevenson-Hinde, J. (2001). Behavioral inhibition: Physiological correlates. In W. R. Crozier & L. E. Alden (Eds.), *International handbook of social anxiety* (pp. 53–76). Chichester, UK: John Wiley.

Matousek, M., & Petersen, I. (1973). Automatic evaluation of EEG background activity by means of age-dependent EEG quotients. *Electroencephalography and Clinical Neurophysiology, 35*, 603–612.

Matsuura, M., Okubo, Y., Toru, M., Kojima, T., He, Y., Hou, Y. et al. (1993). A cross-national EEG study of children with emotional and behavioral problems: A WHO collaborative study in the Western Pacific Region. *Biological Psychiatry, 34*, 59–65.

McGee, T., & Kraus, N. (1996). Auditory development reflected by middle latency response. *Ear and Hearing, 17*, 419–429.

Morr, M. L., Shafer, V. L., Kreuzer, J. A., & Kurtzberg, D. (2002). Maturation of mismatch negativity in typically developing infants and preschool children. *Ear and Hearing, 23*, 118–136.

Muller, M. M., Keil, A., Kissler, J., & Gruber, T. (2001). Suppression of the auditory middle-latency response and evoked gamma-band response in a paired-click paradigm. *Experimental Brain Research, 136*, 474–479.

Mundy, P., Card, J., & Fox, N. (2000). EEG correlates of the development of infant joint attention skills. *Developmental Psychobiology, 36*, 325–338.

Myles-Worsley, M., Coon, H., Byerley, W., Waldo, M., Young, D., & Freedman, R. (1996). Developmental and genetic influences on the P50 sensory gating phenotype. *Biological Psychiatry, 39*, 289–295.

Neylan, T. C., Fletcher, D. J., Lenoci, M., McCallin, K., Weiss, D. S., Schoenfeld, F. B. et al. (1999). Sensory gating in chronic posttraumatic stress disorder: Reduced auditory P50 suppression in combat veterans. *Biological Psychiatry, 46*, 1656–1664.

Niedermeyer, E. (1997). Alpha rhythms as physiological and abnormal phenomena. *International Journal of Psychophysiology, 26*, 31–49.

Orekhova, E. V., Stroganova, T. A., & Posikera, I. N. (1999). Theta synchronization during sustained anticipatory attention in infants over the second half of the first year of life. *International Journal of Psychophysiology, 32*, 151–172.

Orekhova, E. V., Stroganova, T. A., & Posikera, I. N. (2001). Alpha activity as an index of cortical inhibition during sustained internally controlled attention in infants. *Clinical Neurophysiology, 112*, 740–749.

Orekhova, E. V., Stroganova, T. A., Posikera, I. N., & Malykh, S. B. (2003). Heritability and "environmentability" of electroencephalogram in infants: The twin study. *Psychophysiology, 40*, 727–741.

Patrick, G., & Struve, F. A. (2000). Reduction of auditory P50 gating response in marihuana users: Further supporting data. *Clinical Electroencephalography, 31*, 88–93.

Perria, L., Rosadini, G., & Rossi, G. F. (1961). Determination of side of cerebral dominance with amobarbital. *Archives of Neurology, 4*, 173–181.

Picton, T. W., Alain, C., Otten, L., Ritter, W., & Achim, A. (2000). Mismatch negativity: Different water in the same river. *Audiology and Neuro-otology, 5*, 111–139.

Pineda, J. A. (2005). The functional significance of mu rhythms: Translating "seeing" and "hearing" into "doing". *Brain Research Reviews, 50*, 57–68.

Ponton, C. W., Don, M., Eggermont, J. J., Waring, M. D., & Masuda, A. (1996). Maturation of human cortical auditory function: Differences between normal-hearing children and children with cochlear implants. *Ear and Hearing, 17*, 430–437.

Sackeim, H. A., Greenberg, M. S., Weiman, A. L., Gur, R. C., Hungerbuhler, J. P., & Geschwind, N. (1982). Hemispheric asymmetry in the expression of positive and negative emotions. Neurologic evidence. *Archives of Neurology, 39*, 210–218.

Satterfield, J. H., Cantwell, D. P., & Satterfield, B. T. (1974). Pathophysiology of the hyperactive child syndrome. *Archives of General Psychiatry, 31*, 839–844.

Schmidt, L. A., & Fox, N. A. (1998). Electrophysiological studies I: Quantitative electroencephalography. In C. E. Coffey & R. A. Brumback (Eds.), *Textbook of pediatric neuropsychiatry: Section II. Neuropsychiatric assessment of the child and adolescent* (pp. 315–329). Washington, DC: American Psychiatric Press.

Shafer, V. L., Morr, M. L., Kreuzer, J. A., & Kurtzberg, D. (2000). Maturation of mismatch negativity in school-age children. *Ear and Hearing, 21*, 242–251.

Silberman, E. K., & Weingartner, H. (1986). Hemispheric lateralization of functions related to emotion. *Brain and Cognition, 5*, 322–353.

Smith, J. R. (1938). The electroencephalogram during normal infancy and childhood: The nature and growth of the alpha waves. *Electroencephalography and Clinical Neurophysiology, 53*, 455–469.

Strelau, J. (1998). *Temperament: A psychological perspective.* New York: Plenum.

Sutton, S. K., & Davidson, R. J. (1997). Prefrontal brain asymmetry: A biological substrate of the behavioral approach and inhibition systems. *Psychological Science, 8*, 204–210.

Suzuki, T., & Hirabayashi, M. (1987). Age-related morphological changes in auditory middle-latency response. *Audiology, 26*, 312–320.

Tucker, D. A., & Ruth, R. A. (1996). Effects of age, signal level, and signal rate on the auditory middle latency response. *Journal of the American Academy of Audiology, 7*, 83–91.

Urry, H. L., Nitschke, J. B., Dolski, I., Jackson, D. C., Dalton, K. M., Mueller, C. J. et al. (2004). Making a life worth living: Neural correlates of well-being. *Psychological Science, 15*, 367–372.

van der Molen, M. W. (2000). Developmental changes in inhibitory processing: Evidence from psychophysiological measures. *Biological Psychology, 54*, 207–239.

Weinstein, N. D. (1978). Individual differences in reactions to noise: A longitudinal study in a college dormitory. *Journal of Applied Psychology, 63*, 458–466.

Weisser, R., Weisbrod, M., Roehrig, M., Rupp, A., Schroeder, J., & Scherg, M. (2001). Is frontal lobe involved in the generation of auditory evoked P50? *NeuroReport, 12*, 3303–3307.

Wheeler, R. E., Davidson, R. J., & Tomarken, A. J. (1993). Frontal brain asymmetry and emotional reactivity: A biological substrate of affective style. *Psychophysiology, 30*, 82–89.

Woodward, S. A., McManis, M. H., Kagan, J., Deldin, P., Snidman, N., Lewis, M. et al. (2001). Infant temperament and the brainstem auditory evoked response in later childhood. *Developmental Psychology, 37*, 533–538.

Yoshiura, T., Ueno, S., Iramina, K., & Masuda, K. (1995). Source localization of middle latency auditory evoked magnetic fields. *Brain Research, 703*, 139–144.

9 EEG and infant states

Tatiana A. Stroganova
*Psychological Institute RAE,
Moscow, Russia*

Elena V. Orekhova
*Sahlgrenska University Hospital,
Gothenburg, Sweden*

This review is focused on the normal EEG patterns during different functional states of wakefulness in infants. Since the original studies of Smith
(1938a, 1938b) and Lindsley (1939), the majority of infant EEG studies have
reported changes of EEG patterns in the continuum of the sleep–wakefulness
cycle (Dreyfus-Brisac, 1979; Hagne, 1972). Within this framework, wakefulness is considered as a unified functional state with distinct behavioral
correlates (eyes open, vocalization, etc.) and low-amplitude EEG activity, as
compared to the synchronous high-amplitude waves characterizing drowsiness and quiet sleep. Some authors have additionally differentiated quiet
wakefulness (immobile infant with his/her eyes opened) and so-called active
wakefulness (gross body movement, crying, etc.). The latter functional state,
due to the obvious technical obstacles, provides no possibility to obtain
artifact-free EEG recording. It is therefore no surprise that, despite the growing body of infant EEG literature, very little if any attention has been given
to the different functional states during wakefulness. The popular definition
"quiet wakefulness" is technically poor described and theoretically imprecise.
Traditionally, the only criterion defining quiet wakefulness is immobility and
open eyes. In practice it includes several gradations of the functional state,
from being drowsy and uninterested in the environment to having focused
attention, cognitive activity, and emotional arousal. These more fine gradations of functional state strikingly change the mosaic of EEG rhythms. In
this paper we describe the variety of rhythmic activities in the EEG of waking
infants. Some of these rhythms can be observed while an infant is attentive
and immobile; some appear in EEG during overt emotional reactions or
under the peculiar condition of total darkness.

Infants' EEG rhythms of wakefulness can be assigned to one of four
categories depending on their frequency:

1. Rhythms of the "alpha family" (6–10 Hz). These can be recorded over
    posterior or anterior scalp locations with distinct topographical maxima
    at occipital or central electrode sites. The "central rhythm" appears when
    an infant remains behaviorally still, but focuses visual attention on a

target, whereas the "occipital" rhythm is favored by situations of total darkness and eye closure. While the frequencies of these two rhythms may overlap, their origins and especially their behavioral contexts are dissimilar. The former rhythm has been called sensory-motor or *mu rhythm* and the latter the *alpha rhythm*. The identification of these infant EEG rhythms is based on the correspondence of their topographical and functional properties to those of well-known alpha and mu rhythms in adults. Here we use the term "alpha activity" or "alpha band" to address all rhythmic EEG activities of 6–10 Hz range (i.e., both mu and alpha rhythms), while the term "alpha rhythm" is used in the more narrow sense.

2.   Rhythms of the "theta band" (4–6 Hz). These are more widespread over the scalp as compared to the alpha activity. They may appear in different behavioral contexts including: drowsiness, self-stimulation, feeding, positive and negative emotional arousal accompanied by overt affective expression, or cognitive activity (e.g., anticipation).

3.   EEG activity within the 1–3 Hz (delta) frequency band. Although these slow waves have relatively high prevalence and amplitudes over most electrode sites, they are not clearly synchronized in the EEG of healthy awake infants. The great increase in their amplitude and synchronization occurs during sleep.

4.   High-frequency activity (beta and gamma). There is virtually no accumulated knowledge about the cortical topography and conditions of occurrence of high-frequency activity during infancy. Despite the great interest in gamma oscillations in adults, there are only a few recent studies devoted to gamma-band activity in the infant brain (Csibra, Davis, Spratling, & Johnston, 2000; Kaufman, Csibra, & Johnson, 2003; see also Chapter 10, this volume).

In this paper, we concentrate on the first and second categories of rhythms (4–6 and 6–10 Hz bands) in more detail. We describe the most distinctly synchronized EEG patterns of waking infants, present experimental arguments favoring identification of infant EEG rhythms as homologues of theta and alpha rhythms in adults, and discuss their behavioral correlates and possible functional meaning.

THE PROBLEM OF INFANT EEG RHYTHM IDENTIFICATION

The early works using visual inspection of infant EEG did not reveal any visible rhythmic activity in the conventional "adult" alpha band (8–13 Hz). Instead, they described a 3–5 Hz rhythm, which was visible in the EEG at 3–6 months of age (Lindsley, 1939; Smith, 1938a, 1938b), whereas the most prominent rhythmic activity by 12 months of age had a higher frequency (6–7 Hz).

Later studies confirmed these original observations using spectral analysis of EEG (Hagne, 1968, 1972; Hagne, Persson, Magnusson, & Petersen, 1973). These data raised a question—what is the "infant alpha rhythm"? The alpha rhythm is one of the most important grapho-elements and its correct identification is essential for EEG analysis in clinical and research contexts. "Alpha-centrism" dominated the mainstream of infant EEG studies for many years. There are two main viewpoints on the frequency boundaries of the infant alpha rhythm. According to Walter (1950), the alpha rhythm in infants has the same frequency as in adults (8–12 Hz). However, it is of negligible amplitude and is masked by the more pronounced slow rhythms, such as theta. The more commonly accepted opinion is that of Lindsley (1939), who suggested that the alpha rhythm increases in frequency with age, and consequently, that the alpha frequency range in infancy is lower than in childhood.

Currently, there is no final agreement on infant alpha rhythm frequency boundaries, and the choice of frequency boundaries of infant EEG rhythms depends on the researcher's point of view. More recent studies (Bell, 2002; Henderson, Yoder, Yale, & McDuffie, 2002) often refuse to designate the frequency band of interest as delta, alpha, or theta, and prefer to report exact frequency boundaries. In the widely used guidelines for recording and analyzing EEG in research, Pivik and colleagues (Pivik, Broughton, Coppola, Davidson, Fox, & Nuwer, 1993) recommended two approaches for infant EEG studies. According to the first, EEG analysis is accomplished on a wide frequency band that includes all frequencies with non-negligible spectral power. As an example, in a study of infant emotion, Fox and Davidson (1988) computed a frontal EEG asymmetry index in the 3–12 Hz band. According to the second approach, the whole EEG spectrum is examined and a frequency band centered on the dominant peak of the spectrum is analyzed. Such a method has been used in a number of EEG studies of infant emotion and cognition (Bell & Fox, 1992, 1997; Dawson, 1994). Certainly, both above-mentioned techniques disregard the functional meaning of EEG rhythmic activities and do not prevent erroneous interpretation of obtained data. Recent investigations of cortical rhythms in adults have shown that alpha and theta rhythms often demonstrate opposite "behaviors" under the same cognitive or emotional load (Klimesch, 1996). As an example, let us consider the case when both theta and alpha bands are reactive to experimental manipulations. The incorrectly defined band may cover both theta and alpha (e.g., Schmidt, Trainor, & Santesso, 2003). Consequently, an absence of amplitude changes related to a test condition may simply mean that the amplitude of alpha frequencies decreases, whereas the amplitude of theta frequencies increases. Accordingly, a correct interpretation of the results depends on the nature of the EEG rhythm observed in the study and one cannot easily disregard the problem of correct identification of meaningful EEG bands in infants.

An alternative solution to the problem is the fundamental "functional topography" approach (Kuhlman, 1980). It states that identification of rhythmic EEG components should be based on the three main criteria: frequency characteristics, spatial distribution over the cortex, and functional reactivity to specific conditions of registration. Given the probable developmental changes of EEG rhythm frequency, the frequency criterion is not applicable to the infant EEG a priori. Still, it is possible to make some predictions about scalp topography and functional reactivity of alpha and other EEG rhythm in infants. If the rhythmic activity of interest has the known properties of alpha or theta rhythms, such as particular topographical distribution over the scalp and reactive changes under the specific functional loads, it is logical to consider it as alpha or theta. The proposed approach implies that one should analyze narrow frequency bins (of, e.g., 0.4–1 Hz width) (Fernandez et al., 1998; Stroganova, Orekhova, & Posikera, 1999). The identical behavior of the adjacent frequency bins under specific functional loads allows them to be assigned to the same frequency band. In the later section "Alpha and theta rhythms in infant EEG and their correlations with functional states", we review existent infant EEG literature within the framework of the latter approach.

TECHNICAL QUESTIONS

Reliability

It is generally accepted that relatively more reliable estimates of the baseline EEG can be obtained with prolonged (several minutes) EEG registration. However, this may not be the case in infants with rapidly changing behavior and EEG patterns. In infants, "baseline" EEG is usually registered during visual attention to some attractive stimuli. However, the spectrum of infant EEG exhibits regular trends when observed over the course of prolonged visual attention. Figure 9.1 presents a sample of EEG from a 9-month-old infant at the beginning and after 1 minute of attention to soap bubbles. It is evident from the figure that theta activity increases in the course of the registration session. We compared mean alpha and theta spectral power, computed across 20-second artifact-free EEGs, which were sampled during first vs. second 40 seconds of visual attention in 19 infants randomly taken from a greater group of 7–11-month-old infants participating in our earlier study (Stroganova et al., 1999). Repeated measures ANOVA was performed with factors Time (first 40 s vs. second 40 s), Electrode (six levels), and Hemisphere. Between-time differences in alpha power (6–9 Hz) were not significant, while theta power (4–6 Hz) increased with time ($F_{1,18} = 29.4$, $p < .00005$). The observed increase of theta power is probably related to the dynamics of infants' emotional and cognitive processes during stimulus presentation (see later in this chapter). Thus, there are gradual but substantial changes of the brain functional state across the prolonged "baseline" period, and EEG

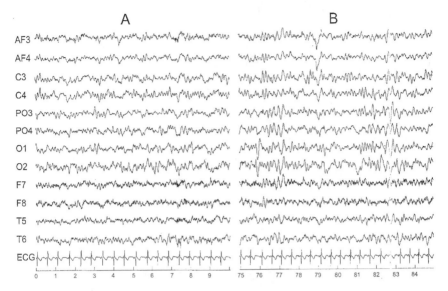

Figure 9.1 EEG samples of a 9-month-old infant during (A) the first seconds and (B) the second minute of attention to soap bubbles. The scale presents time in seconds from the beginning of the experimental situation. The magnitude of theta increases with time.

measures averaged over the long session may give ambiguous information concerning the "baseline" EEG parameters.

Special care should also be taken to avoid speech during EEG recording, unless speech-induced EEG changes are the focus of the study. Speech is a powerful stimulation that can drastically influence the pattern of infant EEG (see Figure 9.5c later). It is therefore mandatory to control for this stimulation if one is interested in the "baseline" EEG characteristics or EEG correlates of mental processes in infants. The combination of child-addressed speech and a cognitive task makes it difficult to decide whether the EEG changes are related to perception of the speech or to the specific stage of the task.

Reference electrode

The most important reason for keeping track of the reference lead is the strong influence it has on scalp topography of EEG oscillations. The ideal reference lead must be electrically neutral, but there are no silent points on a human body. The average reference with a great number of evenly distributed electrodes covering as much as possible of the head surface gives a good approximation of an electrically neutral reference (Junghofer, Elbert, Tucker, & Braun, 1999). Unfortunately, it is not commonly used in infant EEG research. Due to technical convenience, EEG in infants is often registered relative to the vertex—Cz (e.g., Henderson et al., 2002). However, the vertex is

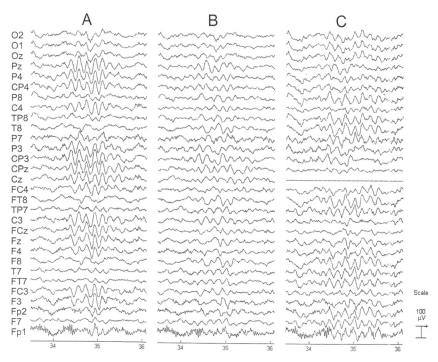

Figure 9.2 The EEG sample of an 18-month-old infant recalculated relative to (A) linked ears, (B) average reference, and (C) Cz. The focus of the theta burst is similar for the linked ears and the average reference montages, and is biased in the case of Cz reference.

the topographical amplitude maximum of a variety of EEG phenomena. As we always record the difference between the potential of an active site and that of a reference site, such a highly active reference may drastically change topographic distribution of EEG signal. Figure 9.2 shows an EEG segment of an 18-month-old infant during attention to emotionally salient computer stimuli. This segment was recalculated with different reference montages. With both linked ears and average reference the prominent theta burst is observed at medial sagittal (Pz, CPz) and parasagittal (CP4, CP3) derivations. With Cz reference montage the picture is just the opposite: theta amplitude is maximal at lateral derivations (e.g., T7, T8, FT8, FT7) and minimal at sagittal and parasagittal electrodes situated closely to Cz. Clearly Cz reference raises considerable problems in regards to topography of the EEG rhythmic activities and its interpretation in infants.

Relative and absolute power

Traditionally, spectral EEG data for analysis are presented as absolute or relative amplitude/power within the particular frequency band. Both these representations of spectral values have advantages and shortcomings of their own. The popular analysis of the EEG absolute spectral power in a single frequency band may lead to erroneous assigning of the possible effect of the overall EEG synchronization/desynchronization to a certain frequency. Indeed, there is evidence that some interindividual EEG spectral differences in infants are due to the factor of wide-band EEG synchronization (Orekhova, Stroganova, & Posikera, 2001). Therefore, when one is interested in the unique relation of the absolute amplitude of a particular frequency band to a behavioral measure, the previous analysis of the whole spectrum is required. Advantages of relative spectra include freedom from among-subject differences in the overall EEG amplitude and better test–retest reliability than absolute power. This measure is recommended by some authors for use in developmental research (Benninger, Matthis, & Scheffner, 1984). However, percentage calculations create interdependencies among spectral values of different bands. The most reliable interpretation of results can be obtained when both absolute and relative EEG powers are taken into consideration (Clarke, Barry, McCarthy, & Selikowitz, 2001; Orekhova et al., 2001).

ALPHA AND THETA RHYTHMS IN INFANT EEG AND THEIR CORRELATIONS WITH FUNCTIONAL STATES

Alpha band of infant EEG

Identification of "alpha-family" rhythms on the basis of their scalp topography and reactivity to homogenous visual field

The discrepancy in opinions concerning the features of the infant alpha rhythm is due to differences in the criteria used for its identification. Some authors suggest that posterior predominance of any rhythmic EEG activity in infants provides enough reason to consider it to be an alpha rhythm (Dreyfus-Brisac, 1979; Lindsley, 1939; Smith, 1938b, 1941). According to another criterion, the dominant EEG rhythm in waking infants should be referred to as alpha, because alpha is the dominant rhythm in adults (Fox & Davidson, 1988). Following this criterion, the 6–9 Hz rhythmic activity registered during visual attention in infants was considered as the functional equivalent of the adult alpha rhythm (Davidson & Fox, 1989; Davidson & Tomarken, 1989), even though it is more prominent over the anterior (central and precentral) cortex (Dawson, 1994; Dawson, Panagiotides, Klinger, & Hill, 1992; Smith, 1939, 1941; Westmoreland & Stockard, 1977). On the other hand, some authors suggest that the 6–9 Hz rhythm registered over the central and precentral cortex in infants is the precursor of the rolandic sensorimotor rhythm (Lairy, 1975; Westmoreland & Stockard, 1977).

From the neurophysiological point of view, not one of the above-mentioned criteria is sufficient for identifying alpha rhythm. According to the "functional topography approach", rhythmic activity can be labeled alpha rhythm if it demonstrates the following properties: First, it should specifically respond to visual input, as the synchronous alpha rhythm reflects an idle state of the visual cortex. It generally emerges during homogenous visual field (e.g., eye closure), and disappears during visual pattern processing (Lehtonen & Lehtinen, 1972; Pfurtscheller, Stancak, & Neuper, 1996). Second, the spatial focus of this rhythmic activity should be located over the occipital cortex and a gradual decrease of amplitude towards the anterior cortical areas (so-called alpha gradient) should be observed. Thus, in order to study the infant alpha rhythm experimentally, it is important to register EEG under conditions as close as possible to those necessary for alpha rhythm occurrence in adults.

However, the majority of developmental EEG studies in waking infants have been performed while infants' eyes were open, basically during sustained visual attention. The problem is that infants cannot close their eyes upon verbal instruction. Some non-systematic observations have been made when gentle, passive occlusion of the eyes was applied for a very short period of time, permitting only non-precise evaluation of the frequency of the induced rhythmic activity (Lairy, 1975). This forced eye closure inevitably provoked crying, protest, and gross body movements. Therefore, such a condition can hardly be considered the baseline quiet state required for the expression of alpha rhythm in adults. Spontaneous eye closure has also been occasionally observed (Lairy, 1975). However, spontaneous eye closure in infants usually reflects drowsiness, which is not acceptable for studying alpha rhythm. In infants and young children, this state is usually accompanied by hypnagogic activity—the EEG pattern that consists of theta and delta waves (Hagne, 1972; Lairy, 1975). More systematic longitudinal study of occipital EEG in infants whose eyes were closed was performed by Mizuno, Yamauchi, Watanabe, Komatsushiro, and Takagi (1970). Unfortunately, the authors did not describe how the eye closure was achieved. In addition, they used only one recording site (O2) that did not permit evaluation of topographical distribution of the rhythmic activity. The frequency distribution of amplitude percentage (with maximum in the 3.46–4.98 Hz band, regardless of infant age) presented by the authors suggests that the EEG was registered during drowsiness. Thus, eye closure is not the appropriate condition under which alpha rhythm in infants should be systematically studied.

It is important to mention that the basic requirement for alpha rhythm registration is a presence of homogenous visual field, rather than eye closure per se. The homogenous visual field can be attained simply by placing the waking infant in total darkness. We (Stroganova et al., 1999) analyzed EEG in a large sample of healthy infants aged 7–12 months of chronological age under two different functional states of wakefulness: (1) attention to patterned visual stimulation and (2) dark homogenous visual field. Figure 9.3 presents EEG samples of two infants (VD, 8 months, and PA, 12 months) participating in the study. The spectral amplitudes between 1.6 and 12 Hz were analyzed in discrete bins of 0.4 Hz. Grand average amplitude spectra for the 8- and 12-month age groups are shown in Figure 9.4. The main result of

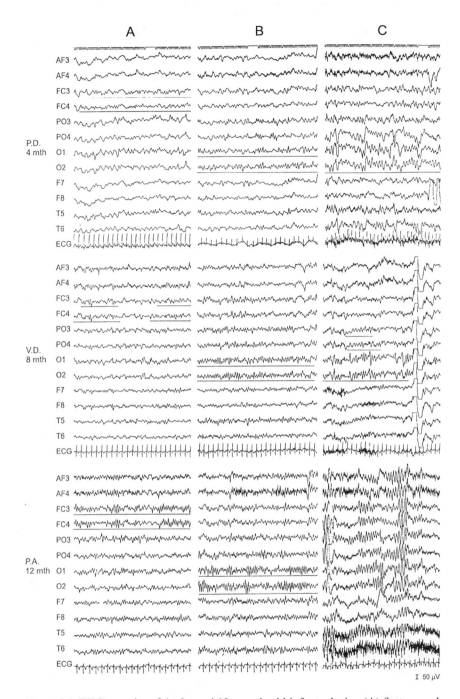

Figure 9.3 EEG samples of 4-, 8-, and 12-month-old infants during (A) first seconds of attention to soap bubbles, (B) total darkness, and (C) crying. Here, and further, one division on the time scale (upper trace) corresponds to 1 second. *Mu rhythm* is seen over the anterior central regions during visual attention. *Alpha rhythm* is maximal over occipital sites during total darkness. Crying is accompanied by *theta rhythm* synchronization. In subjects PD and VD the maximum of theta synchronization is observed over posterior cortex. However, the lower frequency of posterior theta rhythm (4–5 Hz) distinguishes it from posterior alpha rhythm (6–7 Hz).

8 months   11 months

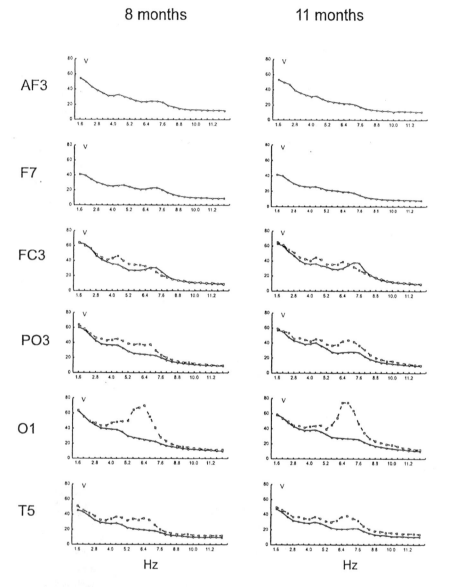

Figure 9.4 Mean amplitude spectra in groups of 8- and 11-month-old infants. Solid line=visual attention; dashed line=total darkness. The distinct spectral peak (6.4–6.8 Hz) over occipital region during darkness reflects *alpha rhythm*. The spectral peak of slightly higher frequency (7.2–7.6 Hz) over anterior central region during visual attention reflects *mu rhythm*.

the study was the discrimination of two rhythmic processes in infant EEG, which have similar frequency characteristics but different distribution over the scalp and opposite functional reactivity to the patterned visual input. The 5.6–9.6 Hz rhythmic activity synchronized over the occipital cortex during darkness and was blocked by visual stimulation. The occipital focus of the darkness-provoked activity was verified by highly significant CONDITION × ELECTRODE interaction for all 0.4 Hz frequency bins within this range (all $Fs_{3, 186} >$ 10.5, $ps < .00001$). Thus, this activity was the only frequency component of infant EEG that had the classical properties of alpha rhythm (Shagass, 1972).

Nevertheless, there are at least two important distinctions between alpha activity in infants and adults. First, the alpha rhythm has lower frequency boundaries during infancy. This observation is in agreement with the well-documented increase of alpha frequency during later childhood (Duffy, 1994; Henry, 1944; Smith, 1941; Surwillo, 1971). Second, the infant alpha rhythm has a rather restricted distribution over the occipito-parietal areas in comparison with adult alpha rhythm, which is more generalized. In infants, the individual alpha peaks were not usually evident at precentral and frontal leads during darkness. These results are in accordance with the data of other authors who found that development of alpha rhythm proceeds from posterior to anterior regions (Gasser, Jennen-Steinmetz, Sroka, Verleger, & Mocks, 1988; Katada, Ozaki, Suzuki, & Suhara, 1981; Lairy, 1975). The lower boundary of the infant alpha rhythm (5.6 Hz) in our study was well under the upper boundary of the conventional adult theta band (4–8 Hz). The dark homogenous visual field led to increase of spectral amplitudes in both 2.8–4.8 Hz and 5.6–9.6 Hz ranges.

Nevertheless, infant alpha and theta rhythms during darkness can be differentiated on the basis of their topographical distribution. In infants, behavioral states characterized by elevated emotional arousal are accompanied by the widespread increase of theta (3–5 Hz) activity (Kugler & Laub, 1971; Maulsby, 1971; Nikitina, Posikera, & Stroganova, 1985; Posikera, Stroganova, Zhurba, & Timonina, 1986; Stroganova & Posikera, 1993). Therefore, the widespread increase of 2.8–4.8 Hz theta activity observed under the condition of total darkness reflects, at least in part, the theta synchronization related to the increase of emotional arousal during the unpleasant "light-turn-off" procedure. On the other hand, the increase of 5.6–9.6 Hz alpha activity during darkness was more local, being limited by posterior scalp regions. The results of this study strongly suggest that alpha and theta rhythms are distinct EEG components during the second half-year of life. The coexistence of alpha and theta rhythms with different functional and topographical properties during infancy implies that the alpha cannot "originate from the early theta" as some authors assert (Lindsley, 1939; Markand, 1990). It should be mentioned, however, that infant theta and alpha bands overlap to some extent and that the borderline frequencies (5.2–6.0 Hz) may display properties of both alpha and theta (Orekhova, Stroganova, & Posikera, 1999).

Another rhythmic component observed in this study (Stroganova et al., 1999) had a frequency similar to that of alpha rhythm and was maximal during sustained visual attention. It was represented by a 6.0–8.8 Hz spectral peak, which was significantly more pronounced at precentral than at frontal and posterior recording sites (Figure 9.4). During darkness, the central rhythm was significantly attenuated in the upper part of this band (7.2–8.0 Hz). There are a few facts indicating that the 6.0–8.8 Hz central rhythm is an infant homologue of the adult rolandic mu rhythm. First, its topographical distribution coincides with the distribution of the mu rhythm in adults. Second, it is registered during immobility, when the infant's attention is captured by visual stimulation. Our earlier study showed that the central rhythmic activity in infant EEG is more pronounced during sustained visual attention than during other behavioral states characterized by a higher level of motor activity (Stroganova & Posikera, 1993). In adults (Koshino & Niedermeyer, 1975; Pfurtscheller & Klimesch, 1992; Pfurtscheller et al., 1996) and animals (Rougeul, Bouyer, Dedet, & Debray, 1979; Rougeul-Buser, Bouyer, & Buser, 1975) the mu rhythm is enhanced during visual processing, when no motor response is required, and reflects an idle state of the sensori-motor cortex. Thus, the central rhythm demonstrates similar reactivity to motor input/output in infants, adults, and animals. Third, the 6.0–8.8 Hz central activity and occipital alpha rhythm in infants demonstrate the recip-rocal behavior during visual processing: synchronization of central rhythm is accompanied by desynchronization of alpha rhythm. The same relationship between alpha and mu rhythms' reactivity to visual input was observed in adults performing a visual task (Pfurtscheller et al., 1996). Fourth, the mean peak frequency of central rhythm in our sample was slightly (about 0.6 Hz), but significantly, above the mean peak frequency of the alpha rhythm. The direction of this difference coincides with the difference between frequencies of alpha and mu rhythms observed in adults (Kuhlman, 1980; Schoppenhorst, Brauer, Freund, & Kubicki, 1980). Fifth, our recent data have shown that in 10–12-month-olds the left-sided predominance of this rhythm correlates with preferential use of the right hand during performance of a motor task (Stroganova, Posikera, Pushina, & Orekhova, 2003). This finding confirms the relation of this anterior rhythmic activity to motor functions.

Taking into account the specific functional reactivity of alpha, mu, and theta rhythms, their correct discrimination is of great importance in infant psychophysiological studies.

Development of alpha and mu rhythms during infancy

Developmental onset of mu and alpha rhythms

Smith (1939, 1941) was the first to observe regular rhythmic activity of approximately 7 Hz over the central cortex in awake infants from 3 months of age. He related the developmental onset of this central EEG activity during wakefulness to the loss of infant primitive reflexes, such as the Babinski and the Moro, and the appearance of voluntary control of neuromuscular behavior. Later, more detailed observations (Posikera & Stroganova, 1983) revealed that 5–7 Hz rhythmic activity of very low amplitude can be observed over the peri-rolandic cortex even at 3–4 weeks of postnatal age. Such an early onset of rhythmic activity over the sensorimotor cortex is in good agreement with the data on earlier maturation of somatosensory evoked potentials comparing to visual and auditory evoked potentials (Hrbek, Karlberg, & Olsson, 1973; Krumholz, 1999) and early (around birth) increases in glucose metabolism in peri-rolandic areas of the infant's brain (Chugani, Phelps, & Mazziotta, 1987). So far, the interpretation of the central rhythmic activity as the sensorimotor (mu) rhythm is in agreement with its possible relation to maturation of motor functions.

In addition to central rhythm, both Smith (1939) and Lindsley (1939) described the short strings of 3–5 Hz rhythmic waves over the occipital area at around 3 months and called them alpha because of their predominance over occipital cortex. Neither Smith nor Lindsley mentioned the condition of occurrence of "occipital alpha" in 3-month-old infants. Other researchers sporadically observed rhythmic slow-wave (3–5 Hz) activity over the posterior cortex in infants not younger than 3 months under the conditions of eye closure and/or crying (Lairy, 1975; Samson-Dollfus, Delapierre, Do Marcolino, & Blondeau, 1997) and also addressed it as "infant alpha". Thus, early reports of EEG changes in young infants during eye closure involved diverse experimental paradigms and produced no statistical data. The change of spectral features of the ongoing EEG during reduction of visual input is a topic that has been largely ignored in the infant EEG literature. Hence, despite consensus regarding the developmental onset of alpha rhythm, the conventional view that alpha appears at 3 months of age at a lower frequency of 3–5 Hz (Markand, 1990) must be experimentally verified. The experimental settings must be modified to take into account the effect of increased theta power over the posterior scalp areas during the same set of conditions (negative affect provoked by unpleasant strained eye closure and/or crying). The posterior 3–5 Hz rhythm that has been sporadically observed in 3–4-month-olds may be not alpha but theta elicited by negative affect.

In our recent study (unpublished data), information was obtained on how a dark homogenous visual field affects spectral features of brain electrical activity in a sample of 20 healthy full-term infants aged 4–5 months. The frequency of alpha rhythm occurring under darkness conditions in 4-month-olds was around 5–6 Hz; i.e., it fell within the lower alpha boundaries determined for older infants. A sample of EEG from a 4-month-old infant (PD) is presented in Figure 9.3. The 5–6 Hz rhythm over occipital areas is seen during darkness (Figure 9.3B), but not during visual attention (Figure 9.3A). Crying of the same infants is accompanied by high-amplitude 4–5 Hz (theta) activity with the same topographical maximum (Figure 9.3C). This finding leads to the following conclusions: (1) one can reliably register alpha rhythm in 4-month-olds, and (2) theta (3–5 Hz) and alpha (5–6 Hz) coexist and can be differentiated even in infants of this early age. No systematic data on alpha rhythm characteristics under the optimal conditions of registration in infants younger than 4 months of age are available.

Whenever alpha developmental onset occurs, it appears to be related to the availability of visual input for the brain. Our studies of infants born between 32 and 41 weeks of gestation revealed that the age-related increase of alpha frequency was due to the duration of the extrauterine experience (i.e., chronological age) rather than to biological (conceptional) age of the infants (Stroganova et al., 1999). This result seems unexpected, because it is commonly acknowledged that brain development proceeds as a function of time from conception, not of time from birth. On the other hand, it is well known that visual stimulation is crucial for the development of the structure and function of the visual cortex (Wiesel, 1982). There is also evidence that the onset of visual stimulation influences development of the P2 component of the visual evoked potentials in human infants (Thomas & Crow, 1994). The importance of early visual input for the development of spontaneous occipital alpha rhythm was confirmed by studying the effect of early visual deprivation in infants with congenital bilateral cataracts (Stroganova & Posikera, 1996). The alpha rhythm was absent during the "blind" period of development. Pattern vision recovery (due to surgery and vision correction) was followed by immediate appearance of the alpha rhythm in EEG. The subsequent increase of alpha peak frequency strongly depended on the time that had passed after the surgical removal of the cataracts (i.e., the duration of visual experience), irrespective of the chronological age of the subject at the time of surgery. In view of these findings, it is apparent that experience of pattern vision influences alpha rhythm development.

Frequency growth

Relatively few developmental data have been reported on the frequency growth of occipital alpha and central mu rhythm throughout infancy. Smith (1941) noted that occipital activity gradually increased from 3–5 Hz at 3 months to 6–7 Hz at 12 months, whereas central activity did not increase in frequency during the first years of life. No meaningful information about frequency can be extracted from the two other longitudinal studies that used spectral analysis or frequency analyzers (Hagne, 1968; Ohtahara, 1981), because the researchers divided the EEG into conventional frequency bands: delta: 1.5–3.5 and theta: 3.5–8 Hz. In addition, no information has been provided about the exact functional state of wakefulness under which the EEG was recorded. We analyzed alpha and mu frequency growth in infants between 7 and 12 months of age (Stroganova et al., 1999). For each subject, the occipital spectral peaks between 5.2 and 9.6 Hz under the condition of total darkness were considered to be the alpha peaks. The spectral peaks in the 6.0–8.8 Hz range at precentral recording sites during visual attention were regarded as mu peaks. There was a highly significant positive correlation between alpha frequency and age, when uncorrected chronological age was employed. The mean peak alpha frequency increased from 6.24 Hz in the 7–9-month-old group to 6.78 Hz in the 10–12-month-old group. The peak frequency of the mu rhythm also significantly increased during the second half-year of life. It changed from 7.03 Hz at 7–9 months to 7.42 Hz at 10–12 months. This means that, unlike later in development, when the age-dependent increase of alpha and mu frequency is slow and gradual, alpha frequency grows rapidly over the short time period between 7 and 12 months of age. This rapid increase of alpha frequency is presumably associated with the spurt in the structural and functional maturation of the cortical (in particular, occipital) neural networks, which takes place during this age period (Huttenlocher, 1994). Given that frequency growth is considered as an operational definition of EEG maturation (Hudspeth & Pribram, 1992), EEG maturation proceeds more quickly in infancy than later. Recently, Marshall and colleagues (Marshall, Bar-Haim, & Fox, 2002) have found that beyond the first year of life mean mu peak frequency steadily increased up to 8 Hz at 14–24 months and reached 9 Hz at 4 years. No data are available on the growth of occipital alpha frequency across the second and third years of life.

Amplitude growth

A number of EEG spectral and frequency analysis studies (Hagne, 1968; Hagne et al., 1973; Mizuno et al., 1970) provided information only about age-dependent amplitude changes into conventional frequency bands: delta: 1.5–3.5 and theta: 3.5–8 Hz during the "background state" (infant visual attention). No visible changes in the former band, concomitant with the rapid amplitude increase in the latter one, gave rise to the widely accepted opinion that the best index of infant EEG maturation is the theta/delta amplitude ratio (Duffy, 1994). However, arguments listed above show that in infants the conventional theta band comprises several neurophysiologically different rhythms—alpha, mu, and theta. Amplitude growth of any of them could potentially explain the developmental changes in the "delta/theta ratio". We found that from 7 to 12 months of age the occipital alpha spectral amplitudes under the "darkness" condition significantly decreased in the lower part of the infant alpha band (5.2–6.0 Hz) and increased in its higher part (7.2–9.6 Hz). The increase of the mean alpha spectral amplitude in the 5.2–9.6 Hz range from 7 to 12 months was marginally significant. The spectral amplitudes of mu rhythm also increased from 7 to 12 months in the upper part of the band (7.6–8.8 Hz), although no age-dependent decrease in the lower part of the mu band was observed. These data are in accordance with the results of a longitudinal study by Marshall and colleagues (2002), who have reported developmental growth of the relative power of the 6–9 Hz band over central recording sites up to 14–24 months during infants' attention to visual stimuli. Thus, unlike in later age periods, amplitudes of alpha and mu rhythms increase during infancy. The possible neurophysiological explanation of this fact relates to the specificity of neuronal synaptic growth during infancy (Huttenlocher, 1994). The number of subcortical-cortical and intracortical synaptic connections rapidly increases during the first months of postnatal life. After the end of the first year the number of synapses substantially decreases (so-called synaptic pruning). Given the importance of neuronal connectivity for the recurrent and lateral inhibition processes that mediate the alpha rhythm's generation (Steriade & Llinas, 1988), one can speculate that the observed increase in alpha and mu amplitude relies on this unique pattern of synaptic growth across the first year of life. The decrease of the *relative* spectral power of 6–9 Hz mu rhythm (Marshall et al., 2002) and the amplitudes of visual and auditory evoked potentials (Krumholz, 1999) from infancy to childhood may be a result of synaptic pruning beyond the infancy period.

The role of alpha and mu rhythms during infant attention

Visual attention is commonly used in infant studies as a baseline state, because it permits prolonged registration of artifact-free EEG. However, this state is not equal to the quiet wakefulness that is basically used as a baseline in adults. First, an active intake and processing of visual input is associated with suppression of the visual *alpha rhythm* over the posterior cortical areas (Steriade, Gloor, Llinas, Lopes de Silva, & Mesulam, 1990). Second, sustaining visual attention for a relatively long time requires behavioral immobility, associated with high level of vigilance. This condition provokes expression of the *mu rhythm* over the peri-rolandic cortical areas (Pfurtscheller et al., 1996). As we have shown above, this dynamic of the alpha and mu rhythms' synchronization/desynchronization characterizes infant visual attention. Third, an infant demonstrates prolonged visual attention if the stimulation is interesting and attractive; i.e., he/she experiences positive affect that is accompanied by expression of *theta rhythm* (see later).

Mu rhythm

EEG rhythms of the alpha family originate from the separate but interconnected thalamo-cortical modules (Lopes da Silva, Vos, Mooibroek, & Van Rotterdam, 1980). During expression of alpha activity the mean membrane potential of thalamo-cortical cells is shifted to the hyperpolarized direction and the transmission of information between thalamus and neocortex is reduced (Lopes da Silva, 1991; Steriade & Llinas, 1988). Therefore, the mu rhythm characterizes an "idling" state of the sensory-motor thalamo-cortical circuits, as the alpha rhythm characterizes an idling state of visual thalamo-cortical circuits (Pfurtscheller et al., 1996). During the state of attentiveness, activity of the thalamo-cortical circuitry is modulated by cholinergic input from the basal forebrain. The modulation via the reticular thalamic nucleus provides the shift in activity (activation/inhibition) between different thalamo-cortical modules, e.g., visual and sensory-motor thalamo-cortical cells (Suffczynski, Kalitzin, Pfurtscheller, & Lopes da Silva, 2001). This shift produces a desynchronization/synchronization pattern of alpha activity over specific cortical areas, and represents one of the neurophysiological mechanisms that regulate the focusing of attention on the specific sensory modality. There is evidence that synchronization of the alpha band rhythms during states of attentiveness is important for active inhibition of irrelevant neural networks (Klimesch, Doppelmayr, Schwaiger, Auinger, & Winkler, 1999; Pfurtscheller & Neuper, 1994). Thus, enhancement of the mu rhythm during sustained processing of visual stimuli reflects not just passive non-involvement of sensory-motor areas, but also an active inhibition of cortical sensorimotor input/output. Such an inhibition helps to avoid interference from the competitive sensory-motor processing and to maintain prolonged visual attention (Rougeul et al., 1979; Rougeul-Buser et al., 1975; Suffczynski et al., 2001). "Behavioral stillness" or demobilization of the movements of behavior (Mulholland, 1995) during prolonged visual attention in infants may stem from the functioning of this important regulatory mechanism. One can assume that mu synchronization during infant visual attention is "a good thing" that reflects the above-mentioned regulatory capacities.

There is a body of evidence that supports this suggestion. First, individual differences in the spectral amplitude of the mu rhythm are significantly influenced by systematic (genetic and/or environmental) factors (Orekhova et al., 2003). This means that the magnitude of mu synchronization is a stable individual trait. Second, the spectral amplitude of the mu rhythm during visual attention increases across the first year of life (Stroganova et al., 1999). This means that infants having more mu rhythm may be more mature. Third, individual differences in mu synchronization during stimulus-driven attention are related to performance on different cognitive tasks. Thus, Bell and Fox (1992, 1997) reported a positive correlation between amplitudes of the "baseline" anterior 6–9 Hz activity and the performance of a frontally mediated A-not-B task. We observed that the "baseline" mu amplitude positively correlated with infants' abilities to maintain anticipatory attention in the peek-a-boo game (Orekhova et al., 2001) and to retrieve a bait in the Detour Reaching task (unpublished data). The later task was specially designed to test the inhibitory motor control capacities of supplementary motor area of the neocortex (Diamond, 1991). Fourth, individual differences in the "baseline" mu synchronization are strongly related to such temperamental traits as regulation of behavioral irritability in different contexts (Stroganova, Tsetlin, Posikera, Orekhova, & Malakhovskaia, 2002) and, more specifically, to tolerance of the distressing "separation from mother" condition (Dawson, 1994). Together these data suggest that mu synchronization tells us little about specific demands of the cognitive task. Rather, it appears that pronounced mu synchronization during stimulus-driven attention in infants reflects a physiological trait that is beneficial in different behavioral domains. Given the neurophysiological mechanisms of mu rhythm synchronization under conditions of visual attention, it is more parsimonious to see this trait as reflecting the effectiveness of thalamo-cortical networks down-regulating the motor activity.

The interpretation of the 6–9 Hz central rhythm as the mu rhythm emphasizes the need for discrimination between two types of EEG events: active enhancement and active blocking. The difference in the amplitude of anterior 6–9 Hz activity between the "baseline" and "test" conditions may have two reasons. First, it may be caused by active inhibition of sensory-motor neural networks during sustained visual attention. This process appears as synchronization of anterior 6–9 Hz rhythm under the "baseline" (actually visual attention) condition. Second, it may stem from activation of sensory-motor cortex or anterior areas of the frontal lobe under the "test" conditions, which unlike the "baseline" condition may require processing of sensorimotor input/output. In this case, the "baseline–test" difference would be the result of anterior 6–9 Hz activity blocking under the "test" conditions. Thus, "the meaningful EEG event" may be cortical inhibition as well as cortical activation. This precaution should be kept in mind when one compares the amplitude of infant "anterior resting activity" over cortical areas of the left and right hemispheres.

Parietal alpha rhythm

Posterior alpha suppression is observed in a variety of tasks requiring visual attention and is thought to reflect activation of cortical areas involved in visual processing. Paradoxically, we have found regionally specific positive correlation between alpha amplitude over the parietal cortex during anticipation and infants' ability to sustain anticipatory visual attention (Orekhova et al., 2001). In older children and adults, "paradoxical" alpha synchronization over parietal cortex also accompanies periods of highly focused attention to the centre of the visual field, and even correlates positively with task performance (Fernandez et al., 1998; Klimesch et al., 1999). Why under some conditions is active visual processing associated with increased parietal alpha? We hypothesized that this task-related increase in alpha amplitude reflects functional disengagement of certain parietal networks that mediate shift of attention to the periphery of the visual field. Participation of posterior parietal cortex in the shift of attention to the peripheral field of view is well documented by PET and MRI studies (Corbetta, Miezin, Shulman, & Petersen, 1993; Vandenberghe et al., 1996) and studies of patients with posterior parietal damage (Farah, 1990; Mennemeier, Chatterjee, Watson, Wertman, Carter, & Heilman, 1994). Moreover, PET studies bear evidence for the inactivation of posterior parietal areas during certain visual tasks demanding focal visual attention to central stimuli (Ghatan, Hsieh, Petersson, Stone-Elander, & Iugvar, 1998). So far, transient inhibition of distinct parietal networks during anticipatory visual attention in infants may be necessary to prevent the attentional shift from the current spatial locus and to maintain prolonged attention. These findings imply that the neurophysiological origin of parietal alpha synchronization under conditions of total darkness (Stroganova et al., 1999) and visual attention (Orekhova et al., 2001) may be quite different. In the former case, the alpha band oscillations over the posterior areas reflect an "idle state" of the respective neural networks due to the absence of visual input. In the latter case, parietal alpha synchronization reflects active inhibition of the information processing interfering with the current focus of visual attention.

To summarize, we assume that the pattern of synchronization of alpha band rhythms during intake of visual information reflects the top-down inhibitory modulation of information processing in the same (visual—parietal alpha rhythm) or other (sensory-motor—mu rhythm) modalities.

Theta band of infant EEG

The theta rhythm was initially described in adult subjects experiencing positive or negative emotions (Walter & Walter, 1949). Subsequently, it was shown that theta in adults can be evoked by purely intellectual activity without any change in mood (Mundy-Castle, 1951). Increase in theta activity has been repeatedly observed in a variety of cognitive tasks requiring mental effort, attention, and memory (Inanaga, 1998; Kahana, Selig, & Madsen, 2001; Kirk & Mackay, 2003). In this section we will show that the functional properties of infant EEG activity in the 4–6 Hz range differ strikingly from those of alpha (6–9 Hz) activity, and resemble functional properties of adult theta rhythm.

Maulsby (1971) was the first to describe the appearance of a peculiar theta rhythm during infant emotional arousal. He reported that, in a 9-month-old girl, the emotional reaction to tactile stimulation was accompanied by a clear-cut enhancement in the amplitude of 4–6 Hz rhythm, simultaneously with the facial expression of positive emotions. Maulsby named this rhythmic activity the "hedonic theta". Later studies described the similar phenomenon of emotional "puppet-show" theta rhythm for a larger sample of toddlers aged from 1 to 3 years (Kugler & Laub, 1971).

Since then, a number of studies have reported the presence of 4–6 Hz waves during different conditions of increased positive arousal, such as feeding (Futagi, Ishihara, Tsuda, Suzuki, & Goto, 1998; Lehtonen, Kononen, Purhonen, Partanen, & Saarikoski, 2002; Paul, Dittrichova, & Papousek, 1996), communication with adults (Nikitina et al., 1985; Posikera et al., 1986; Stroganova & Posikera, 1993), manipulation with toys (Futagi et al., 1998; Stroganova & Posikera, 1993), etc. In addition, synchronization of 4–6 Hz theta activity was observed during negative emotions, e.g., infant crying (Futagi et al., 1998; Hagne, 1972; Stroganova & Posikera, 1993). It is noteworthy that in infants, as well as in adults, the presence of an explicit emotional reaction is not essential for the theta response to occur. For example, theta in infants increases during anticipatory attention, when information processing based on memory traces takes place (Orekhova, Stroganova, & Posikera, 1999; Stroganova, Orekhova, & Posikera, 1998). It is also synchronized during stereotype behaviors (Stroganova & Posikera, 1993), sucking a pacifier (Futagi et al., 1998; Maulsby, 1971; Stroganova & Posikera, 1993), drowsiness (Futagi et al., 1998; Hagne, 1972; Stroganova & Posikera, 1993), and REM sleep (Sterman, McGinty, Harper, Hoppenbrouwers, & Hodgman, 1982).

A few examples of theta synchronization in normal infants during different behavioral states are presented in Figure 9.5. In some cases theta oscillations

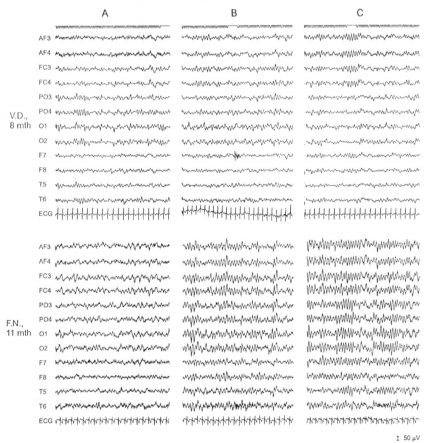

Figure 9.5 EEG samples of 8- and 11-month-old infants during (A) second minute of visual attention to soap bubbles, (B) manipulation with toys, and (C) communication with an adult (attention to infant-addressed speech). Subject NV is the same as in Figure 9.4. She demonstrates moderate synchronization of 4–5 Hz theta rhythm, which is maximal over posterior scalp regions during visual attention and predominates over the anterior electrode sites during manipulation and communication with an adult. Subject FN demonstrates very prominent generalized theta synchronization during situations B and C.

in the EEG of healthy infants may be so pronounced that for 5–10 seconds EEG traces look like sine waves without visually noticeable addition of other frequency components (Figure 9.5B,C, subject FN, 11 months).

Development

The theta response (state-related increase in the amplitude of 3–6 Hz activity) during feeding can already be observed in newborns (Paul et al., 1996). Paul and colleagues have reported significant increases in the mean 3–5 Hz band amplitude at C3–P3 electrode site during feeding as compared to both "prior to feeding" and "after feeding" periods in 2-week-old infants. Incidental observations (Stroganova & Posikera, 1993) show that short periods of low-amplitude rhythmic 4–5 Hz activity over anterior regions during emotionally positive social stimulation (infant-addressed speech) can be detected at 2 months of age (Figure 9.6). The magnitude of "theta response" under theta-provoking conditions dramatically increases across the first year of life. Thus, Paul and colleagues (1996) describe a sharp increase in theta band amplitude and relative abundance of theta waves at C3–P3 channel during feeding between 2.5 and 6.5 months of age. Lehtonen and colleagues (2002) have found that theta amplitude during feeding reaches maximum at temporo-occipital areas, and increases between 3 and 6 months of age. The theta spectral power provoked by attention to a novel visual stimulus (e.g., attractive toys), social interaction (infant-addressed speech, playful communication—gonna-get-you, tickling), or manipulation with toys significantly increases from 4 to 10 months of age, with the sharpest changes taking place from 4 to 6 and from 8 to 10 months of age (Stroganova & Posikera, 1993). These findings have been confirmed by Futagi and colleagues (1998), who

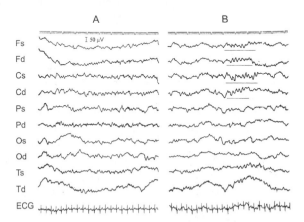

Figure 9.6 EEG samples of a 2-month-old and 4-day-old infant during (A) visual attention to a toy and (B) smiling during eye-to-eye contact with an adult talking to the infant. A short period of 4 Hz anterior theta activity is evident during the second situation.

reported a significant effect of age for the average theta power during feeding, gazing, and handling in infants aged from 2 to 11 months. The developmental course of theta response after 1 year of life is rather difficult to track, because similar experimental manipulations provoking theta rhythm have different affective loads in infants, toddlers, and older children.

No reliable information on the frequency changes of theta rhythm across the infancy period is currently available. Based on inspection of the grand average EEG spectra in different age groups we suggest that, in contrast to theta amplitude, theta frequency does not essentially change between 4 and 12 months of age. Regardless of the infant's age, the maximal spectral peak is always observed between 4 and 5 Hz (Stroganova & Posikera, 1993).

Scalp topography of theta response

During the periods of its distinct synchronization, theta activity in infants is widely distributed over the scalp. Such a wide distribution clearly differentiates theta from the rhythms of the alpha band (6–9 Hz) that are normally more local (see above). Nevertheless, scalp distribution of theta power does depend on the experimental setting (Futagi et al., 1998; Nikitina et al., 1985; Stroganova & Posikera, 1993). In infants younger than 10 months of age theta elicited by relatively simple tactile and audio-visual stimuli (tickling, kissing; attractive new toy; sound of a rattle) is distributed predominantly over parietal regions. The maximum of theta synchronization during attention to infant-addressed speech is located at frontal regions. Manipulation of toys in the absence of an adult is also accompanied by predominantly frontal theta increase. Complex social interactions (e.g., "gonna-get-you") that include both speech and tactile stimulation lead to a more generalized theta response covering both anterior and posterior scalp regions. The topographical differences in theta spectral power between these experimental settings were confirmed statistically (Stroganova & Posikera, 1993). This pattern of results is in general agreement with the later study of Futagi and colleagues (1998), who also observed that the topographical distribution of theta response depended on the type of behavioral activity. They reported that theta synchronization was at its maximum in bilateral parietal regions during attention to attractive visual stimuli and in frontal regions during manipulation of objects (handling). Expression of negative emotions (crying) was accompanied by theta synchronization with predominance over posterior cortical regions (T5, T6, O1, Oz, O2). Although crying could be associated with eye closure, the low peak frequency of the posterior theta activity (4–5 Hz) distinguishes it from that of the infant's occipital alpha rhythm (6–8 Hz) (see Figure 9.3B,C). It should be mentioned that the linked ears reference electrode was used in all studies reviewed in this section.

Based on these findings, one can speculate that the topography of scalp-recorded theta episodes may be indicative of the contribution of different cortical networks in different infant behaviors. The finding of task-related frontal theta oscillations in 7–11-month-old infants (Orekhova et al., 1999; Stroganova et al., 1998) is especially provocative, suggesting that in infants, as in adults, the frontal theta rhythm may be related to frontally mediated cognitive functions.

Frontal theta, states of wakefulness, and infants' performance of cognitive tasks

In adults, frontal theta activity (so-called midline frontal theta rhythm) is repeatedly observed during mental operations involving the frontal lobes (Inanaga, 1998). Do frontal theta oscillations in infants relate to task variables targeting frontal lobe functioning? To answer this question, EEG was recorded in a large sample of infants aged 7–11 months during the anticipatory attention phase of the peek-a-boo game (Orekhova et al., 1999). The need to sustain relatively long periods of anticipatory attention (for more than 4 seconds) in the absence of an attended object requires a certain degree of maturity of the frontal cortex (Fuster, 1990). In human infants, the maturational leap in the development of the frontal cortex takes place between 7 and 10 months (Chugani et al., 1987; Diamond, 1991). We hypothesized that the age dynamic of the frontal theta response may reflect development of the frontal cortex during this age period. As expected, theta significantly increased during the anticipatory attention phase of the game. The increase was maximal at frontal electrode sites and was higher in younger infants. Moreover, in 7–10-month-olds the magnitude of the theta response in the lower part of the band (3.6–4.8 Hz) co-varied with infants' ability to maintain anticipatory attention. Interestingly, the correlation was positive at 7–8 months and negative at 9 and 10 months of age, being restricted to the anterior frontal region for all age groups (Figure 9.7). We believe that frontal theta reflects the amount of frontal lobe *activation* required for task performance. Sustaining anticipatory attention is a demanding task for younger subjects. Infants aged 7–8 months, who failed to maintain prolonged anticipatory attention, exhibited small frontal theta synchronization probably due to immaturity of their frontal cortex. In contrast, at 9–10 months the task becomes easier and does not require widespread activation of the frontal cortex. Therefore, for more mature infants of this age group, maintaining anticipatory attention no longer provokes the great frontal theta response. At the same time, for the less mature 9–10-month-olds it is still a difficult problem that involves more frontal resources and respectively more frontal theta reactive changes. At 11 months the task is easy for all infants. In this age group the theta increase during anticipatory attention was lower than that at 7–8, 9, and 10 months, and did not correlate with the duration of anticipation. This pattern of results strongly suggests that brain maturation during the second half-year of life leads to more economic and more efficient functioning of the frontally dependent attention system.

These findings have important consequences for the interpretation of the

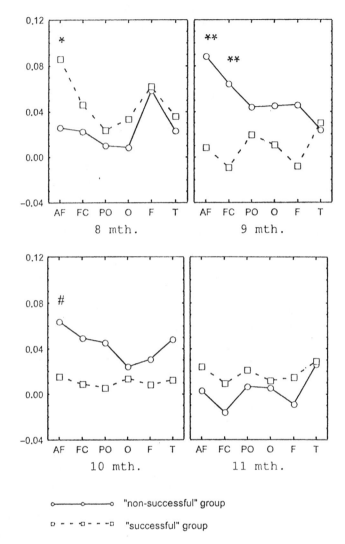

Figure 9.7 Change Scores of θ1 (3.6–4.8 Hz) power in infants who demonstrated short (below age group mean) and long (above age group mean) duration of anticipation during the peek-a-boo game. Positive values reflect relative increase of θ1 power during anticipatory attention as compared to the "baseline". The asterisks denote significant difference between "successful" and "non-successful" subjects: *p < .03, **p < .009, # p < .07. Change Scores of θ1 band at anterior recording sites (mainly anterior frontal) differentiated "successful" and "non-successful" subjects. The difference was significant in three younger age groups only. Note that the relationship between duration of anticipatory attention and Change Scores at 8 (7.28–8.15) months is just the opposite of that at 9 and 10 months.

role of frontal theta activity in infants. The frontal theta rhythm seems to be indicative of frontal processing capacities during performance of a task. Theta synchronization is low if the task is simple for the infant and increases if the task demands become more difficult. This account is consistent with the results obtained in adults (Caplan, Madsen, Raghavachari, & Kahana, 2001; Gevins, Smith, McEvoy, & Yu, 1997; Lang, Lang, Diekmann, & Kornhuber, 1987). Thus, one cannot interpret the magnitude of the task-related theta response as "good" or "bad" without considering the appropriateness of the experimental setting for the infant's age. Increased frontal theta power during the "baseline" (e.g., sustained attention attracted by real visual events) may be associated with heightened effort allocated to a simple task, such as maintenance of attention to real visual stimuli. It may, therefore, reflect *reduced* functional capacities of the frontally mediated attention system. Indeed, recent longitudinal studies of EEG correlates of pre-linguistic communication (joint attention, combined pragmatic functions) have found an inverse relationship between frontal theta power and these behavioral abilities (Card, Mundy, & Schmidt, 1997; Henderson et al., 2002). For example, Henderson and colleagues (2002) reported significant negative correlations between EEG theta power at frontal electrode sites at 14 months and frequency of pointing for joint attention acts at 18 months. Thus, high frontal theta power during a simple "visual attention" task in 14-month-old infants is an unfavorable trait for the development of the ability to initiate joint attention. To interpret this finding the authors invoked the common notion that less power is indicative of cortical (frontal lobe) activation that is favorable for development of cognitive abilities, while more power is indicative of cortical idling. However, this statement is true only for the alpha and not for the theta rhythm (Kirk & Mackay, 2003; Klimesch, 1996). Therefore, given that 4–6 Hz activity should be identified as theta in infants, the explanation proposed by Henderson and colleages is highly improbable.

The finding of a robust frontal theta effect during anticipatory attention in 7–11-month-olds led us to question whether the same effect could be found in younger infants. Studies of oculomotor behavior revealed that infants exhibit anticipatory attention capacities at 3–6 months of age (Gilmore & Johnson, 1995; Haith, Hazan, & Goodman, 1988). However, at this age infants' ability to sustain anticipatory attention is rather limited and, unlike 7–11-month-olds, 6-month-old infants cannot anticipate an incoming stimulus for longer than 5 seconds. Does frontal cortex activation subserve this rudimentary ability to sustain anticipatory attention even in such young infants? If it does, one can expect that the frontal theta would increase in 5-month-olds during anticipatory attention, as it does in 7–11-month-olds. To check this possibility, a modification of the expectation paradigm was used (Stroganova, Bazhenova, & Doussard-Roosevelt, 2000) in which 5-month-old infants attended to a doll that periodically disappeared behind the screen for 3–5 seconds and reappeared again. The subjects sustaining at least 2.5-second periods of anticipatory attention exhibited high-amplitude theta oscillations with 4.8 Hz spectral peak frequency during disappearance periods. However, unlike 7–11-month-old infants, the maximum of theta response in 5-month-olds was located at temporal sites (T5, T6), where theta spectral power positively correlated with anticipatory performance. The notable absence of both frontal maximum of theta and its correlation to performance in young infants points to the difference in the neurophysiological mechanisms of anticipatory attention in younger and older infants. The temporal theta rhythm observed in 5-month-olds during anticipation is likely to be related to the short-term memory processes mediated by the neural networks of temporal cortex (Desimone, 1996). This cortical region may be responsible for maintenance of relatively short periods of anticipatory attention. The later development of frontal cortex makes this originally temporally mediated, short-lived mental representation of the disappeared object less fragile. This possibility is intriguing given the discussion on the sources of mental representation development during infancy (Munakata, McClelland, Johnson, & Siegler, 1997).

Asymmetry of the theta response

There is evidence that the task-related differences in scalp topography of theta response in adults reflect activation of different neural networks (Aftanas, Varlamov, Pavlov, Makhnev, & Reva, 2001; Inanaga, 1998; Kirk & Mackay, 2003). In this relation it is interesting to mention the pronounced right temporal asymmetry of the theta rhythm that has been observed in infants under some conditions. Thus, at 7–9 months, a distinct right-side asymmetry was found for the high-frequency (5.2–6.0 Hz) theta rhythm during periods of anticipation in the peek-a-boo game (Orekhova et al., 1999). Five-month-olds demonstrated significant right-side temporal asymmetry of the theta rhythm at the peak frequency (4.8 Hz) during the ambiguous situation provoked by the still face of the experimenter (Bazhenova, Stroganova, Doussard-Roosevelt, Posikera, & Porges, in press). These right temporal theta asymmetries could be due to relatively greater activation of right limbic system and the related cortical areas of the right hemisphere during (negative) emotional tension. This suggestion is supported by data from adults. Thus, in adults emotionally arousing visual stimuli induce theta response predominantly over the right posterior regions (Aftanas et al., 2001). In a MEG study Nishitani (2003) reported relatively higher increases of theta rhythm and metabolic activity in the right hippocampus during presentation of more arousing unpleasant pictures than pleasant ones.

Functional meaning

Many authors believe that the scalp-recorded theta rhythm originates in limbic structures (Kirk & Mackay, 2003; Klimesch, 1996; Miller, 1991). Indeed, during some behavioral states, theta rhythm can be registered in the human hippocampus (Arnolds, Lopes da Silva, Aitink, Kamp, & Boeijinga, 1980; Cantero, Atienza, Stickgold, Kahana, Madsen, & Kocsis, 2003). Under some specific conditions of memory and cognitive load the limbic and rhinal cortex theta activity can be intercorrelated (Fell, Klaver, Elfadil, Schaller, Elger, & Fernandez, 2003). These recent findings fit Miller's (1991) hypothesis of theta's role in the interplay between cortical and limbic structures. Even if the scalp-recorded theta rhythm may in some cases be transmitted from limbic pacemakers through the subcortical pathways, it is most likely generated in the cerebral cortex (Asada, Fukuda, Tsunoda, Yamaguchi, & Tonoike, 1999; Kirk & Mackay, 2003).

Although the exact neurophysiological origin of the human scalp-recorded theta rhythm is still an open question, its functional properties have become a subject of intensive research. It is well known that in adults the "midline frontal theta" correlates with mental effort during performance of cognitive tasks (see Inanaga, 1998, for review). More recently, the importance of cortical theta oscillations for human memory encoding has been recognized (Klimesch, 1996). However, the role of theta oscillations during memory tasks is hardly likely to be specific for memory function (Caplan et al., 2001; Kahana et al., 2001). In both adults and infants, an increase of scalp-recorded theta rhythm can be observed during behavioral states that are unlikely to load essentially on memory. For example, in adults theta appears during expectation of painful stimuli (Kornhuber, Lang, Kure, & Kornhuber, 1990). In infants, it synchronizes during sucking and stereotype behaviors (Stroganova & Posikera, 1993). It is likely, therefore, that theta synchronization observed during infant "theta-states" reflects a more general process than memory. This process could be essential for encoding and retrieving information, and thereby influence memory performance.

Taking into account similarity of behavioral correlates of human cortical theta rhythm and hippocampal theta in animals (Demiralp, Basar-Eroglu, Rahn, & Basar, 1994), one can suggest similar functional meanings of these two phenomena. Neurophysiological studies in animals have shown that theta synchronization in the hippocampus is observed when attention is highly focused on specific stimulation. Other stimuli, appearing in the background of the ongoing theta, do not evoke responses of hippocampal neurons. Thus, theta synchronization can be regarded as a mechanism of attention, which improves processing of a selected stimulus and simultaneously protects against the interference of other signals (Vinogradova, Kitchigina, & Zenchenko, 1998).

Initially distributed attention becomes focused on a particular stimulus when this stimulus has been evaluated against the internal context and appears to be important for the subject. We suggest that scalp theta response reflects *highly focused attention driven by internal significance of the particular stimulation or of its memory representation*. This interpretation can explain the appearance of the theta rhythm in a number of the infant's behavioral states. For example, the low level of theta synchronization in the beginning of a "visual attention" condition (see Figure 9.1A) is probably related to distribution of attention between incoming stimuli. As soon as an appraisal of the situation occurs, attention becomes more focused on the particular aspect of the stimulation (e.g., face of the experimenter blowing bubbles) and theta (Figure 9.1B) and, occasionally, overt emotional reactions appear. In general, an emotion reflects an appraisal of the internal significance of the current state (Simonov, 1986). Thus, our interpretation of the theta response is in line with the known correlation between emotional arousal (both positive and negative) and the theta rhythm in adults and infants. The intriguing question is which stimuli most effectively provoke theta responses in human infants. Following the above hypothesis, the "theta-provoking" stimuli may be those of the most biological importance, such as food, pacifier, social interaction, cognitive load, etc. Interestingly, Miller (1991) predicted that the theta rhythm is likely to be generated in hippocampus-neocortical circuitry when information important to the species is to be gathered from the environment. He believed that for humans the most potent way of triggering theta activity would be the use of socially significant and novel stimuli. The findings reported above show that these stimuli are indeed very effective in triggering cortical theta synchronization in human infants.

Theta oscillations are crucial for neural plasticity and information coding (see Kahana et al., 2001, for review). This fact has important implications for learning and memory at the behavioral level. During infancy, the most potent theta-provoking behaviors, such as social communication, exploration, and play, are necessary for learning and cognitive development. Thus, it is likely that the abundance of theta activity in young children is not just a sign of immaturity. The limbic system and related cortical structures require considerable social, emotional, perceptual, and cognitive stimulation during infancy and early childhood in order to develop normally and are thus "experience expectant" (Joseph, 1999). Cortical theta rhythm may act as a mechanism for synaptic plasticity (Kahana et al., 2001), and mediate the influence of environmental effects on the development of functional neural networks at a young age.

In line with this suggestion, our genetic twin study (Orekhova et al., 2003) has shown that in 7–12-month-old infants the interindividual variability of theta power during visual attention is determined by environment; in particular, by so-called "shared environmental factors". These factors, shared by the twins in the pair, make them more similar. This finding has been substantiated by positive correlation between theta power and the number of caregivers in the family. The results of this study suggest that even relatively normal variations of social environment at an early age may influence development of brain circuits underlying the theta response. These data are interesting in relation to the hypothetical limbic origin of the cortical theta rhythm. The limbic system and related structures are especially prone to early adverse social environmental influences, such as neglect or abuse (Teicher, Andersen, Polcari, Anderson, Navalta, & Kim, 2003).

There is evidence that, similar to the alpha band, the infant theta band includes different electrophysiological phenomena. First, as already mentioned, the scalp distribution of the theta rhythm is task dependent and may reflect involvement of different neural networks. Second, functional properties of rhythmic activities in the upper and lower theta bands may differ (Klimesch et al., 2001; Orekhova et al., 1999). In particular, in 7–11-month-old infants we reliably distinguished two theta rhythms that had different focuses and different functional properties, and were represented by spectral peaks of different frequency (Orekhova et al., 1999). Both low-frequency (3.6–4.8 Hz) and high-frequency (5.2–6.0 Hz) theta rhythms increased in infants during anticipatory attention. However, the maximal increase of "low theta" was observed over frontal (predominantly left) scalp locations, while "high theta" increased predominantly over the right posterior temporal area. Moreover, "low theta" correlated with task performance, while "high theta" did not. If, as was suggested by Miller (1991), the cortical theta rhythm reflects re-entrant activity in the cortico-hippocampal loops, the different properties of the theta band rhythms could be due to their origination from different cortico-limbic pathways (Duvernoy, 1998; Kirk & Mackay, 2003).

CONCLUDING REMARKS

In conclusion we would like to underline two major points discussed in this chapter. First, we strongly advocate the advantages of selecting functionally meaningful EEG bands over so-called conventional or arbitrarily defined EEG bands in infant EEG studies. Such functionally meaningful EEG bands can be defined through the evaluation of functional reactivity and scalp topography of the rhythmic activity (the so-called functional topography approach). The analysis of brainwave components with known functional properties, rather than of spectral amplitude in the conventional or arbitrarily defined bands, seems to have an important impact on the effectiveness of studying brain development and brain–behavior relationship during infancy. This approach had a profound influence on research topics discussed in this chapter, such as the age-dependent changes in EEG frequency and amplitudes; EEG of the different functional state of wakefulness; EEG indexes of attention and affective processes.

The second point relates to the functional interpretation of EEG parameters. The EEG parameters in waking infants are strongly state dependent. The same EEG parameter may index different neurophysiological processes under different conditions of registration. Therefore, EEG rhythms should be analyzed in the context of the particular functional load. The "spontaneous" oscillations in theta and alpha bands of infant EEG represent unique and quantifiable measures of system-wide activity of distributed brain structures including subcortical circuits. The transmission and processing of incoming sensory information in the entire network is coordinated by the ongoing oscillations. For example, during infant "theta states" the brain "filters in" the information that triggered theta oscillations and "filters out" the other sensory input that is not in the context of the immediate functional state being generated by the brain. From this perspective, infant EEG may be used to study development of regulatory capacities of the brain, rather than to provide "correlates" of psychological variables.

ACKNOWLEDGMENTS

This work was supported by the Russian Fund for Humanitarian Research, grant #03-06-00022a and by the Swedish Medical Research Foundation (proj. no. 12170) and the Gothenburg Medical Faculty.

REFERENCES

Aftanas, L., Varlamov, A., Pavlov, S., Makhnev, V., & Reva, N. (2001). Event-related synchronization and desynchronization during affective processing: Emergence of valence-related time-dependent hemispheric asymmetries in theta and upper alpha band. *International Journal of Neuroscience*, *110*(3–4), 197–219.

Arnolds, D. E., Lopes da Silva, F. H., Aitink, J. W., Kamp, A., & Boeijinga, P. (1980). The spectral properties of hippocampal EEG related to behaviour in man. *Electroencephalography and Clinical Neurophysiology*, *50*(3–4), 324–328.

Asada, H., Fukuda, Y., Tsunoda, S., Yamaguchi, M., & Tonoike, M. (1999). Frontal midline theta rhythms reflect alternative activation of prefrontal cortex and anterior cingulate cortex in humans. *Neuroscience Letters*, *274*, 29–32.

Bazhenova, O. V., Stroganova, T. A., Doussard-Roosevelt, J. A., Posikera, I. N., & Porges, S. W. (in press). Physiological responses of 5-month-old infants to smiling and blank faces. *International Journal of Psychophysiology*.

Bell, M. A. (2002). Power changes in infant EEG frequency bands during a spatial working memory task. *Psychophysiology*, *39*(4), 450–458.

Bell, M. A., & Fox, N. A. (1992). The relations between frontal brain electrical activity and cognitive development during infancy. *Child Development*, *63*(5), 1142–1163.

Bell, M. A., & Fox, N. A. (1997). Individual differences in object permanence performance at 8 months: Locomotor experience and brain electrical activity. *Developmental Psychobiology*, *31*(4), 287–297.

Benninger, C., Matthis, P., & Scheffner, D. (1984). EEG development of healthy boys and girls. Results of a longitudinal study. *Electroencephalography and Clinical Neurophysiology*, *57*(1), 1–12.

Cantero, J. L., Atienza, M., Stickgold, R., Kahana, M. J., Madsen, J. R., & Kocsis, B. (2003). Sleep-dependent theta oscillations in the human hippocampus and neo-cortex. *Journal of Neuroscience*, *23*(34), 10897–10903.

Caplan, J. B., Madsen, J. R., Raghavachari, S., & Kahana, M. J. (2001). Distinct patterns of brain oscillations underlie two basic parameters of human maze learning. *Journal of Neurophysiology*, *86*(1), 368–380.

Card, J. A., Mundy, P. C., & Schmidt, L. A. (1997). *Frontal EEG of social communication skills in 14–18 month old toddlers.* Paper presented at the Biennial Meeting of the Society for Research in Child Development, Washington, DC.

Chugani, H. T., Phelps, M. E., & Mazziotta, J. C. (1987). Positron emission tomography study of human brain functional development. *Annals of Neurology, 22*(4), 487–497.

Clarke, A. R., Barry, R. J., McCarthy, R., & Selikowitz, M. (2001). Age and sex effects in the EEG: Development of the normal child. *Clinical Neurophysiology, 112*(5), 806–814.

Corbetta, M., Miezin, F. M., Shulman, G. L., & Petersen, S. E. (1993). A PET study of visuospatial attention. *Journal of Neuroscience, 13*(3), 1202–1226.

Csibra, G., Davis, G., Spratling, M. W., & Johnson, M. H. (2000). Gamma oscillations and object processing in the infant brain. *Science, 290*(5496), 1582–1585.

Davidson, R. J., & Fox, N. A. (1989). Frontal brain asymmetry predicts infants' response to maternal separation. *Journal of Abnormal Psychology, 98*(2), 127–131.

Davidson, R. J., & Tomarken, A. J. (1989). Laterality and emotion: An electrophysiological approach. In F. Boller & J. Grafman (Eds.), *Handbook of neuropsychology* (Vol. 3, pp. 419–441). Amsterdam: Elsevier.

Dawson, G. (1994). Temperament, affective style, and frontal lobe asymmetry. In G. Dawson & K. W. Fischer (Eds.), *Human behavior and the developing brain* (pp. 347–379). New York: Guilford Press.

Dawson, G., Panagiotides, H., Klinger, L. G., & Hill, D. (1992). The role of frontal lobe functioning in the development of infant self-regulatory behavior. *Brain and Cognition, 20*(1), 152–175.

Demiralp, T., Basar-Eroglu, C., Rahn, E., & Basar, E. (1994). Event-related theta rhythms in cat hippocampus and prefrontal cortex during an omitted stimulus paradigm. *International Journal of Psychophysiology, 18*(1), 35–48.

Desimone, R. (1996). Neural mechanisms for visual memory and their role in attention. *Proceedings of the National Academy of Sciences, USA, 93*(24), 13494–13499.

Diamond, A. (1991). Neuropsychological insights into the meaning of object concept development. In S. Carey & R. Gelman (Eds.), *The epigenesist of mind: Essays on biology and cognition* (pp. 67–110). Hillsdale, NJ: Lawrence Erlbaum Associates Inc.

Dreyfus-Brisac, C. (1979). Ontogenesis of brain bioelectrical activity and sleep organization in neonates and infants. In F. F. Falkner & J. M. Tanner (Eds.), *Human growth* (Vol. 3, pp. 157–182). London: Plenum Publishing Corporation.

Duffy, F. H. (1994). The role of quantified electroencephalography in psychological research. In G. Dawson & K. W. Fischer (Eds.), *Human behavior and the developing brain* (pp. 93–133). New York: Guilford Press.

Duvernoy, H. M. (1998). *The human hippocampus: Functional anatomy, vascularization and serial section with MRI* (2nd ed.). Berlin: Springer.

Farah, M. (1990). *Visuoagnosia: Disorders of object recognition and what they tell us about normal vision.* Cambidge, MA: MIT Press.

Fell, J., Klaver, P., Elfadil, H., Schaller, C., Elger, C. E., & Fernandez, G. (2003). Rhinal-hippocampal theta coherence during declarative memory formation: Interaction with gamma synchronization? *European Journal of Neuroscience, 17*(5), 1082–1088.

Fernandez, T., Harmony, T., Silva, J., Galan, L., Diaz-Comas, L., Bosch, J., et al. (1998). Relationship of specific EEG frequencies at specific brain areas with performance. *NeuroReport, 9*(16), 3681–3687.

Fox, N. A., & Davidson, R. J. (1988). Patterns of brain electrical activity during facial signs of emotion in 10-month-old infants. *Developmental Psychology, 24,* 230–236.

Fuster, M. J. (1990). Prefrontal cortex and the bridging of temporal gaps in the perception/action cycle. In A. Diamond (Ed.), *The development and neural bases of higher cognitive functions* (Vol. 608, pp. 318–336). New York: New York Academy of Sciences.

Futagi, Y., Ishihara, T., Tsuda, K., Suzuki, Y., & Goto, M. (1998). Theta rhythms associated with sucking, crying, gazing and handling in infants. *Electroencephalography and Clinical Neurophysiology, 106*(5), 392–399.

Gasser, T., Jennen-Steinmetz, C., Sroka, L., Verleger, R., & Mocks, J. (1988). Development of the EEG of school-age children and adolescents. II. Topography. *Electroencephalography and Clinical Neurophysiology, 69*(2), 100–109.

Gevins, A., Smith, M. E., McEvoy, L., & Yu, D. (1997). High-resolution EEG mapping of cortical activation related to working memory: Effects of task difficulty, type of processing, and practice. *Cerebral Cortex, 7*(4), 374–385.

Ghatan, P. H., Hsieh, J. C., Petersson, K. M., Stone-Elander, S., & Ingvar, M. (1998). Coexistence of attention-based facilitation and inhibition in the human cortex. *Neuroimage, 7*(1), 23–29.

Gilmore, R. O., & Johnson, M. H. (1995). Working memory in infancy: Six-month-olds' performance on two versions of the oculomotor delayed response task. *Journal of Experimental Child Psychology, 59*(3), 397–418.

Hagne, I. (1968). Development of the waking EEG in normal infants during the first year of life. In P. Kellaway & I. Petersen (Eds.), *Clinical electroencephalography of children* (pp. 97–118). Stockholm: Almquist & Wikell.

Hagne, I. (1972). Development of the EEG in normal infants during the first year of life. A longitudinal study. *Acta Pediatrica Scandinavica Supplement, 232,* 25–53.

Hagne, I., Persson, J., Magnusson, R., & Petersen, I. (1973). Spectral analysis via Fast Fourier Transform of waking EEG in normal infants. In I. Petersen & P. Kellaway (Eds.), *Automation of clinical electroencephalography* (pp. 103–143). New York: Raven Press.

Haith, M. M., Hazan, C., & Goodman, G. S. (1988). Expectation and anticipation of dynamic visual events by 3.5-month-old babies. *Child Development, 59*(2), 467–479.

Henderson, L. M., Yoder, P. J., Yale, M. E., & McDuffie, A. (2002). Getting the point: Electrophysiological correlates of protodeclarative pointing. *International Journal of Developmental Neuroscience, 20*(3–5), 449–458.

Henry, J. R. (1944). Electroencephalograms of normal children. *Monographs of the Society for Research in Child Development, 9,* 1–71.

Hrbek, A., Karlberg, P., & Olsson, T. (1973). Development of visual and somatosensory evoked responses in pre-term newborn infants. *Electroencephalography and Clinical Neurophysiology, 34*(3), 225–232.

Hudspeth, W. J., & Pribram, K. H. (1992). Psychophysiological indices of cerebral maturation. *International Journal of Psychophysiology, 12*(1), 19–29.

Huttenlocher, P. R. (1994). Synaptogenesis in human cerebral cortex. In G. Dawson & K. W. Fischer (Eds.), *Human behavior and the developing brain* (pp. 137–152). New York: Guilford Press.

Inanaga, K. (1998). Frontal midline theta rhythm and mental activity. *Psychiatry and Clinical Neurosciences, 52*(6), 555–566.

Joseph, R. (1999). Environmental influences on neural plasticity, the limbic system, emotional development and attachment: A review. *Child Psychiatry and Human Development*, *29*(3), 189–208.

Junghofer, M., Elbert, T., Tucker, D. M., & Braun, C. (1999). The polar average reference effect: A bias in estimating the head surface integral in EEG recording. *Clinical Neurophysiology*, *110*(6), 1149–1155.

Kahana, M. J., Seelig, D., & Madsen, J. R. (2001). Theta returns. *Current Opinions in Neurobiology*, *11*(6), 739–744.

Katada, A., Ozaki, H., Suzuki, H., & Suhara, K. (1981). Developmental character-istics of normal and mentally retarded children's EEGs. *Electroencephalography and Clinical Neurophysiology*, *52*(2), 192–201.

Kaufman, J., Csibra, G., & Johnson, M. H. (2003). Representing occluded objects in the human infant brain. *Proceedings of the Royal Society of London. B: Biological Sciences*, *270*(Suppl. 2), S140–143.

Kirk, I. J., & Mackay, J. C. (2003). The role of theta-range oscillations in synchronis-ing and integrating activity in distributed mnemonic networks. *Cortex*, *39*(4–5), 993–1008.

Klimesch, W. (1996). Memory processes, brain oscillations and EEG synchronization. *International Journal of Psychophysiology*, *24*(1–2), 61–100.

Klimesch, W., Doppelmayr, M., Schwaiger, J., Auinger, P., & Winkler, T. (1999). "Paradoxical" alpha synchronization in a memory task. *Cognitive Brain Research*, *7*(4), 493–501.

Klimesch, W., Doppelmayr, M., Wimmer, H., Schwaiger, J., Rohm, D., Gruber, W. et al. (2001). Theta band power changes in normal and dyslexic children. *Clinical Neurophysiology*, *112*(7), 1174–1185.

Kornhuber, A. W., Lang, M., Kure, W., & Kornhuber, H. H. (1990). Will and frontal theta activity. In C. H. M. Brunia, A. W. K. Galliard, & A. Kok (Eds.), *Psychophysiological brain research* (Vol. 1, pp. 53–58). Tillburg: Tillburg University Press.

Koshino, Y., & Niedermeyer, E. (1975). Enhancement of Rolandic mu-rhythm by pattern vision. *Electroencephalography and Clinical Neurophysiology*, *38*(5), 535–538.

Krumholz, A. (1999). Evoked potentials in infancy and childhood. In E. Niedermeyer & F. Lopes da Silva (Eds.), *Electroencephalography: Basic principles, clinical appli-cations, and related fields* (pp. 1059–1071). Baltimore: Williams & Wilkins.

Kugler, J., & Laub, M. (1971). "Puppet show" theta rhythm. *Electroencephalography and Clinical Neurophysiology*, *31*, 532–533.

Kuhlman, W. N. (1980). The mu rhythm: Functional topography and neural origin. In G. Pfurtsheller (Ed.), *Rhythmic EEG activities and cortical functioning* (pp. 105–120). Amsterdam: Elsevier.

Lairy, G. C. (1975). The EEG during the first year of life. In A. Remond (Ed.), *Handbook of electroencephalography and clinical neurophysiology* (Vol. 6B, pp. 24–30). Amsterdam: Elsevier.

Lang, M., Lang, W., Diekmann, V., & Kornhuber, H. (1987). The frontal theta rhythm indicating motor and cognitive learning. In R. Johnson, J. W. Rohrbaugh, & R. Parasuraman (Eds.), *Current trends in ERP research* (Vol. EEG Suppl. 40, pp. 322–327). Amsterdam: Elsevier.

Lehtonen, J., Kononen, M., Purhonen, M., Partanen, J., & Saarikoski, S. (2002). The effects of feeding on the electroencephalogram in 3- and 6-month-old infants. *Psychophysiology*, *39*(1), 73–79.

Lehtonen, J. B., & Lehtinen, I. (1972). Alpha rhythm and uniform visual field in man. *Electroencephalography and Clinical Neurophysiology, 32*(2), 139–147.

Lindsley, D. B. (1939). A longitudinal study of the occipital alpha rhythm in normal children: Frequency and amplitude standards. *Journal of Genetic Psychology, 55*, 197–213.

Lopes da Silva, F. (1991). Neural mechanisms underlying brain waves: From neural membranes to networks. *Electroencephalography and Clinical Neurophysiology, 79*(2), 81–93.

Lopes da Silva, F. H., Vos, J. E., Mooibroek, J., & Van Rotterdam, A. (1980). Relative contributions of intracortical and thalamo-cortical processes in the generation of alpha rhythms, revealed by partial coherence analysis. *Electroencephalography and Clinical Neurophysiology, 50*(5–6), 449–456.

Markand, O. N. (1990). Alpha rhythms. *Journal of Clinical Neurophysiology, 7*(2), 163–189.

Marshall, P. J., Bar-Haim, Y., & Fox, N. A. (2002). Development of the EEG from 5 months to 4 years of age. *Clinical Neurophysiology, 113*(8), 1199–1208.

Maulsby, R. L. (1971). An illustration of emotionally evoked theta rhythm in infancy: Hedonic hypersynchrony. *Electroencephalography and Clinical Neurophysiology, 31*(2), 157–165.

Mennemeier, M. S., Chatterjee, A., Watson, R. T., Wertman, E., Carter, L. P., & Heilman, K. M. (1994). Contributions of the parietal and frontal lobes to sustained attention and habituation. *Neuropsychologia, 32*(6), 703–716.

Miller, R. (1991). *Cortico-hippocampal interplay and representation of contexts in the brain.* Berlin: Springer-Verlag.

Mizuno, T., Yamauchi, N., Watanabe, A., Komatsushiro, M., & Takagi, T. (1970). Maturation patterns of EEG basic waves of healthy infants under twelve-months of age. *Tohoku. Journal of Experimental Medicine, 102*(1), 91–98.

Mulholland, T. (1995). Human EEG, behavioral stillness and biofeedback. *International Journal of Psychophysiology, 19*(3), 263–279.

Munakata, Y., McClelland, J. L., Johnson, M. H., & Siegler, R. S. (1997). Rethinking infant knowledge: Toward an adaptive process account of successes and failures in object permanence tasks. *Psychological Review, 104*(4), 686–713.

Mundy-Castle, A. C. (1951). Theta and beta rhythms in the electroencephalogram of normal adults. *Electroencephalography and Clinical Neurophysiology, 3*, 477–486.

Nikitina, G. M., Posikera, I. N., & Stroganova, T. A. (1985). Central organisation of emotional reactions of infants during first year of life. In S. Trojan & F. Stastny (Eds.), *Ontogenesis of the brain* (pp. 223–227). Pragensis, Praga: Universitas Carolina.

Nishitani, N. (2003). Dynamics of cognitive processing in the human hippocampus by neuromagnetic and neurochemical assessments. *Neuroimage, 20*(1), 561–571.

Ohtahara, S. (1981). Neurophysiological development during infancy and childhood. In N. Yamaguchi & F. Fujisawa (Eds.), *Recent advances in EEG and EMG data processing* (p. 369). Amsterdam: Elsevier.

Orekhova, E. V., Stroganova, T. A., & Posikera, I. N. (1999). Theta synchronization during sustained anticipatory attention in infants over the second half of the first year of life. *International Journal of Psychophysiology, 32*(2), 151–172.

Orekhova, E. V., Stroganova, T. A., & Posikera, I. N. (2001). Alpha activity as an index of cortical inhibition during sustained internally controlled attention in infants. *Clinical Neurophysiology, 112*(5), 740–749.

Orekhova, E. V., Stroganova, T. A., Posikera, I. N., Malykh, S. B., Pushina, N. P., Tsetlin, M. M. et al. (2003). Heritability and "environmentability" of electroencephalogram in infants: The twin study. *Psychophysiology, 40*(5), 727–741.

Paul, K., Dittrichova, J., & Papousek, H. (1996). Infant feeding behavior: Development in patterns and motivation. *Developmental Psychobiology, 29*(7), 563–576.

Pfurtscheller, G., & Klimesch, W. (1992). Functional topography during a visuoverbal judgment task studied with event-related desynchronization mapping. *Journal of Clinical Neurophysiology, 9*(1), 120–131.

Pfurtscheller, G., & Neuper, C. (1994). Event-related synchronization of mu rhythm in the EEG over the cortical hand area in man. *Neuroscience Letters, 174*(1), 93–96.

Pfurtscheller, G., Stancak, A. Jr., & Neuper, C. (1996). Event-related synchronization (ERS) in the alpha band—an electrophysiological correlate of cortical idling: A review. *International Journal of Psychophysiology, 24*(1–2), 39–46.

Pivik, R. T., Broughton, R. J., Coppola, R., Davidson, R. J., Fox, N., & Nuwer, M. R. (1993). Guidelines for the recording and quantitative analysis of electroencephalographic activity in research contexts. *Psychophysiology, 30*(6), 547–558.

Posikera, I. N., & Stroganova, T. A. (1983). Electroencephalographic analysis of the functional development of cortical regions of the brain in children under 1 month of age. *Zhurnal nevrologii i psikhiatrii imeni I.P. Pavlova, 33*(4), 624–631. [in Russian]

Posikera, I. N., Stroganova, T. A., Zhurba, L. T., & Timonina, O. V. (1986). Electroencephalographic correlates of positive emotional reactions in children in the first year of life. *Zhurnal nevrologii i psikhiatrii imeni S. S. Korsakova, 86*, 1485–1491. [in Russian]

Rougeul, A., Bouyer, J. J., Dedet, L., & Debray, O. (1979). Fast somato-parietal rhythms during combined focal attention and immobility in baboon and squirrel monkey. *Electroencephalography and Clinical Neurophysiology, 46*(3), 310–319.

Rougeul-Buser, A., Bouyer, J. J., & Buser, P. (1975). From attentiveness to sleep. A topographical analysis of localized "synchronized" activities on the cortex of normal cat and monkey. *Acta Neurobiolia Experimentalis (Warsaw), 35*(5–6), 805–819.

Samson-Dollfus, D., Delapierre, G., Do Marcolino, C., & Blondeau, C. (1997). Normal and pathological changes in alpha rhythms. *International Journal of Psychophysiology, 26*(1–3), 395–409.

Schmidt, L. A., Trainor, L. J., & Santesso, D. L. (2003). Development of frontal electroencephalogram (EEG) and heart rate (ECG) responses to affective musical stimuli during the first 12 months of post-natal life. *Brain and Cognition, 52*(1), 27–32.

Schoppenhorst, M., Brauer, F., Freund, G., & Kubicki, S. (1980). The significance of coherence estimates in determining central alpha and mu activities. *Electroencephalography and Clinical Neurophysiology, 48*(1), 25–33.

Shagass, C. (1972). Electrical activity of the brain. In N. S. Greenfield & R. A. Stenbach (Eds.), *Handbook of psychophysiology* (pp. 263–328). New York: Holt, Rinehart & Winston.

Simonov, P. V. (1986). *The emotional brain: Physiology, neuroanatomy, psychology, and emotion* (M. J. Hall, Trans.). New York: Plenum.

Smith, J. R. (1938a). The electroencephalogram during normal infancy and childhood: I. Rhythmic activities present in the neonate and their subsequent development. *Journal of Genetic Psychology, 53*, 431–453.

Smith, J. R. (1938b). The electroencephalogram during normal infancy and childhood:

II. The nature and growth of the alpha waves. *Journal of Genetic Psychology, 53,* 455–469.

Smith, J. R. (1939). The "occipital" and "pre-central" rhythms during the first two years. *Journal of Psychology, 7,* 223–226.

Smith, J. R. J. P. (1941). The frequency growth of the human alpha rhythms during normal infancy and childhood. *Journal of Psychology, 11,* 177–198.

Steriade, M., Gloor, P., Llinas, R. R., Lopes de Silva, F. H., & Mesulam, M. M. (1990). Report of IFCN Committee on Basic Mechanisms. Basic mechanisms of cerebral rhythmic activities. *Electroencephalography and Clinical Neurophysiology, 76*(6), 481–508.

Steriade, M., & Llinas, R. R. (1988). The functional states of the thalamus and the associated neuronal interplay. *Physiological Review, 68*(3), 649–742.

Sterman, M. B., McGinty, D. J., Harper, R. M., Hoppenbrouwers, T., & Hodgman, J. E. (1982). Developmental comparison of sleep EEG power spectral patterns in infants at low and high risk for sudden death. *Electroencephalography and Clinical Neurophysiology, 53*(2), 166–181.

Stroganova, T., Bazhenova, O., & Doussard-Roosevelt, J. (2000). EEG theta rhythm and internally driven attention in 5-month-old infants. *Psychophysiology, 37*(Suppl. 1), S96–S96.

Stroganova, T. A., Orekhova, E. V., & Posikera, I. N. (1998). Externally and internally controlled attention in infants: An EEG study. *International Journal of Psychophysiology, 30*(3), 339–351.

Stroganova, T. A., Orekhova, E. V., & Posikera, I. N. (1999). EEG alpha rhythm in infants. *Clinical Neurophysiology, 110*(6), 997–1012.

Stroganova, T. A., & Posikera, I. N. (1993). Functional organisation of behavioural states in wakefulness during infancy (EEG study). In O. S. Adrianov (Ed.), *Brain and behaviour in infancy* (pp. 78–166). Moscow: IPRAN Press. [in Russian]

Stroganova, T. A., & Posikera, I. N. (1996). Effect of early visual deprivation on the response to new environmental stimuli in early human ontogeny. *Fiziologija Cheloveka, 22*(5), 20–29. [in Russian]

Stroganova, T. A., Posikera, I. N., Pushina, N. P., & Orekhova, E. V. (2003). Lateralization of motor functions in early human ontogenesis. *Fiziologija Cheloveka, 29*(1), 48–58. [in Russian]

Stroganova, T. A., Tsetlin, M. M., Posikera, I. N., Orekhova, E. V., & Malakhovskaia, E.V. (2002). Biological principles of individual differences in the temperament of children in the second half of the first year of life. III. Psychophysiological principles of "excitability" and "activity". *Fiziologija Cheloveka, 28*(5), 21–33. [in Russian]

Suffczynski, P., Kalitzin, S., Pfurtscheller, G., & Lopes da Silva, F. H. (2001). Computational model of thalamo-cortical networks: Dynamical control of alpha rhythms in relation to focal attention. *International Journal of Psychophysiology, 43*(1), 25–40.

Surwillo, W. W. (1971). Human reaction time and period of the EEG in relation to development. *Psychophysiology, 8*(4), 468–482.

Teicher, M. H., Andersen, S. L., Polcari, A., Anderson, C. M., Navalta, C. P., & Kim, D. M. (2003). The neurobiological consequences of early stress and childhood maltreatment. *Neuroscience and Biobehavioral Reviews, 27*(1–2), 33–44.

Thomas, D. G., & Crow, C. D. (1994). Development of evoked electrical brain activity in infancy. In G. Dawson & K. W. Fischer (Eds.), *Human behavior and the developing brain* (pp. 207–231). New York: Guilford Press.

Vandenberghe, R., Dupont, P., De Bruyn, B., Bormans, G., Michiels, J., Mortelmans, L. et al. (1996). The influence of stimulus location on the brain activation pattern in detection and orientation discrimination. A PET study of visual attention. *Brain, 119*(Pt 4), 1263–1276.

Vinogradova, O. S., Kitchigina, V. F., & Zenchenko, C. I. (1998). Pacemaker neurons of the forebrain medical septal area and theta rhythm of the hippocampus. *Membrane and Cell Biology, 11*, 715–725.

Walter, W. G. (1950). Normal rhythms: Their development, distribution, and significance. In D. Hill & G. Parr (Eds.), *Electroencephalography* (pp. 205–277). London: MacDonald.

Walter, V. J., & Walter, W. G. (1949). The central effects of rhythmic sensory stimulation. *Electroencephalography and Clinical Neurophysiology, 1*, 57–86.

Westmoreland, B. E., & Stockard, J. E. (1977). The EEG in infants and children: Normal patterns. *American Journal of EEG Technology, 17*, 72–103.

Wiesel, T. N. (1982). Postnatal development of the visual cortex and the influence of environment. *Nature, 299*(5884), 583–591.

10 Investigating event-related oscillations in infancy

Gergely Csibra and Mark H. Johnson
Birkbeck College, University of London, UK

Two general approaches have been taken to the electrophysiological study of infant brain function: event-related and evoked potentials (see Chapters 2–8 of this volume) and resting EEG (see Chapters 8 and 9). In this chapter, we introduce a third (intermediate) approach that we term "event-related oscillations". Briefly, event-related oscillations (EROs) are bursts of EEG at particular frequencies that are approximately time-locked to task or stimulus presentation events. For this reason, they are taken to reflect oscillatory activity in the brain related to specific task-relevant computations. While there is a growing literature on EROs in adults, particularly with respect to high-frequency (gamma-band) bursts, the approach has only just begun to be applied to infants. In the first section of this chapter we initially describe (1) how EROs can be analysed from raw EEG data, (2) the potential pitfalls and sources of artefact with EROs, and (3) issues of experimental design. Following this, we review evidence from two areas where we have adopted the ERO approach to study infants' perception and processing of objects. Finally, we discuss potential future avenues for research on infant cognition with EROs.

ERO ANALYSIS AND METHODS

Neurons have the inherent capacity to spontaneously produce oscillatory activity at frequencies above 20 Hz (Llinás, 1988). Sensory stimuli in several modalities (visual, auditory, olfactory) can elicit such oscillations in the gamma-band frequency range (20–80 Hz, most commonly around 40 Hz). When a large number of neurons fire synchronously at the same frequency, these oscillations can be recorded from the scalp by conventional EEG techniques. Recently several laboratories have started to analyse human EEG signals in terms of bursts of oscillatory activities and interpret them in relation to the cognitive functions that the participants performed while their brainwaves were recorded (e.g., Tallon-Baudry & Bertrand, 1999).

The EEG signal can be analysed both in the time domain and in the frequency domain. Analysis in the frequency domain (see Chapters 8 and 9) yields a description of the signal in terms of relative power or amplitude in various frequency bands, each associated with different brain states. Analysis of EEG in the time domain reveals dynamics of brain activity in the milli-second timescale and its relation to cognitive and/or neural events. However, oscillatory neural activities are usually restricted in both time and frequency content; therefore, analyses only in the time or frequency domain tend to be blind to them. To reveal task-related bursts of oscillatory activities, especially if they occur at higher frequency ranges, we need to perform a *time–frequency analysis* that tracks how amplitude (or power) varies at different frequen-cies over time. The relations among time domain, frequency domain, and time–frequency analyses are illustrated in Figure 10.1.

There are several ways to perform a time–frequency analysis on EEG signals. From a mathematical point of view, the best method is to perform a wavelet analysis (Samar, Bopardikar, Rao, & Swarz, 1999). The most

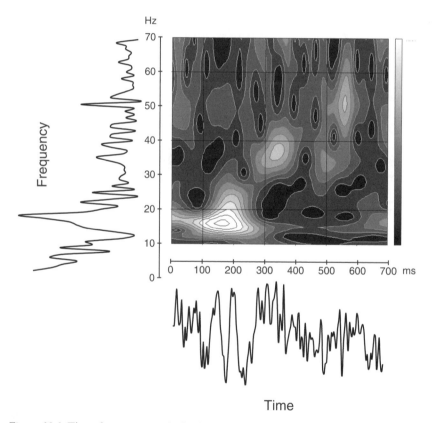

Figure 10.1 Time–frequency analysis. A segment of EEG recording can be analysed both in the time domain (horizontal trace) and in the frequency domain (vertical trace). However, time–frequency analysis of the same recording (contour map) reveals oscillatory activities that are restricted both in time and in frequency domain.

commonly used technique in human EEG research involves a continuous wavelet transformation, with Morlet wavelets appropriately scaled within the frequency range to be explored (Tallon-Baudry, Bertrand, Delpuech, & Pernier, 1996). The result of this transformation is a time-varying function of amplitude power along the frequencies of interest. When these time–frequency functions are interpreted in relation to cognitively important events whose timing can be determined accurately (e.g., stimulus onset, eye-movements), they are called event-related oscillations (EROs).

There are two types of EROs: *evoked* EROs are oscillations that are phase-locked to the corresponding event and can be recovered from averaged, non-filtered event-related potential (ERP) waveforms; *induced* EROs are not phase-locked and are obtained from raw EEG before averaging (Figure 10.2). Evoked oscillations are usually short-latency responses, while induced oscillations can occur both close to and farther away from the corresponding events (Herrmann & Mecklinger, 2000). Time–frequency analyses can also be applied to explore connectivity across brain regions (Lachau, Rodriguez, Martiniere, & Varela, 1999). Long-range phase synchrony between oscillatory activities at two recording sites probably reflects temporary functional connectivity (Varela, Lachaux, Rodriguez, & Martiniere, 2001). Coherence analyses that take temporarily restricted oscillatory activities into account are being developed in various laboratories (e.g., Lachau et al., 2002) but, to our knowledge, have not been applied to infant EEG yet.

EROs are particularly useful tools to study infants' cortical responses for several reasons. Induced EROs may be less sensitive to latency variability than conventional ERPs, and infants' electrophysiological responses to stimuli are known to vary more than those of adults. Also, unlike ERPs, EROs can reflect relatively sustained activation in situations where cognitive processing of certain events cannot be expected to be time-locked well to the event. For example, in a study on "object permanence" that we will discuss later, we found a sustained gamma-band response recorded over temporal regions while 6-month-old infants watched a display in which an object was occluded.

Time–frequency analyses are similarly, if not more, sensitive to electrical and behavioural EEG artefacts than conventional ERPs. Changes in electrical connectivity or sudden eye-movements that create sharp voltage jumps in the recording produce high-amplitude transient responses in a wide range of frequencies. Similarly, muscular artefacts and mains electrical noise may add a sustained high-frequency component to the signal, which is usually filtered out in ERP analyses. Thus, any activity that extends widely in either the temporal or the frequency domain should be treated with suspicion. To avoid such potential artefacts in our own data (1) we video record participants' faces during sessions to allow later rejection of trials with eye or jaw movement, (2) we record EOG from electrodes around the eye to allow identification of saccades, and (3) we have created time–frequency plots from experiments in which we actually induce saccades from infants (see, e.g., Csibra, Tucker, & Johnson, 2001) and we have simulated possible artefacts from mains and

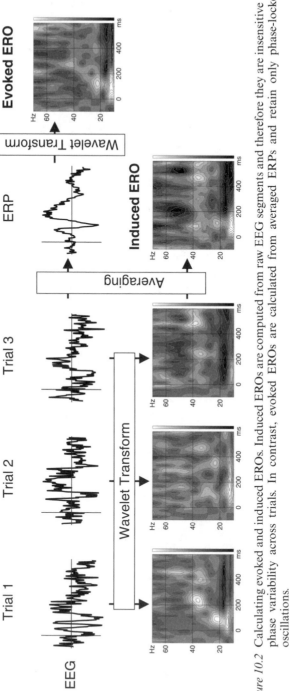

Figure 10.2 Calculating evoked and induced EROs. Induced EROs are computed from raw EEG segments and therefore they are insensitive to phase variability across trials. In contrast, evoked EROs are calculated from averaged ERPs and retain only phase-locked oscillations.

video screens. From the latter approach we have gained experience of the time–frequency signatures of these sources of activity.

PERCEPTUAL "BINDING"

Our perception of coherent, unified objects depends crucially on the brain's ability to 'bind' together various features coded by early stages of vision (Treisman & Schmidt, 1982). One promising recent line of research with adults has demonstrated a close association between gamma-band oscillations of neural activity and visual binding, pointing to a central role for oscillatory neural circuits. This link between oscillations and binding was first evident in recordings from single cells in monkey and cat cortex (Singer & Gray, 1995), but more recent studies have employed electroencephalography (Müller et al., 1996; Tallon-Baudry et al., 1996) and behavioural techniques (Elliott & Müller, 2000) to reveal similar phenomena within the adult human brain. Psychophysical experiments have demonstrated that presentation of stimuli in synchrony with a 40 Hz oscillation helps temporal binding, while electrophysiological studies provided evidence for gamma-band bursts of neural activity contingent on the experience of object perception.

In a previously unrelated line of research, experimenters have sought to determine the extent of object-processing abilities in young infants, and the features and cues they rely on when parsing visual scenes into objects (Kellman & Banks, 1998). One of the ways in which infants' object-processing abilities have been probed is to assess whether or not they are able to perceive static illusory objects composed from a number of separate elements (Bertenthal, Campos, & Haith, 1980; Kavsek, 2002). Results from behavioural studies indicated that while infants of 7 months and older perceive static illusory objects such as the Kanizsa figures, infants of 5 months or less may not. However, more recent studies have suggested that the developmental transition at around 6 months of age is related more to the emerging ability to complete partly occluded objects and to recover depth in illusory figures than to perceiving illusory figures per se (Csibra, 2001; Ghim, 1990; Kavsek, 2004). Studies of object processing in infants have relied on behavioural paradigms such as habituation or preferential looking. Gamma-band electrophysiological responses may provide a more direct measurement for perceptual binding and/or object completion in the infant brain.

With these factors in mind, we (Csibra, Davis, Spratling, & Johnson, 2000) investigated binding-related gamma oscillations in infants while they viewed static illusory objects. To elicit binding-related activation, we presented infants with a Kanizsa subjective-figure pattern (see left side of the first row of Figure 10.3), known to yield the percept of an illusory square, that is sensitive to the binding of the separate "pacmen" elements within the stimulus into a coherent object (Kanizsa, 1976). The Kanizsa Square is therefore an ideal candidate for measuring binding effects and has formed the basis

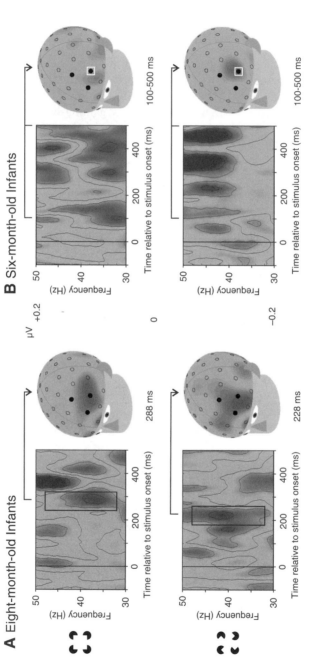

Figure 10.3 Induced gamma-band oscillations to Kanizsa Squares and control stimuli in 8- and 6-month-old infants. Both the increased and reduced activations were restricted to the left frontal area. Adapted from Csibra et al. (2000). Visit http://www.psypress.co.uk/dehaan to see this figure in colour.

of several previous studies of gamma oscillations in adults (Herrmann, Mecklinger, & Pfeifer, 1999; Tallon-Baudry et al., 1996). Furthermore, this pattern has featured prominently in previous *behavioural* studies of perceptual development, such that the current findings can be viewed in the context of a substantial body of other data.

We compared brain activation elicited by the Kanizsa Square to that elicited by a control stimulus (see left side of the bottom row of Figure 10.3) comprising precisely the same "pacmen" elements as the Kanizsa Square. However, in the control stimulus, the pacmen were rearranged so as not to elicit perceptual grouping and consequently no percept of an illusory figure. Any binding-related activation should thus pertain only to the Kanizsa Square, and not to the control stimulus.

Infants aged 6 months and 8 months viewed Kanizsa Squares and control stimuli on a computer screen while EEG was recorded. The recording was then subjected to the time–frequency analysis discussed earlier to yield a measure of induced oscillatory brain activation. Given the results of previous behavioural studies, we predicted that the 8-month-old infants, like adults in previous studies, would show induced gamma-band activations to the Kanizsa Square. In adults, illusory objects induce a burst of 40 Hz oscillations at about 250–300 milliseconds after stimulus onset. This characteristic gamma burst would not be expected following presentation of the control stimulus. In contrast to our predictions for the 8-month-olds, we anticipated that infants of 6 months would not show binding-related gamma oscillations.

In 8-month-olds we found an enhancement of induced gamma-band activity in response to the Kanizsa Square over the left frontal scalp in the 240–320 ms time window, corresponding in time course to results found in adults (Figure 10.3A). No equivalent gamma enhancement was seen in response to the control stimulus. However, intriguingly, the response to the control stimuli showed a significant *decrease* in activity within the gamma band over the same scalp areas and at slightly earlier latency (around 200 ms). This effect has never been reported in adults. Note, however, that in contrast to studies with adults, our test stimuli were preceded by attractive colourful pictures (a cartoon figure, an animal, or a geometric shape), which might also have engaged feature-binding processes. Thus, one plausible interpretation of the suppression of gamma-band activity is that it is a response to the removal of a foveated object that no longer requires active representation. We suggest that the gamma-band activity during presentation of the Kanizsa Square did not show this suppression because the Kanizsa Square acts as an occluder and infants maintain a mental representation of the occluded stimulus. A similar dissociation of gamma-band activation when an occluded object is present or not was also found in our other further studies (see later in this chapter). Kanizsa figures have been shown to be able to act as occluding surfaces (Davis & Driver, 1998), and this account is consistent with evidence from experiments in human adults showing a similar left frontal scalp pattern of 40 Hz oscillation in task situations that require subjects to maintain an object representation while it is not directly visible (Tallon-Baudry, Bertrand, Perronnet, & Pernier, 1998) and with single-cell studies in primates showing activity of neurons in the frontal cortex during "object permanence" tasks (Graziano, Hu, & Gross, 1997).

The time–frequency analysis for the group of 6-month-old infants yielded quite different results from those observed in the older group (Figure 10.3B). While there were some fluctuations in amplitude in the gamma band over the left frontal cortex after presentation of the Kanizsa Squares, these did not come in bursts similar to those observed in adults, but were smeared over long time intervals. The absence of adult-like binding-related gamma oscillation in 6-month-olds is consistent with partial activation of gamma-band oscillatory responses, and probably binding processes, but with a much higher variability in latency, both between and within subjects. This finding suggests that the neural development at around 6–8 months of age that allows infants to perceive static illusory objects involves a decrease in variability of gamma range bursts of oscillatory activity in the frontal cortex. It is also conceivable that, at this transitional age, a subset of the 6-month-old infants in our sample were able to bind the visual elements into a Kanizsa figure.

Our results also indicate that the frontal cortex may play a crucial role in the development of feature binding or object completion. Along with other findings (Csibra, Tucker, & Johnson, 1998; Johnson, Tucker, Stiles, & Trauner, 1998), this suggests a critical role for the frontal cortex in infant visual cognition, although more studies are needed to determine whether the frontal activation is directly related to the binding process, or reflects further attentional processing on the object "bound" elsewhere in the infant brain.

OCCLUDED OBJECTS AND "OBJECT PERMANENCE"

Since Piaget's (1954) original observations, one of the most striking phenomena in cognitive development has been the apparent failure of infants to show "object permanence". When an object is occluded by a cover, infants often behave as if it is no longer present: out of sight is out of mind. In contrast, studies measuring looking times reveal quite sophisticated reasoning about hidden objects even in young infants (for a review see Baillargeon, 2001). In a previously separate line of research, sustained responses in neural circuits have been identified as a mechanism for maintaining representations of objects during a period of occlusion (Rainer & Miller, 2000). In particular, in human adults gamma-band (~40 Hz) activity has been associated with maintaining an object/location in mind (Tallon-Baudry et al., 1998). We (Kaufman, Csibra, & Johnson, 2003) measured infants' electrophysiological responses to occlusion events at the age where reaching behaviour does not yet show evidence of understanding "object permanence".

Prior to examining EROs, it was necessary to determine that our experimental stimuli were realistic enough to be perceived as real objects to the infant participants. Therefore, we created digital video sequences of real objects involved in expected and unexpected events and measured infants' looking time to them in a traditional "violation of expectation" paradigm (von Hofsten & Spelke, 1985). Each infant was shown sequences of video-recorded and digitally edited events depicting an object (a train engine) appearing or failing to appear from under a tunnel when it should or should not have been there. Infants were first familiarized with the situation by watching a repeating event in which the engine entered the screen and then went into, and reversed out from, the tunnel. Following the single familiarization trial, four test events (Expected Appearance, Unexpected Appearance, Expected Disappearance, Unexpected Disappearance) were then presented in counterbalanced order. Each event cycle was 6 seconds (which did not vary across the four video types). Looking time was measured from the point at which infants began to look continuously from the start to the end of the event sequence (thus providing certainty that they had witnessed the expected or unexpected aspects of the event). The event was repeated until infants looked away from the video monitor for 2 seconds. Longer looking times are thought to reflect greater information processing in infant behavioural research (von Hofsten & Spelke, 1985).

Our results were consistent with earlier findings (Wynn & Chiang, 1998) that infants are highly sensitive to the unexpected disappearance of an object (consistent with object permanence) but are less sensitive to an unexpected appearance. A number of possible explanations for the appearance/disappearance discrepancy have been offered—including the idea that infants can infer the existence of two objects behind an occluder (Aguiar & Baillargeon, 2002; Baillargeon, 1994). Whatever the correct explanation for this result, this experiment demonstrated that infants react to our computerized stimuli as if they were watching real objects.

Subsequently, we measured EROs while infants watched the events that we used in the behavioural paradigm. We hypothesized that gamma-band oscillatory activity may be present in the infant brain during object occlusion. Results and analyses are illustrated in Figure 10.4. Statistical analyses on the average gamma-band (20–60 Hz) activity in six consecutive 200-ms windows revealed higher activity in the Unexpected than in the Expected Disappearance condition both before and after a hand lifted the tunnel. Comparing gamma power in each of the two conditions to the preceding baseline revealed that, prior to the tunnel being lifted, gamma power was reduced in the Expected Disappearance condition (Figure 10.4A). After the tunnel was lifted, there was significant enhancement of gamma-band activity in the Unexpected Disappearance condition relative to the baseline. These activity changes were largely restricted to the right, rather than the left, temporal area.

These results demonstrate a sustained period during which gamma power over the right temporal region was consistently higher during an event where infants represented an object despite it being occluded. This response persisted

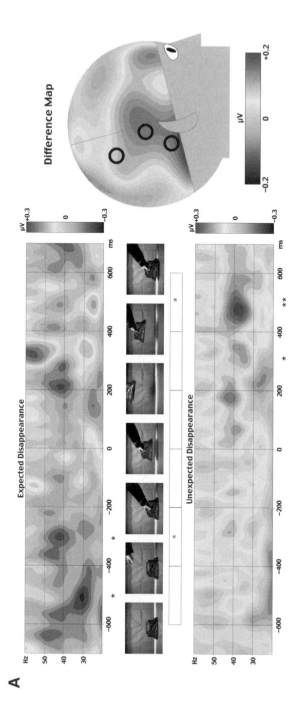

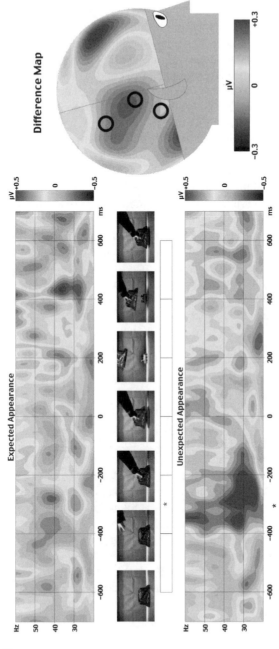

Figure 10.4 Induced gamma-band oscillations to occluded objects in 6-month-old infants. A right temporal activation was elicited both when an object had been hidden and failed to reappear (A), and during hiding before reappearance (B). Visit http://www.psypress.co.uk/dehaan to see this figure in colour.

despite initial visual evidence to the contrary. We propose that this gamma activity provides a neural basis for object permanence in infants. Just before the tunnel was lifted there was a relative (to baseline) decrease in gamma power in the Expected Disappearance condition. This suggests that the visual presence of the engine during the baseline phase partially activated gamma activity, which was then further strengthened during the later periods of occlusion in the Unexpected Disappearance condition. The maximal point of gamma power increase in the Unexpected Disappearance condition occurred around 500 ms after the initial lifting of the tunnel. One interpretation of this finding is that the infant's brain attempts to strengthen further the representation of the "hidden" object to better compete with the (now) direct visual evidence to the contrary. By this view, object permanence is the ability to maintain a sufficiently strong representation of the object, despite competing evidence from visual input (Munakata, 2001).

If this sustained gamma activity is related to representation of non-visible objects, it should also be evident in an ordinary event of temporary hiding, like the Expected Appearance event described above. Furthermore, an alternative explanation for the increase in gamma activity following the uncovering event is that it is correlated with the perception of an *impossible* event—and not directly related to object representation. In order to test these hypotheses we conducted another EEG experiment using only the appearance events.

As in the Unexpected Disappearance condition above, an increased gamma power was evident at right temporal channels during the time and condition where the train should be hidden underneath the tunnel. There was no significant increase in gamma activity time-locked to the Unexpected Appearance event. As before, the differences in oscillatory activity by condition were specific to right temporal channels.

These results bolster the earlier findings, in that infants showed an increase in gamma activity at right temporal leads when the train should have been underneath the tunnel. However, and in contrast to the earlier experiment, following the tunnel being lifted there were no significant differences in gamma power either between the two conditions or from the baseline. This supports the notion that the increase in gamma power following the lifting of the tunnel in the first EEG experiment is related to representing an object in the face of contradictory visual input.

In the latter EEG experiment, because the train was always revealed, there was no need to maintain a representation of the object independent of visual input. These results further advance the interpretation that gamma power in the right temporal area reflects active maintenance of occluded objects.

In a recent experiment we have also demonstrated that the right temporal gamma-band activation does not simply reflect a memory trace of the disappearing object but rather its active maintenance (Kaufman, Csibra, & Johnson, 2005). Six-month-old infants displayed a higher activation when an object disappeared by deletion (consistent with being occluded) than when it disappeared by disintegration. This result supports the view that derives young infants' competence with moving objects from perceptual routines that track objects through space and time (Scholl & Leslie, 1999).

The occlusion-related neural activity also suggests an explanation for the findings of looking-time studies addressing infants' knowledge of objects. We suggest that increased looking time may reflect a conflict between the visual input and the current mental representation of an object. Whatever the exact neural basis of the effects we have observed, our finding that increased gamma-band activity is associated with the representation of hidden objects will inform fundamental issues about how infants process their visual world.

CONCLUSIONS AND FUTURE PROSPECTS

In this chapter we have discussed two applications of ERO to the study of infant cognition. However, this effort to date probably only scratches the surface of the possible applications of the ERO approach for studying typical and atypical brain function. For example, the fact that induced ERO does not require the extent of time-locking to stimulus events that conventional ERPs do means that it can be used in a wider range of experimental paradigms. With Vincent Reid (see Reid, Csibra, Belsky, & Johnson, in press), we have begun to explore the significance of bursts of gamma activity when infants view dynamic video sequences of humans performing actions such as reaching for an object in either an intentional or an accidental manner.

Another potential line of experimentation with EROs concerns the atypical brain responses observed in some developmental disorders. For example, we (Grice, de Haan, Halit, Johnson, Csibra, & Karmiloff-Smith, 2003) have observed that adults with Williams syndrome and autism do not show the same patterns of gamma bursts as adults do in a Kanizsa figure paradigm similar to that described for infants earlier in this chapter. It will be intriguing to see whether these atypical patterns of ERO can be observed in young children or infants "at risk" for autism.

A number of challenges lie ahead for the ERO approach. The first of these is to develop adequate methods for assessing coherence between different regions of the brain in order to determine their patterns of functional connectivity. Another challenge will be to attempt to localize the underlying neural generators of oscillatory activity, since EEG has typically proved harder to localize than conventional ERPs because they do not necessarily occur in coherent clusters on the scalp (Tallon-Baudry, Bertrand, & Pernier, 1999). On a more positive note, high-frequency neural oscillations are more likely to map directly onto regions that show changes in the BOLD signal as detected by functional MRI techniques (Logothetis, Pauls, Augath, Trinath, & Oeltermann, 2001). Thus, we are more likely to find correspondences between results obtained with fMRI and EROs than we are with ERP and fMRI. Despite the challenges of this new approach, we believe that EROs will become a major new thrust in the study of infant brain electrophysiology.

ACKNOWLEDGEMENTS

We acknowledge financial support from MRC Programme Grant G9715587. Some sections of this chapter are adapted from Csibra et al. (2000) and Kaufman et al. (2003), and we thank our collaborators for their contribution.

REFERENCES

Aguiar, A., & Baillargeon, R. (2002). Developments in young infant's reasoning about occluded objects. *Cognitive Psychology*, *45*, 267–336.

Baillargeon, R. (1994). Physical reasoning in young infants: Seeking explanations for impossible events. *British Journal of Developmental Psychology*, *12*, 9–33.

Baillargeon, R. (2001). Infants' physical knowledge: Of acquired expectations and core principles. In E. Dupoux (Ed.), *Language, brain, and cognitive development* (pp. 341–361). Cambridge, MA: MIT Press.

Bertenthal, B. I., Campos, J. J., & Haith, M. M. (1980). Development of visual organization: The perception of subjective contours. *Child Development*, *51*, 1072–1080.

Csibra, G. (2001). Illusory contour figures are perceived as occluding surfaces by 8-month-old infants. *Developmental Science*, *4*, F7–F11.

Csibra, G., Davis, G., Spratling, M. W., & Johnson, M. H. (2000). Gamma oscillations and object processing in the infant brain. *Science*, *290*, 1582–1585.

Csibra, G., Tucker, L. A., & Johnson, M. H. (1998). Neural correlates of saccade planning in infants: A high-density ERP study. *International Journal of Psychophysiology*, *29*, 201–215.

Csibra, G., Tucker, L. A., & Johnson, M. H. (2001). Differential frontal cortex activation before anticipatory and reactive saccades in infants. *Infancy*, *2*, 159–174.

Davis, G., & Driver, J. (1998). Kanizsa subjective figures can act as occluding surfaces in preattentive human vision. *Journal of Experimental Psychology; Human Perception and Performance*, *24*, 169–184.

Elliott, M. A., & Müller, J. (2000). Evidence for 40-Hz oscillatory short-term visual memory revealed by human reaction-time measurements. *Journal of Experimental Psychology: Learning, Memory, and Cognition*, *26*, 703–718.

Ghim, H.-R. (1990). Evidence for perceptual organization in infants: Perception of subjective contours in young infants. *Infant Behavior and Development*, *13*, 221–248.

Graziano, M. S. A., Hu, X. U., & Gross, C. G. (1997). Coding the locations of objects in the dark. *Science*, *277*, 239–241.

Grice, S. J., de Haan, M., Halit, H., Johnson, M. H., Csibra, G., & Karmiloff-Smith, A. (2003). ERP abnormalities of visual perception in Williams syndrome. *NeuroReport*, *14*, 1773–1777.

Herrmann, C. S., & Mecklinger, A. (2000). Magnetoencephalographic responses to illusory figures: Early evoked gamma is affected by processing of stimulus features. *International Journal of Psychophysiology*, *38*, 265–281.

Herrmann, C. S., Mecklinger, A., & Pfeifer, W. (1999). Gamma responses and ERPs in a visual classification task. *Clinical Neurophysiology*, *110*, 636–642.

Johnson, M. H., Tucker, L., Stiles, J., & Trauner, D. (1998). Visual attention in infants with perinatal brain damage: Evidence of the importance of anterior lesions. *Developmental Science, 1*, 53–58.

Kanizsa, G. (1976). Subjective contours. *Scientific American, 234*, 48–52.

Kaufman, J., Csibra, G., & Johnson, M. H. (2003). Representing occluded objects in the human infant brain. *Proceedings of the Royal Society London B: Biology Letters, 270/S2*, 140–143.

Kaufman, J., Csibra. G., & Johnson, M. H. (2005). Oscillatory activity in the infant brain reflects object maintenance. *Proceedings of the National Academy of Sciences of the USA, 102*, 15271–15274.

Kavsek, M. J. (2002). The perception of static subjective contours in infancy. *Child Development, 73*, 331–344.

Kavsek, M. (2004). The influence of context on amodal completion in 5- and 7-month-old infants. *Journal of Cognition and Development, 5*, 159–184.

Kellman, P. J., & Banks, M. S. (1998). Infant visual perception. In W. Damon, D. Kuhn, & R. Siegler (Eds.), *Handbook of child development* (5th ed., Vol. 2, pp. 103–146). New York: John Wiley & Sons.

Lachau, J.-P., Lutz, A., Rudrauf, D., Cosmelli, D., Le Van Quyen, M., Martinerie, J. et al. (2002). Estimating the time-course of coherence between single-trial brain signals: An introduction to wavelet coherence. *Neurophysiologie Clinique/Clinical Neurophysiology, 32*, 157–174.

Lachau, J.-P., Rodriguez, E., Martinerie, J., & Varela, F. J. (1999). Measuring phase synchrony in brain signals. *Human Brain Mapping, 8*, 194–208.

Llinás, R. R. (1988). The intrinsic electrophysiological properties of mammalian neurons: Insights into central nervous system function. *Science, 242*, 1654–1664.

Logothetis, N. K., Pauls, J., Augath, M., Trinath, T., & Oeltermann, A. (2001). Neurophysiological investigation of the basis of fMRI signal. *Nature, 412*, 150–157.

Múller, M. M., Bosch, J., Elbert, T., Kreiter, A., Sosa, M. V., Sosa, P. V. et al. (1996). Visually induced gamma-band responses in human electroencephalographic activity—a link to animal studies. *Experimental Brain Research, 112*, 96–102.

Munakata, Y. (2001). Graded representations in behavioral dissociations. *Trends in Cognitive Sciences, 5*, 309–315.

Piaget, J. (1954). *The construction of reality in the child.* New York: Basic Books.

Rainer, G., & Miller, E. K. (2000). Effects of visual experience on the representation of objects in the prefrontal cortex. *Neuron, 27*, 179–189.

Reid, V. M., Csibra, G., Belsky, J., & Johnson, M. H. (in press). Neural correlates of the perception of goal-directed actions in infants. *Acta Psychologica.*

Samar, V. J., Bopardikar, A., Rao, R., & Swartz, K. (1999). Wavelet analysis of neuroelectric waveform: A conceptual tutorial. *Brain and Language, 66*, 7–60.

Scholl, B. J., & Leslie, A. M. (1999). Explaining the infant's object concept: Beyond the perception/cognition dichotomy. In E. Lepore & Z. Pylyshyn (Eds.), *What is cognitive science?* Oxford, UK: Blackwell.

Singer, W., & Gray, C. M. (1995). Visual feature integration and the temporal correlation hypothesis. *Annual Review of Neuroscience, 18*, 555–586.

Tallon-Baudry, C., & Bertrand, O. (1999). Oscillatory gamma activity in humans and its role in object representation. *Trends in Cognitive Sciences, 3*, 151–162.

Tallon-Baudry, C., Bertrand, O., Delpuech, J., & Pernier, J. (1996). Stimulus specificity of phase-locked and non-phase-locked 40 Hz visual responses in human. *Journal of Neuroscience, 16*, 4240–4249.

Tallon-Baudry, C., Bertrand, O., & Pernier, J. (1999). A ring-shaped distribution of dipoles as a source of induced gamma-band activity. *Clinical Neurophysiology, 110,* 660–665.

Tallon-Baudry, C., Bertrand, O., Peronnet, F., & Pernier, J. (1998). Induced gamma-band activity during the delay of a visual short-term memory task in humans. *Journal of Neuroscience, 18,* 4244–4254.

Treisman, A., & Schmidt, H. (1982). Illusory conjunctions in the perception of objects. *Cognitive Psychology, 14,* 107–141.

Varela, F., Lachaux, J.-P., Rodriguez, E., & Martinerie, J. (2001). The brain web: Phase synchronization and large-scale integration. *Nature Reviews Neuroscience, 2,* 229–239.

von Hofsten, C., & Spelke, E. S. (1985). Object perception and object-directed reaching in infancy. *Journal of Experimental Child Psychology, 114,* 198–212.

Wynn, K., & Chiang, W. C. (1998). Limits to infants' object knowledge: The case of magical appearance. *Psychological Science, 9,* 448–455.

11 Current and future directions in infant electrophysiology

Michelle de Haan
Institute of Child Health,
University College London, UK

The use of electrophysiological measures to study perceptual, cognitive, and emotional development during infancy is on the rise. This trend is illustrated in Figure 11.1, which displays the increase in the number of published papers in this area, particularly over the last decade. With an increasing body of literature also comes an increasing need for integration of the existing findings and a consideration of "what next?" This final chapter aims to address these two points by drawing together some of the diverse findings from the previous chapters and considering the way forward under four main themes/ questions: How and why do ERP components and EEG rhythms change during infancy? How are infant ERP components and EEG rhythms related to those seen in adults? What is the role of behavioural measures in infant ERP/EEG research? How useful are ERPs and EEG for studying atypical infant development?

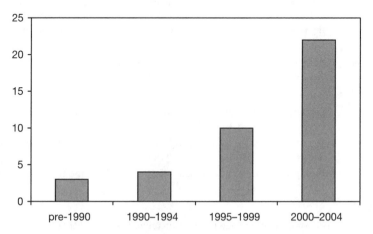

Figure 11.1 Number of citations produce in PubMed search using "infant" and "ERP" as search terms, for the periods prior to 1990, 1990–1994, 1995–1999, and 2000–2004.

HOW AND WHY DO ERPs AND EEG CHANGE OVER INFANCY?

The ERPs and EEG of infants can look strikingly different from those of adults recorded under the same conditions (see Table 11.1 for a list of ERP components and ERO/EEG rhythms in infants according to commonly used labels). The aim of this section is to consider three characteristics of electrophysiological responses that are often noted to differ in infants versus older individuals—amplitude and latency of ERP components, spatial and temporal distribution of responses, and amount of slow wave activity—and to consider the possible brain bases of these changes.

Table 11.1 Labels and brief descriptions of ERP components and EEG/ERO rhythms observed in infants

Component name	Description
Auditory ERP	
P50	Part of the middle-latency response of the auditory evoked potential, peaking at about 50 ms in adults and believed to be involved in the "gating" or suppression of response to irrelevant or repetitive stimuli *Chapter 8*
P2	A large, broad positive deflection over midline electrodes peaking at about 300 ms that is elicited by sounds. Not thought to be equivalent to the P2 elicited by sounds in adults *Chapter 5*
N2	A negative wave following the P2 peaking about 600–900 ms that is elicited by sounds. Not thought to be equivalent to the N2 elicited by sounds in adults
MMN	A pre-attentive change-detection response in the auditory event-related potential that is typically measured as a difference waveform between a standard and deviant stimulus. It is present very early in development although its latency and morphology can vary with age *Chapters 5, 6, 8*
NSW	A negative slow wave that can begin early in recording, overlapping P2, and that may reflect novelty detection *Chapter 5*
Visual EP	
P100	Component of the infant flash visual evoked potential that emerges between term and 15 weeks of age *Chapter 2*
P2	Component of the infant flash visual evoked potential that precedes the N3 and is visible by term *Chapter 2*
N3	Component of the infant visual flash evoked potential that is present in preterms and disappears by 15 weeks of age *Chapter 2*
Visual ERP	
N290	A component in the visual event-related potential that is most prominent over posterior, medial electrodes and may be a developmental precursor of the adult face-sensitive "N170" component *Chapter 3*

P400	A component in the visual event-related potential that is most prominent over posterior electrodes and may be a developmental precursor of the adult face-sensitive "N170" component *Chapter 3*
Pb (or "P2")	A positive component in the infant visual event-related potential that occurs approximately 200–400 ms after stimulus onset that increases across trials and is thought to reflect expectancies as it is sensitive to local probability effects
Nc	A negative component in the infant visual event-related potential that is typically most prominent over anterior sites and is larger in amplitude to salient, attention-getting stimuli *Chapter 4*
PSW or Pc	A positive slow wave that sometimes follows the Nc and is thought to reflect aspects of recognition memory and/or updating of memory representations. Sometimes this late activity is a broad, sustained positivity while other times it is more peaked *Chapters 4, 5*
NSW	A negative slow wave that can follow the Nc, which is thought to reflect detection of novelty *Chapters 4, 5*
ERO	
Gamma	EEG in the gamma range (usually around 40 Hz) that is approximately time-locked to task or stimulus presentation events *Chapter 10*
EEG	
Alpha	A prominent 6–10 Hz rhythm in the infant EEG that is classically most dominant over posterior sites and stronger when eyes are closed than open. It is believed to be inversely proportional to cortical activity *Chapters 8, 9*
Theta	Rhythms in the 4–6 Hz range that are typically more widespread over the scalp compared to alpha rhythms *Chapter 9*
Delta	EEG activity in the 1–3 Hz range that is widespread over the scalp and typically increases amplitude and synchronization with sleep *Chapter 9*
Gamma	EEG activity in the 20–80 Hz range (typically measured around 40 Hz) *Chapters 9, 10*
Mu	A central/anterior rhythm (approximately 6–9 Hz) related to motor functions *Chapter 9*

Note that this list is not necessarily exhaustive and also that terminology for labelling components can vary (the terms used here are those used by the authors in this book). NSW: negative slow wave; PSW: positive slow wave; ERO: event-related oscillation; MMN: mismatch negativity; ERP: event-related potential; EP: evoked potential; EEG: electroencephalogram; ms: milliseconds.

ERP amplitude and latency

ERP components are often said to decrease in latency and increase in amplitude during infancy. However, it is important to note that there are exceptions to this general statement, particularly for amplitude which can show various patterns of developmental change within infancy and beyond. For example, the N3 component in the infant flash visual evoked potential decreases and disappears over the first months of life (see Chapter 2), and some ERP components seem to show a U-shaped pattern with increasing amplitude in infancy but then declining over childhood (see e.g., Chapter 4). Also import-ant to note is that for many components present in the infant ERP there simply have not been enough studies that have used the same procedures and data-processing techniques with different ages to produce a true picture of how amplitude and latency change over the first years of life.

The neurophysiological mechanisms underlying developmental changes in the amplitude and latency of ERP components are not precisely known but could include numerous factors such as myelination, synaptic density and other characteristics of synapses, refractory periods, and the response variability of the generators. With respect to amplitude, the most commonly given mechanism is changes in synaptic density (Courchesne, 1990; Vaughan & Kurtzberg, 1992). Several investigators have noted that developmental changes in synaptic density appear to parallel developmental changes in amplitude of some ERP components, with both showing a U-shaped func-tion of rapid increase in infancy followed by more gradual decline over childhood.

Developmental changes in ERP latency have typically been linked to changes in synaptic efficacy and/or changes in brain myelination (Eggermont, 1998; Ponton, Moore, & Eggermont, 1999). For example, decreases in latency of the Nc component have been related to the myelination of the non-specific thalamic radiation that occurs during the first 7 years of life (Courchesne, 1990), and the rapid decrease in latency of the N1a of the flash VEP around the time of birth has been attributed to the initiation of myelination of the optic radiation (Tsuneishi & Casaer, 2000). While the temporal coincidence of these changes is notable, there is little direct evidence for a developmental connection in humans between degree of myelination and ERP component latency. However, combining brain-imaging techniques with ERPs may pro-vide some more direct support for this view. For example, measures of devel-opmental changes in white matter obtained with diffusion tensor imaging (DTI) could be related to developmental changes in the EEG/ERP, such as changes in the latency of components and/or changes in the EEG coherence across brain areas. A recent case study of full term twins discordant for auditory processing disorder combined the two technologies and showed that the affected twin had both less correlated ERP activity as well as reduced myelin integrity (reduced anisotropy) of the corpus callosum as measured by DTI (Jerger, Martin, & McColl, 2004). These types of investigation will of course be easier in older children or infants with clinical need for MRI, due to the difficulty of obtaining magnetic resonance imaging measures from healthy developing infants.

Several other factors could also cause developmental changes in ERP amplitudes and latencies. For example, an increase in the consistency of the brain's response with age (Thomas & Crow, 1994) could lead to a decrease in latency variability across trials, which could in turn contribute to shortening peak latencies and growing peak amplitudes. Another factor is that maturational changes in one ERP component or slow wave can affect the amplitude or latency of another component with which it overlaps. For example, the decrease of the auditory P150 latency could well be caused by the growing N250 that overlaps with it. Other factors that could contribute include developmental increases or decreases in the neural generators participating in the response, or in physical factors such as skull thickness.

Spatial and temporal distribution

In the ERP and event-related oscillation, several investigators have noted that infant components appear to be more widely distributed in space and in time than their putative mature counterparts. Some specific examples are presented throughout this book: (a) the infant MMN is more widespread in space across studies and not as consistently fronto-centrally focused as in adults, and it is also more spread over time (see Cheour, Chapter 6, this volume). (b) The influence of inversion on the face-selective components observed in infants appears to occur over a prolonged period compared to adults (see de Haan et al., Chapter 3, this volume). (c) Fluctuation in gamma-band in 6-month-olds in an illusory contour task appear as "smeared" over time rather than in the discrete bursts observed in adults (see Csibra & Johnson, Chapter 10, this volume).

Developmental changes in the spatial characteristics of ERP components could occur for many reasons. For example, developmental differences in factors such as skull thickness or bone conductance, or physical changes in the brain might contribute. It is also possible that such changes are in part a reflection of a lesser degree of functional specialisation within the infant brain, with larger regions of cortex being recruited for the same task in infants compared to adults (see Cheour, Chapter 6, this volume or Johnson, 2000, for further discussion). As discussed above, developmental increases in the consistency of the brain's response might account for why in some instances infants' responses seem more protracted. Single trial analysis can help to determine whether the "smeared" responses observed in individuals' averages are due to protracted responses occurring at the single trial level or due to trial-to-trial variability in the timing of the response.

Slow wave activity

Several investigators have noted that there is a predominance of slow wave (delta/theta) activity in the infant ERP and EEG that decreases with development (e.g., Clarke, Barry, McCarthy, & Selikowitz, 2001; Marshall, Bar-Haim, & Fox, 2002; Trainor et al., 2003). The EEG power spectrum is mediated by an anatomically complex and diverse system that involves brainstem, thalamic, hippocampal, and cortical/cortical neuronal pathways.

Specific portions of this system are involved in the generation of EEG within each frequency band, the interaction of activity among these generators being responsible for the frequency distribution of the EEG (Steriade, Gloor, Llinas, Lopes da Silva, & Mesulam, 1990). It is possible that the predominance of lower-frequency activity seen in the infant EEG reflects relatively less cortical/cortical generator activity and more thalmocortical and hippocampal/septal generator activity.

Summary

While there is some information about developmental changes in EEG and in ERP components and the physical bases of these changes, more systematic study in this area is needed. A good grasp of the normative pattern of development is important for application of these measures to the study of developmental disorders to determine, for example, whether a particular condition reflects delayed or deviant development. A better understanding of the neural bases of these developmental changes could be more challenging to achieve. In humans, combining ERPs/EEG with other imaging modalities could prove useful in understanding how physical changes in the brain contribute to changing electrical activity recorded from the scalp, although the options for other imaging methods are somewhat limited when studying normal infant development. Animal models could provide a complementary source of information regarding the particular brain regions and how their developmental changes contribute to the development of scalp-recorded activity. For example, depth recordings in developing monkeys could provide information about the location of generators of surface-recorded ERPs (see e.g., Javitt, Steinschneider, Schroeder, Vaughan, & Arezzo, 1994, for an animal model of adult MMN), or studies of monkeys who have sustained lesions of particular structures at different ages.

HOW DO INFANT ERP COMPONENTS AND EEG RHYTHMS RELATE TO THOSE IN ADULTS?

Given the developmental changes in EEG and ERP described above, an important question for many researchers using ERPs and EEG with infants is how the responses observed in infants relate to those obtained in older children and adults. This is discussed in Chapter 9 with respect to definition of alpha in the EEG, in Chapter 6 with respect to identifying the mismatch negativity (MMN), in Chapter 4 with respect to memory-related ERP components, and in Chapter 3 with respect to identifying face-sensitive ERP components in infants.

In studies of adults, ERP components can be identified by examining their peak latencies, morphology, and spatial distribution. For example, a target-elicited P300 can be defined as a positive component peaking between

300 and 500 ms with a parietal maximum. Similarly EEG activity such as the alpha rhythm can be defined by its bandwidth and spatial distribution. Identifying the infant equivalents of such components and rhythm is not simply a matter of applying the same criteria to the younger age groups. Investigations of ERPs during childhood and old age have clearly shown that timing and topography of components can change across the lifespan (e.g., Taylor & Pang, 1999). One basic approach to identifying the infant and child equivalents of adult ERP components and EEG rhythms has been a functional one: test younger and older participants under the same conditions and look for components/rhythms that show similar stimulus- or task-related modulations across age. This approach has been used, for example, in studies of MMN as described in Chapter 6, or face-selective ERP components in Chapter 4, and is discussed in Chapter 9 for EEG rhythms.

This functional approach in some ways stands in contrast to the typical explanations given for why ERPs and EEG change with age (described in the previous section), which usually focus on physical changes in brain rather than functional changes. While a functional approach may allow developmental tracking of a particular cognitive function, it may not track development of a particular brain region/system. Developmental research has indicated that what appears the same behavioural response or cognitive operation could be mediated by different brain regions at different points in development (Bates, Vicari, & Trauner, 2000; Malkova, Bachevalier, Webster, & Mishkin, 2000). Thus it is possible that a functional approach would result in tapping different neural generators at different ages.

Increasing use of high-density electrode arrays with infants and young children may help better tracking of the neural generators of ERP components with development. High-density arrays allow a better characterisation of spatial distribution of responses as well as source analyses to identify their probable generators. There are some difficulties in applying source analyses to infant ERP data (e.g., the typical available programmes for such analysis use a head model based on adults), a few studies have attempted these analyses and produced interesting results (e.g., Johnson et al., 2005; Reynolds & Richards, 2005). Developments in this area are important, as better understanding of the neural bases of developmental changes in ERP components will also provide insight into the neural bases of the cognitive processes that these components are thought to reflect.

WHAT IS THE ROLE OF BEHAVIOURAL MEASURES IN ERP/EEG RESEARCH?

Use of ERPs in infants is often described as an alternative to behavioural measures, or a technique that is of use because it does not require an overt behavioural response. Indeed, behavioural responses during infant ERP/EEG experiments are often to be avoided to prevent artefacts, and typical infants' behaviour is monitored or controlled in some way so as to minimise movement-related artefact. Typically if behavioural measures are included, they are collected at a separate time and then related to the ERP/EEG results to provide a behavioural correlate for an electrophysiological response. For example, as described in Chapter 4 for the Nc, several investigators have attempted to link Nc amplitude with behavioural measures of visual attention to provide evidence for its putative role in attentional orienting, or to link positive slow wave activity with later tests of visual recognition memory. In some cases responses have actually been successfully incorporated into electrophysiological experiments with infants, such as documenting changes in facial expressions during EEG recording (Davidson & Fox, 1986) and recording eye-movement-locked ERPs in order to investigate the planning of eye movements (Csibra, Tucker, & Johnson, 1998; Csibra, Tucker, Volein, & Johnson, 2000).

More recently, investigators have attempted to devise methods to record ERPs during more traditional tasks of infant cognition, such as the visual paired comparison test of memory. In this task, infants are first familiarised to one stimulus and then presented with the familiar stimulus alongside a novel one. Typically infants demonstrate their memory for the familiar stimulus by looking longer at the novel one. As this task involves switching visual attention from one to the other stimulus, artefact due to eye movement makes recording of ERPs during this task challenging. Reynolds, Courage, and Richards (unpublished data) approached this problem by using independent components analysis to identify and remove eye-movement-related components from the ERP, and they did find a relationship between the size of the Nc component and infants' looking.

Behavioural measures are also important for consideration in study design, as infant electrophysiological studies are often labour intensive and time consuming. Using results from behavioural studies to direct these studies can be very useful, for example with respect to which age to test or which stimuli to use (see also Chapter 1 for further discussion). For example, in Chapter 10 Csibra and Johnson describe an ERO study of perception of illusory contours, which was based in prior behavioural studies demonstrating the ages at which infants appear to begin to "see" the contours. The differences they discovered in the ERO are compelling in part because of their parallel with the behavioural findings.

Summary

Other than measures used to verify that infants are engaging in appropriate behaviour that does not interfere with electrophysiological recordings, most infant ERP/EEG studies do not record behavioural responses during recording sessions. This is mainly due to two factors: (a) the infant's limited response repertoire making response options limited, and (b) responses causing artefacts in the recordings. Behavioural measures remain important in

ERP/EEG research however, as providing an important theoretical framework and background for task design, and providing a link for interpreting the functional significance of ERP components and EEG activity. Future increases in the ingenuity of experimenters in incorporating these measures without interfering with recording, or in devising statistical techniques that allow any resulting unwanted influence on the ERP to be removed, will help to ground electrophysiological responses more solidly in a behavioural framework.

HOW USEFUL ARE ERPs AND EEG FOR THE STUDY OF ATYPICAL DEVELOPMENT?

A question of interest to many researchers is how useful infant ERPs and EEG are for detecting atypical development, either with respect to detecting actual dysfunction in infancy or in identifying those at risk for later-developing impairments. The fact that EEG and ERPs can be obtained passively and do not require an overt behavioural response, and indeed for some measures do not require active attention at all, makes them especially appealing both for studying potentially delayed infants and also for longitudinal study, as the same response could be measured over a wide frame of development (see deRegnier, 2005, for a review of use of ERPs to detect atypical cognitive development in infants).

There have been some remarkably successful applications of EEG and ERPs to detection/evaluation of impairments in young infants. The EEG is a commonly used clinical tool for evaluating brain dysfunction in young infants and diagnosing disorders, e.g., epilepsy. With respect to time-locked responses, their utility in detecting atypical development has been most fully assessed for responses that are relatively easy to obtain, such as auditory MMN and the flash visual evoked potentials that have low attentional demands and in fact can even be obtained from sleeping infants. The visual evoked potential in particular has also provided a very useful clinical tool for assessing whether visual pathways are intact and developing normally (see Chapter 2). The use of EEG and ERPs to detect or predict cognitive or social/emotional impairments is much less well developed. However, Chapters 4–7 do illustrate that ERPs can be useful in differentiating at-risk from typically developing infants and in predicting later cognitive skill, and that at least in some cases they appear more sensitive than traditional, behaviourally based tests. However, the specificity and sensitivity of these measures have not been established, and this area of research has some way to go before ERPs could be used reliably for diagnosis or evaluation of risk at the individual level. As indicated previously, more normative data and information about the consistency of individuals' responses over test sessions are needed for this to be possible.

CONCLUSIONS

The growth of literature using EEG and ERP measures to study infant
perceptual, cognitive, and emotional development is promising, as more
researchers using these tools will result in a more detailed understanding of
the changes in these responses that occur over a period when the brain is
rapidly developing. Although fairly well developed in some cases (e.g., visual
evoked potentials), in many cases more systematic studies tracking the development of electrophysiological responses at frequent points over infancy are
still needed. The feasibility of carrying out such studies will be greatly helped
by ongoing advances in data-processing techniques and experimental design
that will allow as many data as possible to be retained from as many infants
as possible. An important direction for future research efforts is integration
of electrophysiological studies with other measures and approaches, with
respect to a link both with behaviour to understand the functional significance of the responses and their developmental changes, but also with other
imaging modalities or approaches that provide information about how physical changes in the developing brain affect the electrophysiological response.
The growing fields of developmental cognitive neuroscience and developmental social neuroscience provide important theoretical backdrops in this
regard, to allow researchers to frame their work in a broader context than
psychophysiology in isolation. Our better understanding of the interplay
between the functional and neural changes and how they are expressed in the
electrical activity recorded from the scalp will provide important insight into
how the human brain develops during infancy, and will also be an important
backdrop for understanding atypical development.

REFERENCES

Bates, E., Vicari, S., & Trauner, D. (2000). Neural mediation of language development: Perspectives from lesion studies of infants and children. In H. Tager-Flusberg
(Ed.), *Neurodevelopmental disorders* (pp. 533–581). Cambridge, MA: MIT Press.
Clarke, A. R., Barry, R. J., McCarthy, R., & Selikowitz, M. (2001). Age and sex effects in
the EEG: Development of the normal child. *Clinical Neurophysiology, 112,* 806–814.
Courchesne, E. (1990). Chronology of postnatal human brain development: Event
related potential, positron emission tomography, myelinogenesis and synaptogenesis studies. In J. W. Rohrbaugh, R. Parasuraman, & R. Johnson Jr. (Eds.), *Event
related brain potentials: Basic issues and applications* (pp. 210–241). New York:
Oxford University Press.
Csibra, G., Tucker, L. A., & Johnson, M. H. (1998). Neural correlates of saccade
planning in infants: A high-density ERP study. *International Journal of Psychophysiology, 29,* 201–215.
Csibra, G., Tucker, L. A., Volein, A., & Johnson, M. H. (2000). Cortical development
and saccade planning: The ontogeny of the spike potential. *NeuroReport, 11,*
1069–1073.

Davidson, R. J., & Fox, N. A. (1986). Taste-elicited changes in facial signs of emotion and the asymmetry of brain electrical activity in human newborns. *Neuropsychologia, 24,* 417–422.

deRegnier, R. A. (2005). Neurophysiologic evaluation of early cognitive development in high-risk infants and toddlers. *Mental Retardation and Developmental Disabilities Research Review, 11,* 317–324.

Eggermont, J. J. (1998). On the rate of maturation of sensory evoked potentials. *Electroencephalography and Clinical Neurophysiology, 70,* 293–305.

Javitt, D. C., Steinschneider, M., Schroeder, C. E., Vaughan, H. G. Jr, & Arezzo, J. C. (1994). Detection of stimulus deviance within the primate auditory cortex: Intra-cortical mechanisms of mismatch negativity (MMN) generation. Brain Research, 667, 192–200.

Jerger, J., Martin, J., & McColl, R. (2004). Interaural cross correlation of event-related potentials and diffusion tensor imaging in the evaluation of auditory processing disorder: A case study. *Journal of the American Academy of Audiology, 15,* 79–87.

Johnson, M. H. (2000). Functional brain development in infants: Elements of an interactive specialization framework. *Child Development, 71,* 75–81.

Johnson, M. H., Griffin, R., Csibra, G., Halit, H., Farroni, T., de Haan, M. et al. (2005). The emergence of the social brain network: Evidence from typical and atypical development. *Development and Psychopathology, 17,* 599–619.

Malkova, L., Bachevalier, J., Webster, M., & Mishkin, M. (2000). Effects of neonatal inferior prefrontal and medial temporal lesions on learning the rule for delayed nonmatching-to-sample. *Developmental Neuropsychology, 18,* 399–421.

Marshall, P. J., Bar-Haim, Y., & Fox, N. A. (2002). Development of the EEG from 5 months to 4 years of age. *Clinical Neurophysiology, 113,* 1199–1208.

Ponton, C. W., Moore, J. K., & Eggermont, J. J. (1999). Prolonged deafness limits auditory system developmental plasticity: Evidence from an evoked potentials study in children with cochlear implants. *Scandinavian Audiology, 51,* 13–22.

Reynolds, G. D., Courage, M. L., & Richards, J. E. (unpublished). Infant visual preferences within the modified-oddball ERP paradigm. Summary on http://jerlab. psych.sc.edu./richardsinfo/summary3.htm

Reynolds, G., & Richards, J. E. (2005). Familiarization, attention and recognition memory in infancy: An event-related potential and cortical source localization study. *Developmental Psychology, 41,* 598–615.

Steriade, M., Gloor, P., Llinas, R. R., Lopes da Silva, F., & Mesulam, M. M. (1990). Basic mechanisms of cerebral rhythmic activities. *Electroencephalography and Clinical Neurophysiology, 76,* 481–508.

Taylor, M. J., & Pang, E. W. (1999). Developmental changes in early cognitive processes. *Electroencephalography and Clinical Neurophysiology Suppl., 49,* 145–153.

Thomas, D. G., & Crow, C. D. (1994). Development of evoked electrical brain activity in infancy. In G. Dawson & K. Fischer (Eds.), *Human behaviour and the developing brain* (pp. 207–231). New York: Guilford Press

Trainor, L., McFadden, M., Hodgson, L., Darragh, L., Barlow, J., Matsos, L. et al. (2003). Changes in the auditory cortex and the development of mismatch negativity between 2 and 6 months of age. *International Journal of Psychophysiology, 51,* 5–15.

Tsuneishi, S., & Casaer, J. (2000). Effects of preterm extrauterine visual experience on the development of the human visual system: A flash VEP study. *Developmental Medicine and Child Neurology, 42,* 663–668.

Vaughan, H. G. Jr., & Kurtzberg, D. (1992). Electrophysiologic indices of human brain maturation and cognitive development. In M. R. Gunnar & C. A. Nelson (Eds.), *Minnesota Symposia on Child Psychology Vol. 24* (pp. 1–36). Hillsdale, NJ: Lawrence Erlbaum Associates Inc.

Glossary of ERP/EEG terminology

Jane Cownie
Institute of Child Health,
University College London, UK

A/D board   analogue/digital board—hardware that converts the analogue signal from the electrodes to digital format in order for the signal to be displayed, manipulated, and saved through computer software.

aliasing   a distortion in the data that occurs when the sampling frequency is set too low. Typically avoided by setting the high-frequency filter at or below the **Nyquist frequency**.

amplifier   equipment located at the end of the electrode leads, which acts to magnify the relatively weak electrical signal coming from the brain.

amplitude (average)   a measure of the size (level of deflection) in an ERP **component** or **slow wave** calculated by taking the average amplitude across time points over the period during which the component occurs.

amplitude (peak)   a measure of the size (level of deflection) in an ERP **component** calculated as the amplitude value at the single time point at which the component shows the greatest microvolt deflection; this can be either positive or negative.

area scores   a measure of the size of an ERP **component** or **slow wave** calculated as the area above or below baseline of the component or slow wave.

artefact   an event on the ERP output that is not the result of the surface brain activity being measured. This may be caused by factors such as eye movements, including blinks, other bodily movement, or by electrical equipment in the testing room.

average   the combination of all trials from the same condition, and the same subject, to form a representative response for that subject, under that condition.

average reference   the referencing of data to an average of all the channels, rather than the arbitrary value provided by a **reference electrode**. Typically used only for high-density recordings.

baseline   a selected length of time on the ERP waveform usually immediately preceding the time point at which the stimulus is presented. The amplitude of an ERP **component** is typically computed relative to this baseline.

baseline correction   a procedure performed after data collection to normalise the baseline on an ERP trial so that it is close to zero. For example, if a waveform is shifted up, a value of microvolts may be subtracted from the waveform that will result in the baseline being close to zero. Note that this will not skew the magnitude of neurophysiological effect because the same calculation is performed uniformly to the entire waveform.

bipolar recording   recording of electrical current by referencing one active electrode to another to produce a differential value; mostly used in **EOG**.

blink correction   the process of removing **artefacts** caused by eye blinks from ERP data.

channel   the term used for any single electrode and/or its output.

component   a constituent part of the EEG output that, after averaging, remains prominent and represents brain processing in response to the time-locked stimuli. Terming of a component refers to its charge and its latency, for example the P300 is a positively deflected component, which peaks approximately 300 ms after stimulus onset.

current sink and source   the sink is where current flows in, and the source is where current flows out.

current source density   (surface Laplacian)—a type of topographical mapping of electrophysiological data, displayed in a similar way as a **spline map**, but in which the data have been recalculated in such a way as to emphasise **current sinks and sources**.

dipole   an entity with both a positive and negative charge.

endogenous   said of electrophysiological activity that is dependent on the participant's mental state and cognitive processes, for example attention or memory, rather than being solely determined by the physical parameters of the stimuli being presented.

EOG   Electro-oculogram—a measure of eye function utilised by recording the electrical charge produced as the eye moves. In ERP recording this is used in order to track eye movements that may produce **artefacts** in the data.

epoch   any stretch of continuous EEG output.

exogenous   said of electrophysiological activity that is elicited automatically by the stimuli presented to a participant externally.

filter   a function used to eliminate from the waveform activity above and/or below a certain frequency range. A high-pass (or low-frequency) filter excludes activity below a given frequency, while a low-pass (or high-frequency) filter excludes activity above a given frequency.

fontanel   membranous structure situated between the various bones of the skull, which develops to fuse these bones together in neonates. The largest fontanel, at the top centre of the skull, is the last to fuse, leaving an opening well after birth.

Fourier analysis   a computation by which real-world signals such as EEG can be approximated as a series of sine or cosine waves of varying frequencies.

gain   the value by which the electrical signal from the brain is amplified, for example a gain of 50 would increase amplitude by 50 times.

grand average the combination of all subjects' averaged ERPs, from the same conditions, to produce a cross-subject ERP.

ground electrode a recording point connected in such a way as to conduct electrical current to the ground to include it in the electrical circuit.

head room the data range that the **A/D board** is set to accept. This may differ between populations being tested, for example adults often have a headroom of $\pm$ 100 μV and infants' $\pm$ 250 μV.

high density refers to the coverage of the scalp by a recording system with more than 32, and up to 256, electrodes.

impedance the resistance level that affects the transfer of the brain's electrical activity to the receiving electrodes. A high level of impedance is susceptible to encouraging the reception of external electrical sources, which will distort EEG output.

independent component analysis a form of **source separation**.

inion protuberance at the back centre of the skull; a reference point used for taking measurements in the **International 10–20 system**.

International 10–20 system a common measurement and labelling system used to provide systematic and consistent placement of electrodes in certain locations on the scalp.

interpolation the process of assigning voltage values to the space between electrodes based on the surrounding electrodes' voltage. Spherical splines and three-dimensional splines are two calculation methods commonly used for interpolation in EEG/ERP.

latency refers to the time lag between the display of a stimulus and the resulting peak in EEG activity.

mastoids bony protuberance of the skull located behind each ear.

monopolar recording recording of electrical current from single active electrodes referenced to a set scalp location, producing differential values.

morphology the form and structure of the EEG waveform.

nasion area of the face where the top of the nose and forehead meet; a reference point used for taking measurements in the **International 10–20 system**.

noise the general term given to any irrelevant, excessive activity in the EEG output.

notch filter a **filter** process selected to block a given frequency range, allowing frequencies above and below this set parameter to pass. Typically notch filters are used to selectively filter out mains frequency.

nyquist frequency the highest frequency that can be accurately sampled at a given sampling rate; it is calculate as one-half the sampling frequency.

oddball paradigm a procedure for presenting stimuli where one stimulus is presented frequently and a second is presented infrequently.

offline the term given to viewing the data collected after an ERP recording has been completed.

online the term given to viewing, and possibly intervening in, data collection as an ERP recording is ongoing, or active.

oscillations   fluctuations in electrical signal recorded from the brain, regularly changing from a maximum to a minimum point.

reference electrode   an electrode, positioned at a given point such as the vertex, nose tip, or ear lobe, and given an arbitrary value of zero. The other active electrodes are compared to the reference and a difference value assigned as their activity level.

re-reference   a mathematical calculation that allows for changing, by recalculating, the site of the reference electrode used, or to another method such as **average reference**.

sampling rate   the frequency with which the analogue signal from the electrodes is converted, by the **A/D board**, to the digital signal displayed on the computer.

signal-to-noise ratio   A measure of the strength of the signal (e.g., ERP **component**) relative to non-relevant content. Typically ERPs for an individual are averaged over a number of presentations in order to increase the signal-to-noise ratio.

slow wave   large-amplitude, low-frequency EEG output. In the ERP, broad, sustained deflections with prominent peaks are also often called slow waves.

source localisation   a process that infers the magnitude, orientation, and location of dipoles in the brain from the ERP **components** recorded.

source separation   a statistical process that attempts to analyse and split simultaneous ERP activity into its distinctly generated elements.

spike   a type of transient EEG abnormality that is seen as a sharp deflection, usually of less than 70 ms duration.

spline map   a type of topographical mapping of the amplitude of the EEG/ ERP signal at a given time point. Typically it displays the voltages as different colours over a model head. Positive and negative voltages are displayed as different colours, with the intensity of the colour representing the magnitude of the positive or negative voltage, and with values between electrodes **interpolated**.

time window   a time frame identified within which a known **component** can occur.

topography   the distribution of electrical activity across the surface of the scalp.

vertex   the highest, central point of the head, obtained by measuring the half-way point on the skull between the **inion** and **nasion**, and also that between the area directly in front of both ears.

volume conduction   the propagation of electrical signal through brain tissue; the latter may differ in density and conductivity, therefore affecting the signal's strength.

Author index

Aaltonen, O. 173, 179, 184
Abrams, J. M. 22, 23
Abramson, A. S. 211
Acebo, C. 173
Achim, A. 236
Ackles, P. K. 85, 91, 101, 103, 104, 106, 114, 115, 126
Adelman, C. 150
Adler, L. E. 240, 241
Adrien, J. L. 179
Aftanas, L. 276
Agarwal, N. 179
Aguiar, A. 297
Ahonen, T. 210
Ahonniska, J. 155
Ainsworth, A. R. 50
Aitink, J. W. 277
Aiyer, A. D. 55
Akaho, R. 173
Alain, C. 236
Algazi, A. 171, 172
Alho, K. 171, 172, 173, 174, 176, 177, 178, 182, 183, 184, 185, 199, 200, 236, 237
Alku, P. 110, 177, 179, 199, 237, 238
Allen, D. 51, 54
Allen, J. J. 234
Allen, M. 179
Allik, J. 174, 176, 177, 178, 200
Allison, T. 77, 78, 81, 82, 84, 85, 91, 92
Almqvist, F. 181
Alvarez, A. 230
Alvarez, T. D. 88
Amaral, D. G. 146, 147
Amin, S. B. 149, 150
Amlie, R. N. 145, 149, 150
Amry, S. E. 60
Anderer, P. 173
Andersen, S. L. 278
Anderson, A. W. 78, 79, 152
Anderson, C. M. 278
Anderson, G. F. 181
Andreason, P. 179
Andrew, C. 179
Andrews Espy, K. 205, 216
Anker, S. 54
Anllo-Vento, L. 81
Apkarian, P. 43, 44, 61, 62
Appelbaum, L. G. 88
Aprile, T. 39
Arai, M. 50, 51
Archbold, S. 181

Archbold, S. M. 181
Arciniegas, D. 240
Arden, G. B. 58, 59
Arezzo, J. C. 39, 310
Armstrong, C. A. 50
Arnolds, D. E. 277
Aro, M. 209, 220
Aronen, E. 110, 237, 238
Aronen, E. T. 181
Ary, J. P. 56
Asada, H. 277
Aslin, R. N. 56
Aso, J. 46
Astikainen, P. 171
Atienza, M. 173, 277
Atkin, A. 63
Atkinson, J. 51, 54, 55, 57, 63
Augath, M. 301
Auinger, P. 267, 268
Austin, G. 179
Aylward, E. 212

Bach, M. 40, 41, 43, 44, 46, 48, 59
Bachevalier, J. 118, 121, 311
Badier, J. M. 241
Baillargeon, R. 296, 297
Baillet, S. 177, 178
Baitch, L. 56
Baitch, L. W. 56
Baker, N. 240
Baker, P. 152
Baker, R. S. 56
Balan, P. 150, 174, 176, 238
Baldeweg, T. 6, 9, 17, 26, 27
Ball, A. K. R. 185
Ballantyne, J. 47
Bane, M. C. 48, 50
Banks, M. S. 50, 54, 293
Barber, C. 41, 46, 59
Bargallo, N. 160
Bar-Haim, Y. 7, 9, 181, 228, 229, 236, 237, 240, 265, 266, 309
Barkley, R. A. 180
Barlow, J. 309
Barnard, W. M. 58, 59
Barnet, A. B. 63
Baron-Cohen, S. 179
Barrett, S. E. 80, 87
Barry, R. J. 229, 257, 309
Barthelemy, C. 173, 179, 236, 237
Bartling, J. 182
Bartussek, D. 234
Basar, E. 277
Basar-Eroglu, C. 277

Bastien, C. 173
Bates, E. 311
Battin, M. 162
Bauer, P. J. 12, 101, 107, 108, 109, 110, 119, 128, 130, 134, 137, 160, 161, 163
Bazhenova, O. 275
Bazhenova, O. V. 276
Beers, A. P. A. 48
Beke, A. 178
Bell, A. J. 32
Bell, I. 173
Bell, M. A. 1, 12, 227, 229, 233, 253, 255, 267
Bellugi, U. 88
Belsky, J. 86, 104, 106, 133, 301
Benasich, A. A. 173, 174
Benninger, C. 257
Benson, P. 199
Bentin, S. 17, 21, 27, 77, 82, 92
Berezovsky, A. 61
Berg, P. 17, 21, 22, 27, 33, 213
Bergman, E. 179, 212
Berman, J. L. 56
Bernard, C. 82
Berninger, V. 212
Bertenthal, B. I. 293
Berti, S. 110
Bertolasi, L. 56
Bertrand, O. 289, 291, 293, 295, 296, 301
Bieber, M. L. 54
Binder, J. R. 208
Birch, D. G. 46, 60
Birch, E. 50, 57
Birch, E. E. 46, 48, 50, 55, 59, 60
Bissenden, J. G. 43, 46, 57
Blanchfield, B. 181
Blomberg, A. P. 172
Blondeau, C. 263
Bloom, D. 103, 104, 108, 109, 110, 114, 119, 126
Bodis-Wollner, I. 57, 63
Boeijinga, P. 277
Bongiovanni, L. G. 56
Boothe, R. 55
Bopardikar, A. 290
Borchert, M. 61
Bormans, G. 268
Borscheid, A. J. 160, 163
Bosch, J. 254, 268, 293
Bosser, J. 185
Bouchet, P. 179

Bouyer, J. J. 262, 267
Bozic, V. S. 80
Braddick, O. 63
Braddick, O. J. 51, 54, 55, 57
Bradlow, A. R. 183
Bradnam, M. S. 47, 48
Brady, S. 212
Braff, D. L. 240
Brammer, M. 179
Brauer, F. 262
Braun, C. 255
Brecelj, J. 46, 60
Breier, J. I. 179, 212
Bremer, D. L. 60
Brent, H. P. 93
Briassoulis, G. 145, 150
Brigell, J. 41, 46
Brigell, M. 41, 46, 59
Broadbent, N. J. 145, 147
Brooks, B. B. 231
Broughton, R. J. 253
Brown, C. III 9
Brown, G. 43
Brown, R. J. 56, 59
Bruder, G. E. 199
Bruneau, N. 173, 179, 236, 237
Bruyer, R. 82
Buitelaar, J. K. 180
Bullier, J. 39
Buncic, J. R. 50
Buncic, R. J. 63
Bunge, S. A. 241
Burns, T. 17
Burr, D. C. 54
Burton, A. M. 80, 82, 92
Burton, L. C. 61
Busby, K. A. 174
Buser, P. 262, 267
Buss, K. A. 8, 12, 233
Butler, B. 200, 214
Butler, S. 171
Buwalda, B. 160
Buzzonetti, L. 61
Byatt, G. 78
Byerley, W. 240

Cacioppo, J. T. 234
Cadena, C. 178
Calkins, S. D. 7, 27, 228, 233, 236, 237
Camfferman, G. 179, 180
Cammann, R. 173
Campanella, S. 81
Campbell, K. 173
Campbell, K. B. 173
Campos, J. J. 293
Candy, R. C. 51
Candy, T. R. 50, 54, 56, 57
Cannistraci, C. J. 162
Cantell, M. 155
Cantero, J. L. 173, 277
Cantwell, D. P. 180, 229
Caplan, J. B. 275, 277
Card, J. 12, 229
Card, J. A. 275
Carey, S. 78, 79
Carlesimo, G. A. 88
Carmel, D. 27, 82
Carrell, T. 173, 177
Carrell, T. D. 172, 174, 177, 181, 183, 208
Cartee, C. 241
Carter, L. P. 268
Carver, L. 87

Carver, L. J. 12, 16, 86, 107, 108, 109, 110, 119, 128, 130, 131
Casaer, J. 308
Casaer, P. 43
Casey, B. J. 107, 152, 179, 241
Castellanos, F. X. 179, 180
Castelloe, P. 234
Catts, H. 212
Cawthra, E. 240
Ceponiene, R. 110, 150, 162, 173, 174, 176, 177, 178, 179, 181, 182, 183, 185, 200, 236, 237, 238
Chabot, R. J. 229, 230
Chandna, A. 55, 59
Chaney, L. 103, 104, 108, 109, 110, 114, 119, 126
Chang, S. 46, 50
Chao, L. L. 241
Chatterjee, A. 268
Chatterjee, S. 57
Chauvel, P. 241
Cheatham, C. L. 101, 108, 110, 137
Chemtob, S. 46
Cheng, A. K. 181
Cheng, J. 237
Cheour, M. 11, 171, 173, 174, 175, 176, 177, 178, 182, 183, 185, 200, 208, 210, 219, 236, 237
Cheour-Luhtanen, M. 173, 174
Chiang, W. C. 297
Chichon, S. 183
Chien, S. H. L. 54
Chiron, C. 179
Cho, N. H. 162
Chong, W. K. 160, 161
Christophe, A. 200
Chugani, H. T. 263, 273
Chun, M. M. 78
Cigánek, L. 59
Clare, S. 152
Clark, R. E. 145, 147
Clarke, A. R. 229, 257, 309
Clarke, M. P. 63
Clementz, B. A. 240
Coan, J. A. 234
Cohn, R. 199
Coles, M. G. H. 25, 208, 235
Collins, A. D. 56
Collins, P. F. 103, 104, 106, 113, 114, 118, 124, 155
Colson, E. R. 152
Connell, S. 202
Cook, E. H. Jr 180
Cook, K. G. 101, 103, 104, 106, 114, 115, 126
Coon, H. 240
Cooper, F. 212
Coppola, R. 253
Corbetta, M. 268
Corina, D. 212
Corkin, S. 117
Cornblatt, B. 9
Cosmelli, D. 291
Cottrell, G. W. 82
Counsell, S. J. 162
Counter, S. A. 149
Courage, M. L. 117, 312
Courchesne, E. 1, 9, 85, 86, 103, 104, 107, 112, 114, 115, 123, 179, 308
Cowan, N. 171, 237
Cox, N. J. 180
Crepin, G. 153

Crognale, M. A. 46, 50, 54, 58
Crommelinck, M. 79
Crow, C. D. 172, 264, 308
Csépe, V. 172, 174, 177, 178, 179, 208
Csibra, G. 82, 84, 92, 230, 252, 291, 293, 294, 296, 300, 301, 311, 312
Cunningham, J. 181, 183
Cunningham, N. 207, 212
Cuperus, J. M. 179
Curry, S. H. 172
Curtis, W. J. 160, 161
Cycowicz, Y. M. 237, 238
Czigler, I. 177

Dabholkar, A. S. 148
Dager, S. 212
Dahl, R. E. 60
Dale, N. 59
Dalton, K. M. 233
Dalzell, L. E. 149, 150
Danahy, T. 154
D'Angio, G. 63
Darragh, L. 309
Das, A. 181
Daseleer, S. M. 146, 160
Davalos, M. 8
Davidoff, J. 82
Davidson, M. 152
Davidson, M. L. 28–9
Davidson, R. J. 8, 12, 26, 231, 232, 233, 234, 253, 257, 312
Davis, G. 230, 252, 293, 294, 295
Davis, M. 102, 103, 104, 110, 114, 138
Davis, R. 103, 104, 108, 109, 110, 114, 119, 126
Dawson, G. 8, 11, 86, 87, 107, 108, 110, 131, 234, 253, 257, 267
Day, J. 57
Day, R. E. 47
De Bruyn, B. 268
De Courten, C. 172
de Haan, M. 8, 16, 21, 22, 26, 32, 33, 77, 79, 80, 81, 82, 83, 84, 85, 86, 88, 90, 91, 92, 101, 102, 103, 104, 106, 107, 108, 109, 112, 114, 115–16, 117, 121, 125, 128, 133, 160, 161, 230, 301, 311
De Meirlier, L. J. 62, 63
deRegnier, R. 86, 104, 107, 108, 110, 114, 115, 120, 129, 160, 163
deRegnier, R.-A. 102, 113, 120, 126, 155, 160, 313
De Renzi, E. 78
de Schonen, S. 8, 86, 88, 114, 115, 128
de Vries, L. 145, 150
Deacon, D. 171
Debatisse, D. 81
DeBoer, T. 134, 163
Debray, O. 262, 267
DeCasper, A. J. 153, 157
Dedet, L. 262, 267
Deecke, L. 80, 87, 90
Degiovanni, E. 81, 82, 84, 85, 91
Dehaene, S. 152, 174, 176
Dehaene-Lambertz, G. 85, 152, 174, 176, 177, 178, 200
Deimel, W. 182
Delapierre, G. 263
Deldin, P. 235
Delinte, A. 81

Delon-Martin, C. 39
Delpuech, J. 291, 293, 295
Demiralp, T. 277
Denno, S. 50, 51
Deouell, L. Y. 27, 82
deRegnier, R. 149, 150, 155, 159, 160, 162, 163
deRegnier, R.-A. 11, 17, 132, 150, 151, 155, 156, 160, 162, 163
deRegnier, R. A. O. 155, 157, 160, 161
Derek, R. J. 60
Desimone, R. 276
Desjardins, R. N. 176
Desmond, J. E. 179
Despland, P. 82
Despland, P. A. 1
deUngria, M. 162
di Michele, F. 229, 230
Di Russo, F. 39
Diamond, A. 267, 273
Diamond, R. 78, 79
Diaz, R. 172
Diaz de Leon, A. E. 230
Diaz-Comas, L. 254, 268
Dickmann, A. 61
Diekmann, V. 275
diSumma, A. 56
Dittmann-Balcar, A. 180, 181
Dittrichova, J. 269, 271
Do Marcolino, C. 263
Dobson, V. 1, 60, 63
Dodd, K. L. 60
Dojat, M. 39
Dolan, R. J. 146, 155, 160
Dolberg, A. 162
Dolski, I. 8, 12, 233
Don, M. 181, 241
Donchin, E. 17, 21, 25, 27
Doneshka, P. 180
Donohoe, B. 179
Dooley, S. L. 162
Doppelmayr, M. 267, 268, 279
Doran, S. 173
Dorey, S. E. 61
Dorman, M. F. 177
Doussard-Roosevelt, J. 275
Doussard-Roosevelt, J. A. 276
Douthwaite, W. A. 47
Doyle, M. C. 90
Draganova, R. 173
Drew, K. J. 59
Dreyfus-Brisac, C. 251, 257
Driver, J. 295
Dubowitz, L. M. S. 145, 150
Dubowitz, V. 145, 150
Duchowney, M. S. 63
Dudkovic, N. M. 241
Duffy, F. H. 261, 265
Duggan, P. J. 162
Dukette, D. 115
Dulitzky, M. 162
Dunbar, J. 181
Duncan, C. C. 152
Duncan, K. 152
Dupont, P. 268
Dupoux, E. 176
Dutton, G. N. 43
Duvernoy, H. M. 279

Eckhardt, P. G. 61
Eden, G. 212
Edmonds, G. E. 77, 81, 82, 84, 85, 91, 92

Eerola, O. 179
Eggermont, J. J. 148, 150, 172, 181, 241, 308
Eggers, C. 180, 181
Eifuku, S. 77, 92
Eilers, R. 211
Eimas, P. 211
Eimer, M. 27, 77, 80, 82, 87, 90, 92
Eisner, W. 57
Eizenman, M. 48, 57
Ek, M. 184
Eklund, K. 210
Eklund, K. M. 173, 174, 176, 185, 208, 209, 210, 219, 220
Ekman, P. 232
Elbert, T. 22, 255, 293
Eldredge, L. 150
Elfadil, H. 277
Elger, C. E. 277
Elia, M. 179
Ellingson, M. L. 208
Ellingson, R. J. 43, 44, 154
Elliott, L. L. 185
Elliott, M. A. 293
Elton, M. 173
Endo, S. 77, 92
Engel, R. 200, 201, 214, 215
Eriksen, K. J. 56
Erkkola, R. 173, 174, 175, 200
Erlenmeyer-Kimling, L. 9
Escera, C. 171, 172, 179, 237
Eswaran, H. 173
Evans, J. 82
Eysenck, H. J. 229, 242
Eysenck, M. W. 229, 242

Fabiani, M. 208, 235
Fabre-Thorpe, M. 82
Fagan, J. F. III 145, 157
Faidherbe, J. 47
Fantz, R. 101
Farah, M. 268
Farah, M. J. 78, 79
Farghaly, W. M. A. 60
Faria, J. D. 50, 51
Farrell, K. 63
Farroni, T. 84, 92, 311
Fawcett, S. 55
Fay, W. 200, 201, 214
Fazio, F. 78
Feldman, J. 181
Feldman, J. F. 117, 160, 161
Feldt, L. S. 27
Fell, J. 277
Fellman, V. 150, 162, 174, 176, 238
Fendick, M. G. 62
Ferguson, M. 212
Fernandez, G. 277
Fernandez, T. 254, 268
Ferree, T. C. 13
Ferri, R. 179
Ferstl, R. 171
Fey, M. 212
Field, T. 8
Fielder, A. R. 39, 58, 60
Fiensod, M. 60
Fifer, W. P. 153
Filipek, P. A. 179
Filley, C. M. 240
Fiorentini, A. 46, 50, 51, 54
Fiori, N. 82
Fischer, C. 172, 179
Fishbeck, K. 179
Fisher, S. E. 183

Fletcher, A. M. 162
Fletcher, D. J. 240
Fletcher, J. M. 179, 212
Fletcher, P. F. 146, 160
Flieger, K. Z. 173, 174, 179, 185, 185, 239
Flodman, P. 180
Floodmark, O. 63
Fock, J. M. 43
Foerster, M. H. 60
Fonaryova Key, A. 207
Foorman, B. R. 179
Fowler, B. 173
Fox, N. 12, 229, 253
Fox, N. A. 1, 7, 8, 9, 12, 27, 181, 227, 228, 229, 230, 231, 232, 233, 234, 236, 237, 240, 253, 257, 265, 266, 267, 309, 312
Francis, H. W. 181
Franco, P. 174
Frank, Y. 63
Franks, R. D. 240
Freedman, M. H. 63
Freedman, R. 240, 241
Freeman, D. N. 47, 63
Freeman, R. 199, 202
Frees, T. E. 180
French, J. 51
Freund, G. 262
Frey, K. 234
Friederici, A. D. 174, 176, 178, 185
Friedman, D. 9, 115, 199, 237, 238
Friedrich, M. 174, 176, 178, 185
Fries, T. 240
Friesen, W. V. 232
Friston, K. J. 161
Frodl-Bauch, T. 184
Fukai, R. 62
Fukuda, Y. 277
Fulton, A. B. 39, 41, 60
Furune, S. 46
Fuster, M. J. 273
Futagi, Y. 269, 270, 271, 272

Gabrieli, J. D. 241
Gadian, D. G. 117, 161, 162
Gaeta, H. 237, 238
Gaillard, A. W. K. 171
Galambos, R. 1, 123, 199
Galan, L. 254, 268
Gallant, T. 63
Ganel, T. 92
Ganz, L. 1, 85, 86, 103, 104, 107, 114, 115, 123
Garcia, H. 55
Gardner, E. 181
Garey, L. G. 172
Gary, J. W. 16
Gasser, T. 261
Gauthier, I. 78, 79, 82
Geer, I. 57
Geffen, L. B. 179
Geisler, M. W. 17
Geisser, S. 27
George, N. 82
George, S. R. 62
Georgieff, M. 86, 104, 107, 108, 110, 114, 115, 120, 129, 160, 162, 163
Georgieff, M. K. 11, 17, 120, 126, 132, 150, 151, 155, 156, 159, 160, 161, 162, 163
Gerhardt, G. A. 240
Geschwind, N. 231

Geva, D. 60
Gevins, A. 275
Geyer, M. A. 240
Ghatan, P. H. 268
Ghim, H.-R. 293
Giard, M. H. 110, 172, 173, 179, 236, 237
Gibbs, C. 185
Gibson, M. 63
Gibson, R. A. 60
Giedd, J. 241
Giedd, J. N. 179
Gill, L. A. 217
Gilmore, R. O. 275
Givre, S. J. 39
Glabe, C. 180
Gliga, T. 85
Gloor, P. 266, 310
Glorieux, J. 17
Glover, G. H. 179
Goffaux, V. 79
Goldman, D. Z. 101, 102, 104, 106, 110, 133
Goldschmidt, L. 60
Goldsmith, H. H. 233
Goldstein, P. J. 47, 63
Goldwein, J. L. 63
Gomes, H. 171, 237
Gomez, C. 8
Gomez, C. M. 81, 173
Gomot, M. 173, 179, 236, 237
Gonsalves, B. 80
Good, W. V. 51
Goodman, G. S. 275
Gordon, G. E. 58
Gordon, J. 48, 57
Gordon-Salant, S. 181, 236, 237
Gore, J. C. 78, 79
Goshen-Gottstein, Y. 92
Gosselin, J. 46
Goto, M. 269, 270, 271, 272
Gottlob, I. 62
Gout, A. 176
Grabowecky, M. 80
Grady, C. L. 89
Graf, E. W. 54
Gratton, G. 25, 208, 235
Gray, C. M. 293
Gray, J. 86, 107, 108, 110, 131
Graziani, L. J. 150
Graziano, M. S. S. 296
Green, M. 50, 62
Greenbaum, C. 162
Greenberg, M. S. 231
Greenfield, P. 50
Greenhouse, S. W. 27
Grice, S. J. 230, 301
Griffin, R. 92, 311
Grimm, T. 183
Grose, J. 43, 45, 57
Grose, J. H. 185
Gross, C. G. 296
Groswasser, J. 174
Groswasser, Z. 61
Gruber, R. 173
Gruber, T. 241
Gruber, W. 279
Gruetteer, R. 162
Guan, Z. 17
Guillemot, J. P. 58
Guillet, R. 149, 150
Gumenyuk, V. 237
Gunnar, M. R. 236
Guo, A. 62

Gur, R. C. 231
Gustafson, E. C. 22, 23
Guttorm, T. 210
Guttorm, T. K. 174, 176, 183, 185, 209, 210, 219, 220

Haapanen, M. L. 182, 183, 185
Habib, R. 146
Hackley, S. A. 172
Haegerstrom-Portnoy, G. 62
Hafer, A. 173
Hagemann, D. 234
Hagne, I. 251, 253, 258, 264, 265, 269, 270
Hahne, A. 174, 176, 178, 185
Haight, J. C. 101, 107, 108, 109, 110, 119, 134, 137
Hains, S. M. J. 153
Haith, M. M. 275, 293
Halgren, E. 87, 90
Halit, H. 77, 79, 81, 82, 83, 84, 85, 91, 92, 230, 301, 311
Hall, A. 62
Hall, J. W. 185
Halliday, A. M. 61
Hämäläainen, H. 171
Hamburger, S. 241
Hamburger, S. D. 179
Hamer, R. D. 50, 51, 55, 56, 60
Hamilton, R. 48
Hammarrenger, B. 58
Hampson, S. 208
Handy, T. C. 6, 26, 27
Hanna, N. 46
Hansen, R. M. 39, 41, 60
Hansen, V. 58
Hansen, V. C. 48
Hardin, M. G. 236
Harding, G. F. A. 43, 45, 54, 57
Harmony, T. 230, 254, 268
Harms, L. 179
Harper, R. M. 270
Harrad, R. A. 56, 59
Harris, C. 58
Harris, L. 63, 202
Hartel, S. 60
Harter, M. R. 9, 63
Hartmann, E. E. 39, 41, 48, 57
Harwerth, R. 59
Harwerth, R. S. 56
Hassid, S. 174
Hatzakis, H. 16, 21, 22, 26, 32, 33, 88
Haxby, J. V. 89
Hazan, C. 275
He, Y. 229
Hegerl, U. 184
Heide, A. 212
Heikki, L. A. 181
Heilman, K. M. 268
Held, R. 55
Helenius, H. 181
Helwig, S. 202
Henderson, H. A. 12, 27, 228, 233, 237
Henderson, L. M. 253, 255, 275
Henderson, N. 200, 201, 215
Henry, J. R. 227, 228, 261
Henson, R. N. 92
Hepper, P. G. 149
Herbert, A. M. 48, 50
Hernell, O. 60
Herrgård, E. 180
Herrmann, C. S. 291, 295

Hersey, M. A. 22, 23
Hertz-Pannier, L. 152
Hessl, D. 234
Hevnar, R. F. 148
Hill, D. 257
Hill Goldsmith, H. 8, 12
Hill-Karrer, J. 103, 104, 108, 109, 110, 114, 119, 126
Hillyard, S. A. 17, 21, 27, 81, 172
Hilpert, P. L. 150
Hirabayashi, M. 241
Hirano, S. 43
Hirasawa, K. 173, 174
Hirayasu, Y. 17
Hirose, T. 47, 48, 50, 51
Hiruma, T. 171
Hitchcox, S. M. 57
Hodgman, J. E. 270
Hodgson, L. 309
Hoenig, K. 240
Hoffman, D. R. 60
Hoffmann, M. B. 43
Hoke, M. 208
Holder, G. E. 60, 61
Holmes, A. 55
Holopainen, I. 179, 181
Holopainen, I. E. 182
Holtzman, M. 60
Honbolygó, F. 178
Hood, B. 54
Hood, B. M. 16, 33
Hopf, J. M. 81
Hopkins, B. 174
Hoppenbrouwers, T. 270
Hornhuber, H. H. 277
Horwitz, B. 89
Hotakainen, M. 173
Hou, C. 57
Hou, Y. 229
Howe, M. L. 117
Hoyt, C. S. 50, 59, 60
Hrbek, A. 263
Hsieh, J. C. 268
Hsu-Winges, C. 56
Hu, X. U. 296
Huang, H. 153
Hubel, D. 57
Hudspeth, A. J. 146, 147
Hudspeth, W. J. 265
Hughes, E. L. 60
Hui, R. 48
Hukki, J. 182, 183, 185
Humphry, R. 55
Hungerbuhler, J. P. 231
Hunt, M. J. 177
Hunter, S. 103, 115, 124
Huotilainen, M. 150, 173, 174, 176, 177, 184, 208
Huttenlocher, P. R. 148, 172, 265, 266
Huynh, H. 27
Hykin, J. 152

Iarossi, G. 61
Ichikawa, I. 173
Iglesias, J. 88
Ilmoniemi, R. J. 184, 237
Ilvonen, T. 184, 199
Inanaga, K. 269, 273, 276, 277
Ingvar, M. 268
Iramina, K. 241
Irwin, R. J. 185
Isaacs, E. B. 160, 161
Ishihara, T. 269, 270, 271, 272

Itier, R. J. 80, 81, 82, 84, 92

Jackson, D. C. 233
Jambaque, I. 179
Jan, J. E. 63
Jandeck, C. 60
Jankowski, J. J. 160
Jaramillo, M. 199
Jasper, H. H. 13, 155
Jastak, S. 206
Jastrzebski, G. 60
Javitt, D. C. 171, 180, 310
Jenkins, T. C. 47
Jenkins, W. M. 183
Jennen-Steinmetz, C. 261
Jensen, D. R. 200
Jensen, P. S. 180
Jentzsch, I. 80, 92
Jerger, J. 308
Jessen, F. 240
Jiang, D. 172
Jing, H. 173, 174
John, E. R. 229, 230
Johnson, C. L. 152, 160, 161
Johnson, M. B. 206
Johnson, M. H. 16, 21, 22, 26, 32,
    33, 77, 79, 80, 81, 82, 83, 84, 85,
    86, 88, 91, 92, 93, 104, 106, 110,
    133, 230, 252, 275, 276, 291,
    293, 294, 296, 300, 301, 309,
    311, 312
Johnson, R. Jr 13, 17, 21, 27
Johnston, P. 183
Johnston, V. S. 17
Johnstone, S. J. 229
Jones, K. 48, 59
Jones, N. A. 8
Jonkman, L. M. 180
Jorgensen, M. H. 50, 60
Jorgenson, L. A. 162
Joseph, R. 278
Joyce, C. A. 82
Julez, B. 56, 57
Jung, T.-P. 32
Junghöfer, M. 22, 255
Junque, C. 160
Juottonen, K. 182
Jusczyk, P. 211

Kaartinen, J. 173
Kagan, J. 235, 236
Kahana, M. J. 269, 275, 277, 278
Kahn, A. 174
Kaila, K. 184
Kalin, N. H. 8, 12, 233
Kalitzin, S. 267
Kamp, A. 277
Kane, N. M. 172
Kaneko, S. 171
Kanizsa, G. 293
Kanno, O. 173
Kanwisher, N. 78
Karlberg, P. 263
Karmiloff-Smith, A. 230, 301
Karmos, G. 171, 172
Karrer, R. 8, 11, 85, 86, 91, 101,
    102, 103, 104, 106, 108, 109,
    110, 114, 115, 119, 121, 124,
    125, 126, 138
Kaski, S. 184
Kasmann-Kellner, B. 61
Katada, A. 261
Kathmann, N. 184
Kato, M. 50, 62

Katsumi, O. 47, 50, 51
Katz, D. R. 185
Kaufman, J. 252, 296, 300
Kaufmann, J. M. 80, 82, 92
Kavsek, M. J. 293
Kay, N. 185
Kayser, J. 199
Kazmerski, V. A. 238
Keenan, N. K. 63
Keil, A. 241
Kekoni, J. 171
Kellman, P. J. 293
Kellner, U. 60
Kelly, J. P. 46, 50, 54, 60
Kelly, S. 207, 212, 213
Kemner, C. 179, 180, 240
Kenemans, J. L. 173
Kennedy, J. 180
Kennedy, J. L. 180
Kero, P. 173, 174, 175, 200
Key, A. F. 212
Khedr, E. H. M. 60
Khosla, D. 181
Kieffer, J. E. 180
Kiesila, P. 179
Kilpeläinen, R. 180
Kim, D. M. 278
King, A. C. 179
King, C. 172, 177
King, N. 180
Kinney, H. C. 148
Kirjavainen, J. 11, 173, 174, 176,
    200
Kirk, I. J. 275, 276, 277, 279
Kirkorian, G. 179
Kisilevsky, B. S. 153
Kisley, M. 241
Kisley, M. A. 240
Kissler, J. 241
Kitchigina, V. F. 277
Klaver, P. 277
Klimesch, W. 253, 262, 267, 268,
    275, 276, 277, 279
Klinger, L. G. 8, 11, 234, 257
Knight, R. T. 241
Knowlton, B. J. 117
Kobayashi, T. 62
Koch, D. B. 172, 181, 183
Kocsis, B. 277
Koelega, H. S. 180
Kojima, T. 229
Kok, A. 173
Kok, L. L. 182
Komatsushiro, M. 258, 265
Konishi, Y. 173, 174
Kononen, M. 269, 271
Koren, G. 60
Korhonen, T. 171, 172
Korman, M. 154
Kornhuber, A. W. 277
Kornhuber, H. 275
Korpilahti, P. 179, 181, 182, 237
Korzyukov, O. 237
Koshino, Y. 262
Koskinen, M. 183, 185
Kovacs, I. 59
Kozuch, P. 179
Krasowski, M. D. 180
Krauel, K. 171
Kraus, H. 60
Kraus, N. 171, 172, 173, 174, 177,
    181, 182, 183, 184, 208, 239, 241
Krause, C. M. 181
Kreiter, A. 293

Kreuzer, J. A. 150, 173, 174, 176,
    179, 185, 185, 236, 238, 239
Krick, C. M. 61
Kriss, A. 41, 58, 60, 61
Kronheim, J. K. 47, 51
Kropfl, W. 56, 57
Krumholz, A. 263, 266
Kubicki, S. 262
Kucharski, C. 240
Kuefner, D. 85
Kugler, J. 261, 269
Kuhl, P. 177
Kuhl, P. K. 178
Kuhlman, W. N. 254, 262
Kujala, A. 173, 184
Kujala, T. 173, 199, 200
Kulju, P. 210
Kure, W. 277
Kurihara, M. 173, 174
Kuriowa, Y. 62
Kuritatashima, S. 50
Kurjenluoma, S. 182
Kurtzberg, D. 9, 103, 115, 150,
    173, 174, 176, 179, 185, 185,
    236, 237, 238, 239, 308
Kushnerenko, E. 150, 162, 173,
    174, 176, 238
Kutas, M. 27, 87
Kwong, B. 181

Laakso, M. L. 210
Labrosse, M. 58
Lacerda, W. F. 178
Lachau, J. P. 291
Lachaux, J.-P. 291
Ladish, C. 17
LaHoste, G. 180
LaHoste, G. J. 180
Lähteenmäki, P. M. 181
Lairy, G. C. 257, 258, 261, 263
Lalonde, R. 82
Landrieu, P. 200
Lang, A. H. 179, 181, 184, 237
Lang, H. 181, 182
Lang, J. 57
Lang, M. 275, 277
Lang, W. 80, 87, 90, 275
Lanuzza, B. 179
Lara-Ayala, L. 178
Larson, E. W. 47
Larsonpark, E. W. 50
Lary, S. 145, 150
Lathrop, G. H. 154
Latinus, M. 82, 84
Laub, M. 261, 269
Lauritzen, L. 50
Lavoie, M. E. 17
Le Grand, R. 93
Le Van Quyen, M. 291
Leboyer, M. 179
Lecaunet, J.-P. 145, 148, 149, 152
Lee, G. P. 231
Lee, K. 153
Lefebvre, C. 153
Lefebvre, F. 17
Leguire, L. E. 60
Lehnann, D. 57
Lehtinen, I. 258
Lehtokoski, A. 174, 176, 177, 178,
    184, 200, 208
Lehtonen, J. 269, 271
Lehtonen, J. B. 257
Leiderer, P. 22
Leinonen, S. 210

Leipälä, J. 162
Leiwo, M. 209
Lennanen, P. H. 209
Lenneberg, E. 202
Lennes, M. M. 177, 208
Lenoci, M. 240
Leon, F. 179
Lepage, M. 146
Lepisto, T. 110, 179, 181, 237, 238
Lepore, F. 58
Leppanen, P. 173, 182
Leppänen, P. H. 173, 174, 176, 185, 208, 209, 210, 219, 220
Leppanen, P. H. T. 174, 176, 179, 183, 185, 219, 220
Leslie, A. M. 301
Levi, D. M. 56, 59
Levi, H. 150
Levin, A. V. 60, 61
Levisohn, P. M. 240
Lewis, C. 154
Lewis, M. 235
Lewis, T. 172
Lewy, A. 234
Liard, L. 81
Liberman, A. 212
Liebenthal, E. 208
Liegeois-Chauvel, C. 241
Lincoln, A. J. 179
Lindblom, B. 178
Lindeke, L. L. 160, 161
Linder, N. 150
Lindsley, D. B. 1, 228, 251, 252, 253, 257, 261, 263
Linotte, S. 82
Lippe, S. 58
Lisker, L. 211
Liu, G. 79
Livingstone, M. S. 57
Livonen, A. 177, 208
Llinás, R. R. 266, 289, 310
Loewy, D. H. 173
Logan, W. J. 62, 63
Logothetis, N. 78
Logothetis, N. K. 301
Long, J. D. 8, 86, 101, 102, 107, 110, 115, 136
Lopes da Silva, F. H. 266, 267, 277, 310
Loring, D. W. 231
Lowery, C. 173
Luaute, J. 172
Lucas, A. 160, 161
Luciana, M. 5, 8, 9, 162
Luidten, P. G. 160
Lukowski, A. F. 101, 107, 108, 109, 110, 119, 134, 137
Luoma, L. 180
Lurquin, P. 174
Lutz, A. 291
Luu, P. 13
Luuk, A. 174, 176, 177, 178, 200
Lyytinen, H. 155, 172, 173, 174, 176, 179, 183, 185, 208, 209, 210, 219, 220

Maalouf, E. F. 162
Macchi Cassia, V. 85
Mace, M. J. 82
Mackay, A. M. 48
Mackay, J. C. 275, 276, 277, 279
Mackie, R. T. 39, 47, 58
MacMillan, L. J. 43
Madrid, M. 54, 58

Madsen, J. R. 269, 275, 277, 278
Maffei, L. 51
Magnusson, R. 253, 265
Maier, W. 240
Maisog, J. M. 89, 179
Maiste, A. C. 177
Majlessi, H. 63
Makeig, S. 32
Makhnev, V. 276
Makrides, M. 60
Malakhovskaia, E. V. 267
Malcolm, C. A. 60
Malkova, L. 311
Malmstadt Schumacher, J. R. 8, 12
Malykh, S. B. 229, 267
Manahilov, V. 50, 54
Manara, A. R. 172
Maneru, C. 160
Mangun, G. R. 81
Manny, R. E. 55
Mäntysalo, S. 171
Marechal, L. 47
Marg, E. 47, 59, 60, 63
Markand, O. N. 261, 263
Markowitsch, H. J. 146, 147
Marlow, N. 62
Marmor, M. F. 41, 46, 59, 60
Marois, R. 152
Marosi, E. 230
Marquis, P. 241
Marsh, W. L. 179
Marshall, D. H. 181
Marshall, J. C. 146, 147
Marshall, P. J. 7, 9, 181, 228, 229, 230, 234, 235, 236, 237, 240, 265, 266, 309
Marshall, T. R. 7, 228, 233, 236
Martin, B. A. 173
Martin, J. 308
Martin, W. H. 145, 149, 150
Martinerie, J. 291
Martynova, O. 11, 173, 174, 175, 176, 185, 200, 237
Mason, A. J. S. 55
Mason, J. I. 63
Masuda, A. 241
Masuda, K. 241
Mathivet, E. 86
Matousek, M. 227, 229
Matsos, L. 309
Matsui, Y. 47
Matsuura, M. 229
Matthis, P. 257
Mattia, F. 150, 155, 159
Mattia, F. R. 157, 160, 161
Maulsby, R. L. 261, 269, 270
Maurer, D. 84, 93
Maurer, J. P. 48
May, P. 184
Mayer, M. J. 60
Mazziotta, J. C. 263, 273
McCallin, K. 240
McCarthy, G. 27, 77, 78, 81, 82, 84, 85, 91, 92
McCarthy, R. 257, 309
McCarton, C. M. 161
McClelland, J. L. 276
McCloud, V. 171
McColl, B. 308
McCormack, G. 50, 51
McCormack, G. L. 48
McCormick, A. Q. 63
McCulloch, D. L. 39, 43, 44, 46,

47, 48, 50, 54, 56, 58, 59, 60, 61, 62, 63
McDermott, J. 78
McDonald, W. I. 61
McDuffie, A. 253, 255, 275
McEvoy, L. 275
McFadden, M. 309
McGee, T. 172, 173, 174, 177, 183, 184, 239, 241
McGee, T. J. 172, 177, 181, 183, 208
McGinty, D. J. 270
McIsaac, H. 90, 116
McKean, C. M. 149
McManis, M. H. 235
McPartland, J. 86, 87, 107, 108, 110, 131
McRae, K. 240
Meader, K. J. 231
Meadows, A. T. 63, 181
Mecklinger, A. 291, 295
Meek, J. 1
Mehta, M. C. 47, 50, 51
Meigen, T. 40, 48
Meister, L. A. 181
Mellon, N. K. 181
Mellor, D. H. 39, 58, 60
Meltzoff, A. N. 86, 87, 107, 108, 110, 131, 177
Mennemeier, M. S. 268
Mentis, M. J. 89
Menzies, R. 43
Mercier, L. 174
Mercuri, E. 55
Merle, K. S. 149, 150
Merzenich, M. M. 183
Mesulam, M. M. 266, 310
Metzger, B. E. 162
Micco, A. 174, 208
Micco, A. G. 181
Michaelsen, K. F. 60
Michiels, J. 268
Miezin, F. M. 268
Mikkelsen, T. B. 50
Mikkola, K. 162
Miller, C. 241
Miller, E. K. 296
Miller, R. 276, 277, 278, 279
Miller, S. L. 183
Mills, D. L. 88
Milner, B. 117
Mirmiran, M. 43
Mishkin, M. 116, 117, 161, 162, 311
Mitchell, K. W. 63
Mitsudome, A. 148
Miyamoto, L. 77, 92
Miyazaki, M. 112
Mizuno, T. 258, 265
Mocks, J. 261
Modglin, A. 205, 207, 213, 216
Molenaar, P. C. M. 17
Molfese, D. 205, 207, 212, 216
Molfese, D. L. 199, 200, 201, 202, 203, 204, 205, 206, 207, 210, 211, 212, 213, 215, 216, 217, 218
Molfese, V. J. 201, 202, 203, 204, 205, 206, 207, 210, 211, 215, 217, 218
Molholm, S. 237
Molnár, M. 172, 179
Monaco, A. P. 183
Mondloch, C. J. 93

Monk, C. 9
Montgomery, C. 60
Monti, L. A. 8, 11, 86, 101, 103, 106, 110, 114, 115, 121, 125
Mooibroek, J. 266
Moon, C. M. 153
Moore, J. 211
Moore, J. K. 308
Moore, R. 152
Moraes, N. S. B. 61
Morillion, M. 153
Morlet, D. 172, 179
Morong, S. E. 63
Morr, M. L. 173, 174, 176, 236, 238
Morrell, L. K. 199
Morrone, M. C. 54
Morrongiello, B. A. 185
Mortelmans, L. 268
Morton, J. 80
Moscovitch, M. 118
Moskowitz, A. 41, 46, 48, 50, 51, 57, 58
Moss, T. 172
Moyzis, R. 180
Muehleck, A. J. 101, 108, 110, 137
Mueller, C. J. 233
Mulholland, T. 267
Müller, J. 293
Muller, M. M. 241, 293
Muller-Myhsok, B. 183
Munakata, Y. 276, 300
Mundy, P. 12, 229
Mundy, P. C. 275
Mundy-Castle, A. C. 269
Murias, M. 180
Murphy, P. 173
Murray, E. A. 116
Mushin, A. S. 59
Musolino, A. 241
Mustari, M. J. 55
Musumeci, S. A. 179
Myles-Worsley, M. 240, 241
Mylin, L. 63

Näätänen, R. 110, 150, 162, 171, 172, 173, 174, 175, 176, 177, 179, 181, 182, 183, 184, 185, 200, 208, 237, 238
Nace, K. 179
Naegele, J. R. 55
Nagamoto, H. T. 241
Nagy, W. 212
Nakagome, K. 173
Nakayamahiromatsu, M. 50
Naumann, E. 234
Navalta, C. P. 278
Negro, T. 46
Nelson, B. 154
Nelson, C. A. 5, 8, 9, 11, 12, 17, 22, 23, 24, 25, 26, 79, 80, 81, 85, 86, 88, 89, 90, 91, 92, 101, 102, 103, 104, 106, 107, 108, 109, 110, 112, 113, 114, 115, 118, 119, 120, 121, 123, 124, 125, 126, 128, 129, 130, 132, 133, 134, 135, 136, 137, 145, 148, 150, 151, 155, 156, 159, 160, 161, 162, 163. 236
Neumann, M. A. 60
Neuper, C. 258, 262, 266, 267
Neveu, M. M. 61
Neville, H. 88, 176, 199
Newton, P. 171

Neylan, T. C. 240
Nicholas, T. W. 180
Nicol, T. 173, 174, 177, 184
Nicol, T. G. 172, 177, 183, 208
Niedermeyer, E. 229, 262
Nikitina, G. M. 261, 269, 272
Nikkel, L. 106, 108, 114, 124
Niparko, J. K. 181
Nishijo, H. 77, 92
Nishitani, N. 276
Nitschke, J. B. 233
Nold, J. 162
Norcia, A. M. 1, 48, 50, 51, 54, 55, 56, 57, 59, 85, 86, 103, 104, 107, 114, 115, 123
Normand, C. 181
Nothen, M. M. 183
Novak, G. 172
Novak, G. P. 150
Novick, B. 179
Noyd, W. W. 55
Nozza, R. J. 174
Nultin, C. 179
Nunez, P. 207
Nunez, P. L. 33
Nusinowitz, S. 61
Nuwer, M. R. 253
Nyakas, C. 160
Nyrke, T. 184

Oades, R. D. 179, 180, 181
Odom, J. V. 41, 46, 50, 59, 62
O'Donoghue, G. M. 181
Oeltermann, A. 301
Ogura, C. 17
Ohn, Y. H. 47
Ohta, H. 17
Ohtahara, S. 264
Okazaki, M. 148
Okubo, Y. 229
Oldfield, R. C. 17
Olincy, A. 240
Olivares, E. I. 88
Oliver, A. 16, 21, 22, 26, 32, 33, 88
Oliver-Rodriguez, J. C. 17
Olkon, D. M. 180
Olondo, M. 160
Olsen, S. F. 50
Olsson, T. 263
O'Neill, C. 181
Oranje, B. 240
Orbach, H. 46
Orekhova, E. V. 228, 229, 254, 257, 258, 261, 262, 264, 267, 268, 269, 270, 273, 276, 278, 279
Orel-Bixler, D. 55
Orel-Bixler, D. A. 51, 62
Orlando, M. S. 149, 150
Ornoy, A. 162
Orquin, J. 46
Osier, H. 199
Osman, A. A. A. 60
Otten, L. 236
Otten, L. J. 92
Ozaki, H. 261

Paavilainen, P. 172, 173
Pachtman, E. 240
Packer, R. J. 63
Palermo, D. 199, 202
Paller, K. A. 80
Palmer, J. 80
Panagiotides, H. 8, 11, 16, 86, 87, 107, 108, 110, 131, 234, 257

Pang, E. W. 90, 173, 311
Pantev, C. 208
Panton, C. M. 57, 60, 61
Papanicolaou, A. C. 179, 212
Papassotiropoulos, A. 240
Papousek, H. 269, 271
Pardou, A. 174
Paris-Delrue, L. 152
Parker, D. M. 51
Parker, S. W. 102, 110, 135
Parkkonen, L. 173
Partanen, J. 180, 269, 271
Pascalis, O. 8, 77, 80, 82, 83, 84, 85, 88, 108, 114, 115, 121, 128
Pascual, R. 230
Paterson, A. D. 180
Patria, F. 39
Patrick, G. 240
Paul, K. 269, 271
Pauls, J. 301
Pause, B. M. 171
Pavlov, S. 276
Pecevich, M. 240
Peedle, J. E. 47
Pekkonen, E. 184
Peltzman, P. 47, 63
Pena, M. 200
Pennefather, P. M. 59
Pennington, B. F. 183
Penttonen, M. 172
Perani, D. 88
Pereverzeva, M. 54
Perez, E. 77, 82, 92
Pernier, J. 291, 293, 295, 296, 301
Peronnet, F. 296
Perrett, D. I. 87
Perria, L. 231
Persson, J. 253, 265
Petersen, I. 227, 229, 253, 265
Petersen, S. E. 106, 268
Peterson, B. S. 152, 162
Petersson, K. M. 268
Petrie, A. 59
Petrig, B. 46, 50, 56, 57
Pettet, M. W. 51, 57
Pfeifer, W. 295
Pfurtscheller, G. 258, 262, 266, 267
Phelps, M. E. 263, 273
Phillips, J. O. 60
Piaget, J. 296
Piccardi, M. 61
Pickering, E. C. 80, 82, 92
Picton, T. W. 17, 21, 27, 177, 236
Pieh, C. 44
Pihko, E. 174, 176, 185, 208, 209, 210, 219, 220
Pike, A. A. 62
Pineda, J. A. 229
Pinkhasov, E. 57
Pirchio, M. 50, 51
Pitzalis, S. 39
Pivik, R. T. 174, 253
Pohjavuori, M. 173, 174, 176, 185, 200, 236
Poiroux, S. 82
Polcari, A. 278
Polich, J. 17, 90, 116
Polk, S. D. 240
Polka, L. 178
Polo, A. 56
Ponton, C. W. 181, 241, 308
Porciatti, V. 46, 51, 53
Porges, S. W. 276
Porjesz, B. 80

Posikera, I. N. 228, 229, 254, 257, 258, 261, 262, 264, 267, 268, 269, 270, 271, 272, 273, 276, 277, 278, 279
Posner, M. I. 106, 180
Powe, N. R. 181
Powers, J. C. 50
Preissl, H. 173
Prescott, P. A. 157
Prestidge, C. 60
Pribram, K. H. 265
Prichep, L. 229, 230
Prieto, T. E. 208
Proffitt, F. 78
Prunte Glowazki, A. 48
Puce, A. 77, 78, 82, 92
Pugh, K. R. 179
Purhonen, M. 269, 271
Pushina, N. P. 262, 267
Putnam, L. E. 9, 13

Quayle, A. 92
Querleu, D. 152, 153
Quinn, G. E. 79
Quinn, P. C. 106, 137

Raab, E. 57, 63
Rabinowitz, C. 79
Raghavachari, S. 275, 277
Ragó, A. 178
Rahn, E. 277
Raichle, M. E. 180
Raimo, I 184
Rainer, G. 296
Ramos, A. 230
Ranta, R. 182
Rao, R. 162, 290
Rapin, I. 199
Rashotte, C. 212
Ratliff, F. 57
Ratzon, C. 162
Raviv, A. 173
Raz, A. 173
Rebai, M. 82
Reed, J. M. 145
Reed, N. L. 241
Regal, D. M. 44, 63
Regan, D. 6, 48, 59, 63
Reid, V. 86, 104, 106, 133
Reid, V. M. 301
Reimslag, F. C. 48
Reinikainen, K. 171, 173, 174, 176, 184, 185, 200, 236
Reis, R. 181
Reith, W. 61
Remschmidt, H. 182
Renard, X. 152, 153
Renault, B. 82
Renecke, R. D. 62
Renlund, M. 173, 174, 176, 200
Reva, N. 276
Reynolds, G. D. 26, 32, 89, 103, 104, 105, 107, 109, 110, 111, 113, 115, 120, 121, 135, 311, 312
Rhodes, G. 78
Riccardi, R. 61
Richards, A. 212
Richards, J. E. 26, 32, 33, 86, 89, 102, 103, 104, 105, 107, 109, 110, 111, 113, 115, 120, 121, 132, 135, 311, 312
Richards, T. 212
Richardson, G. A. 60
Richardson, U. 183, 209, 219, 220

Ridder, W. H. III 48, 50, 56
Ridlehuber, H. W. 179
Rinaldi, J. A. 16
Ring, H. A. 179
Rinne, T. 173, 174, 184, 200
Ritter, W. 27, 171, 172, 236, 237
Ritters, W. 199
Rivera-Gaxiola, M. 178
Rizzo, T. A. 162
Roark, L. B. 63
Robaey, P. 17
Robinson, A. J. 86
Robles, N. 60
Robson, J. 41, 46
Rockstroh, B. 22
Rodinguez-Holquin, S. 88
Rodriguez, E. 291
Roehrig, M. 241
Rogers, G. L. 60
Rohm, D. 279
Róna, Z. 178
Ropella, K. M. 208
Rosadini, G. 231
Rosburg, T. 208
Rose, G. M. 240
Rose, S. A. 117, 160, 161
Rosen, B. 152
Ross, B. 208
Ross, R. G. 240
Rossi, G. F. 231
Rossion, B. 79, 81, 82
Roth, W. T. 13
Rother, C. 61
Rothstein, M. 237
Rougeul, A. 262, 267
Rougeul-Buser, A. 262, 267
Rousselet, G. A. 82
Roux, S. 173, 236, 237
Rovet, J. F. 60
Rowlands, C. A. 172
Roy, M. S. 46, 58
Rubel, E. W. 172
Rubia, K. 179
Rubin, H. R. 181
Rubin, K. H. 12, 27, 228, 233, 237
Ruddick, G. A. 54
Rudrauf, D. 291
Rugg, M. D. 80, 87, 90, 92
Rumage, C. 207
Rumsey, J. M. 179
Rupp, A. 241
Ruprecht, K. W. 61
Russell, G. S. 13
Russell-Eggitt, I. 41, 58
Russell-Eggitt, I. R. 60
Ruth, R. A. 241
Rutherford, M. A. 162
Ruusuvirta, T. 171, 172

Saarikoski, S. 269, 271
Sackeim, H. A. 231
Sadeh, A. 173
Saher, M. 184
Sainio, K. 173, 174, 176, 185, 200, 236
Saino, K. 173, 174
Salamy, A. 149, 150
Salamy, J. G. 199
Salapatek, P. 103, 115, 123
Salerno, J. A. 89
Saletu, B. 173
Salgado-Pineda, P. 160
Saliba, E. 81, 82, 84, 85, 91
Sallinen, M. 173

Salmi, T. T. 181
Salmond, C. H. 161
Salo, S. 179
Salomao, S. R. 59, 61
Salonen, O. 179
Salzen, E. A. 51
Samar, V. J. 290
Sampath, V. 57
Sams, M. 173
Samson-Dollfus, D. 263
Samuel, S. S. 176
Samura, M. 17
Sanders, S. 145, 149, 150
Santesso, D. L. 8, 9, 253
Saron, C. D. 232
Satterfield, B. T. 180, 229
Satterfield, J. H. 180, 229
Saunders, K. J. 43, 47
Scabini, D. 241
Scanlon, D. 211
Schaal, B. 145, 148, 149, 152
Schacter, D. L. 118
Schafer, T. 61
Schaller, C. 277
Scheffner, D. 257
Schell, A. M. 180
Schepker, R. 180, 181
Scher, M. S. 60
Scherg, M. 33, 177, 213, 241
Schiller, P. H. 57
Schmeisser, E. T. 56
Schmidt, H. 293
Schmidt, L. A. 1, 8, 9, 27, 227, 233, 237, 253, 275
Schmitz, B. L. 61
Schmolck, H. 145, 147
Schneider, B. A. 185
Schneider, S. 57
Schnieder, K. C. 162
Schoenfeld, F. B. 240
Scholl, B. J. 301
Schoppenhorst, M. 262
Schorr, E. A. 181, 236, 237
Schott, P. 171
Schreiner, C. 183
Schroeder, C. E. 39, 310
Schroeder, J. 241
Schröger, E. 110, 172, 184, 237
Schubert, A. B. 179
Schuck, S. 180
Schulman-Galambos, C. 123, 199
Schulte-Korne, G. 182, 183
Schumacher, J. R. 233
Schwab, A. 146, 147
Schwaiger, J. 267, 268, 279
Schweinberger, S. R. 80, 82, 87, 92
Scoville, W. B. 117
Searock, K. 201, 203, 216
Seelig, D. 269, 277, 278
Seeliger, M. W. 60
Segebarth, C. 39
Seifer, R. 173
Sejnowski, T. J. 32
Self, J. 234
Selikowitz, M. 257, 309
Semelin, R. 179
Semlitsch, H. 173
Senulis, J. A. 232
Serafini, S. 212
Seress, L. 148
Sergeant, A. 180
Sergeant, J. A. 179
Serra, J. M. 172
Serra-Grabulosa, J. M. 160

Service, E. 179
Seufert, P. 43
Shafer, V. L. 173, 174, 176, 236, 238
Shagass, C. 261
Shah, N. J. 146, 147
Shahani, U. 44, 50, 54
Shahidullah, B. S. 149
Shankweiler, D. 212
Shapiro, E. G. 101, 102, 104, 106, 110, 133
Sharma, A. 173, 174, 177, 181, 208
Shawkat, F. S. 58
Shaywitz, B. A. 179
Shaywitz, S. E. 179
Shea, S. J. 55
Shea, S. L. 56
Sheldon, S. H. 174
Shepherd, A. 60
Shepherd, A. J. 43
Shestakova, A. 173, 179
Shibasaki, H. 112
Shibata, T. 77, 92
Shinozaki, N. 171
Shors, T. J. 56
Shulman, G. L. 268
Sidappa, A. 160, 162
Siegler, R. S. 276
Silberman, E. K. 231
Silipo, G. S. 180
Sillanpää, M. 173, 174, 175, 182, 200
Silva, J. 254, 268
Silveri, M. C. 88
Simion, F. 84
Simmer, K. 60
Simonov, P. V. 278
Simos, P. 205, 216
Simos, P. G. 179, 212, 217
Simson, R. 199
Singer, W. 293
Sinkkonen, J. 184
Sipilä, P. 180
Siqueland, E. 211
Skarf, B. 39, 41, 43, 46, 48, 50, 56, 58, 59, 63
Skladzien, C. J. 47, 50
Skoczenski, A. 51
Skoczenski, A. M. 50, 55
Skoczenski, M. 54, 57
Skovgaard, I. M. 50
Skudlarski, P. 78, 79, 179
Sloper, J. J. 56, 61
Smith, D. I. 241
Smith, E. L. III 56
Smith, J. R. 1, 228, 251, 252, 257, 261, 262, 263, 264
Smith, K. 57
Smith, M. E. 87, 90, 275
Smith, S. D. 183
Smith, T. S. 199
Smith, W. 16, 21, 22, 26, 32, 33, 88
Snead, O. C. 63
Snidman, N. 235, 237
Snyder, K. 25, 26, 88, 101, 110, 114, 115, 120, 129
Snyder, K. A. 11
Sohmer, H. 150
Soinen, K. 174
Soininen, M. 110, 181, 237, 238
Sojka, B. 171
Sokol, S. 1, 46, 48, 50, 51, 57, 58, 59, 63
Solman, R. T. 182

Somer, M. 182
Sommer, W. 87
Sonksen, P. M. 59
Sonnadara, R. R. 176
Sonuga-Barke, E. J. S. 180
Soong, F. 61
Sosa, M. V. 293
Sosa, P. V. 293
Spanaki, M. V. 208
Spekreijse, H. 48
Spelke, E. S. 297
Spence, M. A. 180
Spence, M. J. 153
Spieker, S. 8, 11
Spieth, F. 80, 87, 90
Spinelli, D. 39, 50, 51
Spitoni, G. 39
Spratling, M. W. 230, 252, 293, 294
Squire, L. R. 116, 117, 145, 147
Srebro, R. 56
Sroka, L. Verleger, R. 261
St George, M. 88
Stager, D. 55
Staib, L. H. 162
Staines, W. R. 241
Stancak, A. Jr 258, 262, 266
Stark, S. M. 145, 147
Starr, A. 145, 149, 150
Stauder, J. E. A. 17
Stein, J. F. 183
Stein, L. K. 241
Stein, M. A. 180
Steiner, C. A. 181
Steinschneider, M. 310
Steriade, M. 266, 310
Sterman, M. B. 270
Stern, L. M. 179
Steury, K. 212
Stevens, J. L. 56
Stevens, K. N. 178
Stevenson-Hinde, J. 235
Stickgold, R. 277
Stiles, J. 296
Stiller, R. M. 87
Stillman, J. A. 185
Stirn-Kranjc, B. 60
Stockard, J. E. 257
Stolarova, M. 17, 132
Stone-Elander, S. 268
Stout, A. U. 61
Straarup, E. M. 50
Stranger, B. A. 155
Strelau, J. 242
Stroganova, T. 275
Stroganova, T. A. 228, 229, 254, 257, 258, 261, 262, 264, 267, 268, 269, 270, 271, 272, 273, 276, 277, 278, 279
Struve, F. A. 240
Studdert-Kennedy, M. 212
Suffczynski, P. 267
Suhara, K. 261
Suitt, C. D. 63
Sukuki, H. 261
Summerfield, A. Q. 181
Sunohara, G. A. 180
Suominen, K. 176
Surwillo, W. W. 261
Suter, P. S. 50
Suter, S. 50
Sutoh, T. 171
Suttle, C. M. 50, 54
Sutton, S. K. 233

Suzuki, M. 173
Suzuki, T. 241
Suzuki, W. A. 117, 146, 147
Suzuki, Y. 269, 270, 271, 272
Swanson, J. 180
Swanson, J. M. 180
Swarz, K. 290
Swick, D. 241
Syrota, A. 179

Takaetsu, E. 46
Takagi, T. 258, 265
Takahashi, I. 46
Takano, K. 148
Takazawa, S. 173
Takkinen, S. 174, 176, 185
Tales, A. 171
Tallal, P. 183
Tallon-Baudry, C. 289, 291, 293, 295, 296, 301
Tamura, R. 77, 92
Tan, A. 217
Tang, Y. 48
Tarr, M. J. 78, 79, 82
Taylor, A. 179
Taylor, D. 58
Taylor, E. 179, 180
Taylor, M. J. 6, 9, 17, 26, 27, 39, 43, 58, 62, 63, 77, 80, 81, 82, 84, 85, 90, 91, 92, 311
Teder, W. 171
Tees, R. C. 178
Teicher, M. H. 278
Teller, D. Y. 46, 50, 54
Teneke, C. E. 39
Tenke, C. 199
Terrell, S. 212, 213
Tervaniemi, M. 184, 199
Tetsuka, H. 47, 48, 51
Teuber, H.-L. 117
Thayer, J. F. 234
Therien, J. M. 157, 161
Thoman, E. B. 154
Thomas, D. G. 172, 264, 308
Thomas, K. 11, 17, 90, 150, 151, 155, 156, 160, 162, 163
Thomas, K. M. 86, 104, 107, 108, 110, 114, 115, 120, 129, 160, 163
Thomason, M. E. 241
Thomson, J. 212
Thorpe, L. A. 185
Tiitinen, H. 171, 172, 184
Tijssen, R. 43, 62
Till, C. 60
Timonina, O. V. 261
Tinazzi, M. 56
Titran, M. 153
Tkac, I. 162
Tobimatsu, S. 50, 62
Tolvanen, A. 155, 176, 183, 220
Tomarken, A. J. 232, 257
Tombin, J. 212
Tomlinson, A. 48
Tonoike, M. 277
Topkoff, J. 240
Torgesen, J. 212
Tormene, A. P. 41, 46, 59
Torres, F. 63
Toru, M. 229
Towle, V. L. 50
Townsend, E. L. 162
Trainor, L. 309
Trainor, L. J. 8, 9, 176, 253
Trainor, R. 241

Trauner, D. 296, 311
Travis, L. 202
Trehub, S. E. 185
Treisman, A. 293
Tremblay, K. 177
Tribbles, J. A. R. 63
Tribby-Walbridge, S. 86, 104, 107, 108, 110, 114, 115, 120, 129, 160, 163
Tribby-Walbridge, S. R. 16
Tricklebank, J. 54
Trimarchi, C. 46
Trinath, T. 301
Trisciuzzi, M. T. S. 61
Troscianko, T. 171
Tsetlin, M. M. 267
Tsuda, K. 269, 270, 271, 272
Tsukada, T. 47
Tsuneishi, S. 43, 308
Tsunoda, S. 277
Tuchman, R. F. 179
Tucker, D. 15
Tucker, D. A. 241
Tucker, D. M. 13, 255
Tucker, L. 296
Tucker, L. A. 16, 21, 22, 26, 32, 33, 88, 291, 296, 312
Tulving, E. 117, 146
Tyler, C. W. 48, 50, 51, 56
Tzischinsky, O. 173

Uauy, R. 46, 60
Ueno, S. 241
Uhl, F. 80, 87, 90
Ungerleider, L. G. 89
Urry, H. L. 233
Utsunomiya, H. 148
Uutela, K. 179
Uwer, R. 182, 184

Vaal, J. 174
Vaidya, C. J. 179, 241
Vainio, M. 177
Vaituzis, C. K. 241
van Boxtel, G. 27
van der Gaag, R. J. 180
van der Loos, H. 172
van der Molen, M. W. 17, 240
van Engeland, H. 179, 180, 240
Van Petten, C. 87
Van Rotterdam, A. 266
van Soest, A. J. 174
Vandenberghe, R. 268
Vanhala, R. 179
Vanni, S. 39
Vanschooneveld, M. J. 61
Varela, F. 291
Varela, F. J. 291
Vargha-Khadem, F. 117, 118, 121, 161, 162
Varlamov, A. 276
Vaughan, H. G. Jr 1, 9, 103, 115, 150, 171, 172, 173, 174, 176, 179, 185, 185, 237, 239, 308, 310
Vaughn, H. G. 39
Vauss, Y. 241
Veltman, D. J. 146, 160
Verbaten, M. N. 179, 180, 240
Versyp, F. 152
Vervoort, P. 152
Vicari, S. 311

Vigorito, J. 211
Vinogradova, O. S. 277
Vizzoni, L. 51
Vogt, I. R. 183
Vohr, B. 162
Volbrecht, V. J. 54
Volein, A. 82, 86, 104, 106, 133, 312
Volpe, J. J. 145
von Hofsten, C. 297
von Suchodoletz, W. 182, 184
vonBerger, G. P. 51
Vos, J. E. 266

Wagner, R. 212
Waldo, M. 240
Waldo, M. C. 240
Walker, M. 102, 103, 104, 110, 114, 138
Walker, M. K. 179
Walter, V. J. 269
Walter, W,G 253, 269
Wang, T. 185
Wang, W. 80
Waring, M. D. 181, 241
Warnking, J. 39
Watanabe, A. 258, 265
Watanabe, K. 46
Waters, J. M. 107, 108, 109, 119, 130
Watkins, K. E. 161
Watson, R. T. 268
Wattam-Bell, J. 54, 55, 57
Weaver, L. T. 60
Webb, S. 17, 88, 132
Webb, S. J. 8, 25, 26, 33, 86, 87, 101, 102, 107, 108, 110, 114, 115, 118, 120, 129, 136
Weber, C. 174, 176, 178, 185
Webster, M. 311
Wechsler, D. 205
Weiman, A. L. 231
Weingartner, H. 231
Weinstein, N. D. 242
Weiss, A. H. 46, 50, 54, 60
Weiss, D. S. 240
Weiss, I. P. 63
Weiss, S. 63
Weisbrod, M. 241
Weisser, R. 241
Weitzman, E. D. 150
Welch, J. 57
Werker, J. F. 178
Werner, J. S. 54
Wertman, E. 268
Wesemann, W. 55
Westall, C. A. 50, 57, 60, 61,. 63
Westerlund, A. 22, 23, 85, 106, 137
Westmoreland, B. E. 257
Wetzel, M. 110
Wewerka, S. 11, 17, 86, 90, 104, 107, 108, 110, 114, 115, 120, 129, 150, 151, 155, 156, 159, 160, 162, 163,
Wewerka, S. S. 16, 116, 127, 160, 163
Wheeler, R. E. 232
Wheelwright, S. 179
Whiting, S. 63
Whitney, H. 17, 132
Whyte, H. E. 43
Widmann, A. 110

Wiebe, S. A. 101, 107, 108, 109, 110, 119, 130, 134, 137
Wiens, A. S. 177
Wiesel, T. N. 264
Wigal, S. B. 180
Wigal, T. 180
Wilkinson, G. 206
Wilkinson, G. S. 205
Williams, K. A. 177, 178
Williams, S. C. 179
Wilner, E. 63
Wilson, J. R. 55
Wilson, W. 211
Wilton, A. Y. 43, 45, 57
Wimmer, H. 279
Winkler, I. 171, 172, 177, 237
Winkler, T. 267, 268
Winsberg, B. G. 180
Winter, O. 173
Wise, D. 179
Witter, M. P. 146, 160
Wobken, J. D. 162
Woldorff, M. G. 172
Wolf, A. 162
Wolfe, M. E. 48
Wolff, C. 110, 172
Wolfson, A. R. 173
Wolfson, J. 161
Wolkstein, M. 63
Wong, P. K. H. 63
Wong, V. C. 63
Wood, S. J. 160, 161
Woodcock, R. W. 206
Woods, D. L. 171, 172, 241
Woodward, S. A. 235
Worwa, C. 160, 162
Worwa, C. T. 157, 161
Wright, K. W. 56, 59
Wynn, K. 297

Xie, X. 153

Yabe, H. 171
Yago, E. 172
Yale, M. E. 253, 255, 275
Yamada, E. 234
Yamada, S. 80
Yamaguchi, M. 277
Yamamoto, S. 60
Yamauchi, N. 258, 265
Yaple, K. 202
Ye, H. H. 153
Yoder, P. J. 253, 255, 275
Yonelinas, A. 117
Yoshiura, T. 241
Young, D. 240
Yppärilä, H. 180
Yu, D. 275

Zafiris, O. 146, 147
Zanette, G. 56
Zecker, S. G. 172, 183, 208
Zeffiro, T. 212
Zemon, V. 48, 57
Zenchenko, C. I. 277
Zerbin, D. 180, 181
Zhang, X. 212
Zhurba, L. T. 261
Zilles, K. 146, 147
Zola, S. 145, 147
Zubcov, A. A. 62

Subject Index

absolute power (EEG) 26–7
achromatopsia 60
active wakefulness 251
acuity charts 50
adult/infant comparisons in ERPs 115–16, 310–11
affective development, ERPs and 234–42
afferent visual pathways 61–2
age, EEG/ERPs study design and 16–17
age-related changes in EEG 8
age-related differences in ERPs 9
albinism, afferent visual pathways 61
alcoholism 179
alpha activity 252
alpha band 252
   see also alpha rhythm
alpha gradient 258
alpha power 228
alpha rhythm 228–9, 251–2
   adult vs infant 261
   adult/infant frequency boundaries 252–3
   amplitude growth 265–6
   developmental onset 252–4
   frequency growth 264–5
   identification 257–62
   paradoxical 268
   parietal 268–9
   role during infant attention 266, 268–9
Alzheimer's disease, P50 suppression in 240
amblyopia 55, 56, 58, 59
ANOVA 26, 27, 29, 254
approach–withdrawal tasks 7
ataxias, hereditary 62
Attention Deficit Hyperactivity Disorder (ADHD) 179
   methylphenidate (MP) therapy in 180
   MMN in 180–1
auditory awakening threshold (AAT) 174
auditory brainstem response (ABR) methodology 149
auditory novelty processing 235–9
auditory recognition memory 145–64
   anatomic development of neural pathway 148–9
   behavioral and evoked potential measures of auditory processing 149–53
   event-related potentials 154–60
      long-term memory abilities of newborn 154–5
      negative slow wave response 155
      postmenstrual age and memory development 155–7
      postnatal experience and maternal voice recognition 155–7
      sleep and 154
   in the fetus and newborn 153–60
   high-risk populations 160–4
   infants of diabetic mothers 162–4
   neural pathway 146–7
   premature infants 160–2
   psychophysiologic and behavioral studies 153–4
autism
   ERP studies 179
   gamma activity 301
   hemispheric asymmetry in 234
   MMN studies 179–80
   NC in 87
   P50 suppression in 240

Batten's disease 62
Bayley Scales of Infant Development 120
   Mental Developmental Index Score 162
behavioral measures, role in ERP/EEG research 311–13
behavioral stillness 267
Bender Gestalt test 201
beta band 252
binocular vision 56–7
blindness 179
blood oxygenation level dependent (BOLD) imaging 152
Brain Electrical Source Analysis (BESA) 33, 213

cancer survivors, MMN 181
cataract, congenital 59, 60
central rhythm 251, 262, 263
cerebral palsy 59
cerebral visual impairment 62
ceroid lipofucinosis (Batten's disease) 62
cleft lip 182
cleft palate 182
cochlear implants 179, 181
cognitive functioning, ERPs as predictors of 201–2
coherence (EEG) 26, 27
colour vision 54
coma
   childhood, flash VEPs in 63
   MMN in 179
'Conlern' 80
'Conspec' 80
contrast sensitivity thresholds, maturation of 50–1
cortical visual impairment 62–3
cortisol, EEG and 12

data collection, EEG/ERPs study design and 18–26
data recording, EEG/ERPs study design and 18–19
declarative memory 116
deferoxanmine 63
deferred limitation memory task, ERP responses 12
definition of visual evoked potentials 39
delayed visual maturation 58
delta amplitude 265

delta band 252
depression
  MMN in 179
  maternal, infant EEG activation and 11
developmental electrophysiology, definition 6
difference-waveform 171
diffusion tensor imaging (DTI) 308
dishabituation procedure 11–12
dopamine-related disorders 180
Downs syndrome 119
dynamic random dot correlogram 56–7
dyslexia 179, 182, 183
  infant brain responses 208–11
  MMN 181
dysphasia 182–3
  MMN studies 181–2

Early Childhood Vigilance test 106
EEG 5, 6, 251–80
  adult/infant 310–11
  asymmetry 26, 27, 230–4, 242
  band power 227–30
  baseline 254–5
  change over infancy 306–10
  infant rhythm identification 252–4
  reference electrode 255–6
  relative and absolute power 256–7
  reliability 254–5
  see also EEG/ERPs, development, study design
EEG/ERPs, development, study design
  age 16–17
  artifact rejection 24–5
  averaging 25–6
  data collection 18–26
  data recording 18–19
  data reduction 24–6
  hypotheses 7
  participants 16–18
  reference montages 21–2
  sample size 17–18
  screening 17
  source localization in ERPs 32–3
  source separation in ERPs 32–3
  statistical analysis 26–32
  task design 7–8
  testing session specifics 19–21
    infants 20–1
    newborns 20
electrode caps 14, 15
electrodes, optimum numbers of 22
electroencephalography (EEG) *see* EEG
electrooculogram (EOG) activity 24
electroretinogram 60–1
epilepsy 313
epsilon 27
ERPs 5–6
  in affective development 234–42
  change over infancy 306–10
  in developmental outcomes 199–213
  face-sensitive 77–89
  in visual attention and recognition memory 101–21
  see also EEG/ERPs, development, study design
event-related oscillations 289–301
  evoked 291
  induced 291
  methods 289–93
  occluded objects and object permanence 296–7
  perceptual binding 293–6
event-related potentials (ERPs) *see* ERPs
event-related synchronization/desynchronization 6
explicit memory 116, 117
eye disorders 60–1

face processing 77–93

by adults 78–9
development 79–80
event-related potential studies 80–90
familiarity-based recognition 117
fast Fourier transform 27
fetal hearing 149–53
  BOLD signaling 152
  fMRI response 152
  hearing thresholds 150
  latency 150
  maturity, scoring system 150
  uterus and 152–3
flash luminance 41
flash VEPs 41, 43, 61, 62, 63, 308
frequency bands, EEG 8
frontal EEG asymmetry 232–4
frontal EEG rhythm 253–4
functional lateralization, speech and 202
functional magnetic resonance imaging (fMRI) 5, 146, 301
functional topography approach 257, 279

gamma band 230, 252, 296–301
gender 17
Geodesic Sensor Net (GSN) 15–16
glaucoma, congenital 59
glioma 61
Grass-Astromed amplifier 18

habituation paradigm 7, 8, 11–12
handedness 17
head size 17
hedonic theta 269
hemispheric asymmetry (EEG) 26, 27, 230–4, 242
hierarchical linear modeling (HLM) 26, 31–2, 206
hippocampal development 148
HIV 179
HM anterograde amnesia case 116–17
hydrocephalus, visual pathways and 62
hyperkinetic disorder (HKD) *see* Attention Deficit Hyperactivity Disorder

implicit memory 116–17
incidental memory 116
independent components analysis (ICA) 26, 32–3, 110
infant electrophysiology, frequency of use 305
infantile nystagmus 58
infants of diabetic mothers (IDMs)
  auditory recognition memory 162–4
  visual memory 120–1
intelligence assessment 17
intelligence quotient, full-scale (FSIQ) 205
intentional memory 116
inverse problem 32
iron deficiency 17
isoluminance 54

joint attention, EEG and 12

Kanizsa Square 293–6

language outcome prediction, ERPs and 200–4
learning disabilities 183
Leber's amaurosis 60
left frontal asymmetry, social and emotional development and 232
leucodystrophy 62
leukemia, childhood, MMN 181
low-density EEG/ERPs, recording methods 13–15
luminance VEPs (flash and flicker) 40, 43–4, 54, 60

macular hypoplasia 59
magnetic resonance imaging (MRI) 148–9, 154, 308
MANOVA 26, 28–9

mastoid electrodes 22
McCarthy Scales of Children's Abilities 204
McCarthy Verbal Index 203
medial temporal lobe development 148–9
memory span 17
midline frontal theta rhythm 273–6
mismatch negativity (MMN) paradigm
    in adults and children 172–6
    in clinical pediatric populations 179–83
    cognitive mechanisms 172
    development during infancy 171–85, 236–8, 309
    filtering 176
    infants without 185
    in laboratory animals 172
    language outcome and 208
    language-specific memory 177–8
    latency 174–6
    pediatric/adult differences 184–5
    size of response 184
    sleep and 173–4
    social and emotional development 236–8
    speech-processing 177–8
motion perception 55
motion-reversal-specific VEPs 55
motor development, EEG and 12
mu rhythm 229, 252, 262
    amplitude growth 265–6
    developmental onset 262–4
    frequency growth 264–5
    role during infant attention 266–8
    baseline 267, 268

N1 184
    responses to speech stimuli and 204–7
N2, adult 115
N3 308
N160, encoding of faces 80
N170 27, 77
    adult 91–2, 93
    face recognition 81–2, 84, 85
N250 309
N250r, encoding of faces 80
N290 81–5, 91, 92, 93
    encoding of faces 82–5
N400, face and language processing 77, 87–8
N500 component (ERP) 27
Nb 241
Nc (negative central) 85–8, 92, 93, 101–4, 112–13,
        120–1, 312
    Nc1 and Nc2 109–10, 113
    age and 108
    recognition memory and 107–9
    repetition priming and 108
    underlying generators 110–12
    visual attention and 104–7
        heart rate 107
        looking time 104–6
night blindness, congenital stationary 60
non-declarative memory 116
novelty P3 237–8
nursery rhyme games 211
nystagmus, infantile 58

object permanence, EEG and 12
obsessive-compulsive disorder 179
occipital rhythm 252
oddball paradigm 8
    auditory 236
    Nc and 103–4
    vowel duration change in 210
onset/offset VEPs 41–3
optic nerve atrophy 61
optic nerve hypoplasia, congenital 61
optimal MMN paradigm studies 184

orientation sensitivity 54–5

P1
    encoding of faces 80, 81, 93
    suppression 239–42
P2 264
P3 179
P3a 184
P50 suppression 239–42
P150 309
P300 27, 90, 310–11
    adult 115–16
P400 85, 91, 92, 93, 291
P600 77
Pa 241
Pb suppression 239–42
passive paradigms 9
pattern VEPs 40, 41, 45–6, 56, 61, 62, 63
pattern-reversal VEPs 41, 56
Pc 115
Peabody Picture Vocabulary Test (PPVT) 203
periventricular leucomalacia 62
phonetic contrasts 211
phonological awareness 212
phonological memory 212
photic latency responses 200–1
positive slow wave 88–90
post-traumatic stress disorder (PTSD), P50
        suppression in 240
pre-explicit infant memory 118
prematurity
    auditory recognition memory and 160–2
    ERPs and 17
principal components analysis (PCA) 26, 32
proton echo-planar spectroscopic imaging (PEPSI)
        212
ptosis 59

quiet wakefulness 251

rapid eye movement (REM) sleep 174
reading, ERPs as predictors of 204–7
recognition memory 7, 116
recollection-based recognition 117
relative power (EEG) 26, 27
reorienting negativity 110
retinal dystrophy 60
right frontal asymmetry 232, 242

sample size, EEG/ERPs study design and 17–18
schizophrenia
    MMN in 179
    P50 suppression in 240, 241
screening, EEG/ERPs study design and 17
sensory gating 239–42
signal-to-noise ratio 26, 48, 184
sleep
    auditory recognition memory and 154
    flash VEPs and 43
    rapid eye movement (REM) 174
slow waves 309–10
    late 113–14
    early negative (eNSW) 114
    generators of 115
source analysis 110
source localization 32–3
source separation 32
specific language impairment (SLI) 182
speech discrimination tasks 7
speech perception 199–200
standardised VEP tests 41–3
Stanford-Binet Intelligence Test 201, 204
steady-state VEPs 40, 48
step VEP technique 48, 49

stereograms 56, 57
stereopsis 56, 57
strabismus 55, 56
sweep VEPs 48–50, 51, 52, 55, 59
synaptic density 308
synaptic pruning 266
synaptogenesis 148

temperament
    auditory novelty processing and 235–9
    EEG and 12
    P50 suppression 239–42
    sensory gating and 239–42
temporal resolution limit 44
theta amplitude 265
theta band 252
    see also theta rhythms
theta rhythms 229–30, 261, 266
    adult vs infant 277
    asymmetry of response 276
    development 271–2
    frontal theta 273–6
    functional meaning 276–9
    humans vs animals 277
    of infant EEG 269–79
    neural plasticity 278
    scalp topography of response 272–6
time of day 17
time–frequency analysis 290
Tourette syndrome 180–1

Velcro headband procedure 13, 15
Velo Cardio Facial (VCF) 182
Vernier offset 54–5
vertex-positive potential (VPP), adult 22, *23*
vigabatrin 63
violation of expectation paradigm 297
visual acuity 53, 59
visual attention and recognition memory in infancy 101–38
visual evoked potentials in infants 39–63
    binocular vision 56–7
    clinical applications 58–63
    colour vision 54

    definition 39
    flash 41, 43, 61, 62, 63, 308
    functional sub-systems 57–8
    luminance (flash and flicker) 40, 43–4, 54, 60
    motion perception 55
    motion-reversal-specific 55
    onset/offset 41–3
    orientation sensitivity and Vernier offset 54–5
    pattern 40, 41, 45–6, 56, 61, 62, 63
    pattern-reversal 41, 56
    standard tests 41–3
    steady-state 40, 48
    step technique 48, 49
    stimuli 40
    sweep 48–50, 51, 52, 55, 59
    testing strategies 40–1
    visual resolution and contrast sensitivity thresholds 50–1
    visual threshold assessment 46–50
visual maturation 60
visual paired comparison procedure 101
visual recognition memory development 116–19
    adult, neuroanatomy 116–17
    infant memory 117–21
visual resolution, maturation of 50–1
visual system functional sub-systems 57–8
    excitatory vs lateral inhibitory dimension 57
    magnocellular/parvocellular dimension 57–8
    ON/Off dimension 57
visual threshold assessments from VEPs 46–50

wakefulness, states of, and infants' performance of cognitive tasks 273–6
Wechsler Intelligence Scales for Children
    WISC-3 205
    WISC-R 201
Wide Range Achievement Test (WRAT) – Revised 205, 206, 207
Williams syndrome 301
'windmill-dartboard' stimuli 57
withdrawal-related behaviors, EEG and 12
Woodcock-Johnson Psychoeducational Battery–Revised
    Word Attack subtest 205, 206, 207